D·N·ANGEL

BY YUKIRU SUGISAKI

VOLUME 9

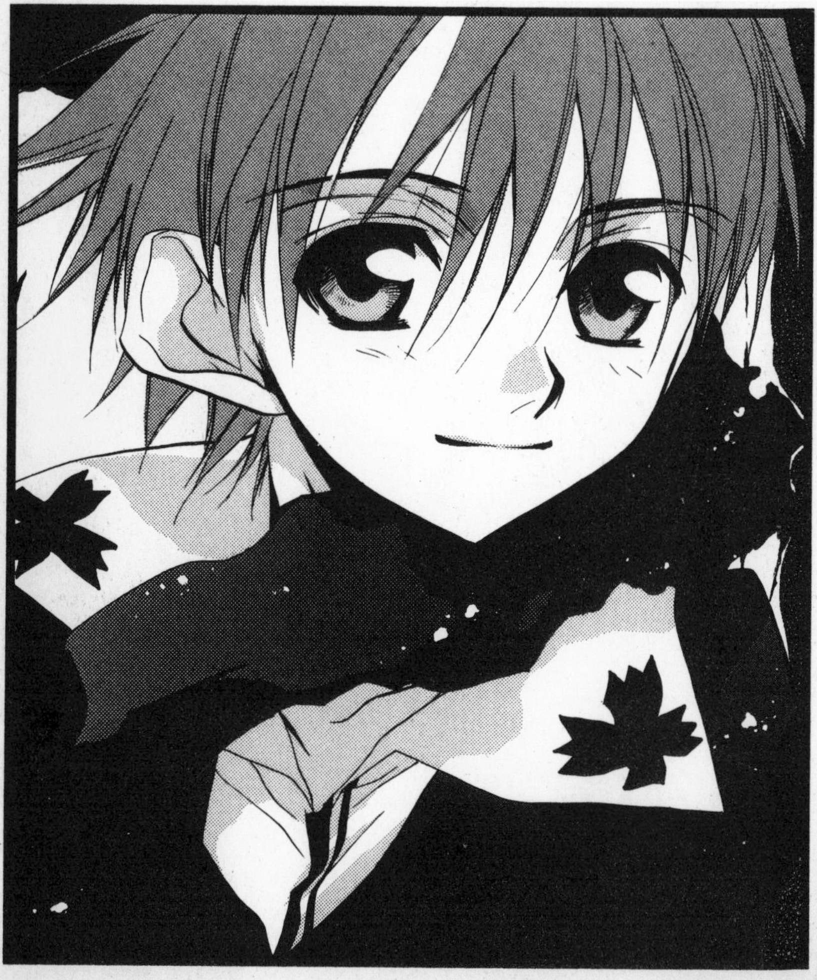

& STORY

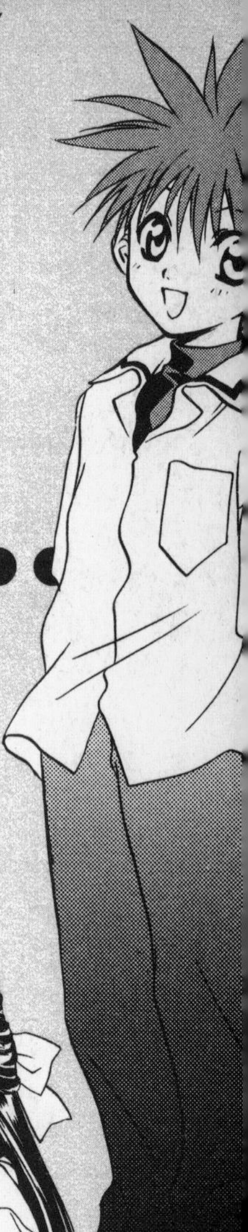

Daisuke and Riku have finally resolved their relationship and are happily in love...but the connection between Dark, Daisuke, and Satoshi is still unresolved. When Daisuke was pulled into the world inside his painting by the Toki no Byoushin, he learned the tragic story of the love between Princess Freedert and her lover, Elliot. The power of the Toki no Byoushin was coming to an end, but with Satoshi's help he was able to reunite Freedert and Elliot at the last moment. They vanished along with the Toki no Byoushin, and even though they were finally together, Daisuke couldn't stop wishing he could have done more for them...

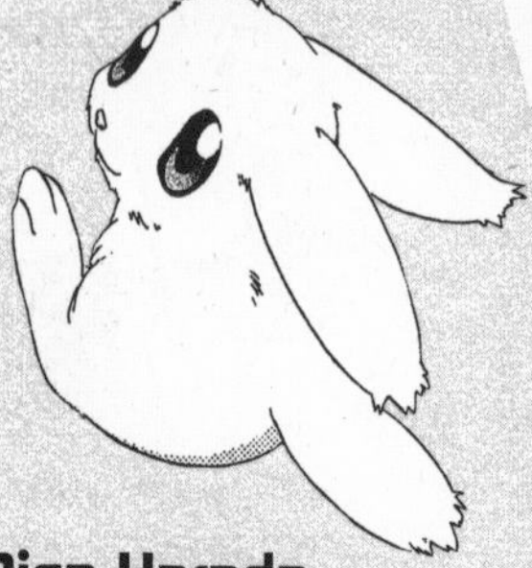

Wiz

A mysterious animal who acts as Dark's familiar and who can transform into many things, including Dark's black wings. He can also transform himself into Dark or Daisuke.

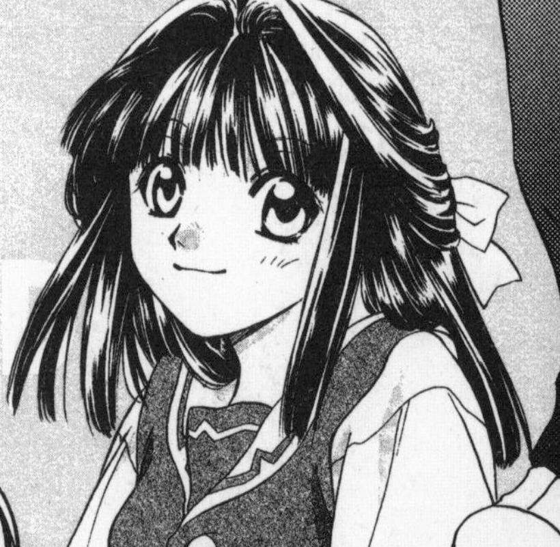

Risa Harada (younger sister)

Daisuke's first crush. Daisuke confessed his love to her...but she rejected him. She's been in love with Dark since the first time she saw him on TV.

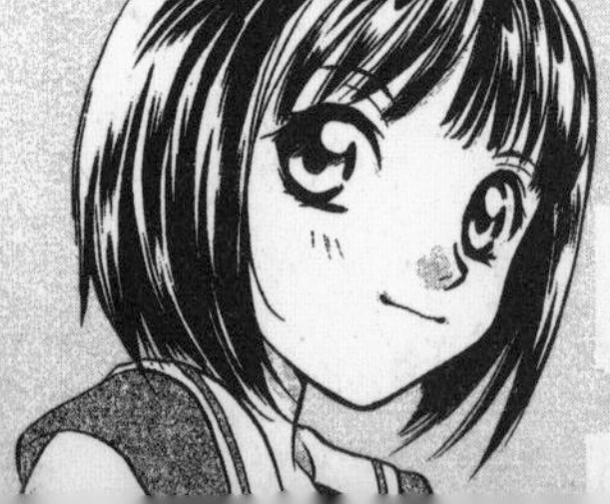

Riku Harada (older sister)

Risa's identical twin sister. She and Daisuke have fallen for each other.

Daisuke Niwa

A 14-year-old student at Azumano Middle School. He has a unique genetic condition that causes him to transform into the infamous Phantom Thief Dark whenever he has romantic feelings.

CHARACTERS

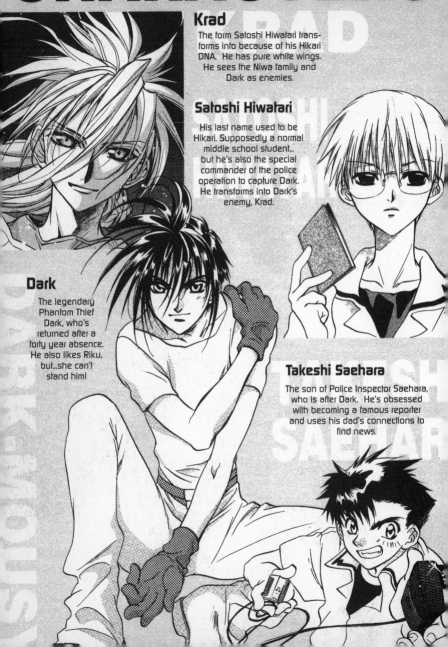

Krad

The form Satoshi Hiwatari transforms into because of his Hikari DNA. He has pure white wings. He sees the Niwa family and Dark as enemies.

Satoshi Hiwatari

His last name used to be Hikari. Supposedly a normal middle school student... but he's also the special commander of the police operation to capture Dark. He transforms into Dark's enemy, Krad.

Dark

The legendary Phantom Thief Dark, who's returned after a forty year absence. He also likes Riku, but...she can't stand him!

Takeshi Saehara

The son of Police Inspector Saehara, who is after Dark. He's obsessed with becoming a famous reporter and uses his dad's connections to find news.

D•N•ANGEL Vol. 9
Created by Yukiru Sugisaki

Translation - Alethea and Athena Nibley
English Adaptation - Sarah Dyer
Copy Editor - Suzanne Waldman
Retouch and Lettering - Adriana Rivera
Production Artist - Irene Woori Choi
Cover Layout - Thea Willis

Editor - Bryce P. Coleman
Digital Imaging Manager - Chris Buford
Production Managers - Jennifer Miller and Mutsumi Miyazaki
Managing Editor - Jill Freshney
VP of Production - Ron Klamert
Publisher and E.I.C. - Mike Kiley
President and C.O.O. - John Parker
C.E.O. - Stuart Levy

A  Manga

TOKYOPOP Inc.
5900 Wilshire Blvd. Suite 2000
Los Angeles, CA 90036

E-mail: info@TOKYOPOP.com
Come visit us online at www.TOKYOPOP.com

ISBN: 1-59532-794-0

First TOKYOPOP printing: September 2005
10 9 8 7 6 5 4 3 2 1
Printed in the USA

D•N•ANGEL•

Volume 9

By
Yukiru Sugisaki

TOKYOPOP®

HAMBURG // LONDON // LOS ANGELES // TOKYO

CONTENTS

CHARACTERS & STORY 2

THE SECOND HAND OF TIME PART 11 7

STAGE 3, PART 1 45

STAGE 3, PART 2 77

STAGE 3, PART 3 121

STAGE 3, PART 4 147

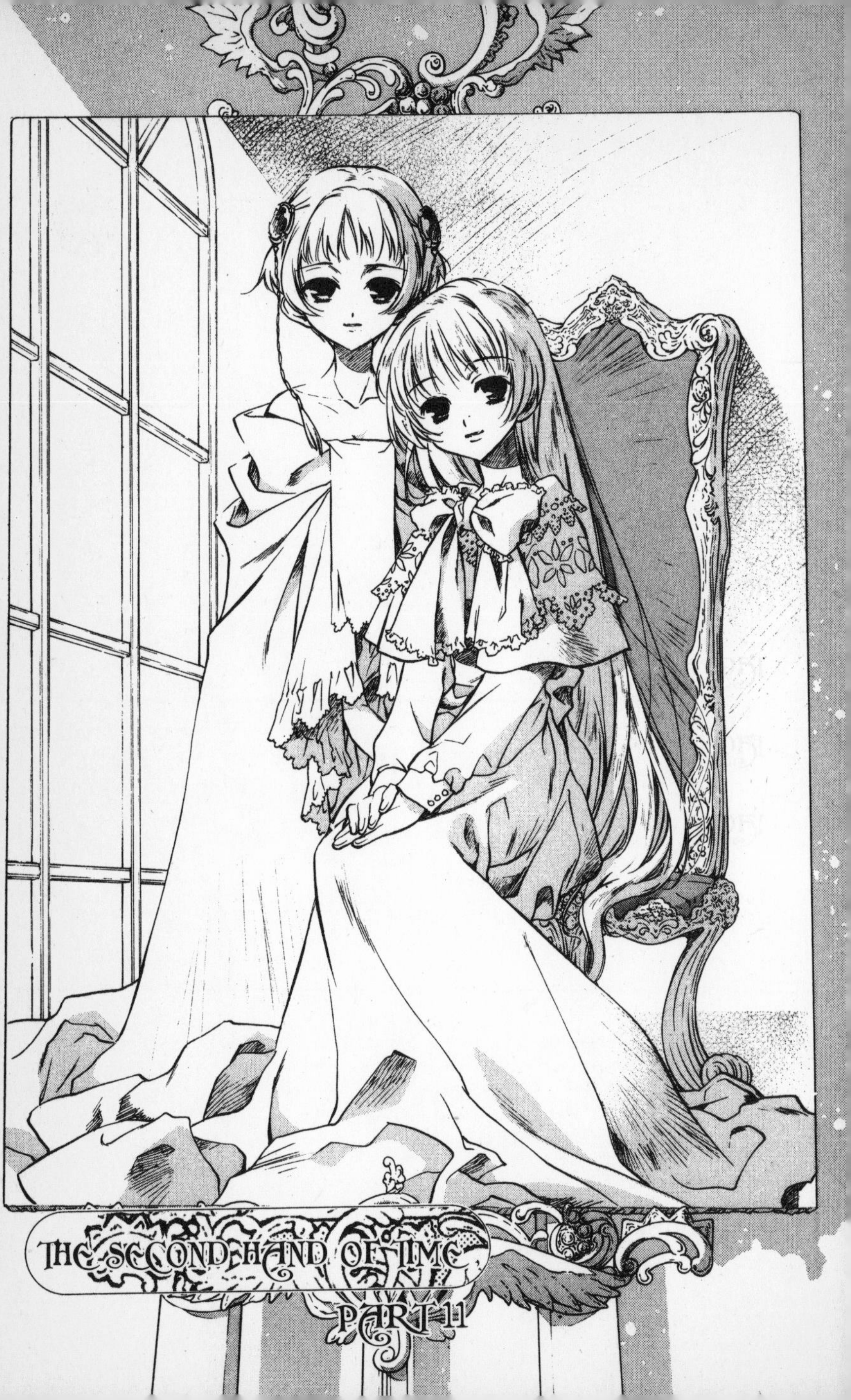
THE SECOND HAND OF TIME
PART 11

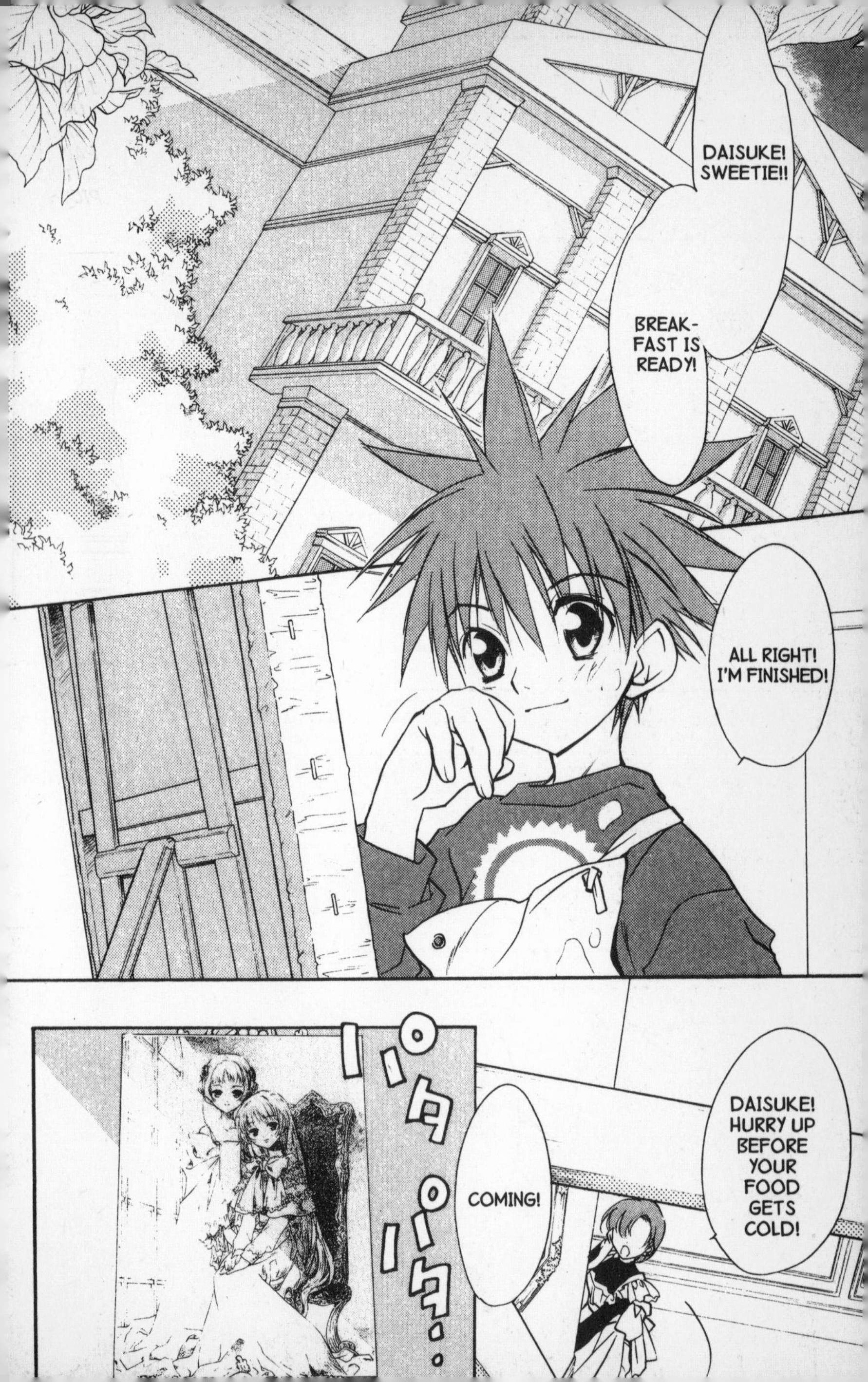
DAISUKE! SWEETIE!!
BREAK-FAST IS READY!
ALL RIGHT! I'M FINISHED!
DAISUKE! HURRY UP BEFORE YOUR FOOD GETS COLD!
COMING!
パタパタ…

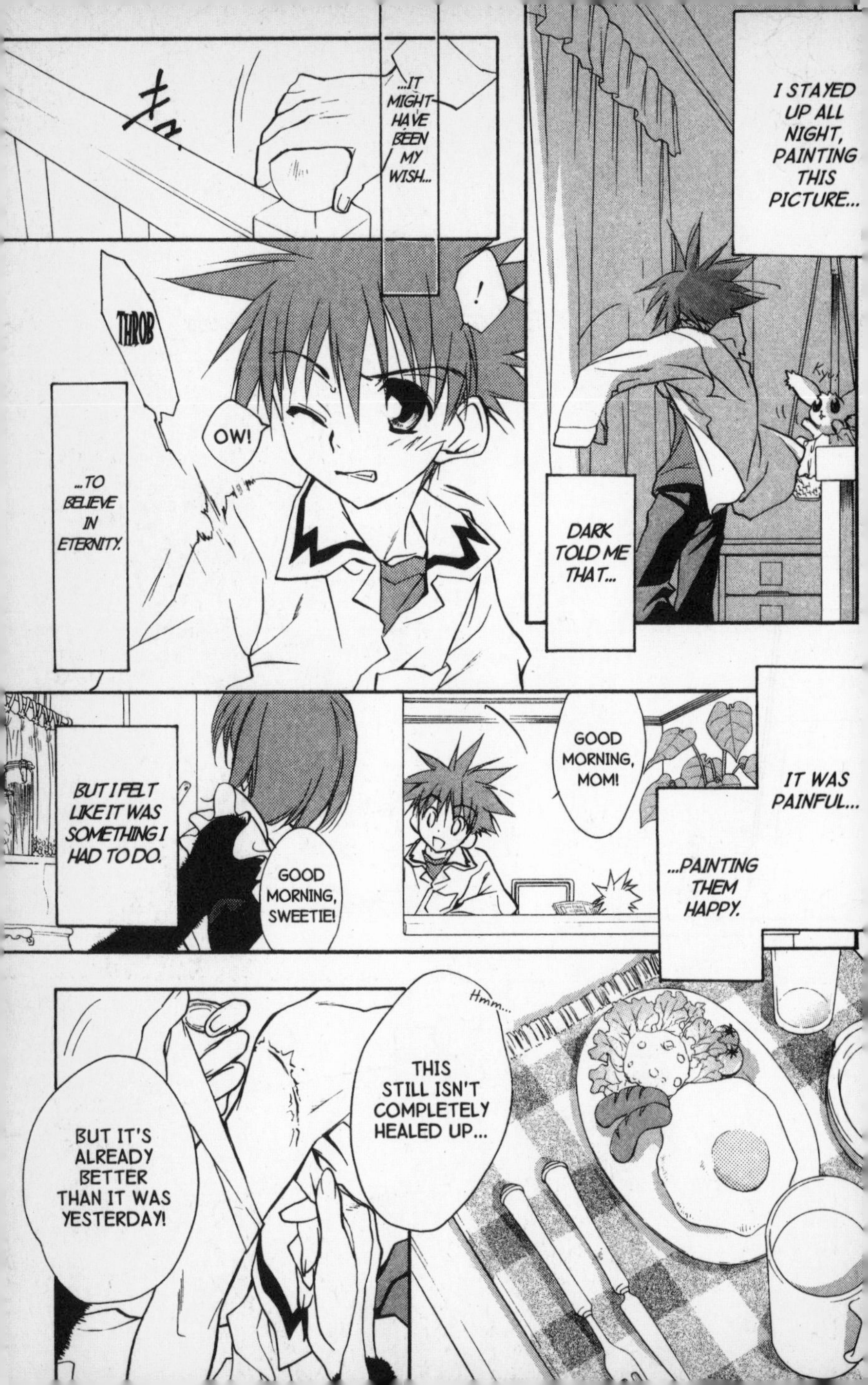
I STAYED UP ALL NIGHT, PAINTING THIS PICTURE...
DARK TOLD ME THAT...
Kyu!
...IT MIGHT HAVE BEEN MY WISH...
!
THROB
OW!
...TO BELIEVE IN ETERNITY.
IT WAS PAINFUL...
...PAINTING THEM HAPPY.
GOOD MORNING, MOM!
GOOD MORNING, SWEETIE!
BUT I FELT LIKE IT WAS SOMETHING I HAD TO DO.
Hmm...
THIS STILL ISN'T COMPLETELY HEALED UP...
BUT IT'S ALREADY BETTER THAN IT WAS YESTERDAY!

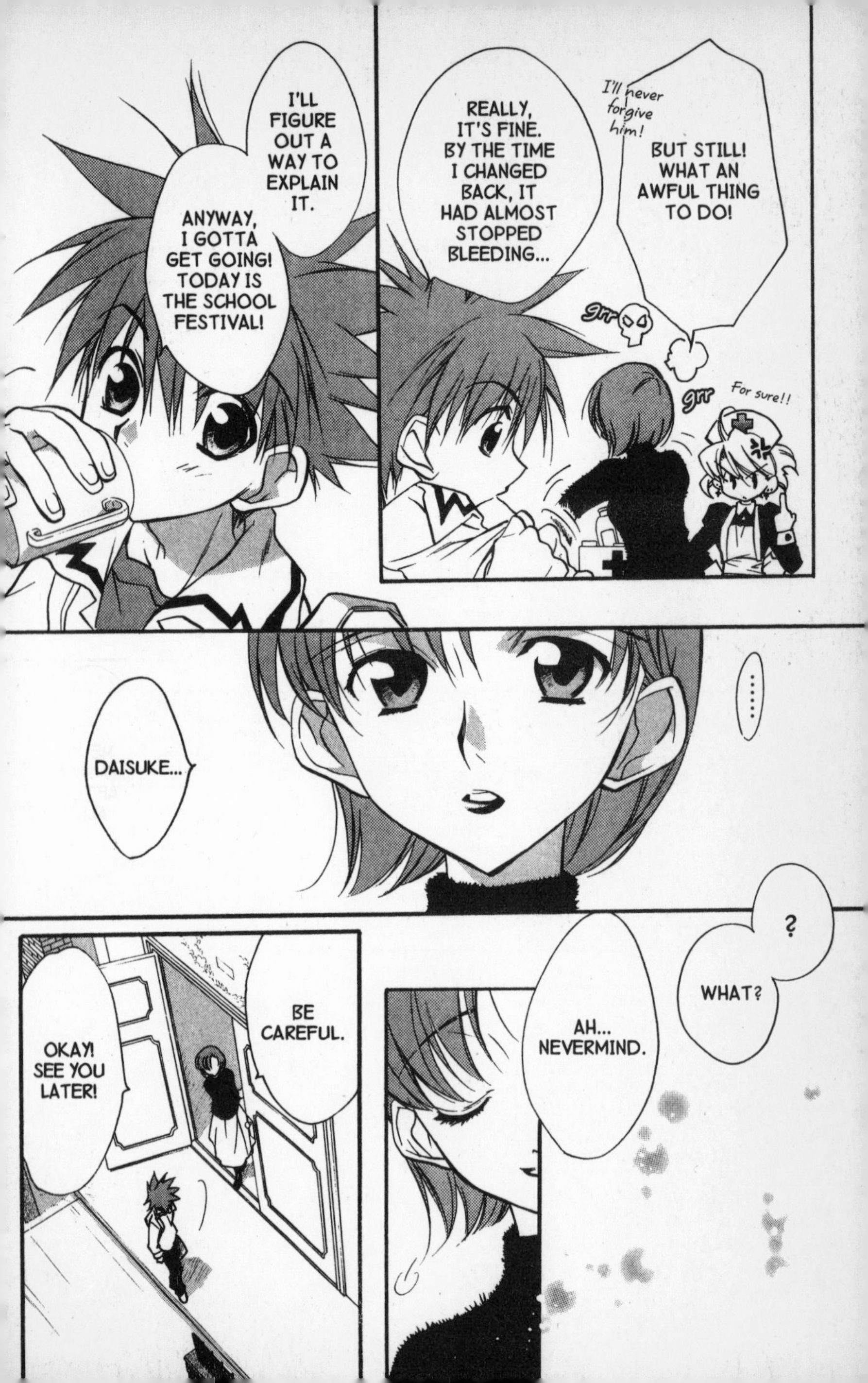
BUT STILL! WHAT AN AWFUL THING TO DO!
I'll never forgive him!
grr
grr
For sure!!
REALLY, IT'S FINE. BY THE TIME I CHANGED BACK, IT HAD ALMOST STOPPED BLEEDING...
I'LL FIGURE OUT A WAY TO EXPLAIN IT.
ANYWAY, I GOTTA GET GOING! TODAY IS THE SCHOOL FESTIVAL!
......
DAISUKE...
?
WHAT?
AH... NEVERMIND.
BE CAREFUL.
OKAY! SEE YOU LATER!

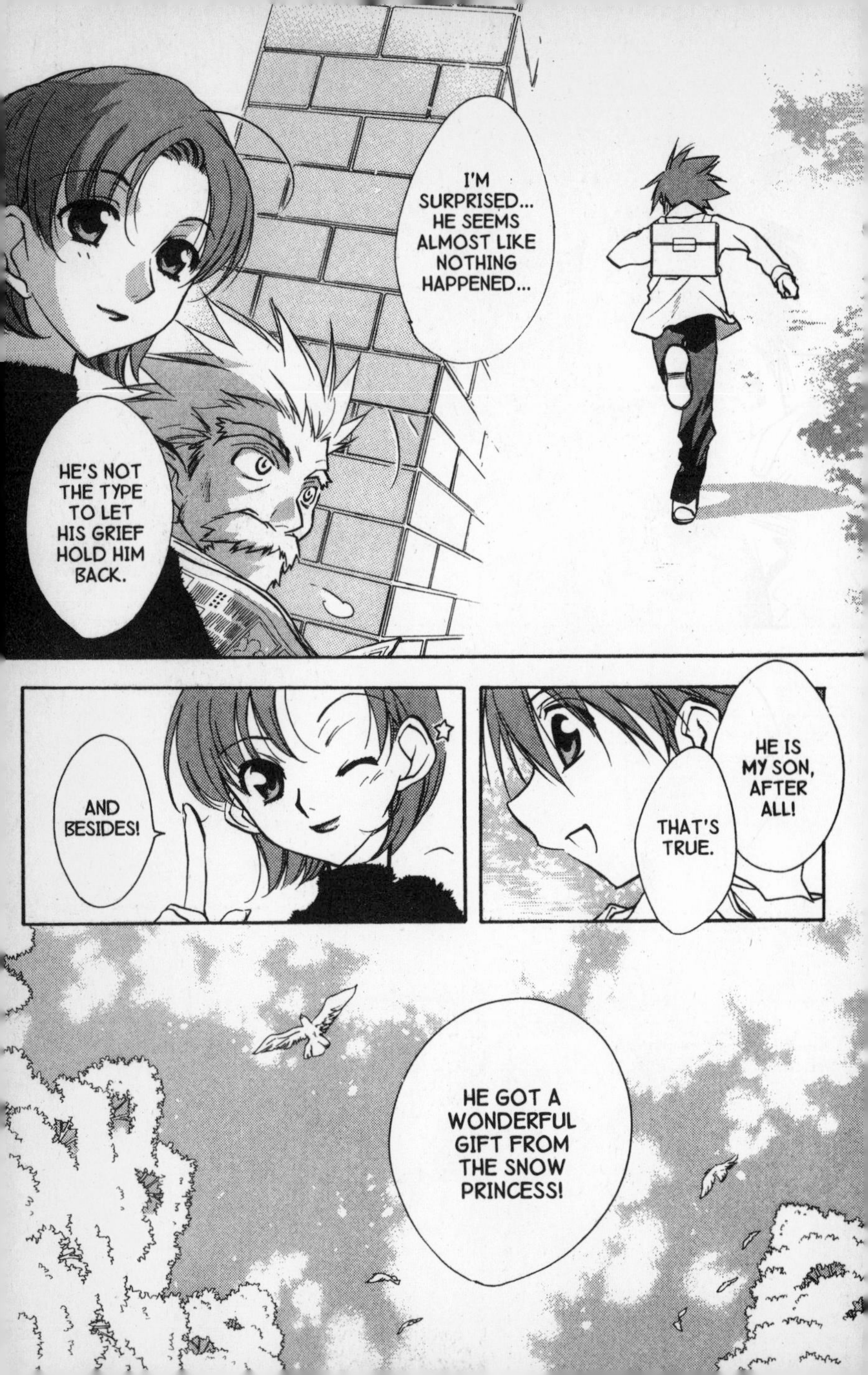
I'M SURPRISED... HE SEEMS ALMOST LIKE NOTHING HAPPENED...
HE'S NOT THE TYPE TO LET HIS GRIEF HOLD HIM BACK.
HE IS MY SON, AFTER ALL!
THAT'S TRUE.
AND BESIDES!
HE GOT A WONDERFUL GIFT FROM THE SNOW PRINCESS!

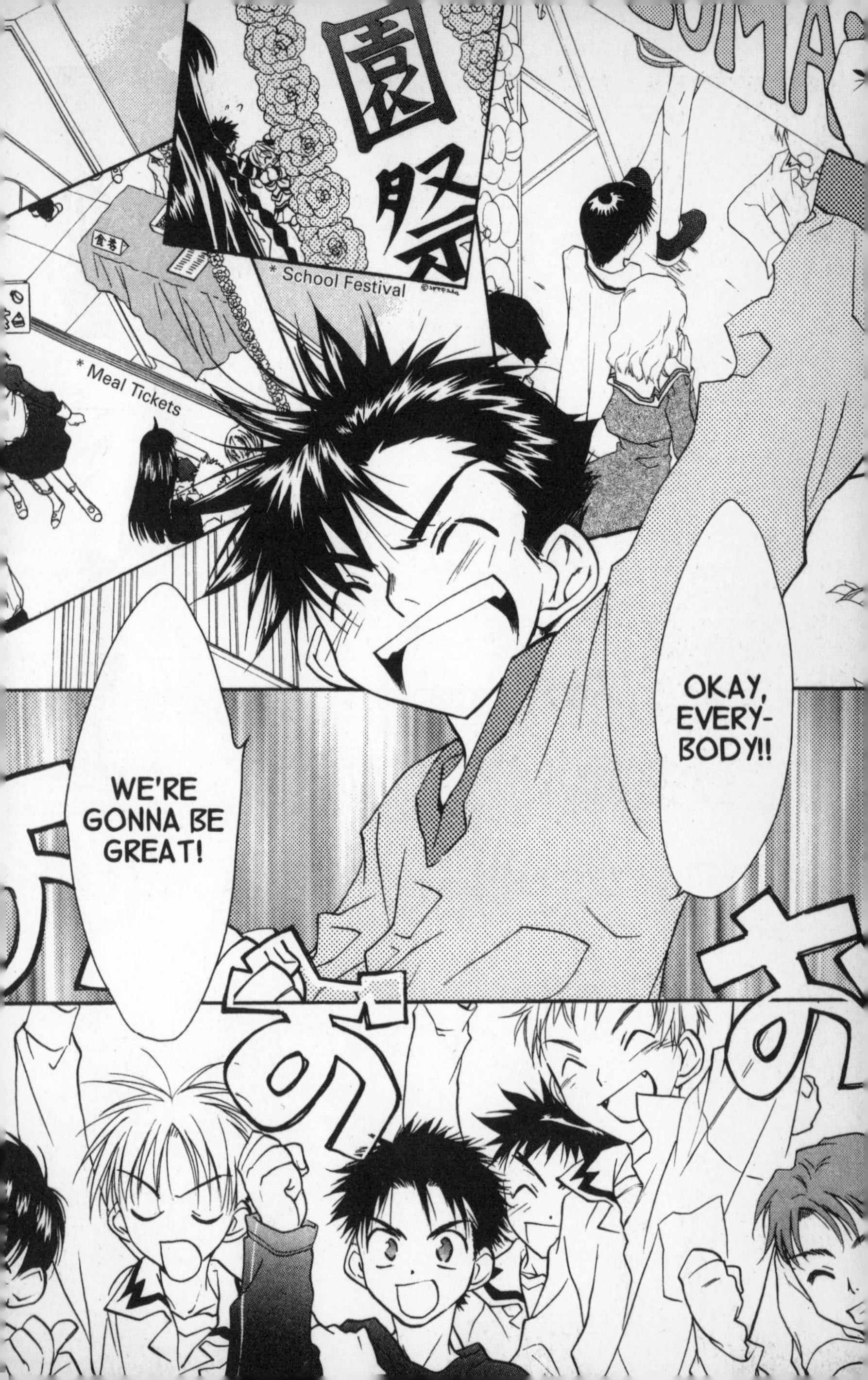
* School Festival
* Meal Tickets
OKAY, EVERY-BODY!!
WE'RE GONNA BE GREAT!

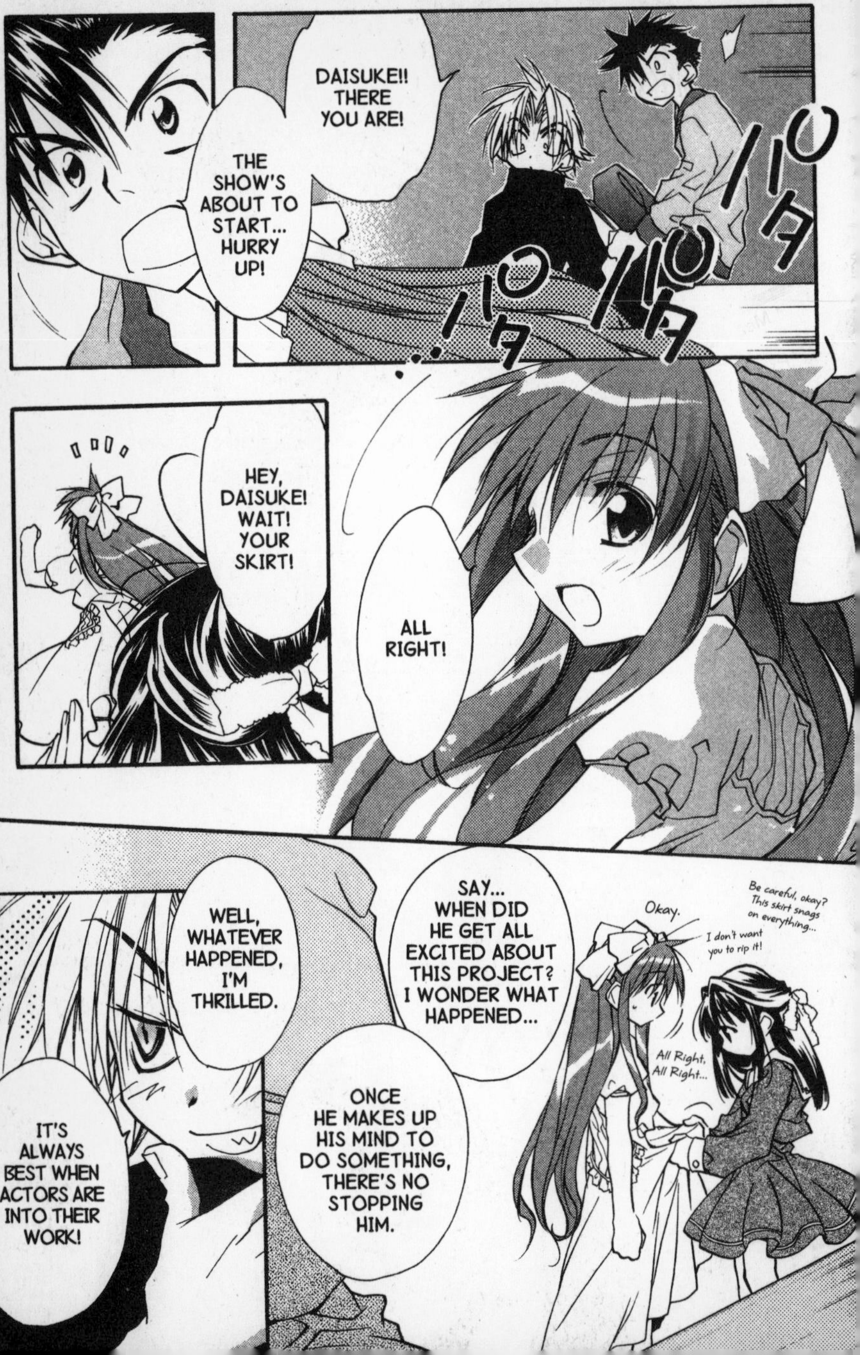
DAISUKE!! THERE YOU ARE!
THE SHOW'S ABOUT TO START... HURRY UP!
パタ
パタ
パタ...
ALL RIGHT!
HEY, DAISUKE! WAIT! YOUR SKIRT!
Be careful, okay? This skirt snags on everything...
I don't want you to rip it!
Okay.
All Right, All Right...
SAY... WHEN DID HE GET ALL EXCITED ABOUT THIS PROJECT? I WONDER WHAT HAPPENED...
ONCE HE MAKES UP HIS MIND TO DO SOMETHING, THERE'S NO STOPPING HIM.
WELL, WHATEVER HAPPENED, I'M THRILLED.
IT'S ALWAYS BEST WHEN ACTORS ARE INTO THEIR WORK!

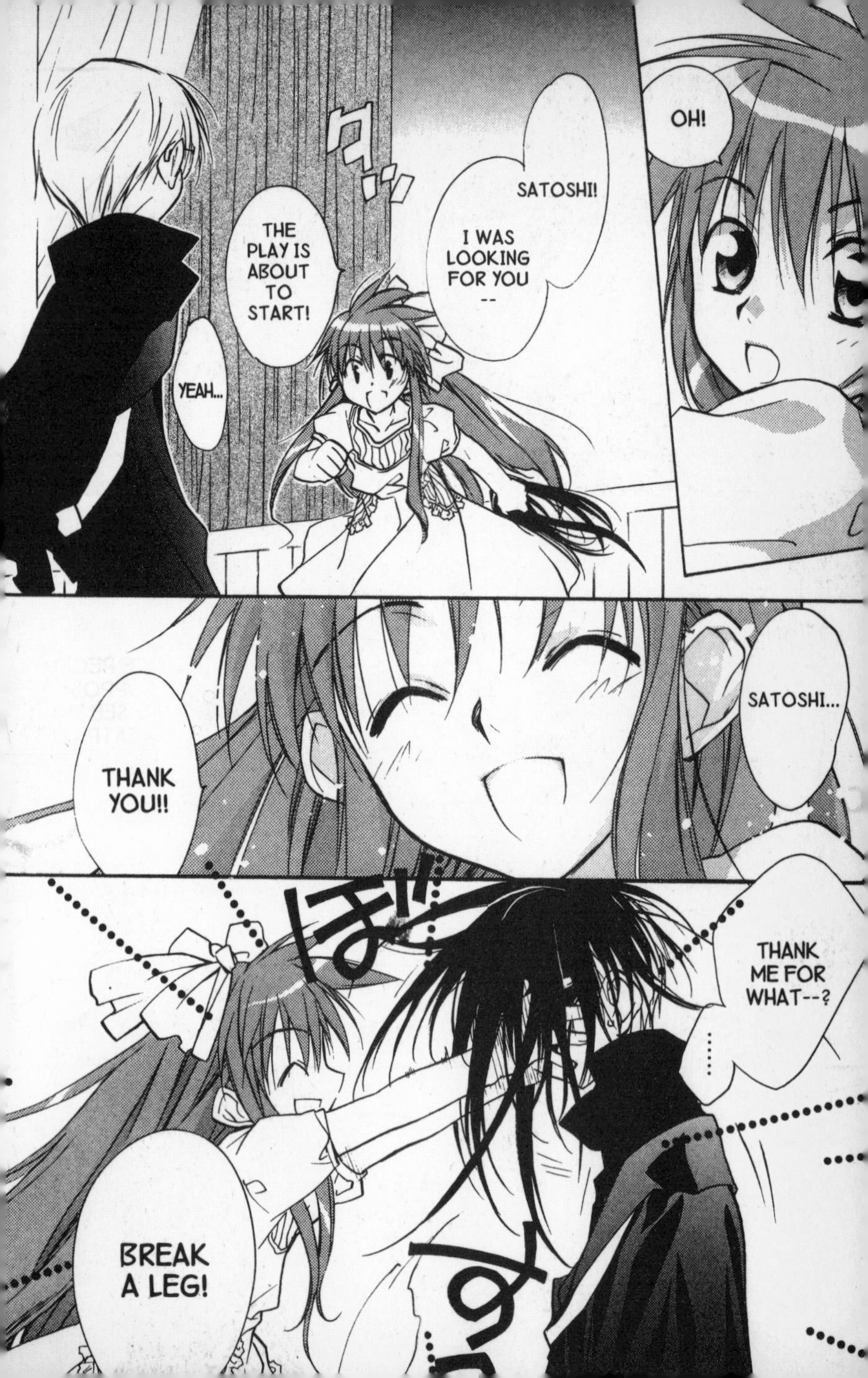
OH!
SATOSHI!
I WAS LOOKING FOR YOU --
THE PLAY IS ABOUT TO START!
YEAH...
SATOSHI...
THANK YOU!!
THANK ME FOR WHAT--?
......
BREAK A LEG!

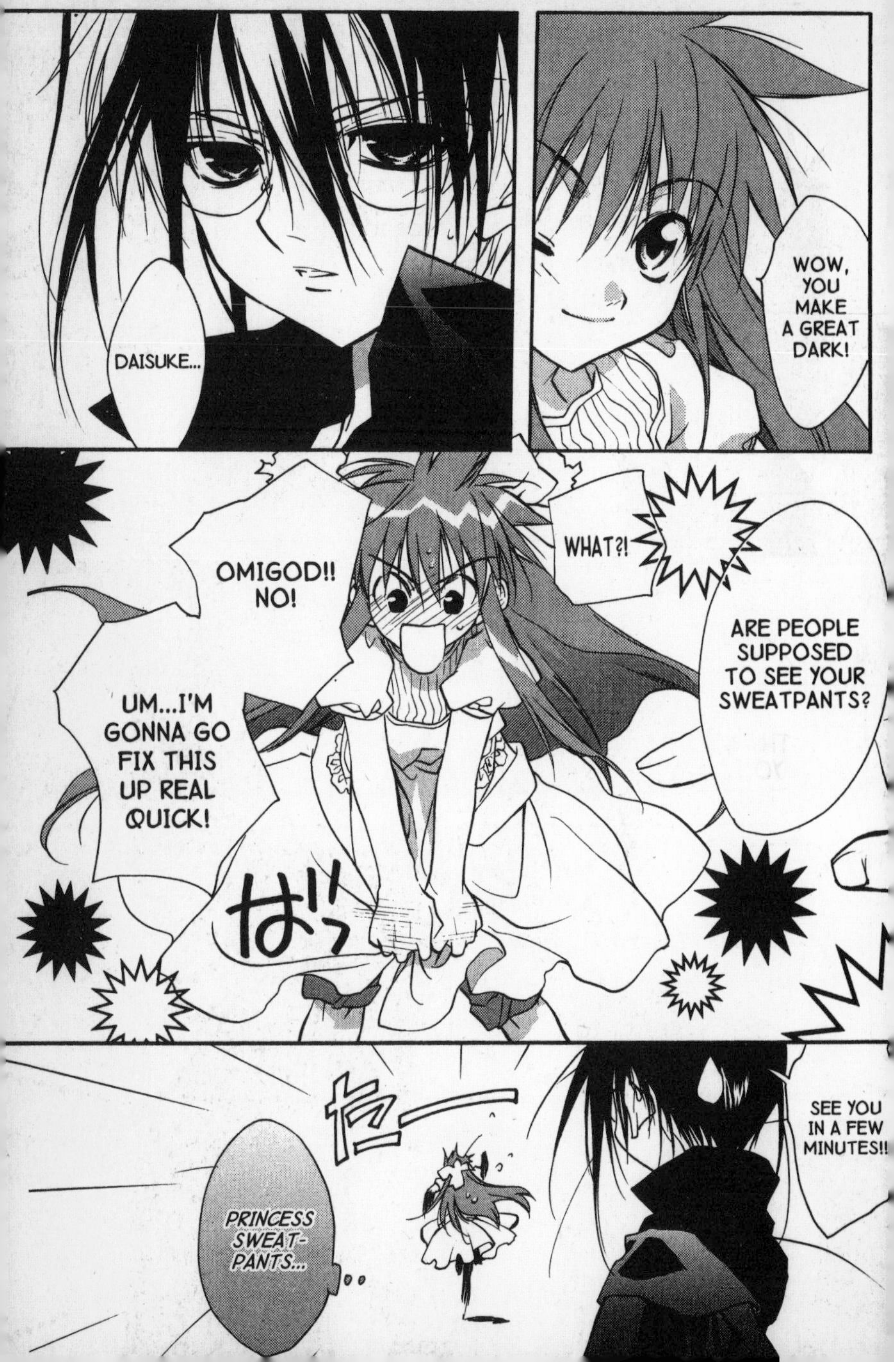
WOW, YOU MAKE A GREAT DARK!
DAISUKE...
ARE PEOPLE SUPPOSED TO SEE YOUR SWEATPANTS?
WHAT?!
OMIGOD!! NO!
UM...I'M GONNA GO FIX THIS UP REAL QUICK!
はっ
SEE YOU IN A FEW MINUTES!!
たーー
PRINCESS SWEAT-PANTS...

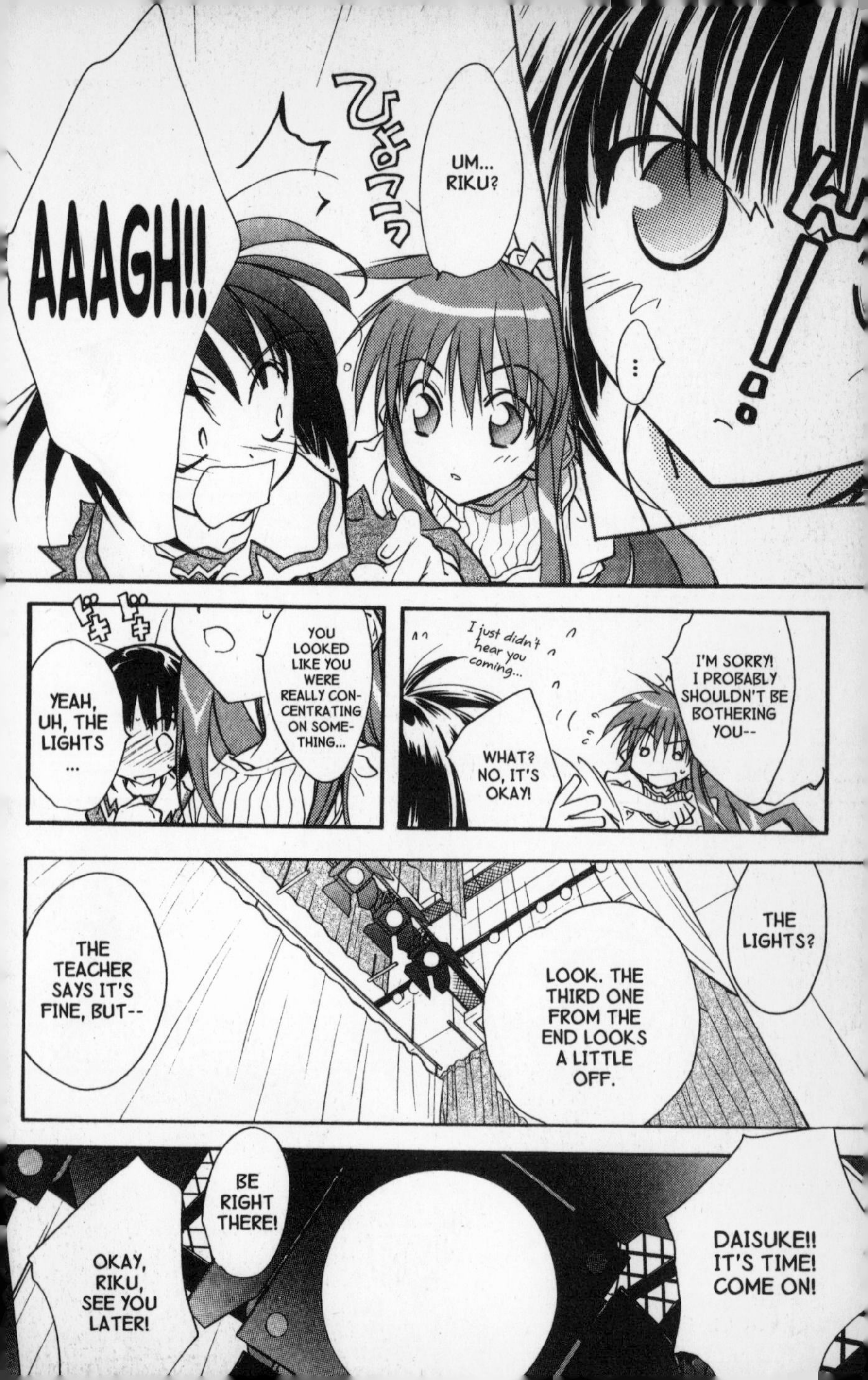
!!
...
UM... RIKU?
ひよっ
AAAGH!!
I'M SORRY! I PROBABLY SHOULDN'T BE BOTHERING YOU--
WHAT? NO, IT'S OKAY!
I just didn't hear you coming...
YOU LOOKED LIKE YOU WERE REALLY CONCENTRATING ON SOMETHING...
YEAH, UH, THE LIGHTS ...
THE LIGHTS?
LOOK. THE THIRD ONE FROM THE END LOOKS A LITTLE OFF.
THE TEACHER SAYS IT'S FINE, BUT--
DAISUKE!! IT'S TIME! COME ON!
BE RIGHT THERE!
OKAY, RIKU, SEE YOU LATER!

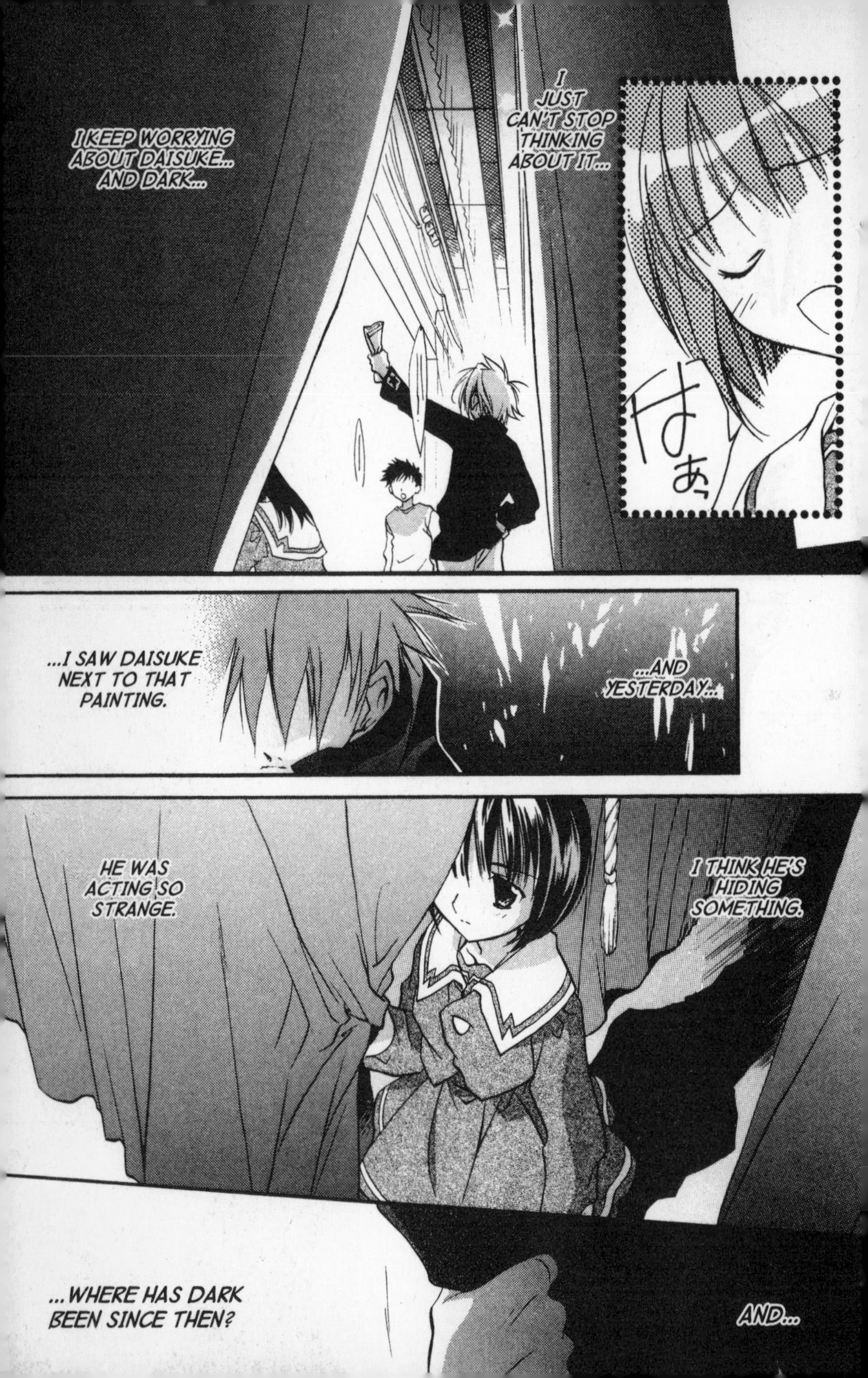
はぁ
I JUST CAN'T STOP THINKING ABOUT IT...
I KEEP WORRYING ABOUT DAISUKE... AND DARK...
...AND YESTERDAY...
...I SAW DAISUKE NEXT TO THAT PAINTING.
I THINK HE'S HIDING SOMETHING.
HE WAS ACTING SO STRANGE.
AND...
...WHERE HAS DARK BEEN SINCE THEN?

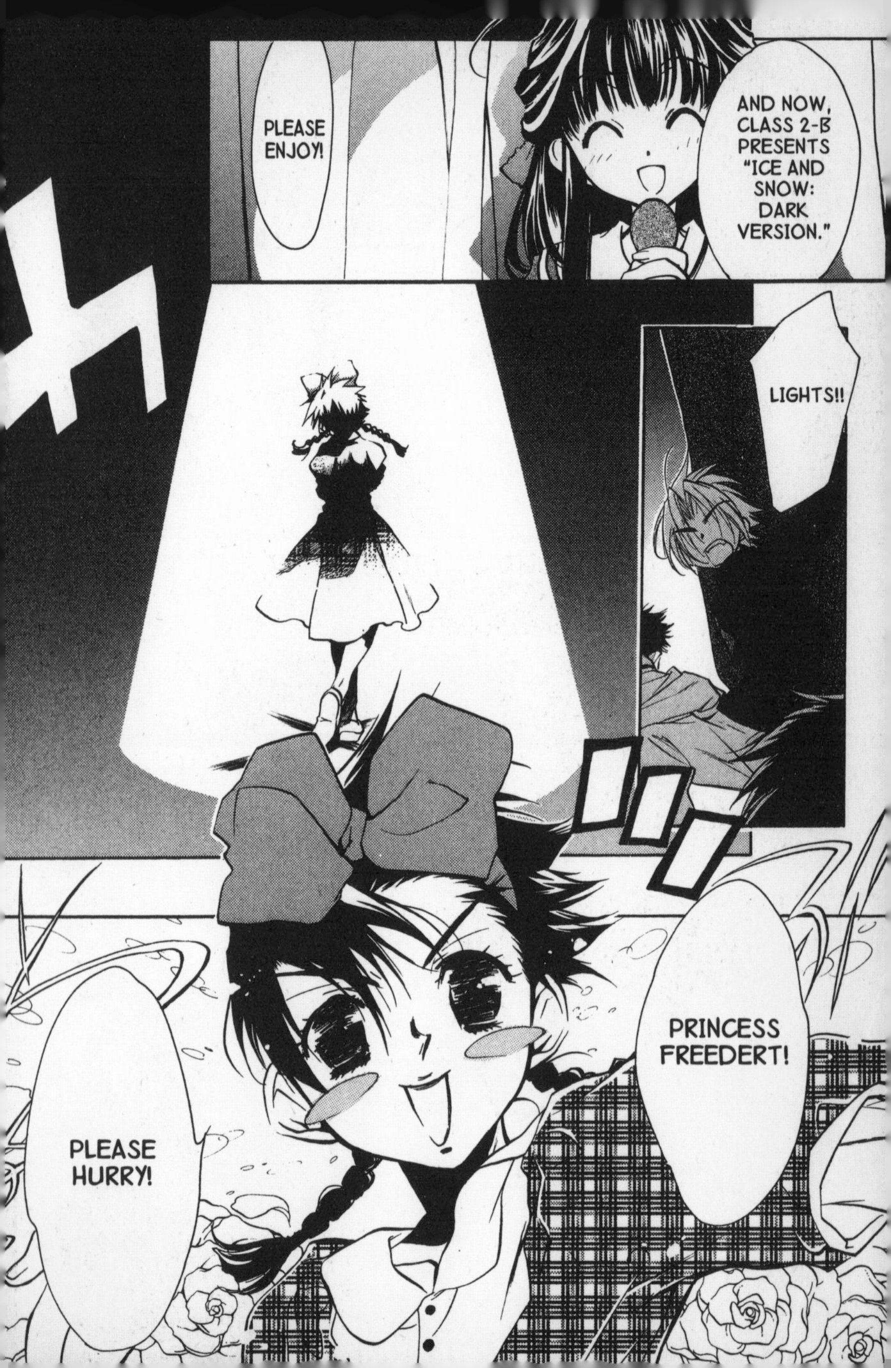
AND NOW, CLASS 2-B PRESENTS "ICE AND SNOW: DARK VERSION."
PLEASE ENJOY!
LIGHTS!!
PRINCESS FREEDERT!
PLEASE HURRY!

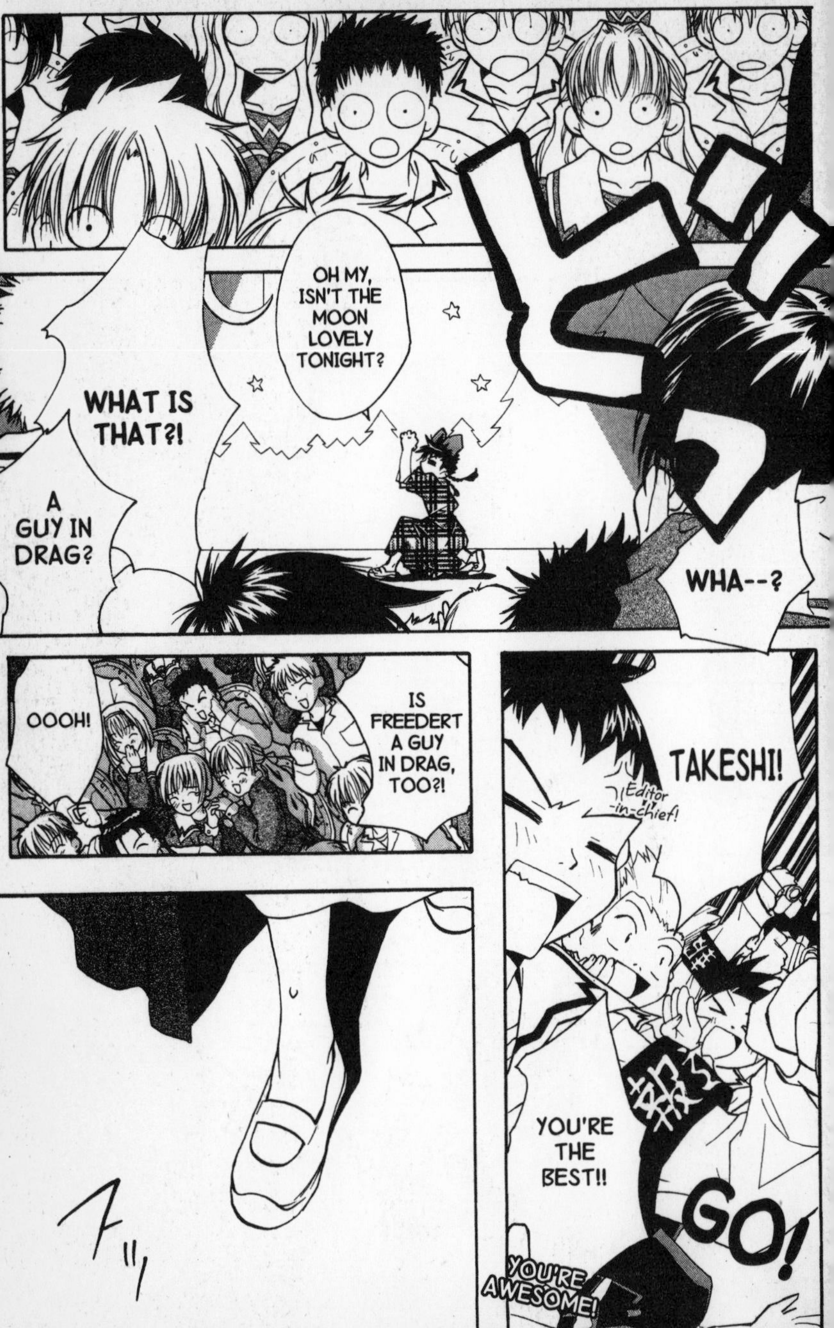
WHA--?
OH MY, ISN'T THE MOON LOVELY TONIGHT?
WHAT IS THAT?!
A GUY IN DRAG?
TAKESHI!
Editor-in-chief!
YOU'RE THE BEST!!
GO!
YOU'RE AWESOME!
IS FREEDERT A GUY IN DRAG, TOO?!
OOOH!

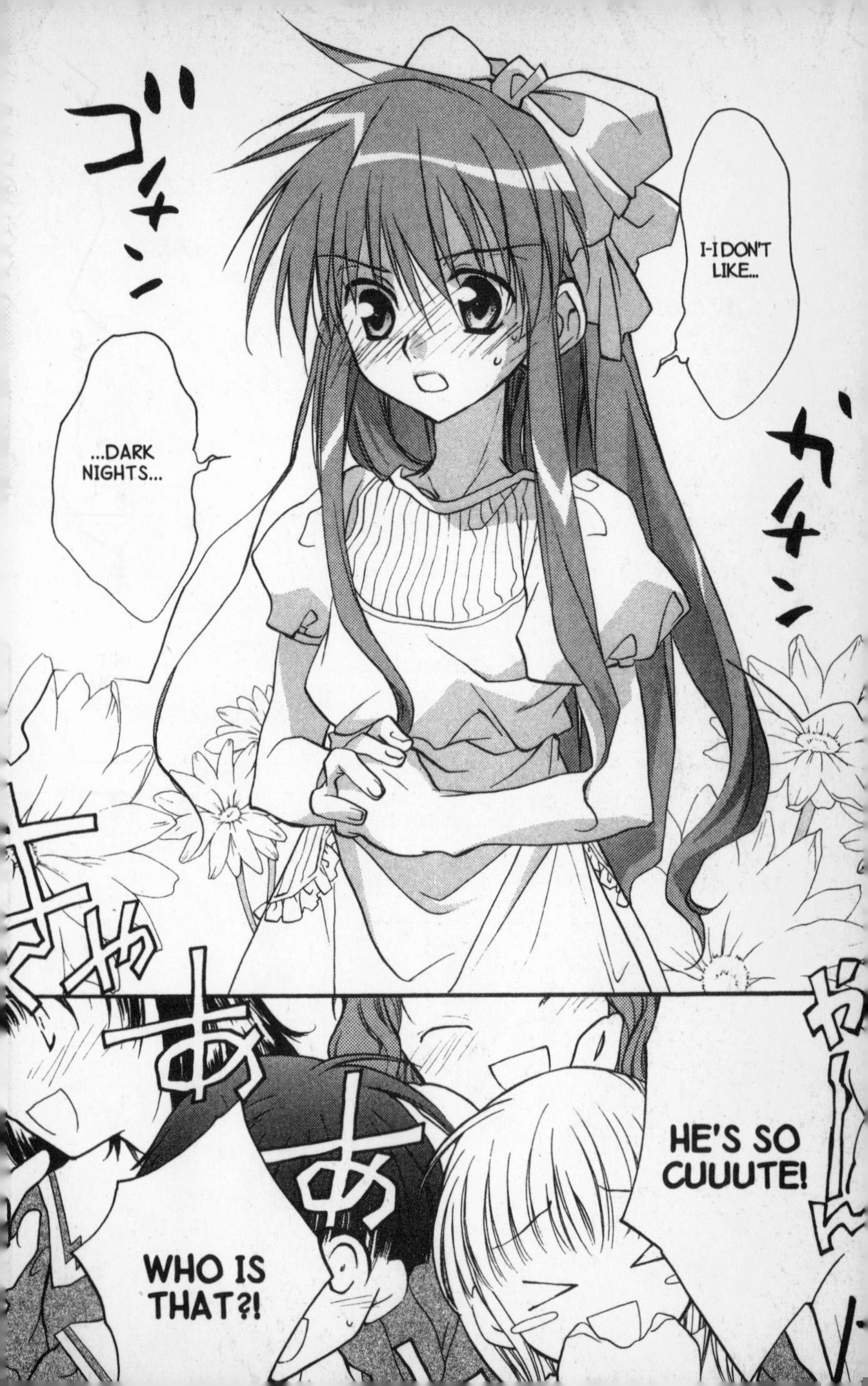
I-I DON'T LIKE...
...DARK NIGHTS...
HE'S SO CUUUTE!
WHO IS THAT?!

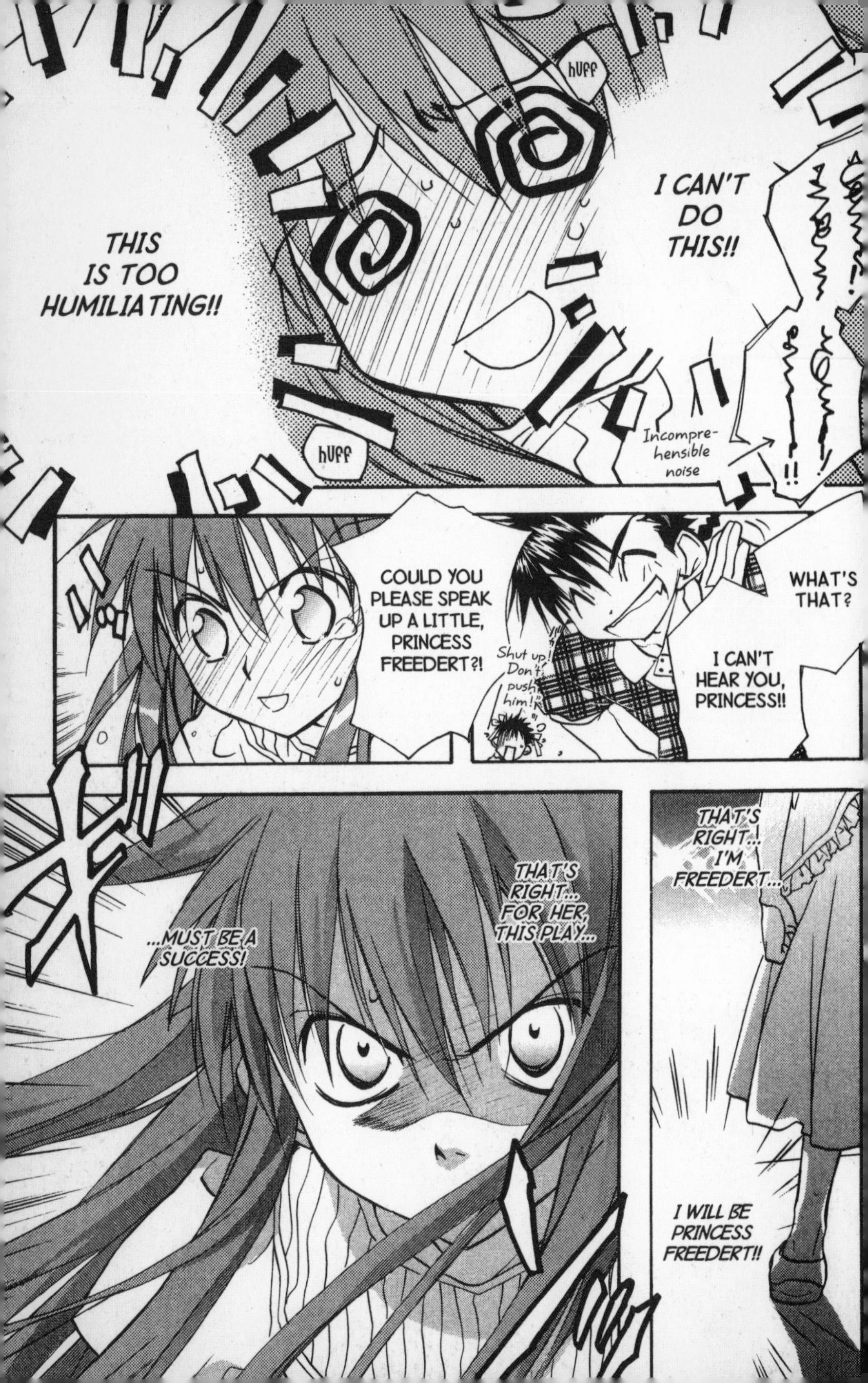
I CAN'T DO THIS!!
THIS IS TOO HUMILIATING!!
huff
huff
Incompre-hensible noise
WHAT'S THAT?
I CAN'T HEAR YOU, PRINCESS!!
COULD YOU PLEASE SPEAK UP A LITTLE, PRINCESS FREEDERT?!
Shut up! Don't push him!
THAT'S RIGHT... I'M FREEDERT...
I WILL BE PRINCESS FREEDERT!!
THAT'S RIGHT... FOR HER, THIS PLAY...
...MUST BE A SUCCESS!

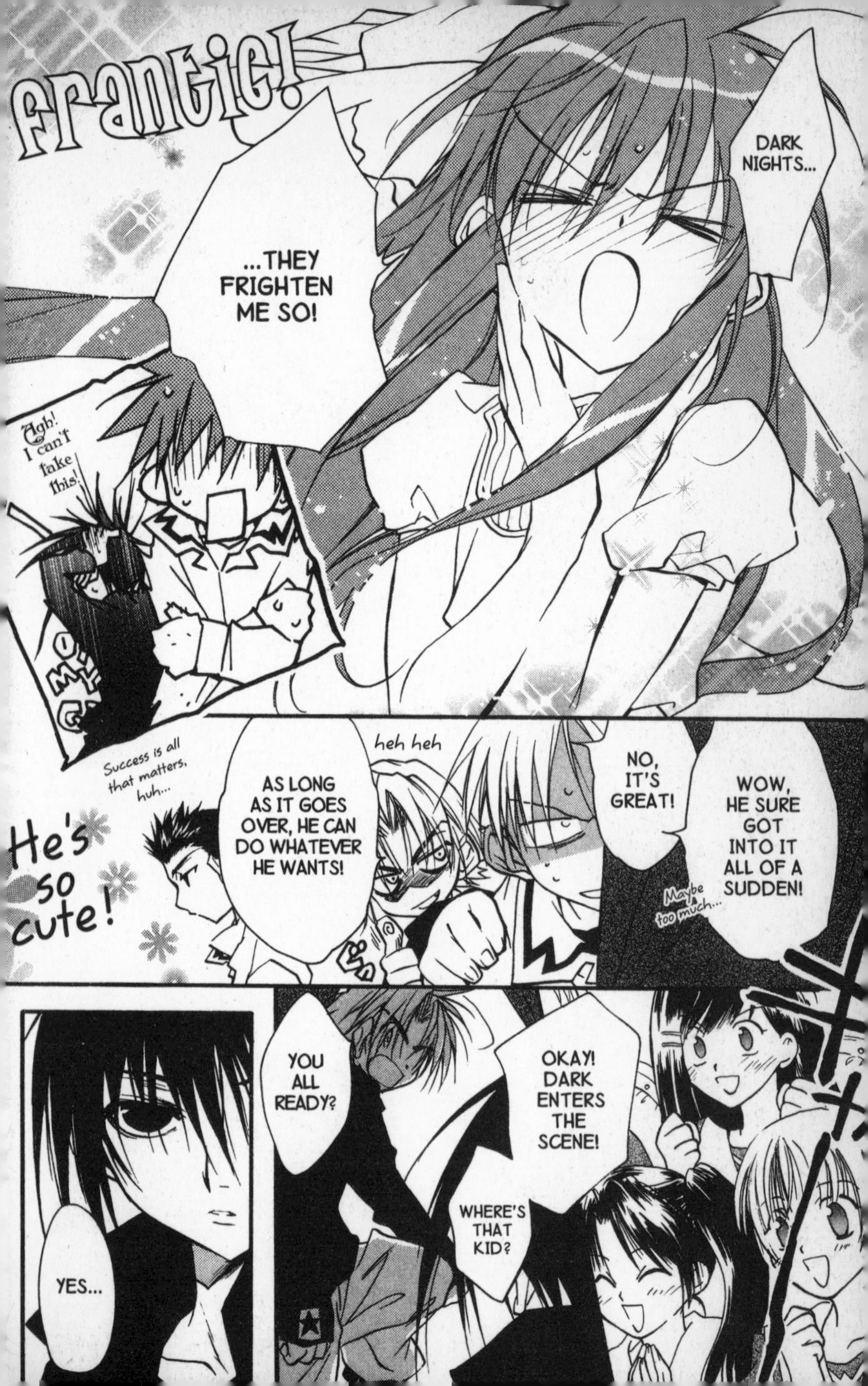
DARK NIGHTS...
...THEY FRIGHTEN ME SO!
Frantic!
Agh! I can't take this!
WOW, HE SURE GOT INTO IT ALL OF A SUDDEN!
Maybe too much...
NO, IT'S GREAT!
heh heh
AS LONG AS IT GOES OVER, HE CAN DO WHATEVER HE WANTS!
Success is all that matters, huh...
He's so cute!
OKAY! DARK ENTERS THE SCENE!
YOU ALL READY?
WHERE'S THAT KID?
YES...

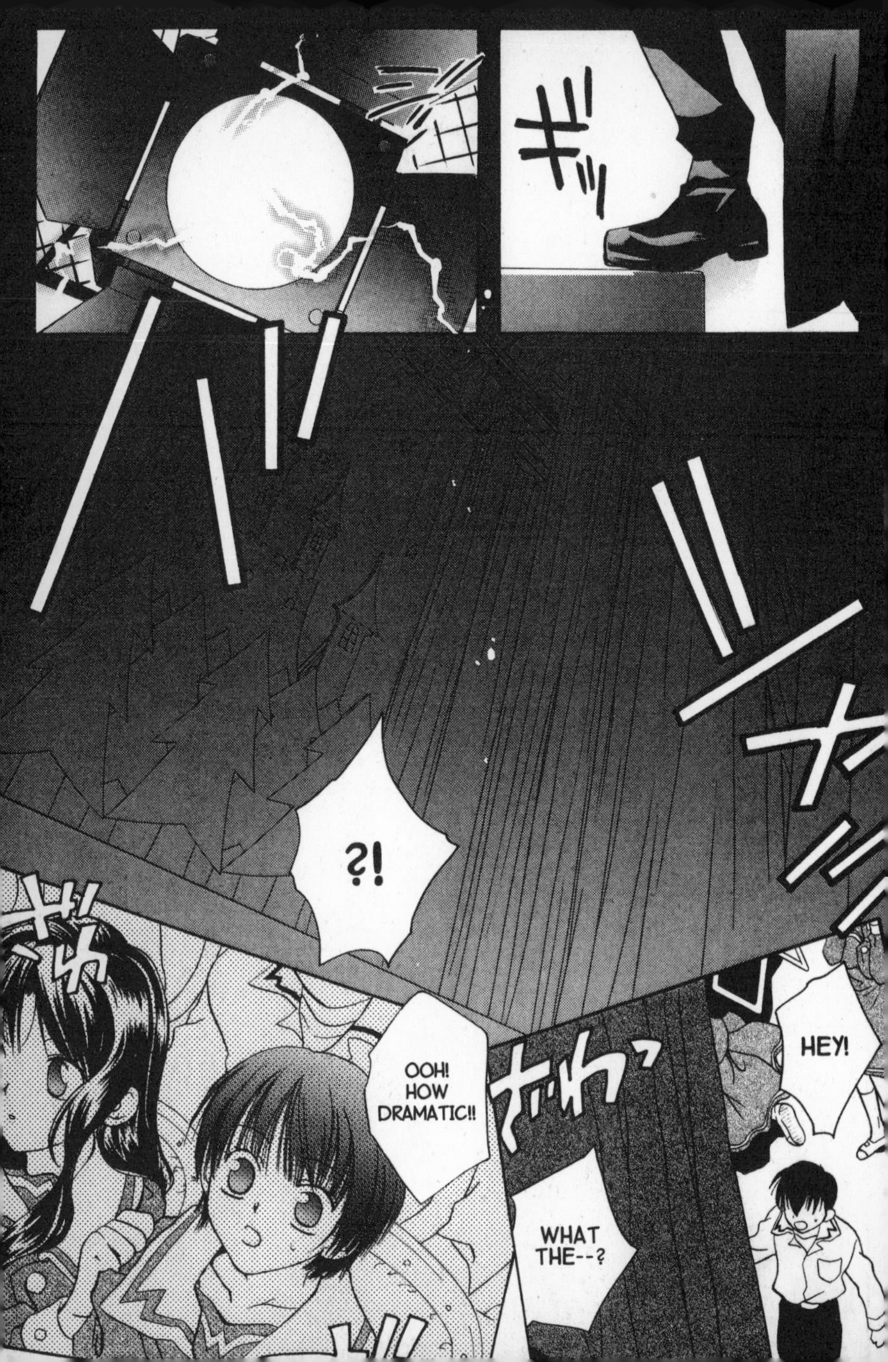
ギッ
?!
HEY!
ざわっ
OOH! HOW DRAMATIC!!
WHAT THE--?

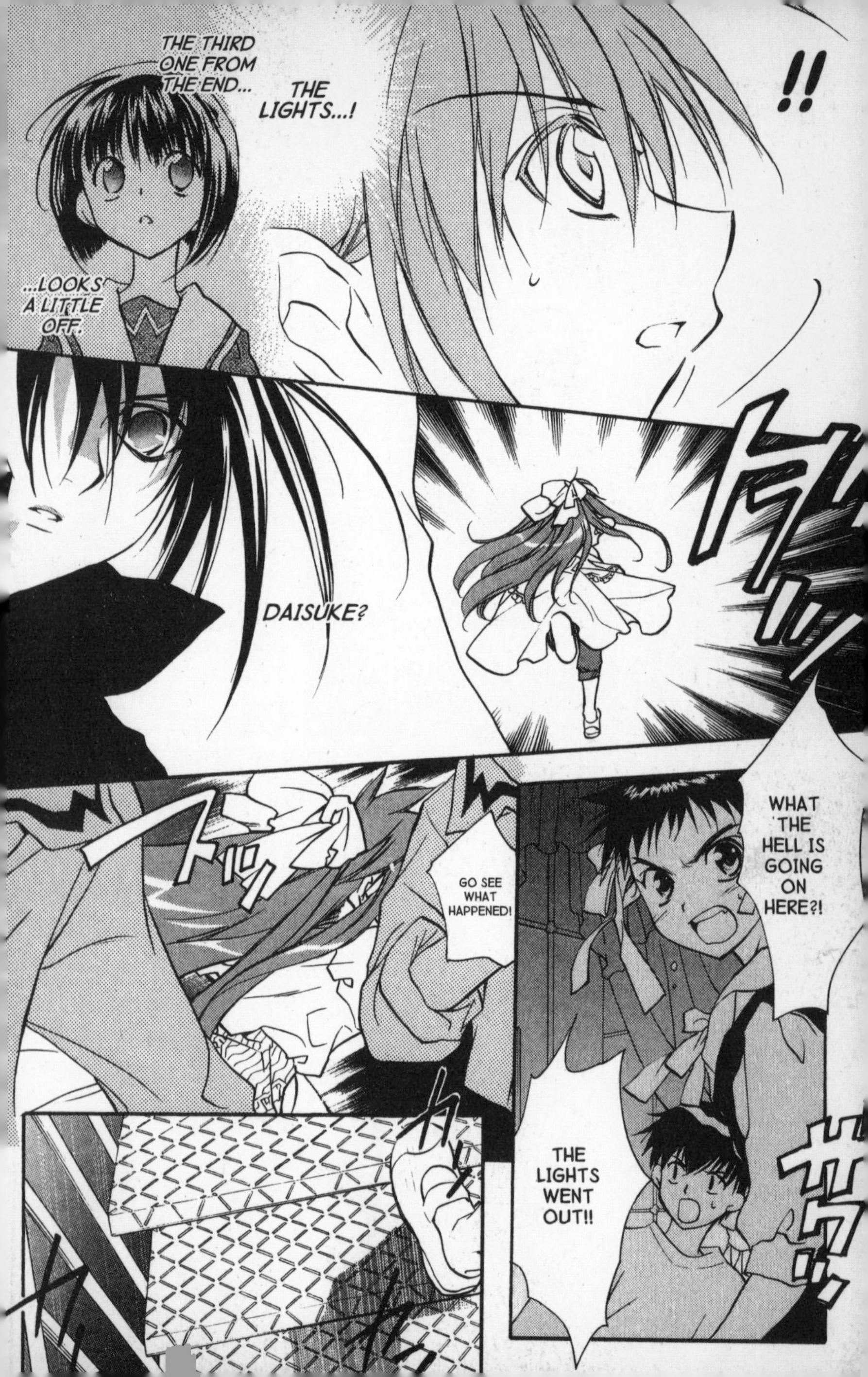
!!
THE LIGHTS...!
THE THIRD ONE FROM THE END...
...LOOKS A LITTLE OFF.
DAISUKE?
WHAT THE HELL IS GOING ON HERE?!
GO SEE WHAT HAPPENED!
THE LIGHTS WENT OUT!!

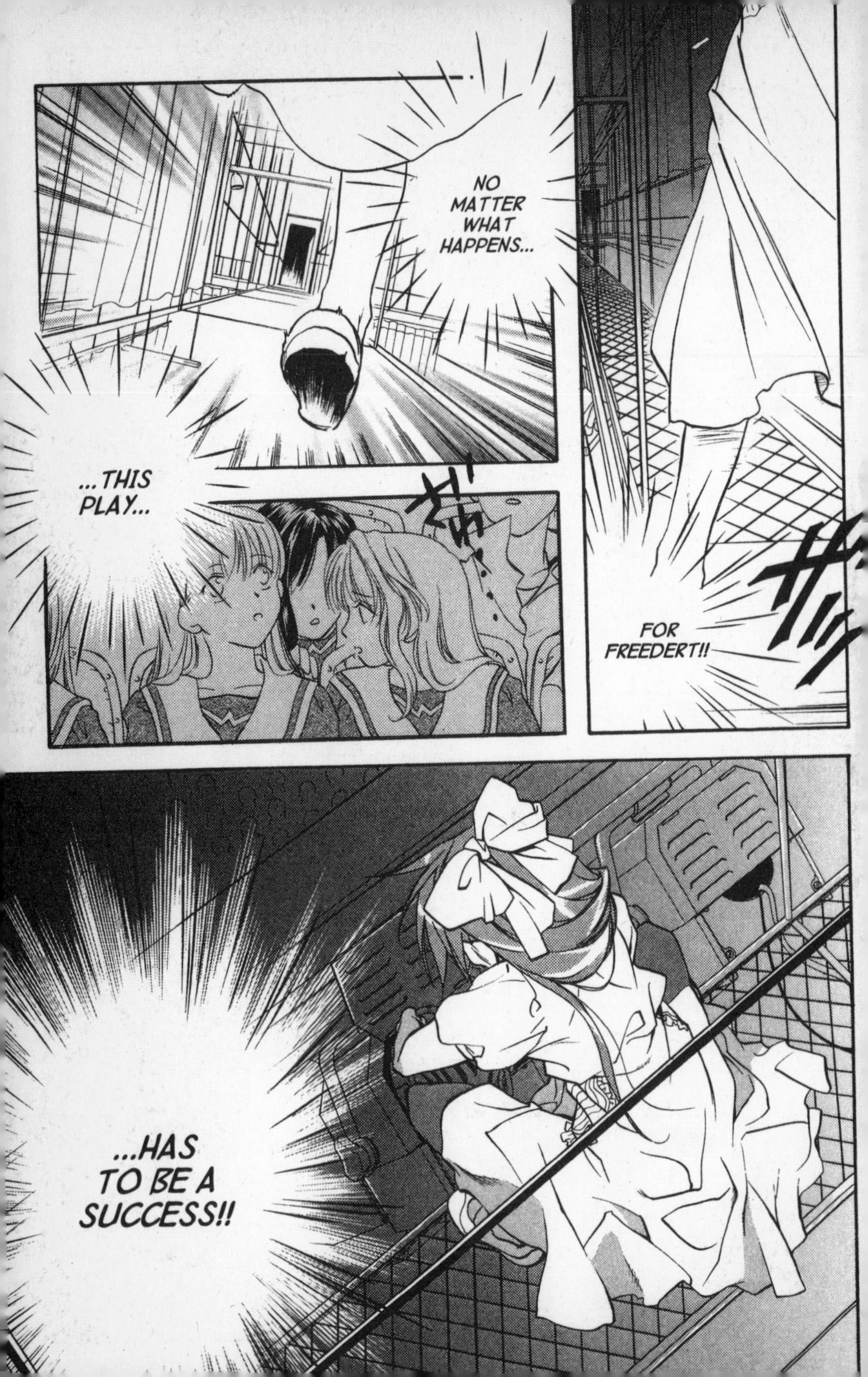
NO MATTER WHAT HAPPENS...
FOR FREEDERT!!
...THIS PLAY...
...HAS TO BE A SUCCESS!!

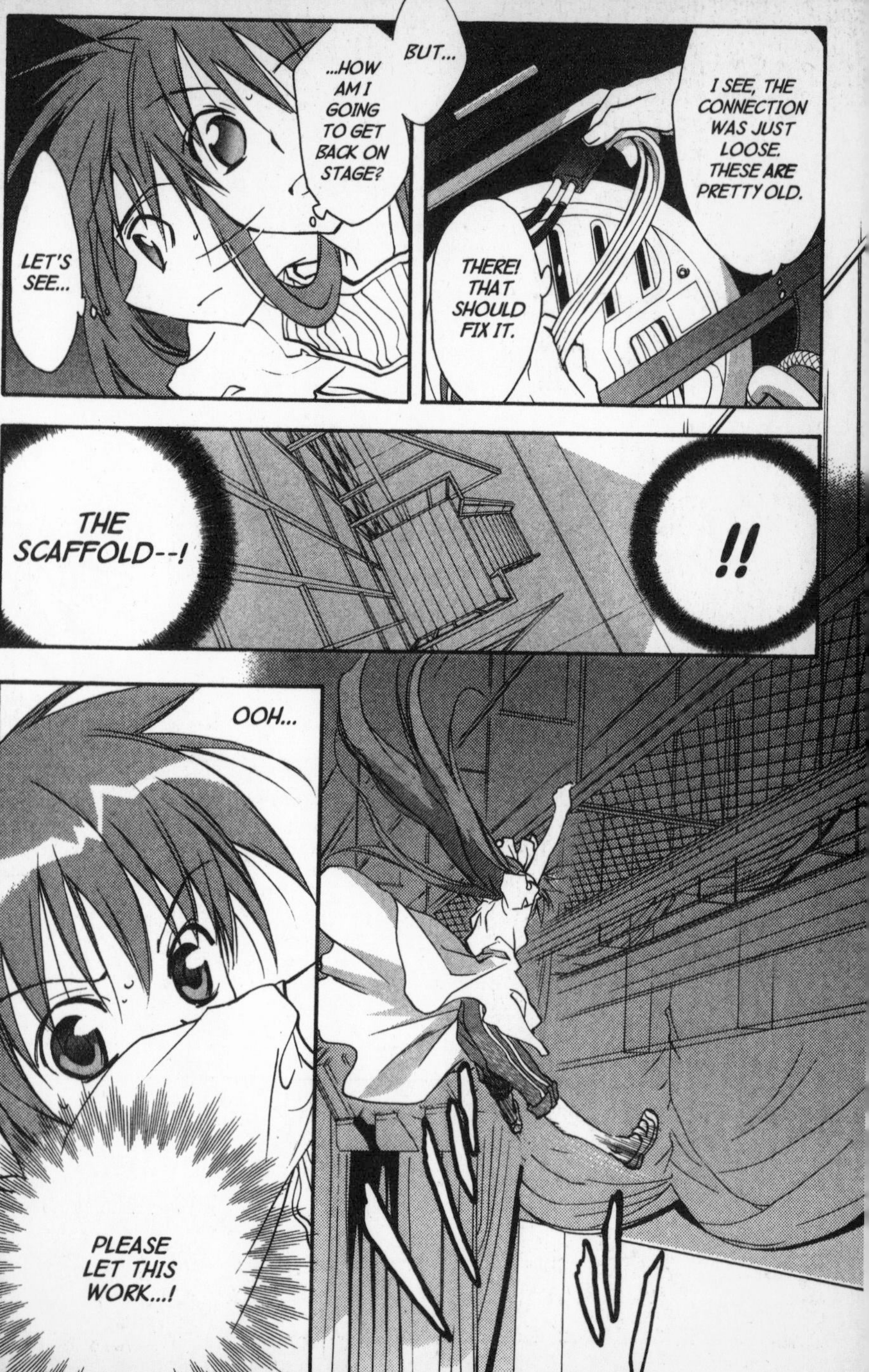
I SEE, THE CONNECTION WAS JUST LOOSE. THESE ARE PRETTY OLD.
THERE! THAT SHOULD FIX IT.
BUT...
...HOW AM I GOING TO GET BACK ON STAGE?
LET'S SEE...
!!
THE SCAFFOLD--!
OOH...
PLEASE LET THIS WORK...!

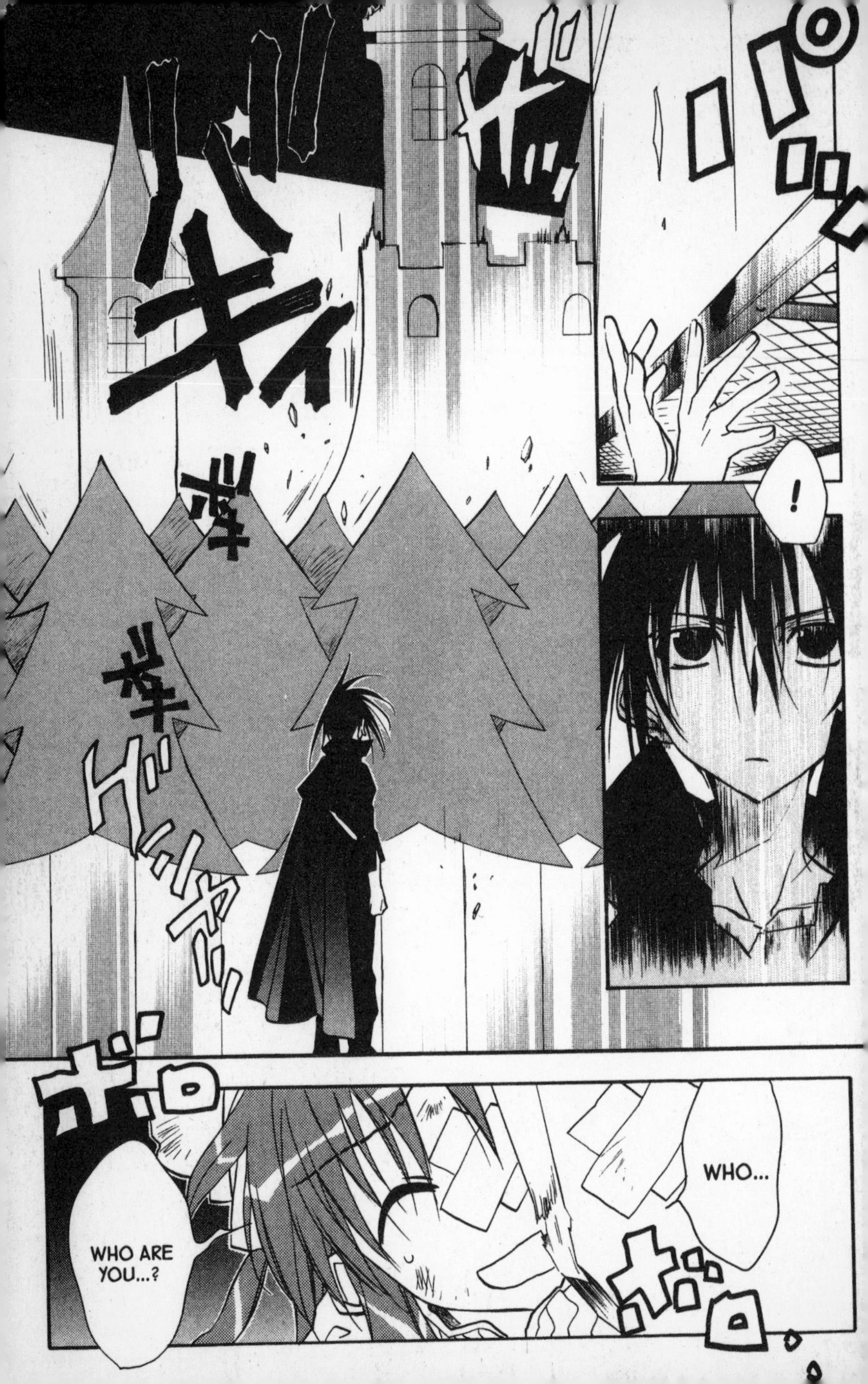

!
WHO...
WHO ARE YOU...?
ボロ

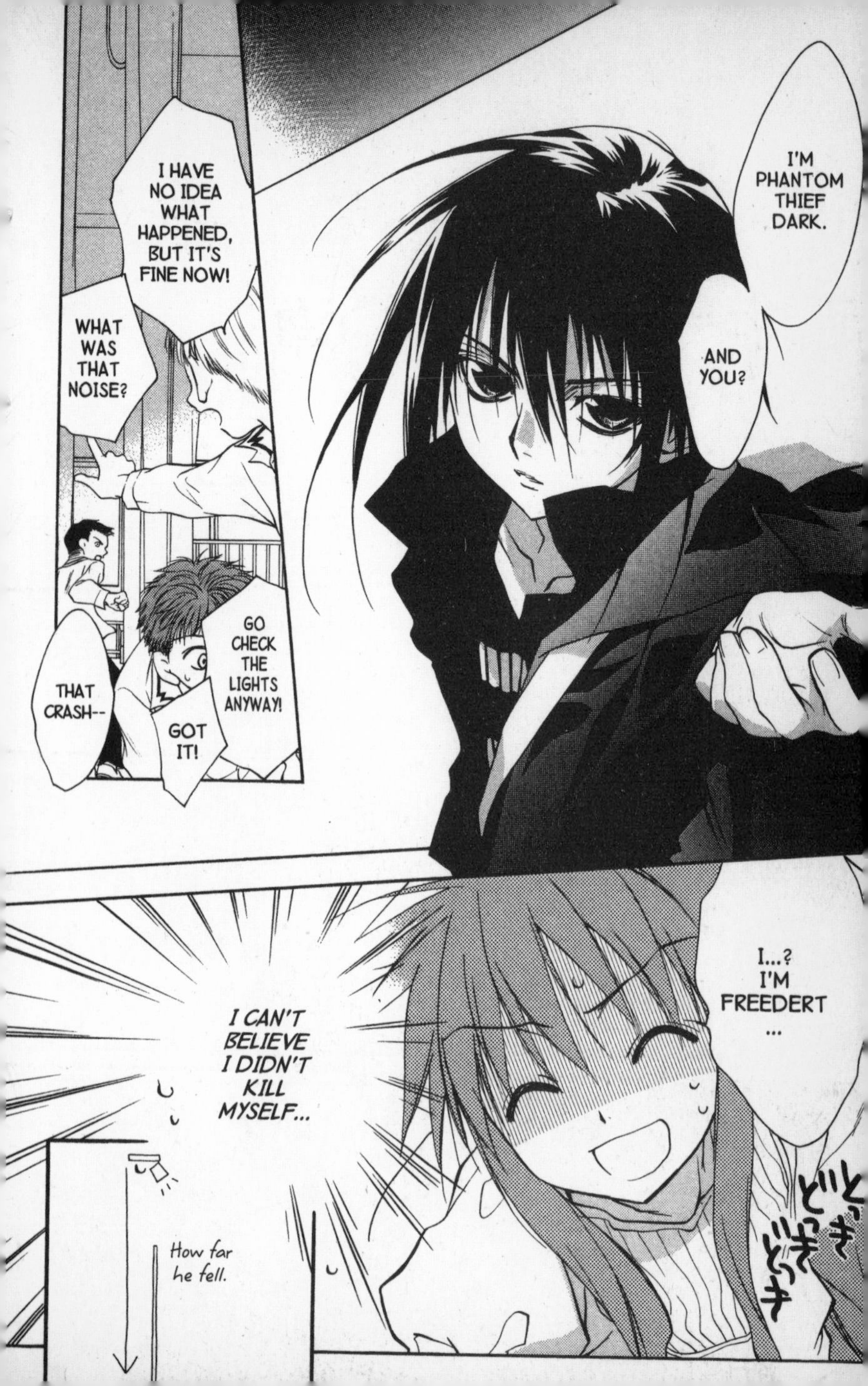
I'M PHANTOM THIEF DARK.
AND YOU?
I HAVE NO IDEA WHAT HAPPENED, BUT IT'S FINE NOW!
WHAT WAS THAT NOISE?
GO CHECK THE LIGHTS ANYWAY!
THAT CRASH--
GOT IT!
I...? I'M FREEDERT ...
I CAN'T BELIEVE I DIDN'T KILL MYSELF...
How far he fell.

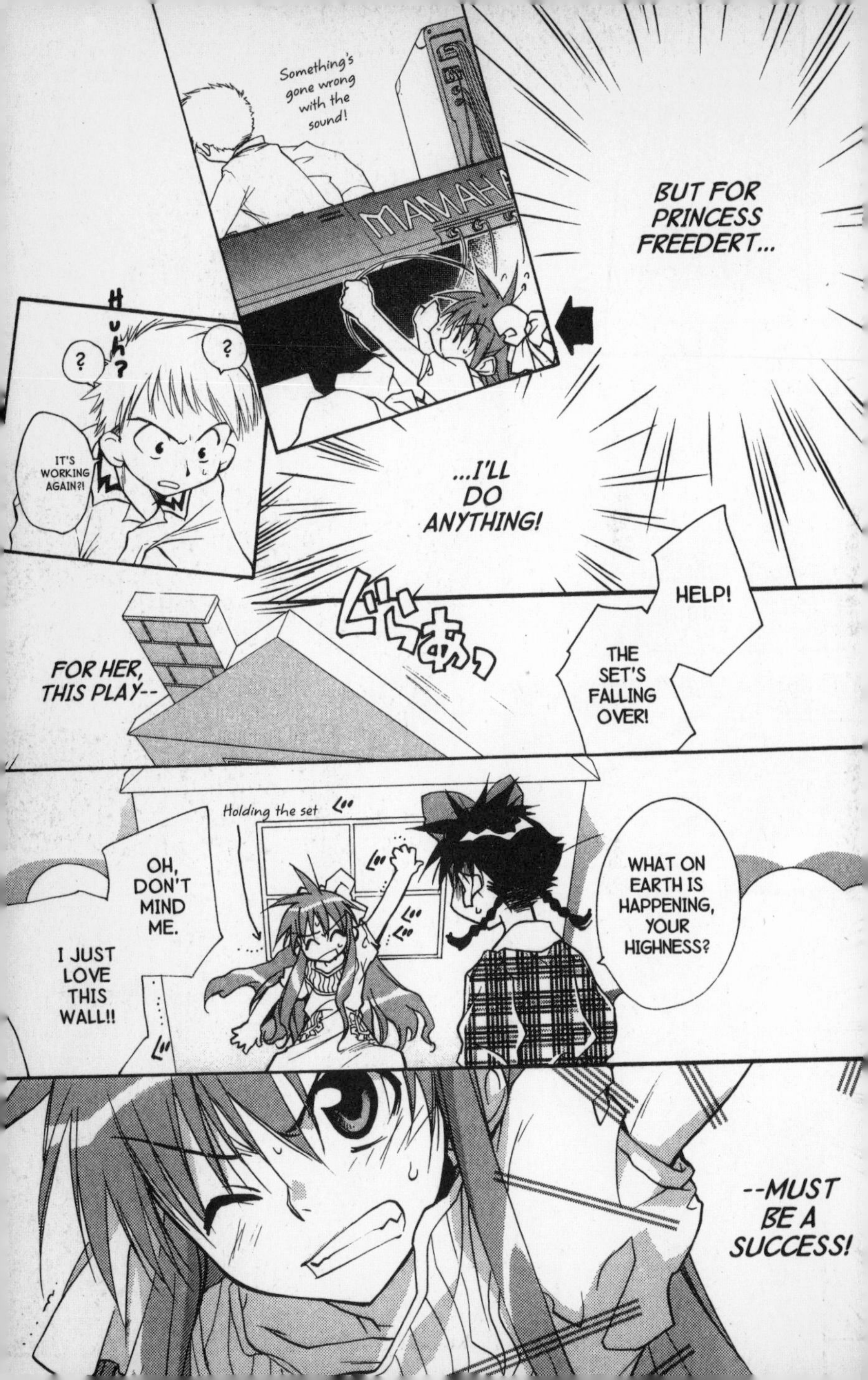

Something's gone wrong with the sound!
MAMAHA
BUT FOR PRINCESS FREEDERT...
Huh?
?
?
IT'S WORKING AGAIN?!
...I'LL DO ANYTHING!
HELP!
THE SET'S FALLING OVER!
ぐらあっ
FOR HER, THIS PLAY--
WHAT ON EARTH IS HAPPENING, YOUR HIGHNESS?
Holding the set
OH, DON'T MIND ME.
I JUST LOVE THIS WALL!!
--MUST BE A SUCCESS!

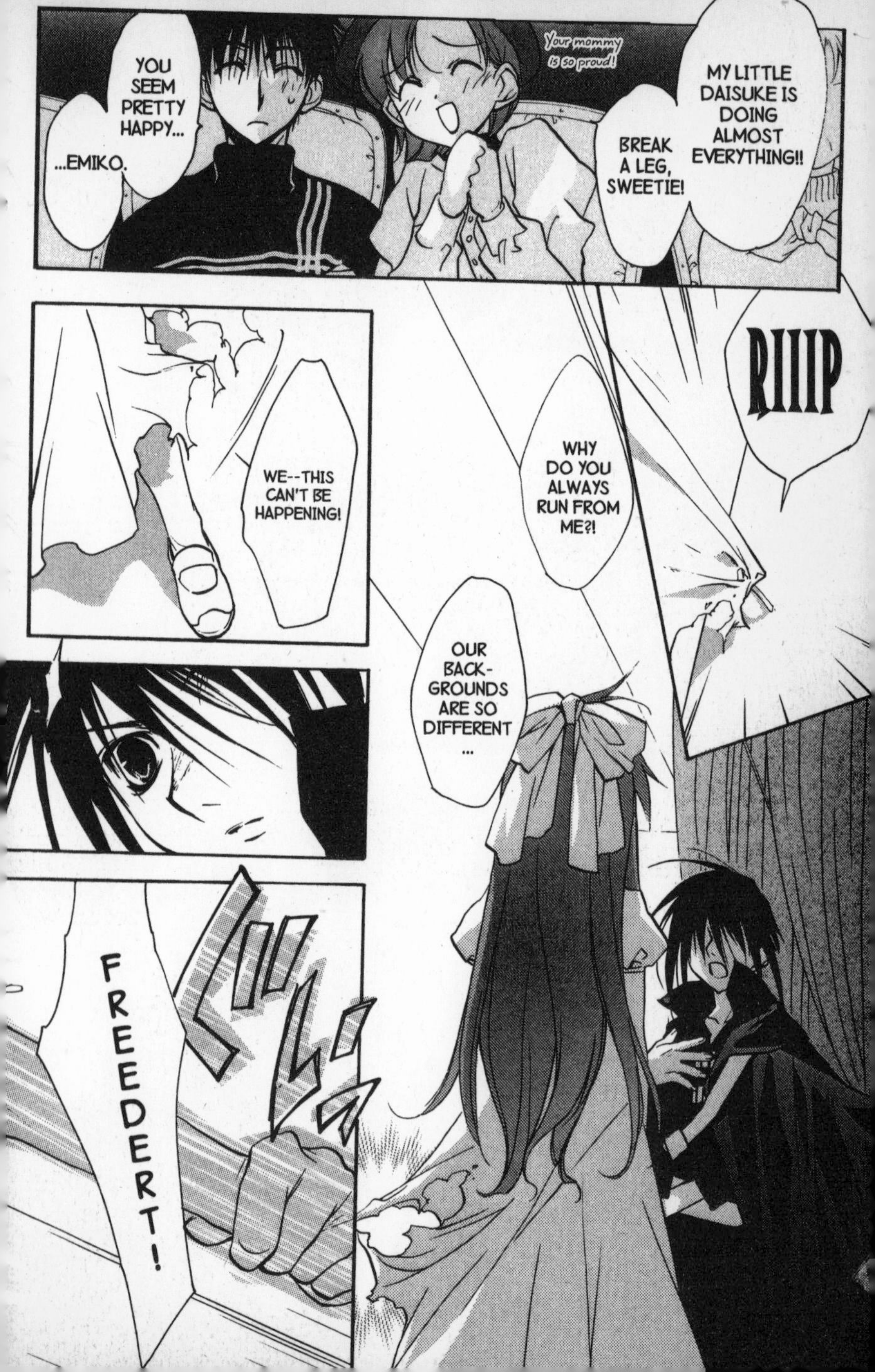
MY LITTLE DAISUKE IS DOING ALMOST EVERYTHING!!
BREAK A LEG, SWEETIE!
Your mommy is so proud!
YOU SEEM PRETTY HAPPY...
...EMIKO.
RIIIP
WHY DO YOU ALWAYS RUN FROM ME?!
WE--THIS CAN'T BE HAPPENING!
OUR BACK-GROUNDS ARE SO DIFFERENT ...
FREEDERT!

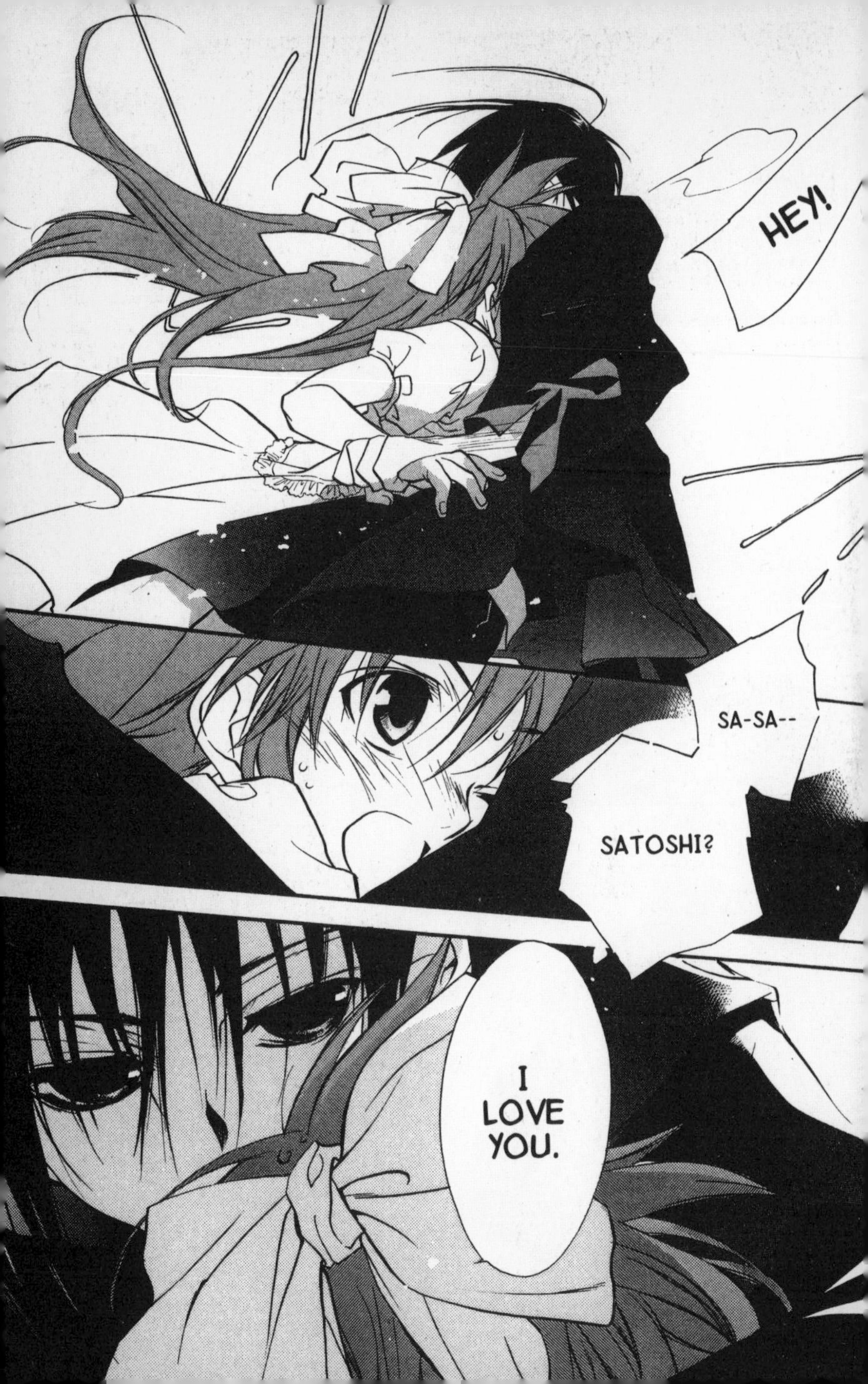
HEY!
SA-SA--
SATOSHI?
I LOVE YOU.

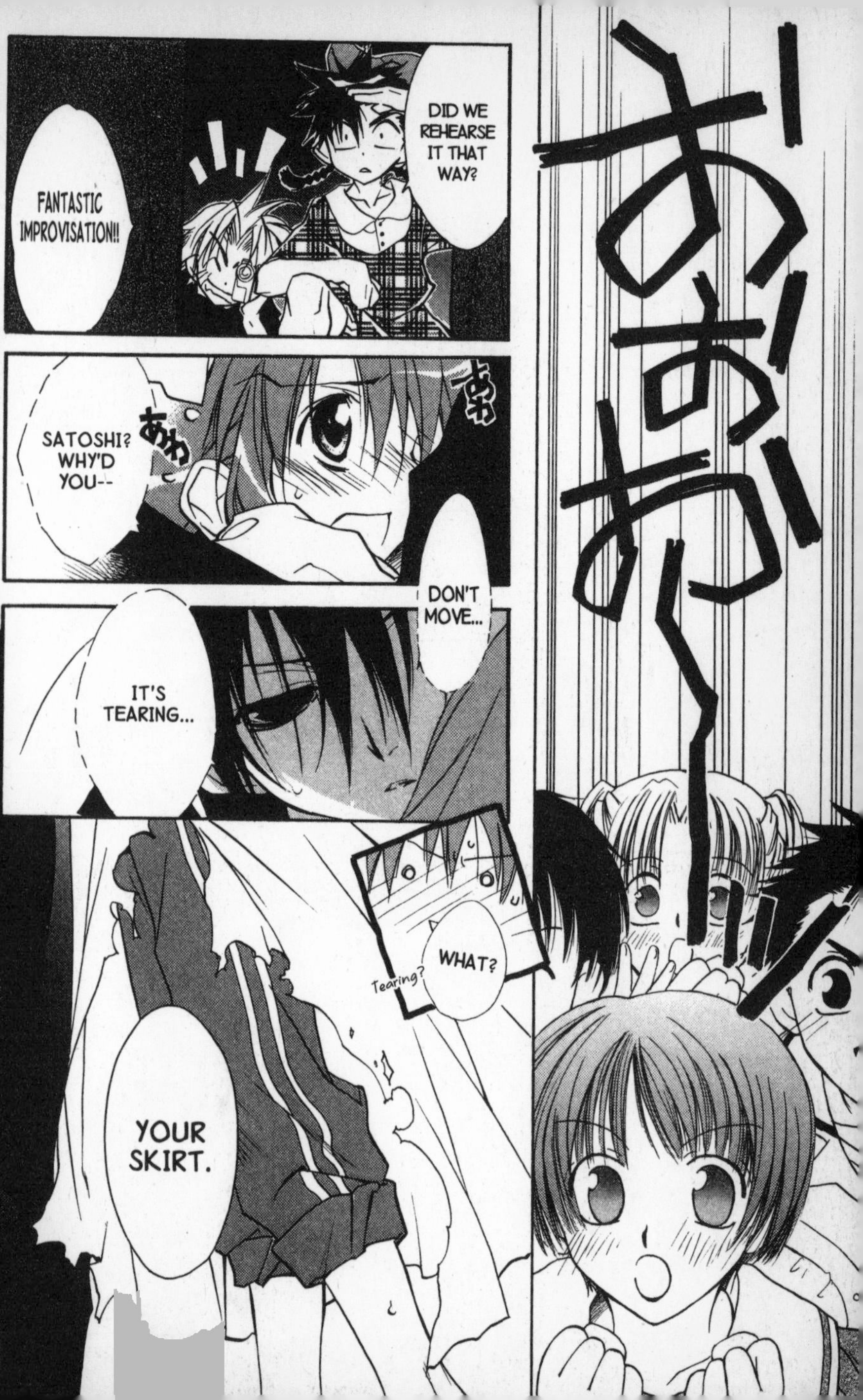

DID WE REHEARSE IT THAT WAY?
FANTASTIC IMPROVISATION!!
あわ
あわ
SATOSHI? WHY'D YOU--
DON'T MOVE...
IT'S TEARING...
WHAT?
Tearing?
YOUR SKIRT.

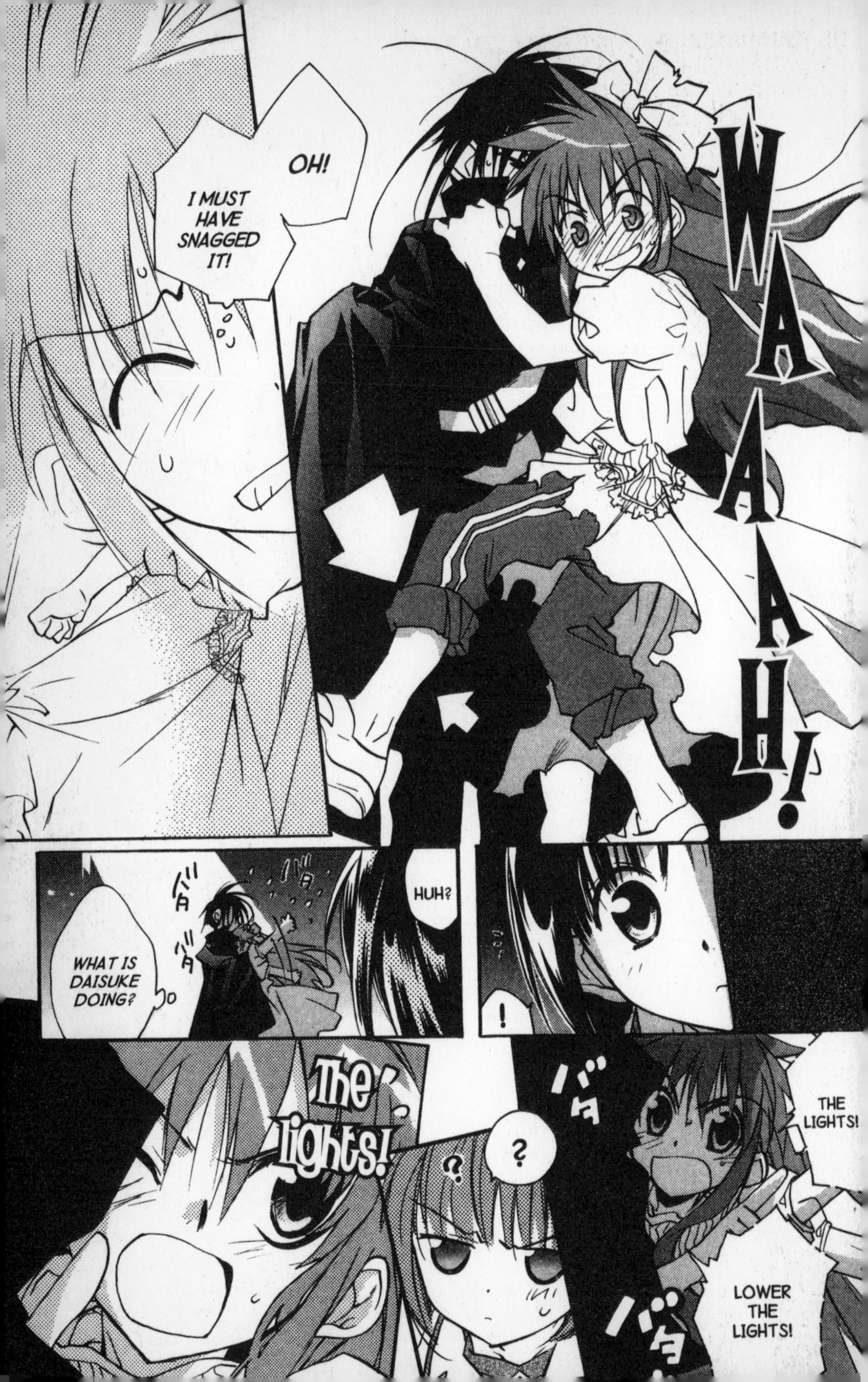
WAAAH!
OH!
I MUST HAVE SNAGGED IT!
HUH?
WHAT IS DAISUKE DOING?
!
THE LIGHTS!
LOWER THE LIGHTS!
?
The lights!

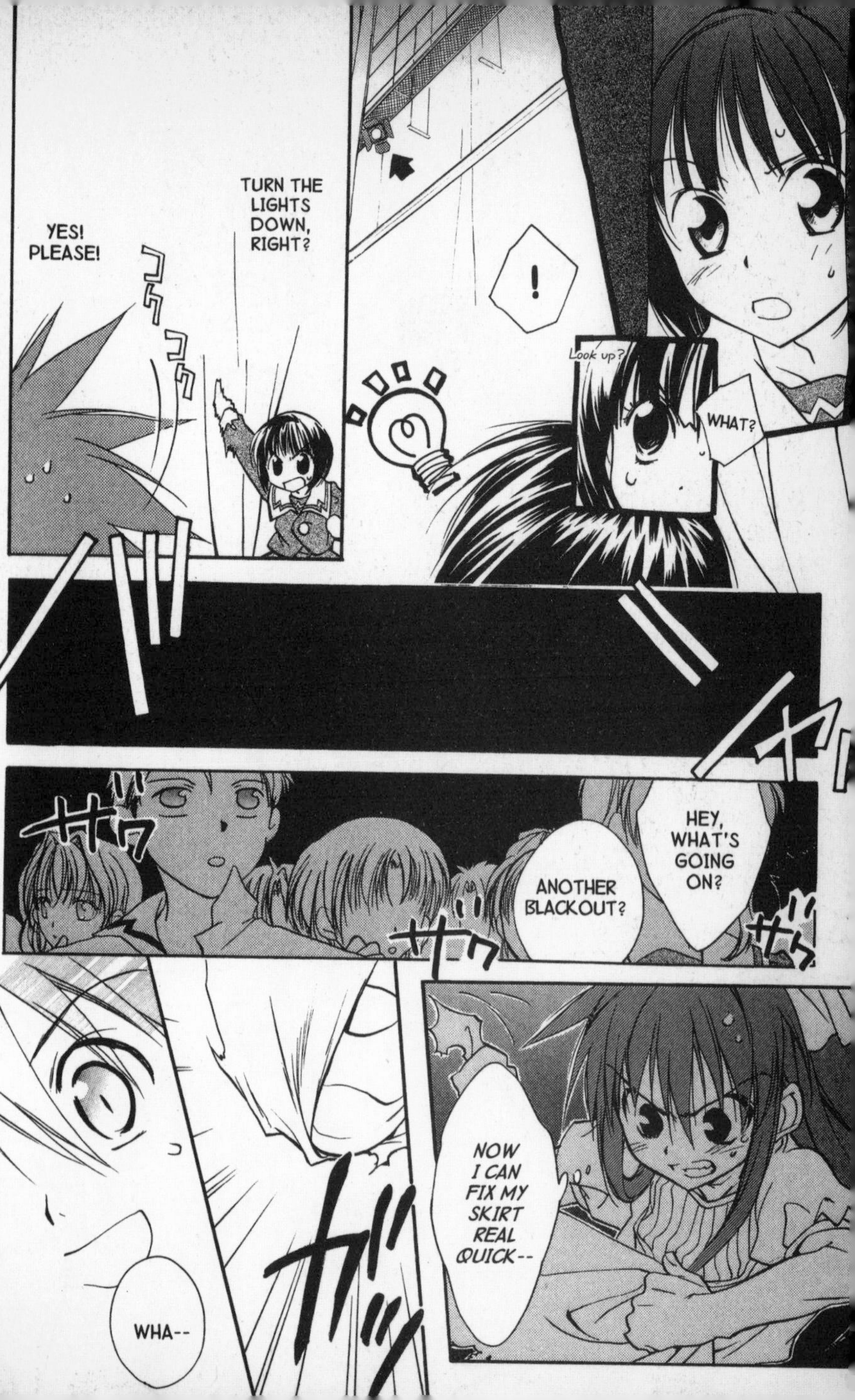
!
WHAT?
Look up?
TURN THE LIGHTS DOWN, RIGHT?
YES! PLEASE!
HEY, WHAT'S GOING ON?
ANOTHER BLACKOUT?
NOW I CAN FIX MY SKIRT REAL QUICK--
WHA--

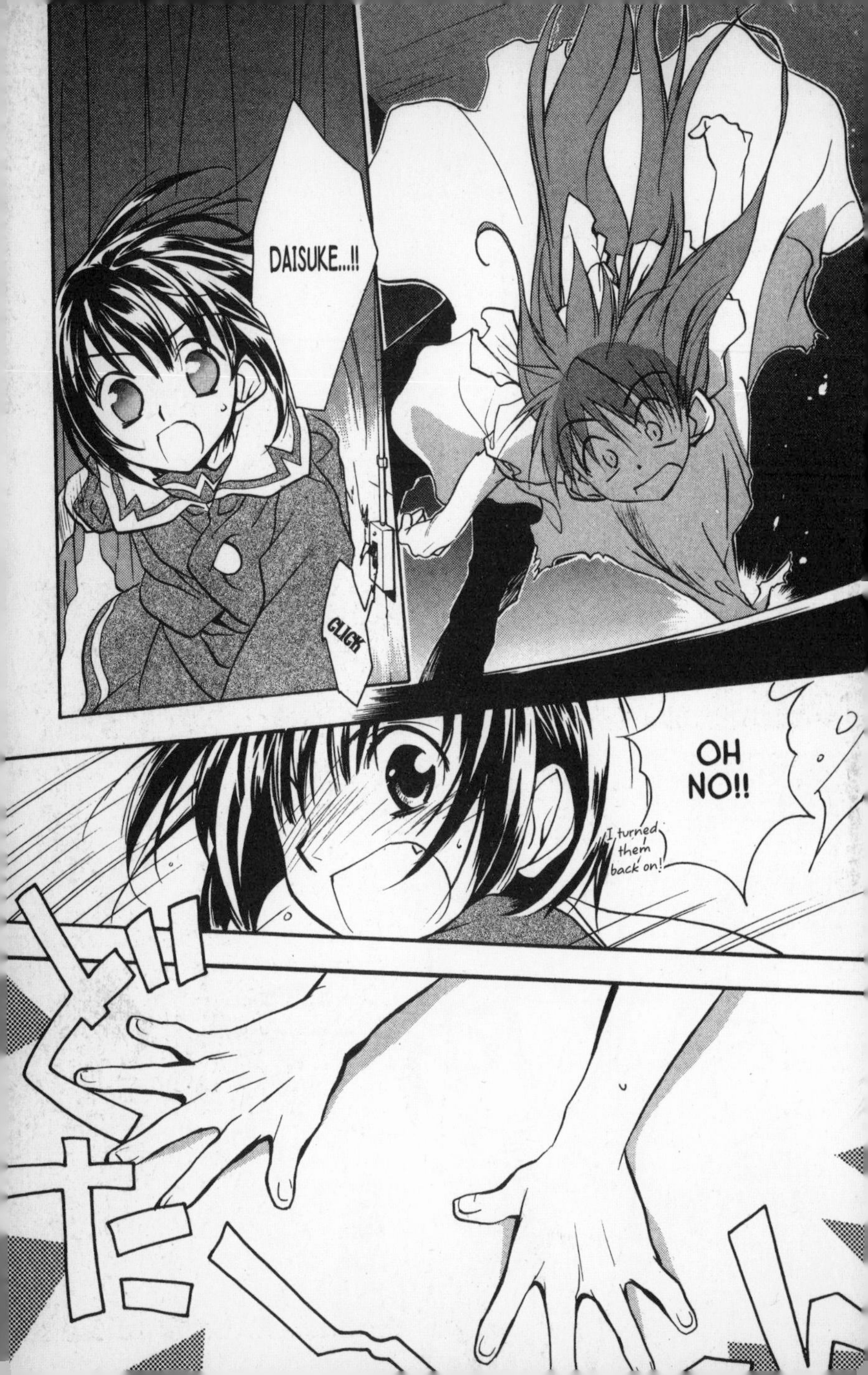
DAISUKE...!!
CLICK
OH NO!!
I turned them back on!

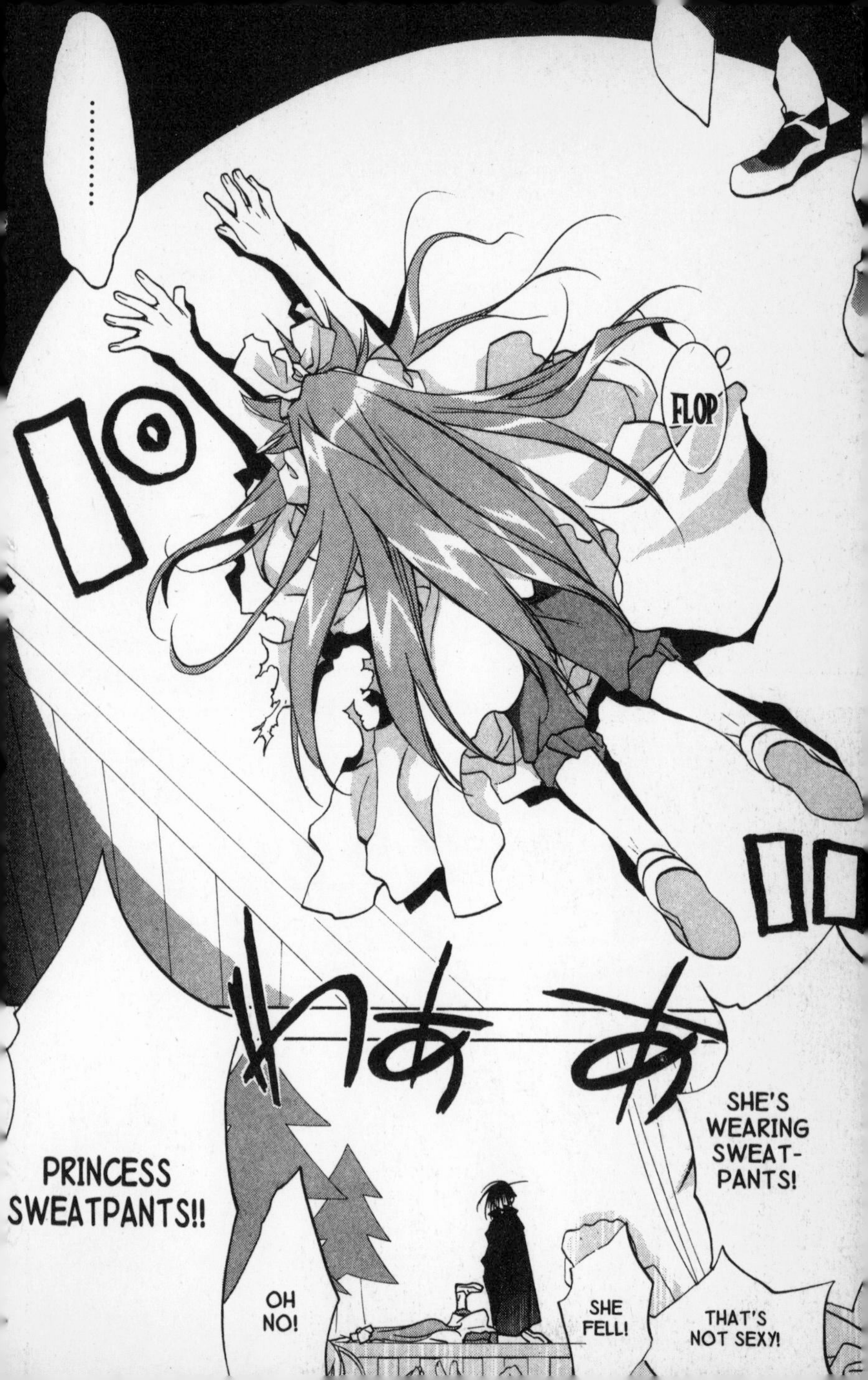
......
FLOP
わああ
SHE'S WEARING SWEAT-PANTS!
PRINCESS SWEATPANTS!!
THAT'S NOT SEXY!
SHE FELL!
OH NO!

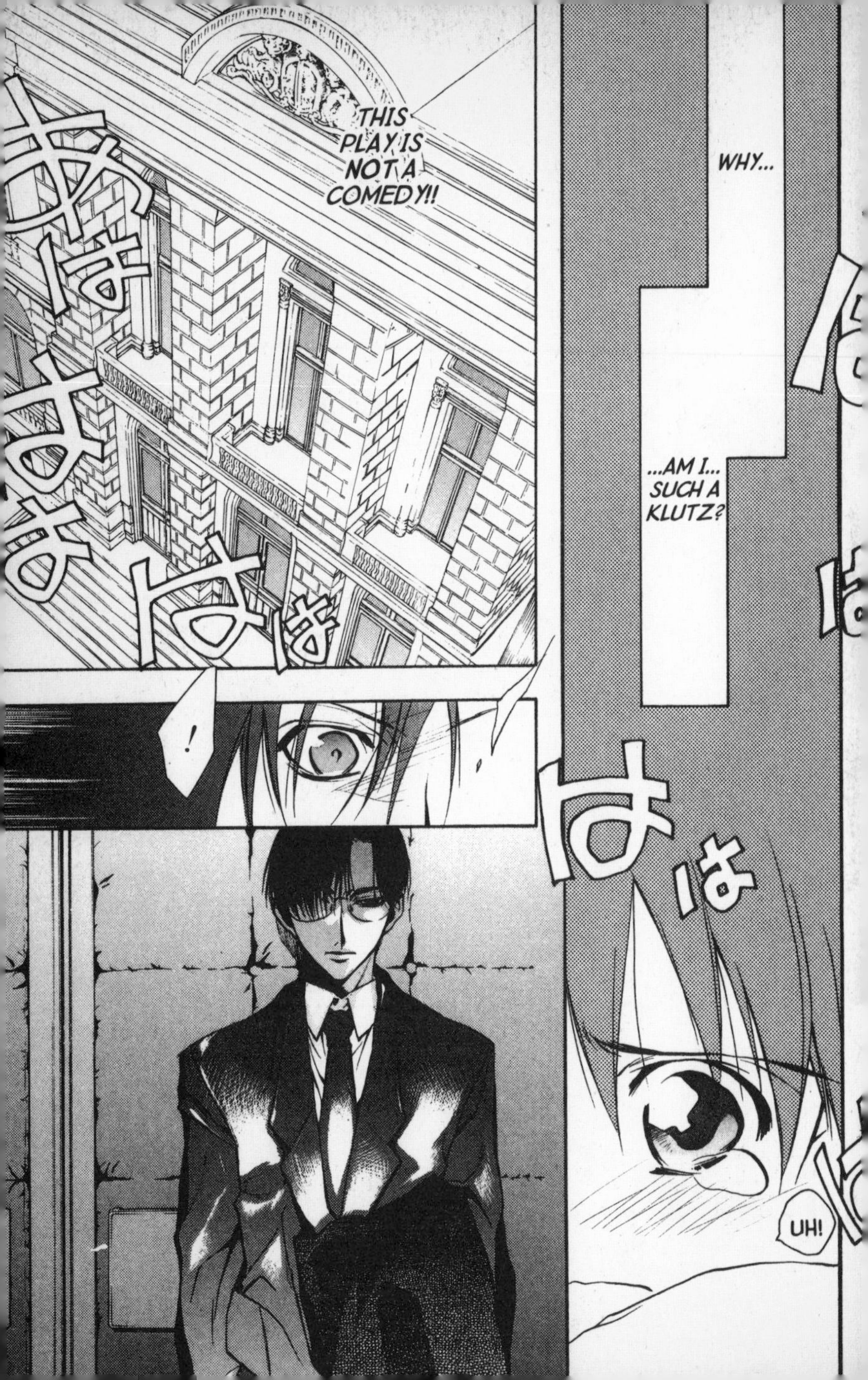
WHY...
...AM I... SUCH A KLUTZ?
UH!
THIS PLAY IS NOT A COMEDY!!
!

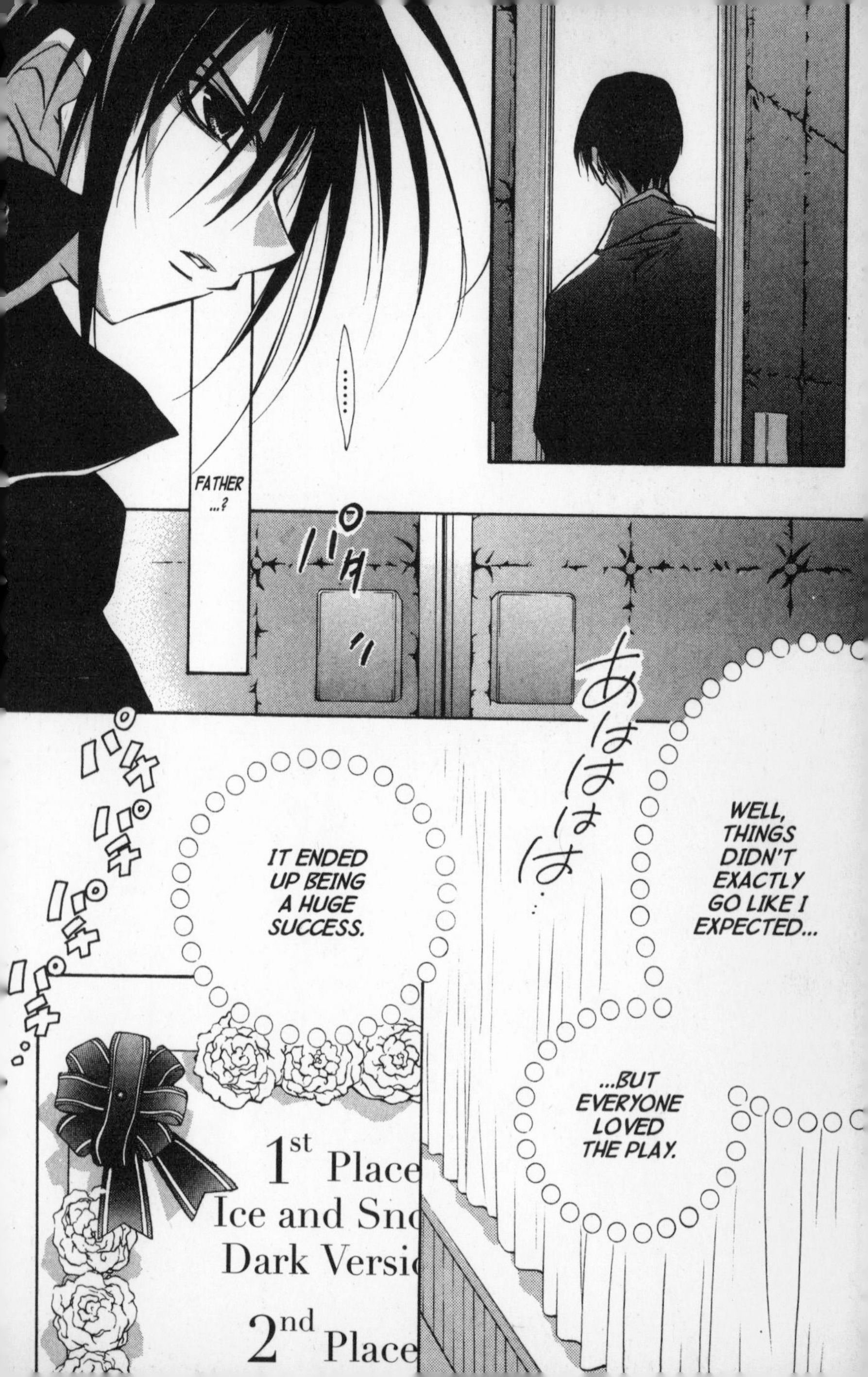
......
FATHER ...?
パタッ
あははは...
WELL, THINGS DIDN'T EXACTLY GO LIKE I EXPECTED...
IT ENDED UP BEING A HUGE SUCCESS.
パチパチパチパチ...
...BUT EVERYONE LOVED THE PLAY.
1st Place
Ice and Sno
Dark Versi
2nd Place

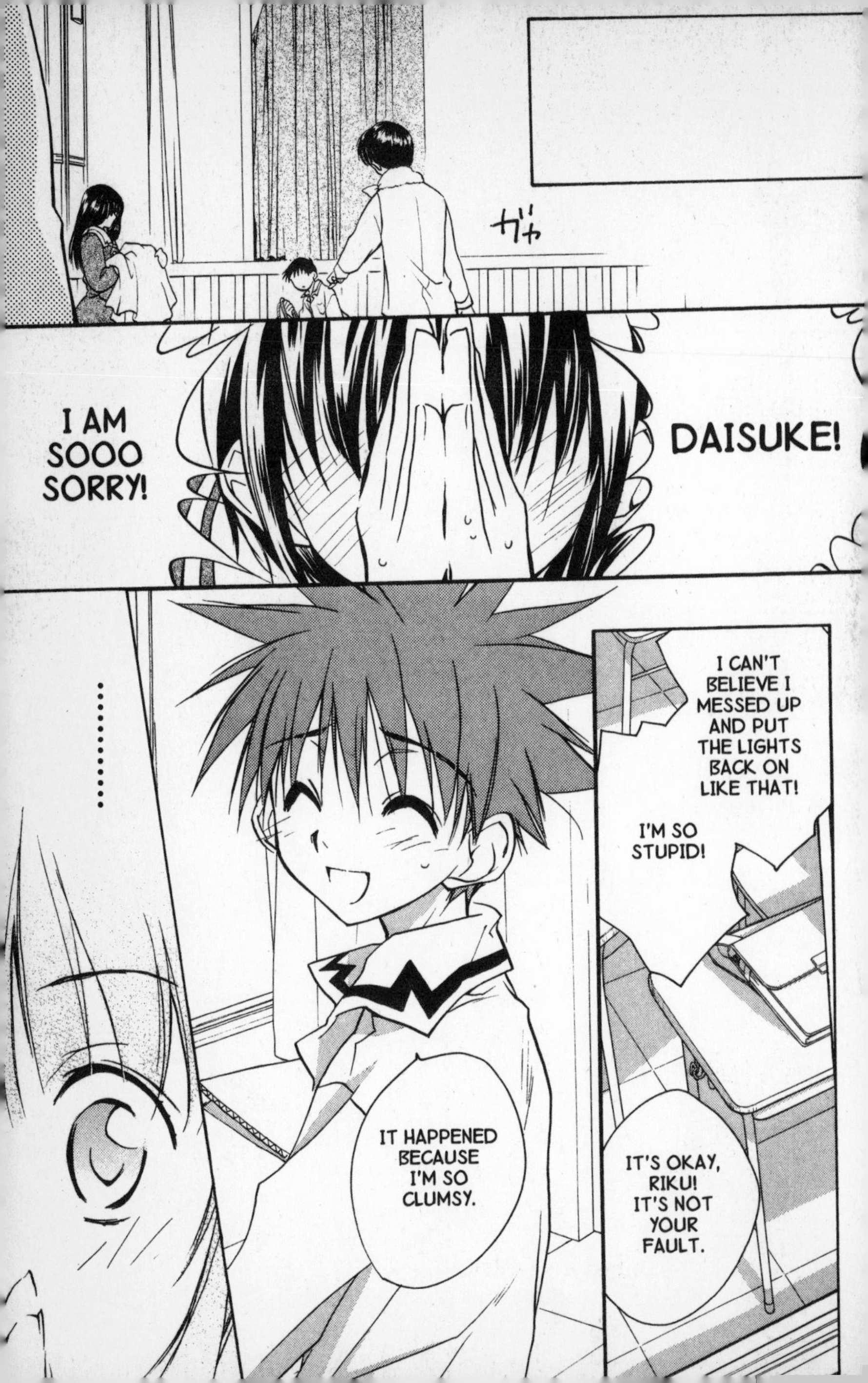
ガチャ
DAISUKE!
I AM SOOO SORRY!
I CAN'T BELIEVE I MESSED UP AND PUT THE LIGHTS BACK ON LIKE THAT!
I'M SO STUPID!
IT'S OKAY, RIKU! IT'S NOT YOUR FAULT.
IT HAPPENED BECAUSE I'M SO CLUMSY.
....

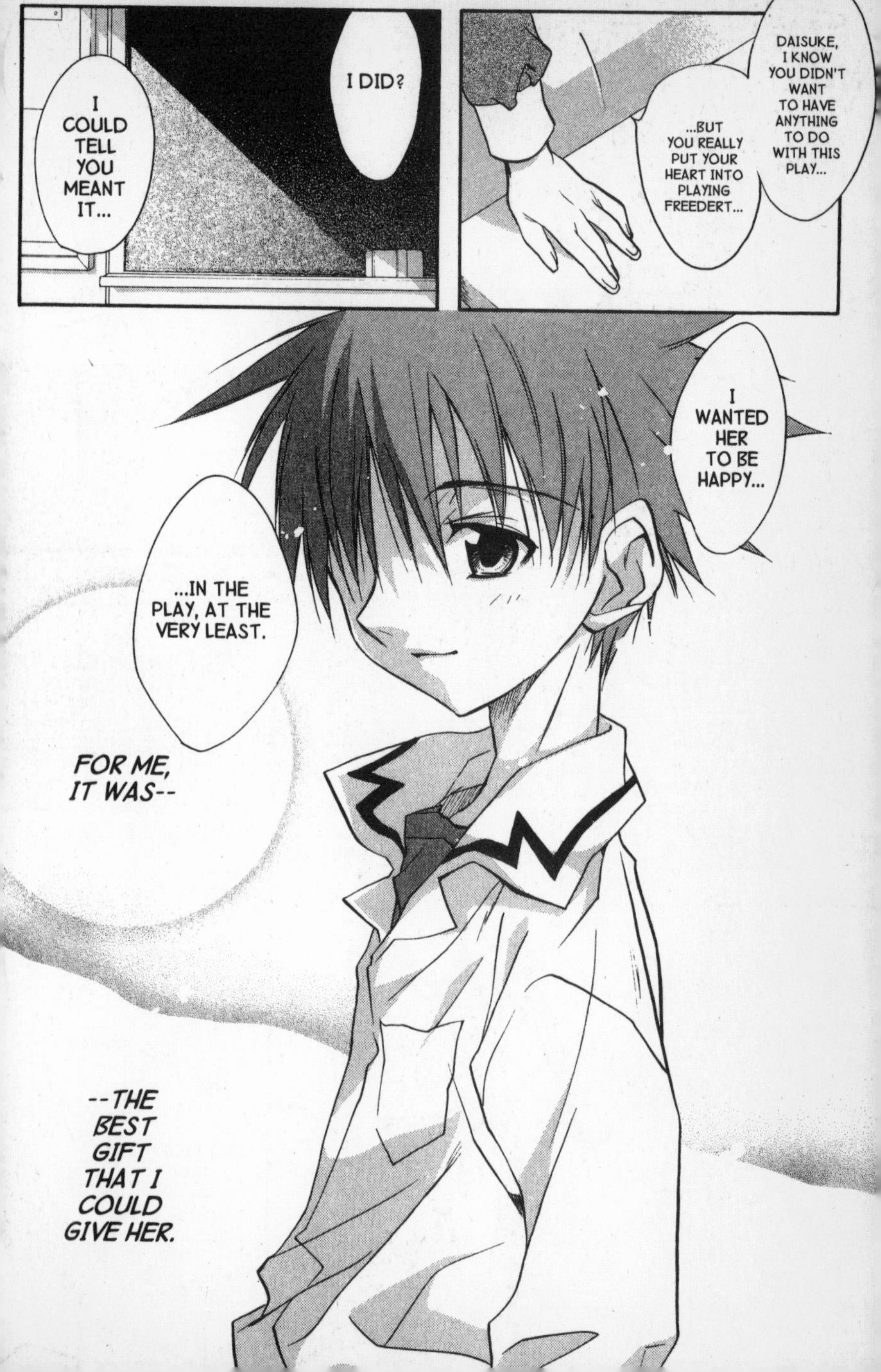
DAISUKE, I KNOW YOU DIDN'T WANT TO HAVE ANYTHING TO DO WITH THIS PLAY...
...BUT YOU REALLY PUT YOUR HEART INTO PLAYING FREEDERT...
I DID?
I COULD TELL YOU MEANT IT...
I WANTED HER TO BE HAPPY...
...IN THE PLAY, AT THE VERY LEAST.
FOR ME, IT WAS--
--THE BEST GIFT THAT I COULD GIVE HER.

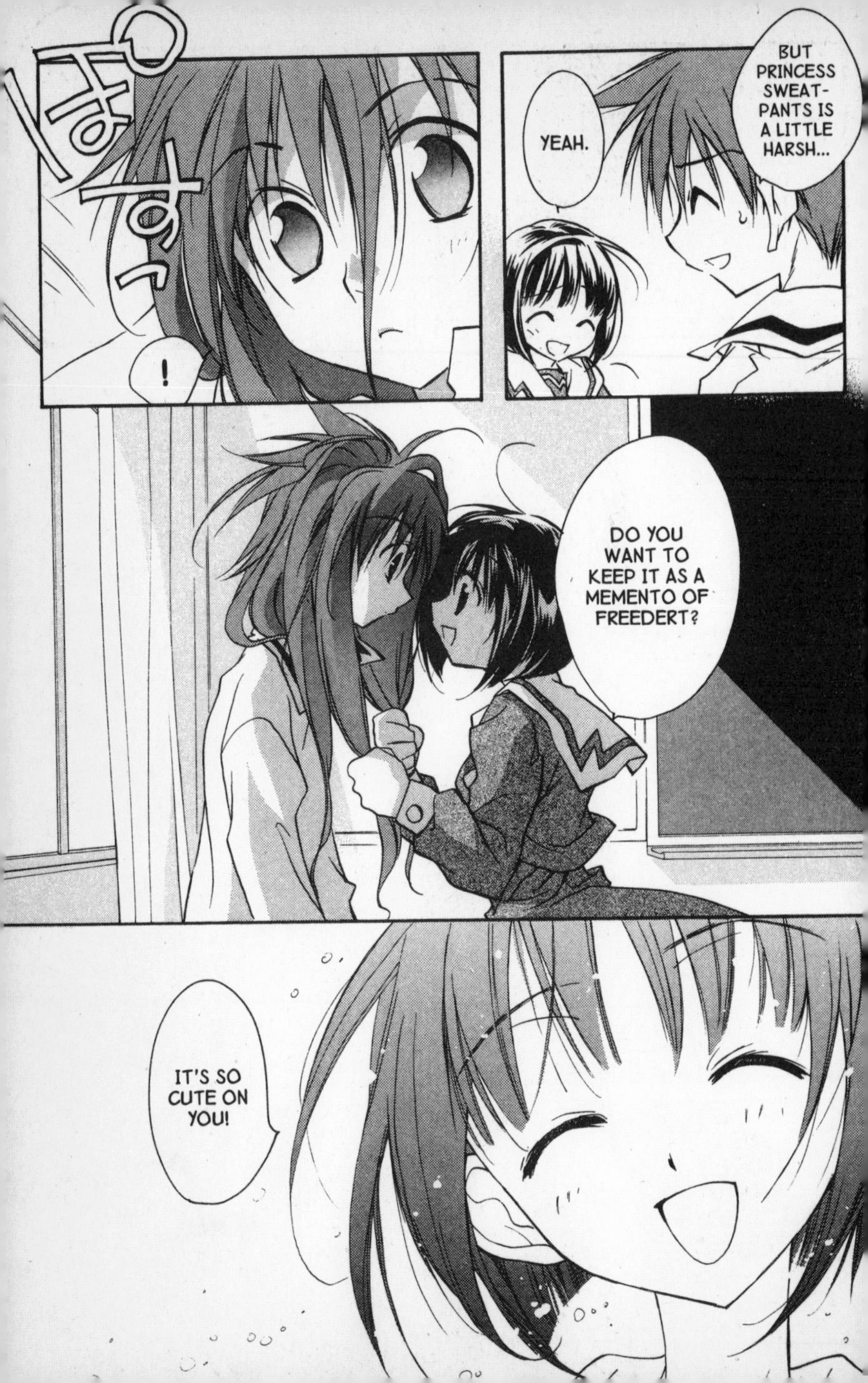
BUT PRINCESS SWEAT-PANTS IS A LITTLE HARSH...
YEAH.
ぽすっ
!
DO YOU WANT TO KEEP IT AS A MEMENTO OF FREEDERT?
IT'S SO CUTE ON YOU!

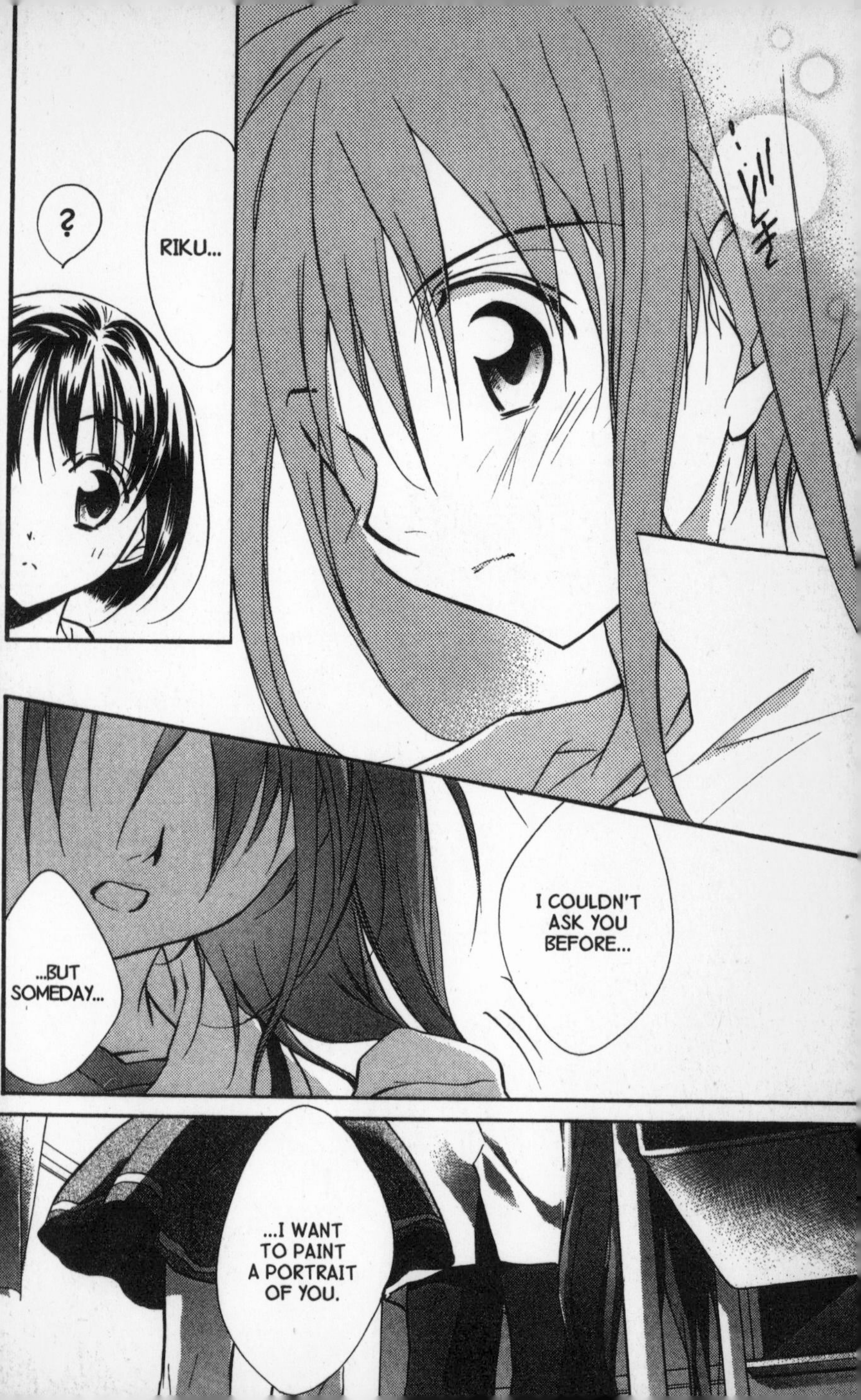
RIKU...
?
I COULDN'T ASK YOU BEFORE...
...BUT SOMEDAY...
...I WANT TO PAINT A PORTRAIT OF YOU.

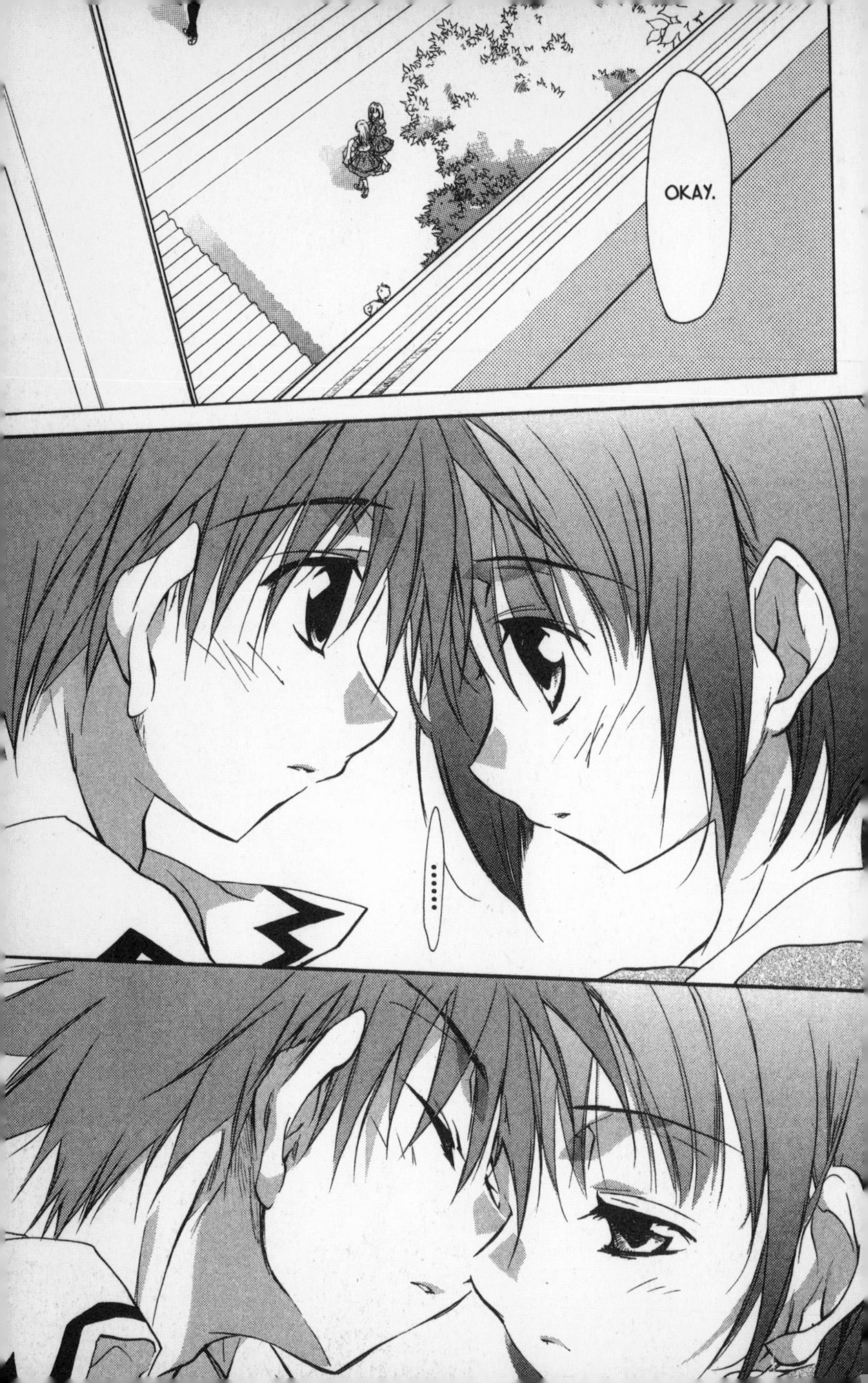
OKAY.
......

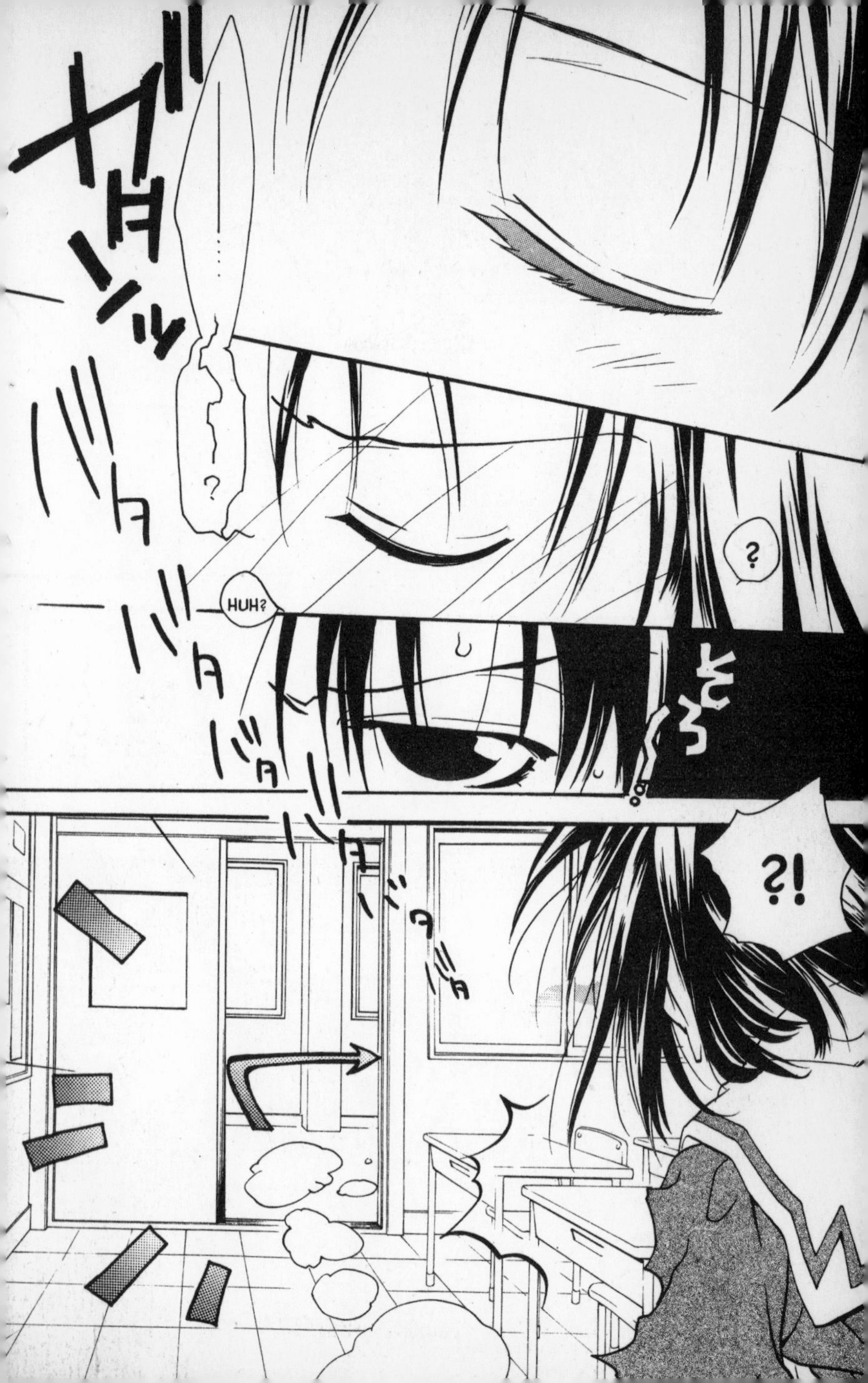
ガタンッ
......
?
?
HUH?
バタバタバタバタバタバタ
?!

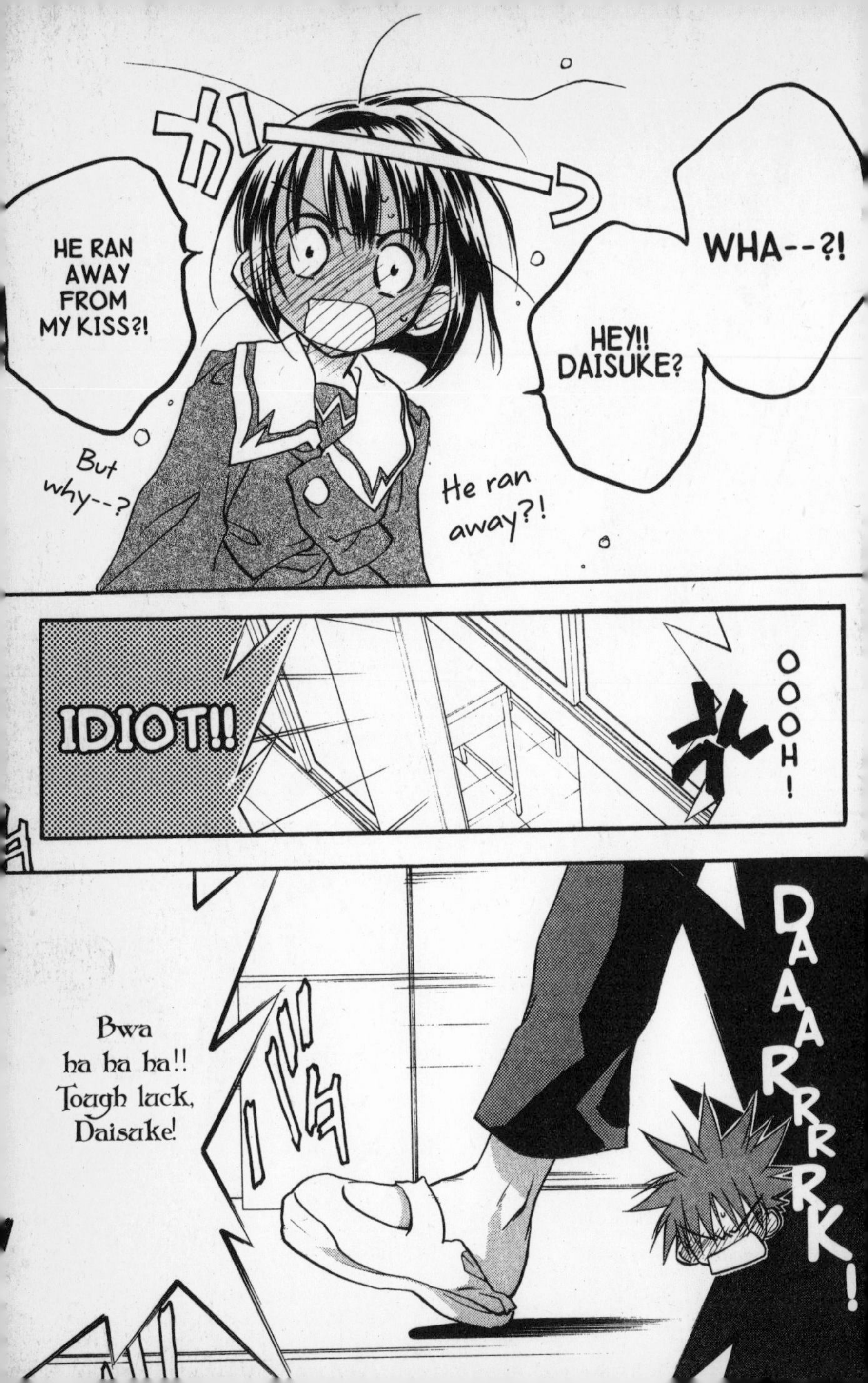
WHA--?!
HEY!! DAISUKE?
HE RAN AWAY FROM MY KISS?!
He ran away?!
But why--?
OOOOH!
IDIOT!!
DAAARRRRK!
Bwa ha ha ha!! Tough luck, Daisuke!

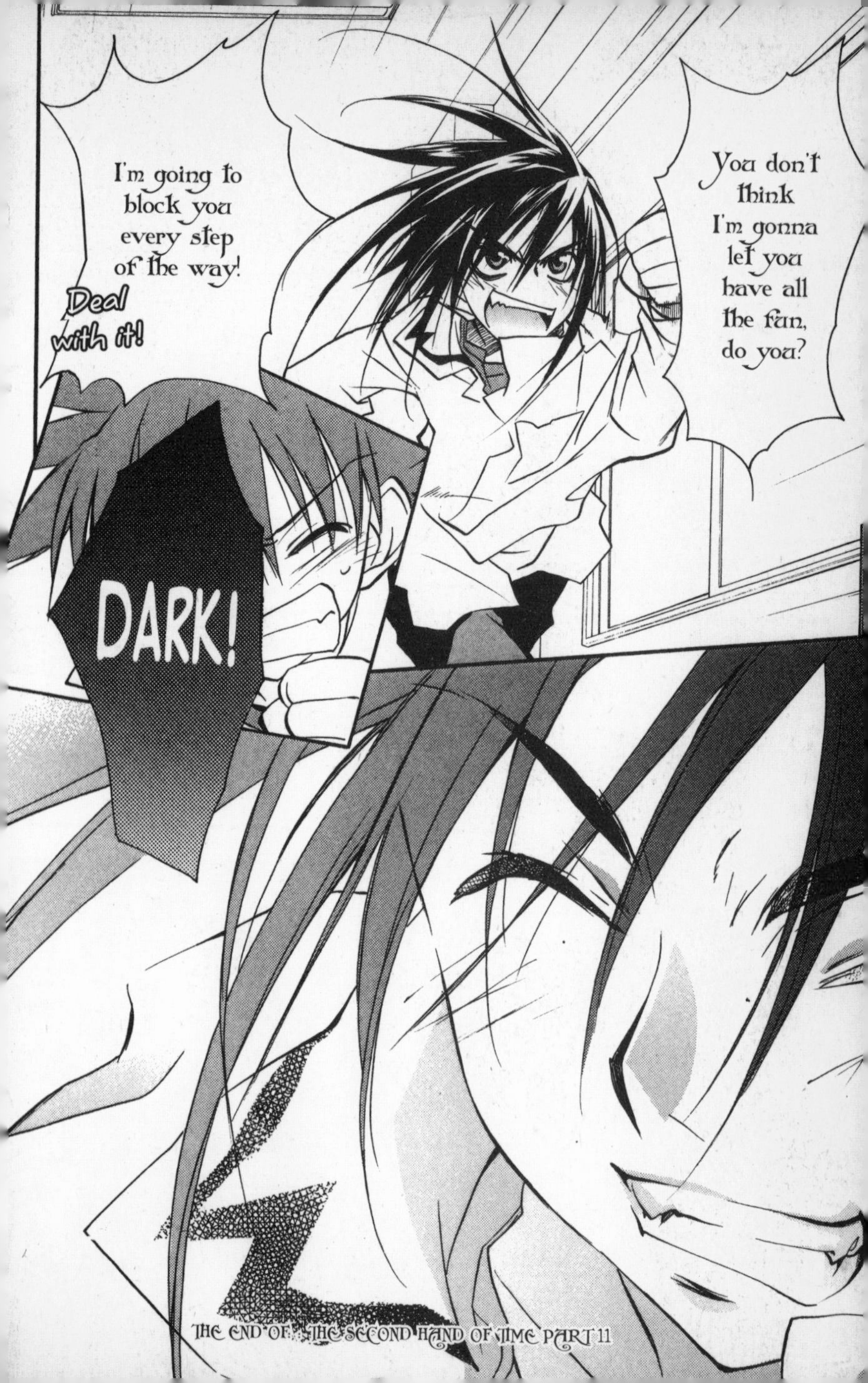
You don't think I'm gonna let you have all the fun, do you?
I'm going to block you every step of the way!
Deal with it!
DARK!
THE END OF THE SECOND HAND OF TIME PART 11

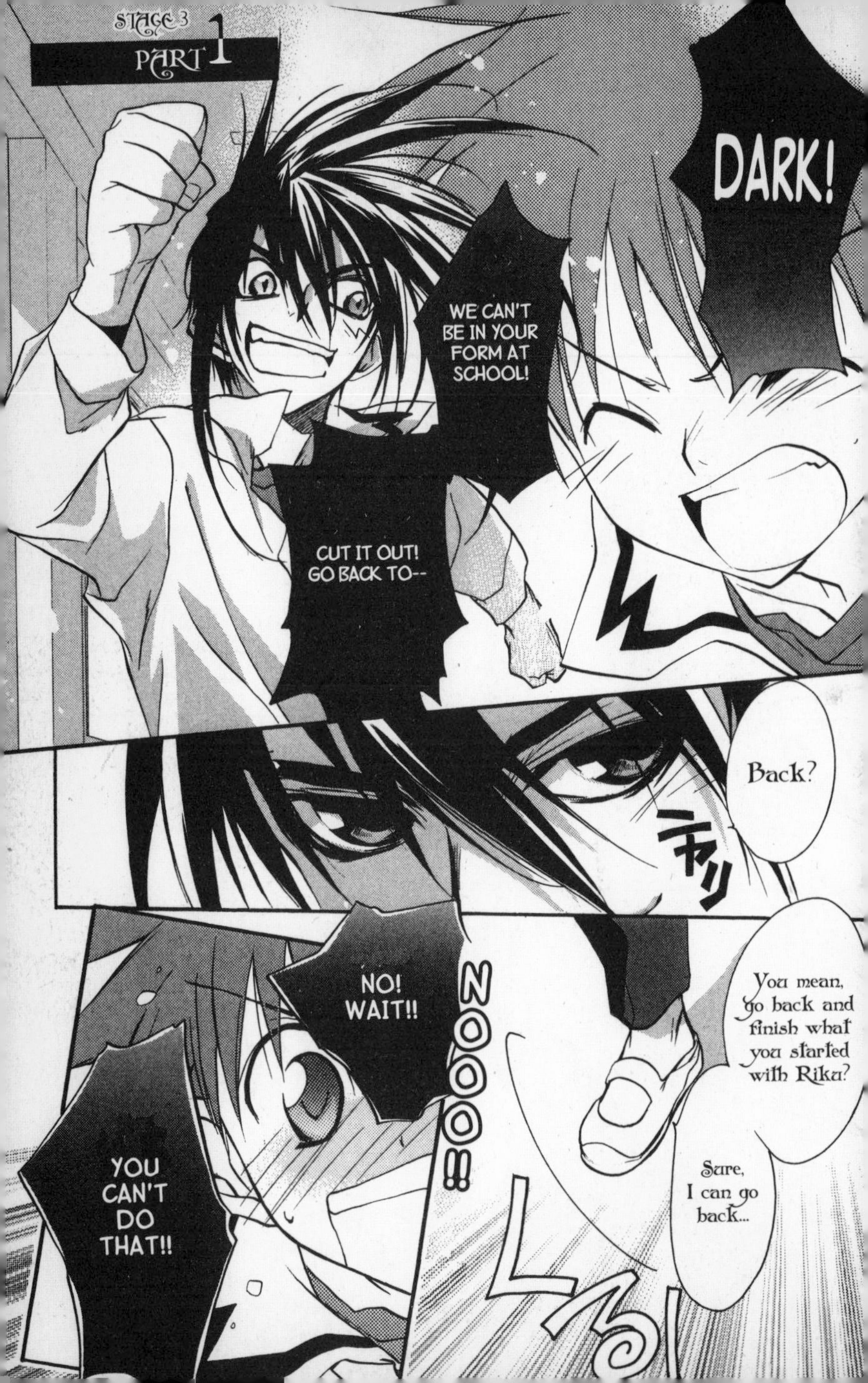
STAGE 3
PART 1
DARK!
WE CAN'T BE IN YOUR FORM AT SCHOOL!
CUT IT OUT! GO BACK TO--
Back?
ニヤリ
You mean, go back and finish what you started with Riku?
Sure, I can go back...
NO! WAIT!!
NOOOOO!!
YOU CAN'T DO THAT!!

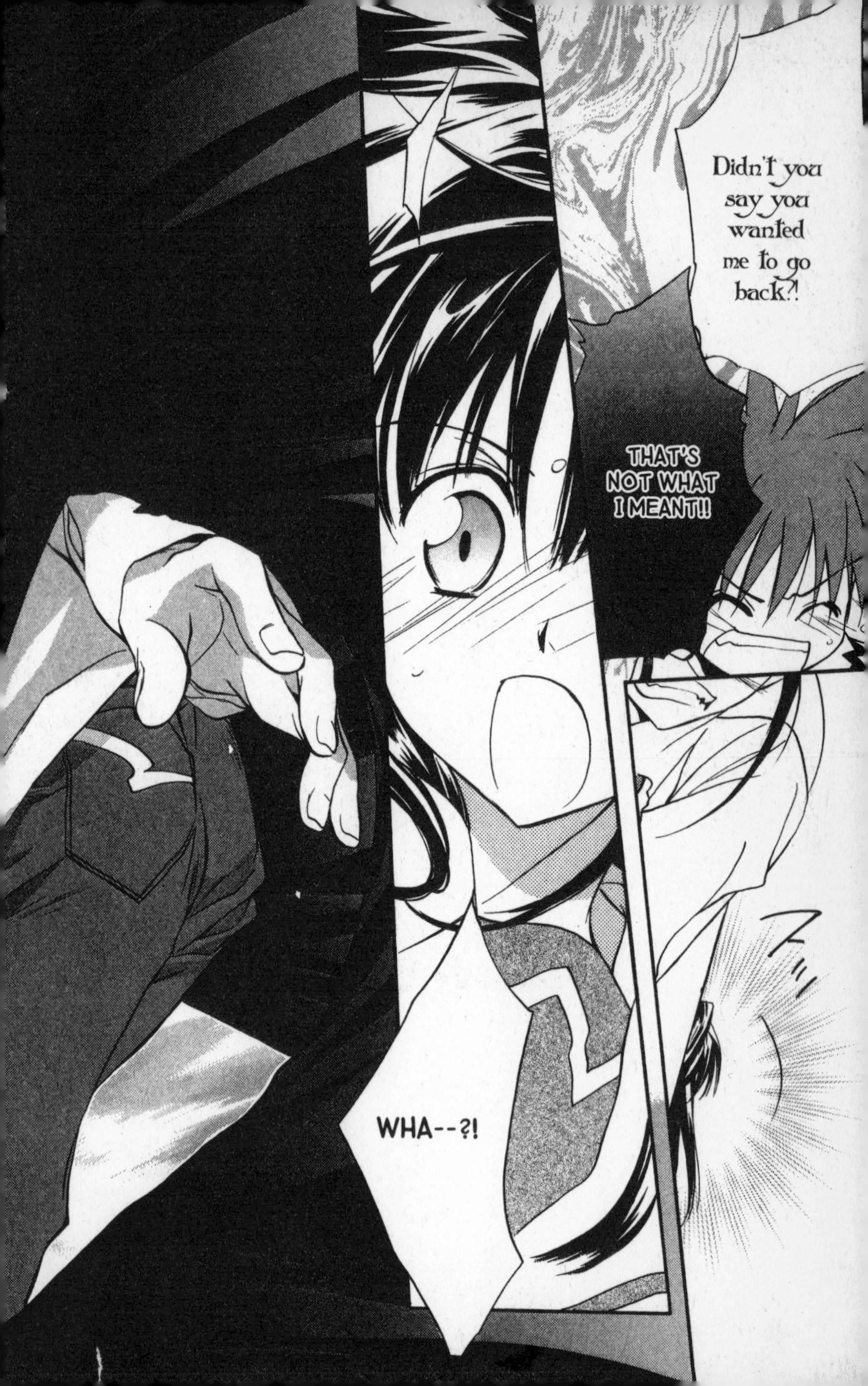
Didn't you say you wanted me to go back?!
THAT'S NOT WHAT I MEANT!!
WHA--?!

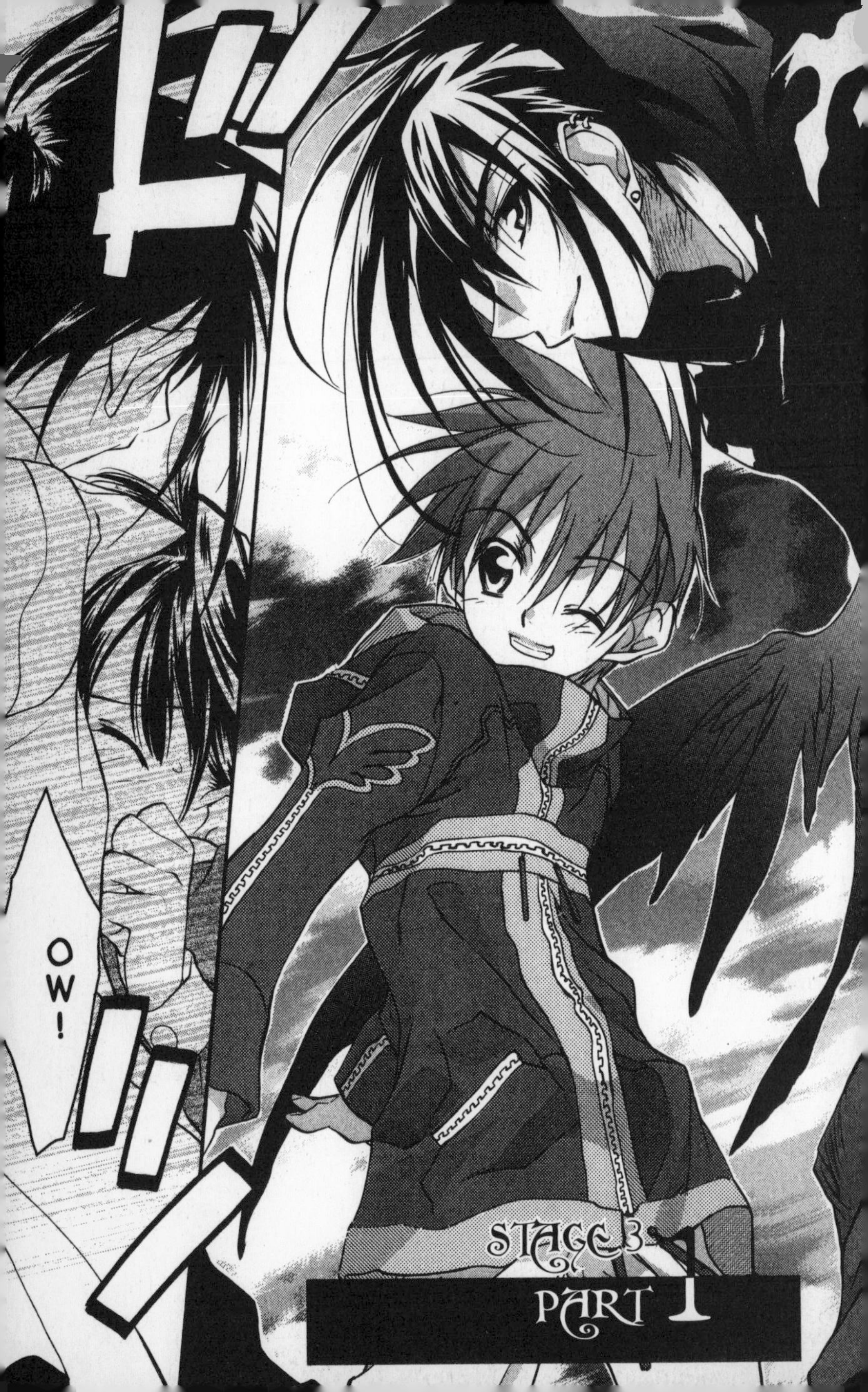
OW!
STAGE 3
PART 1

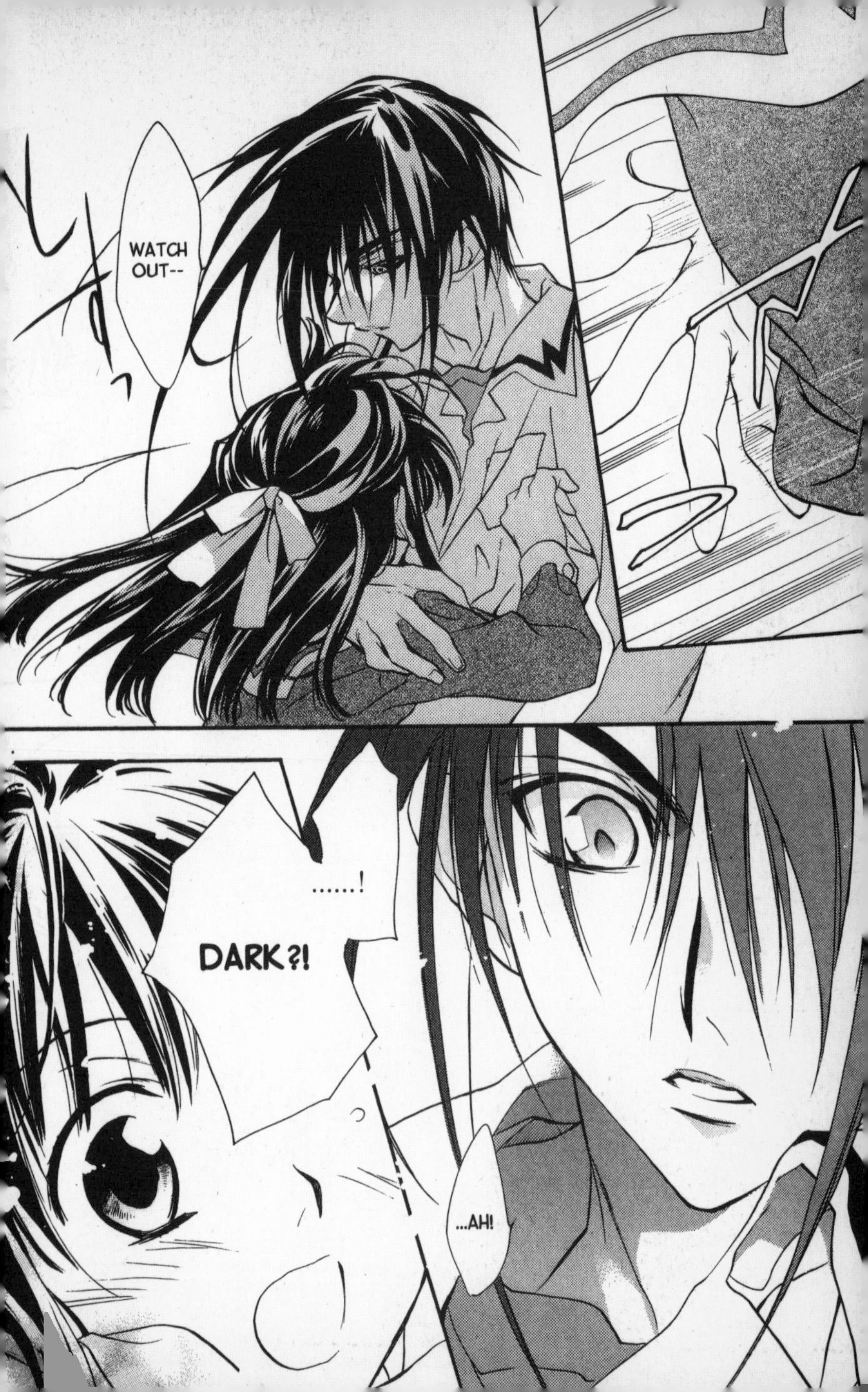
WATCH OUT--
.......!
DARK?!
...AH!

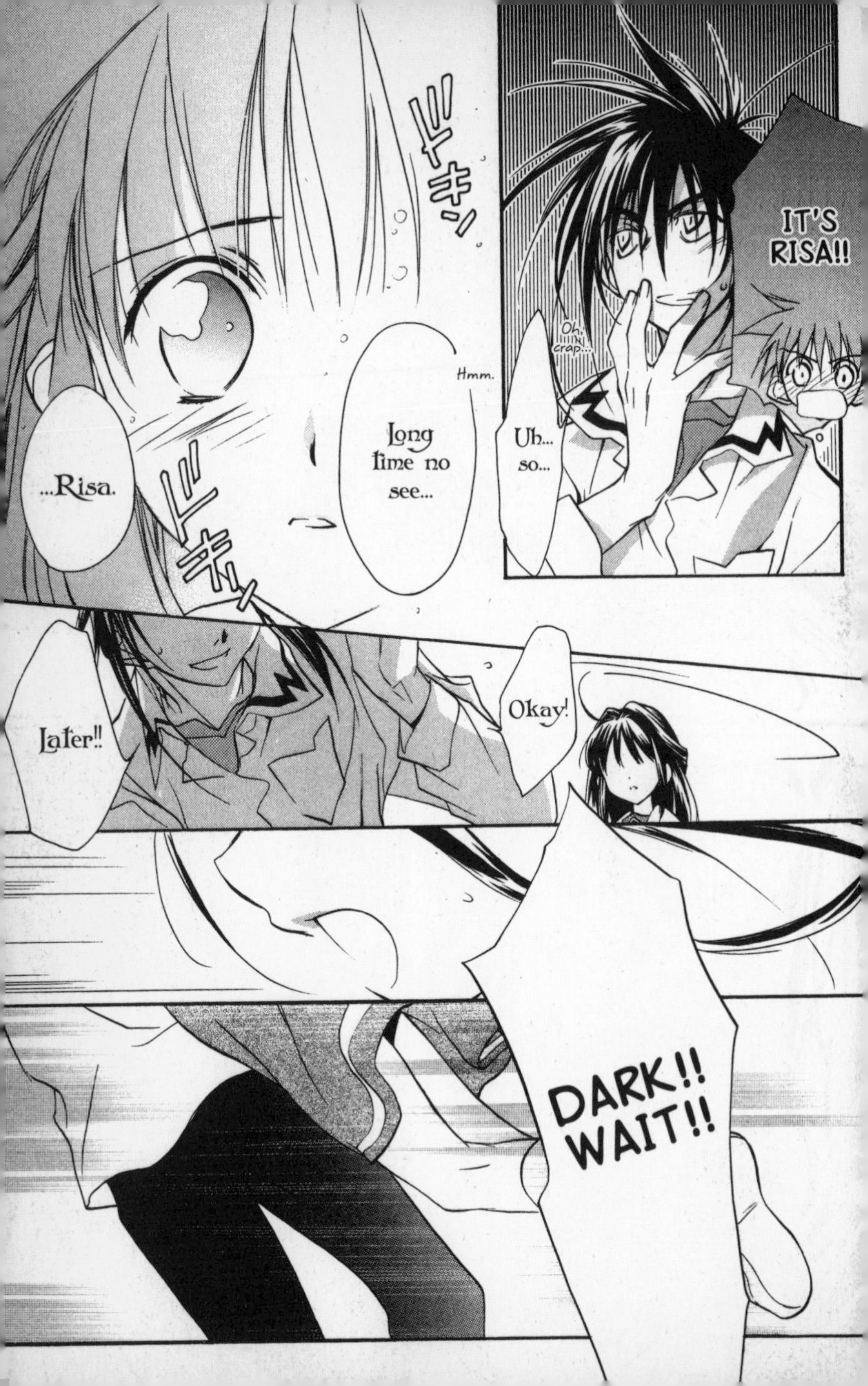
IT'S RISA!!
Oh, crap...
Uh... so...
Hmm.
Long time no see...
...Risa.
Okay!
Later!!
DARK!! WAIT!!

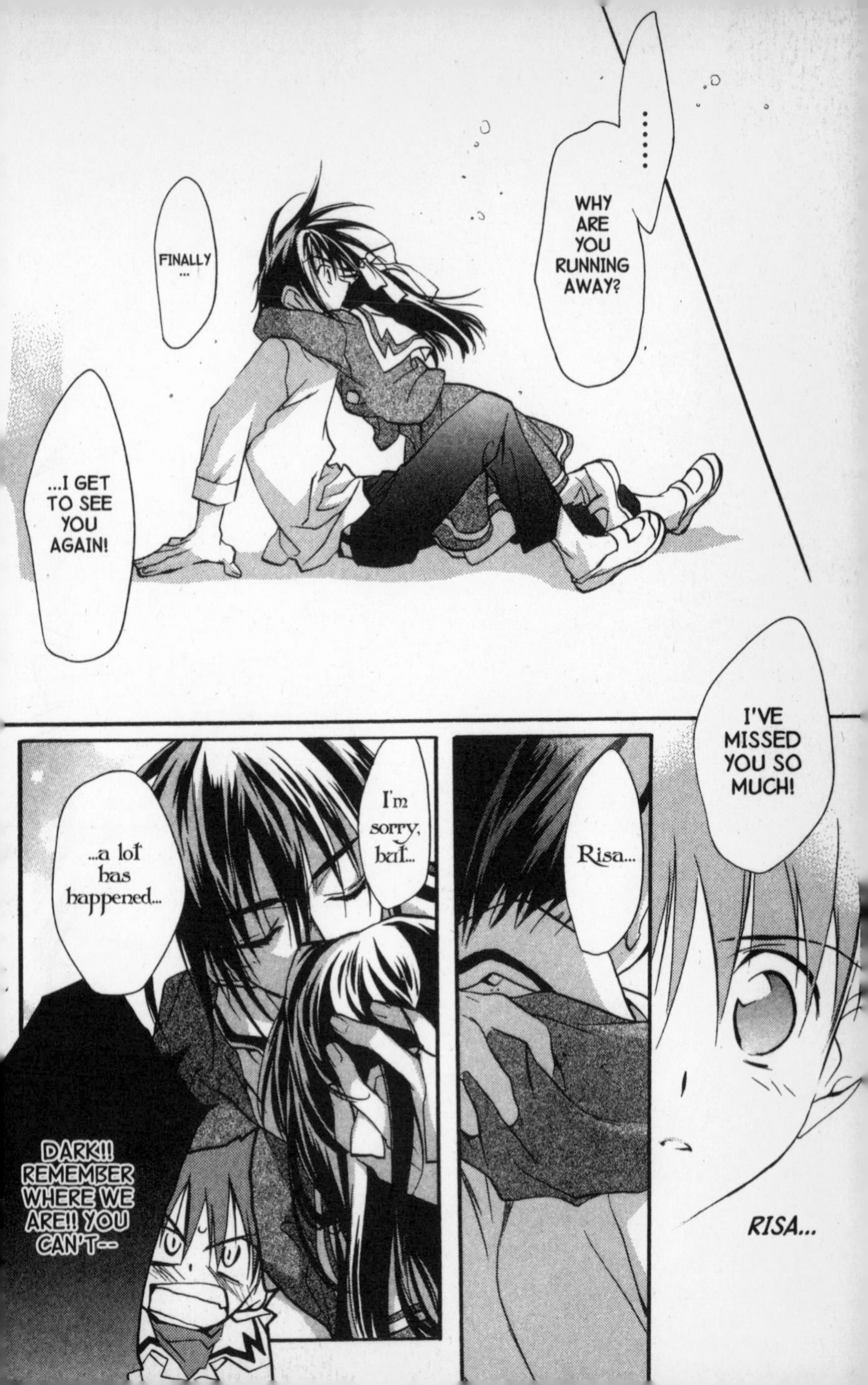
......
WHY ARE YOU RUNNING AWAY?
FINALLY...
...I GET TO SEE YOU AGAIN!
I'VE MISSED YOU SO MUCH!
RISA...
Risa...
I'm sorry, but...
...a lot has happened...
DARK!! REMEMBER WHERE WE ARE!! YOU CAN'T--

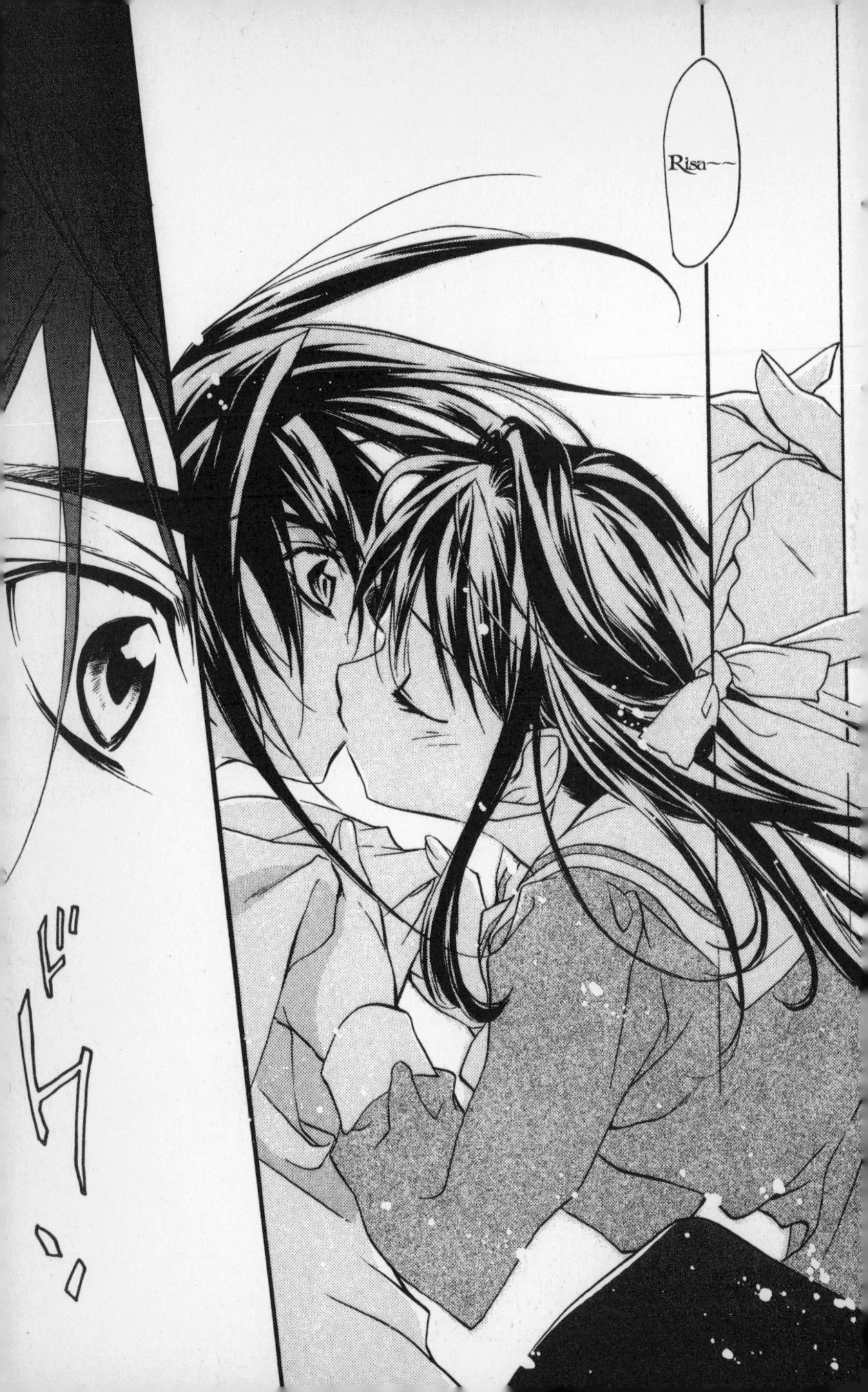
Risa~~

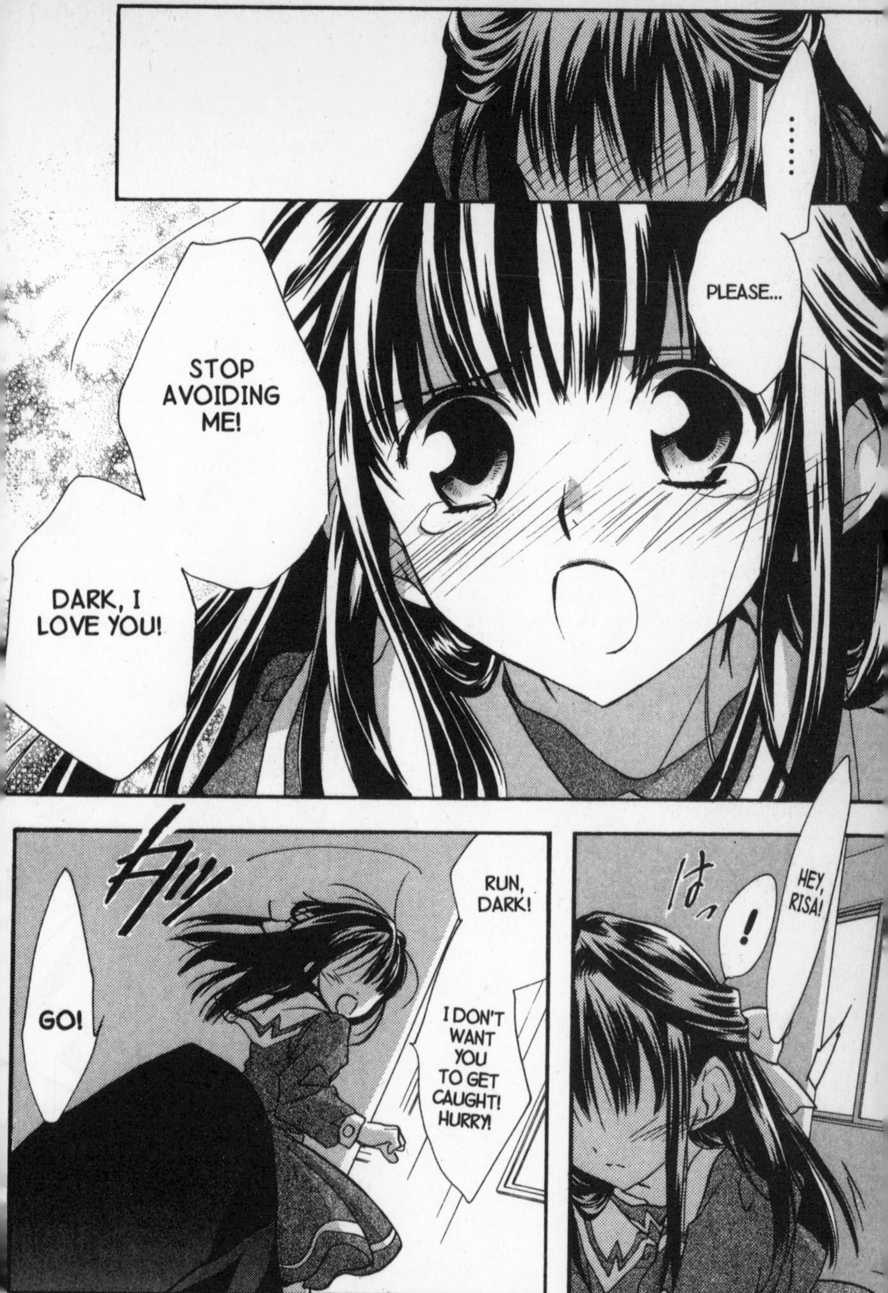
......
PLEASE...
STOP AVOIDING ME!
DARK, I LOVE YOU!
HEY, RISA!
はっ
!
RUN, DARK!
I DON'T WANT YOU TO GET CAUGHT! HURRY!
ダッ
GO!

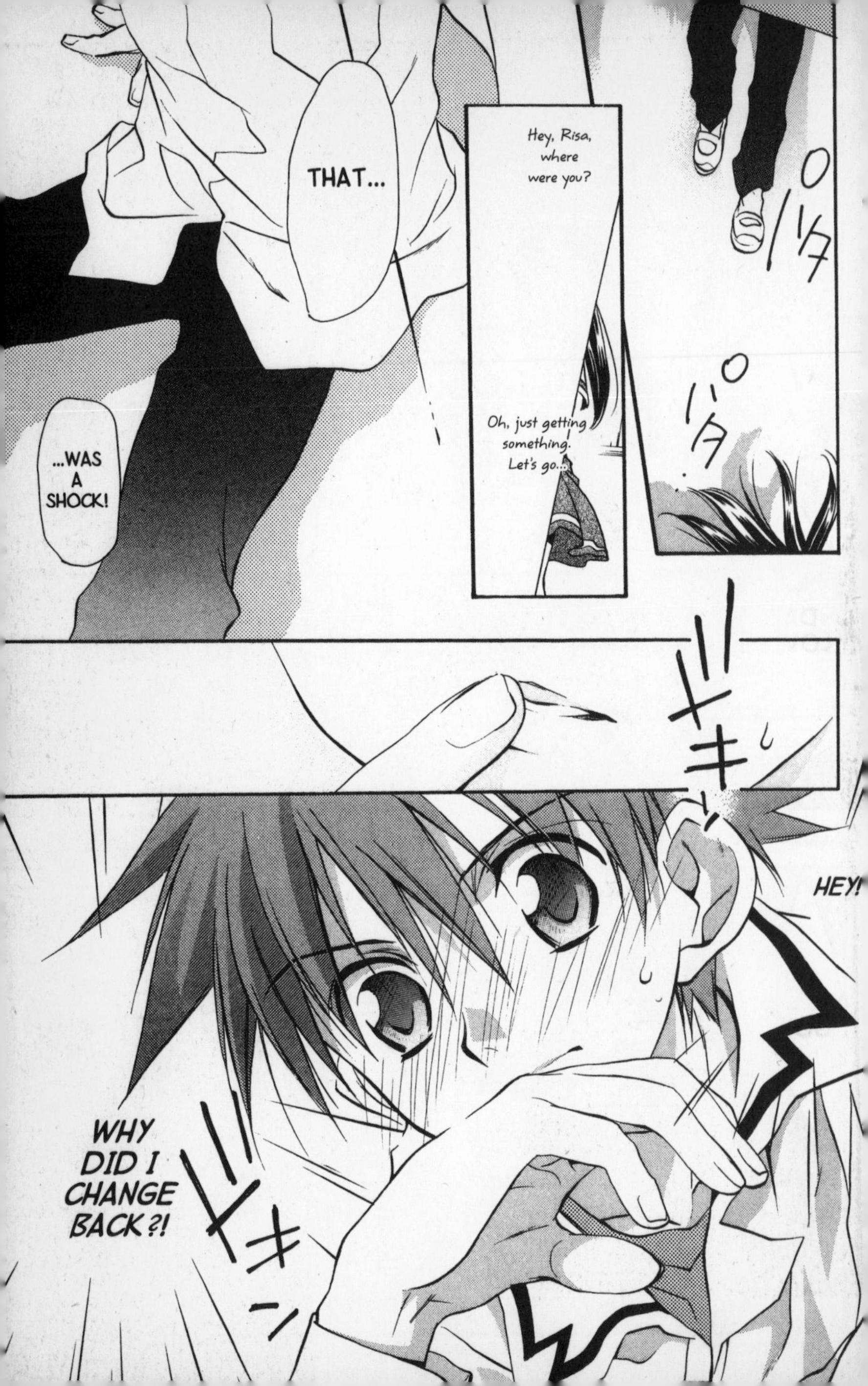

Hey, Risa, where were you?
Oh, just getting something. Let's go...
THAT...
...WAS A SHOCK!
HEY!
WHY DID I CHANGE BACK?!

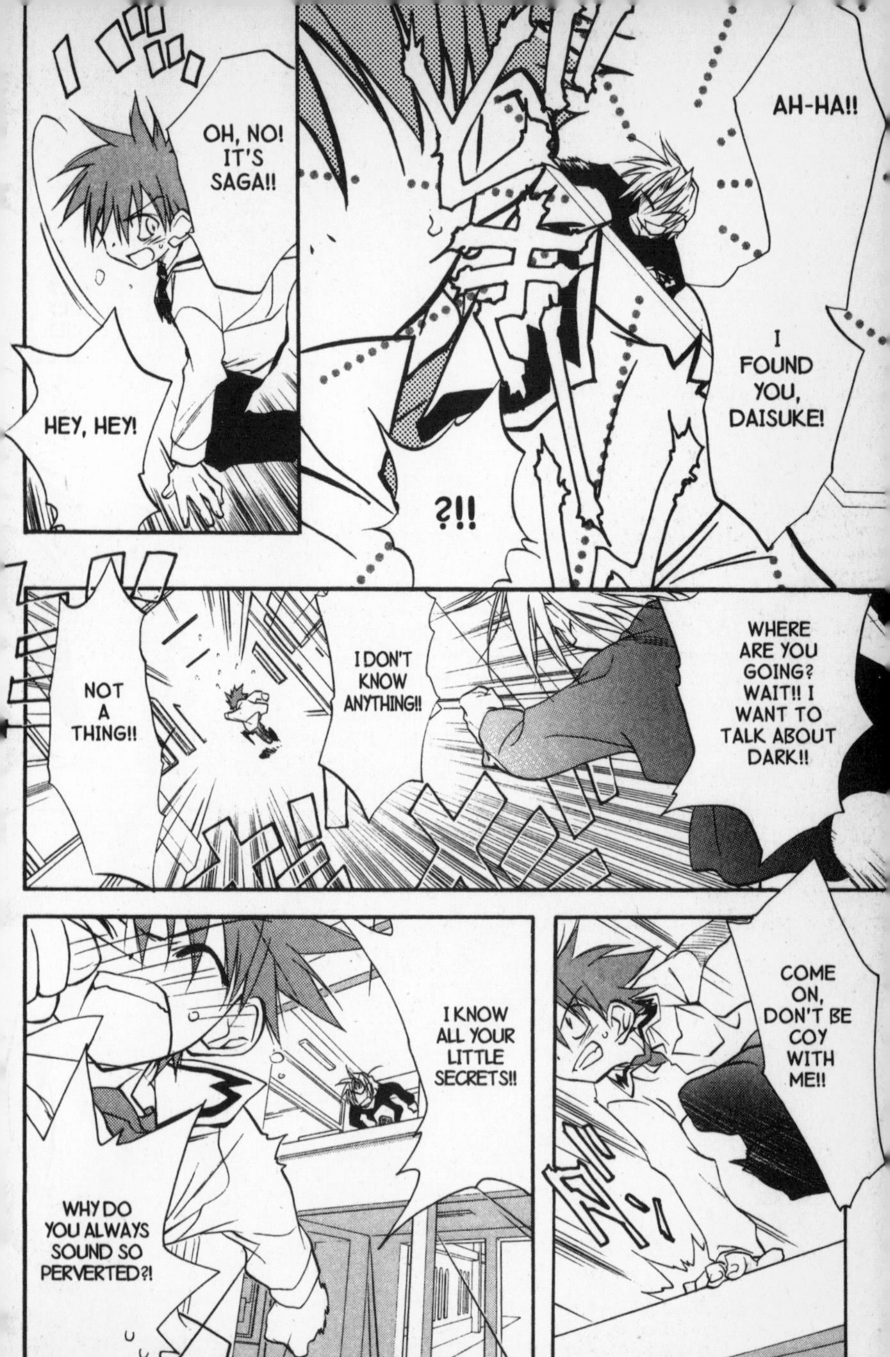
AH-HA!!
I FOUND YOU, DAISUKE!
?!!
OH, NO! IT'S SAGA!!
HEY, HEY!
WHERE ARE YOU GOING? WAIT!! I WANT TO TALK ABOUT DARK!!
I DON'T KNOW ANYTHING!!
NOT A THING!!
COME ON, DON'T BE COY WITH ME!!
I KNOW ALL YOUR LITTLE SECRETS!!
WHY DO YOU ALWAYS SOUND SO PERVERTED?!

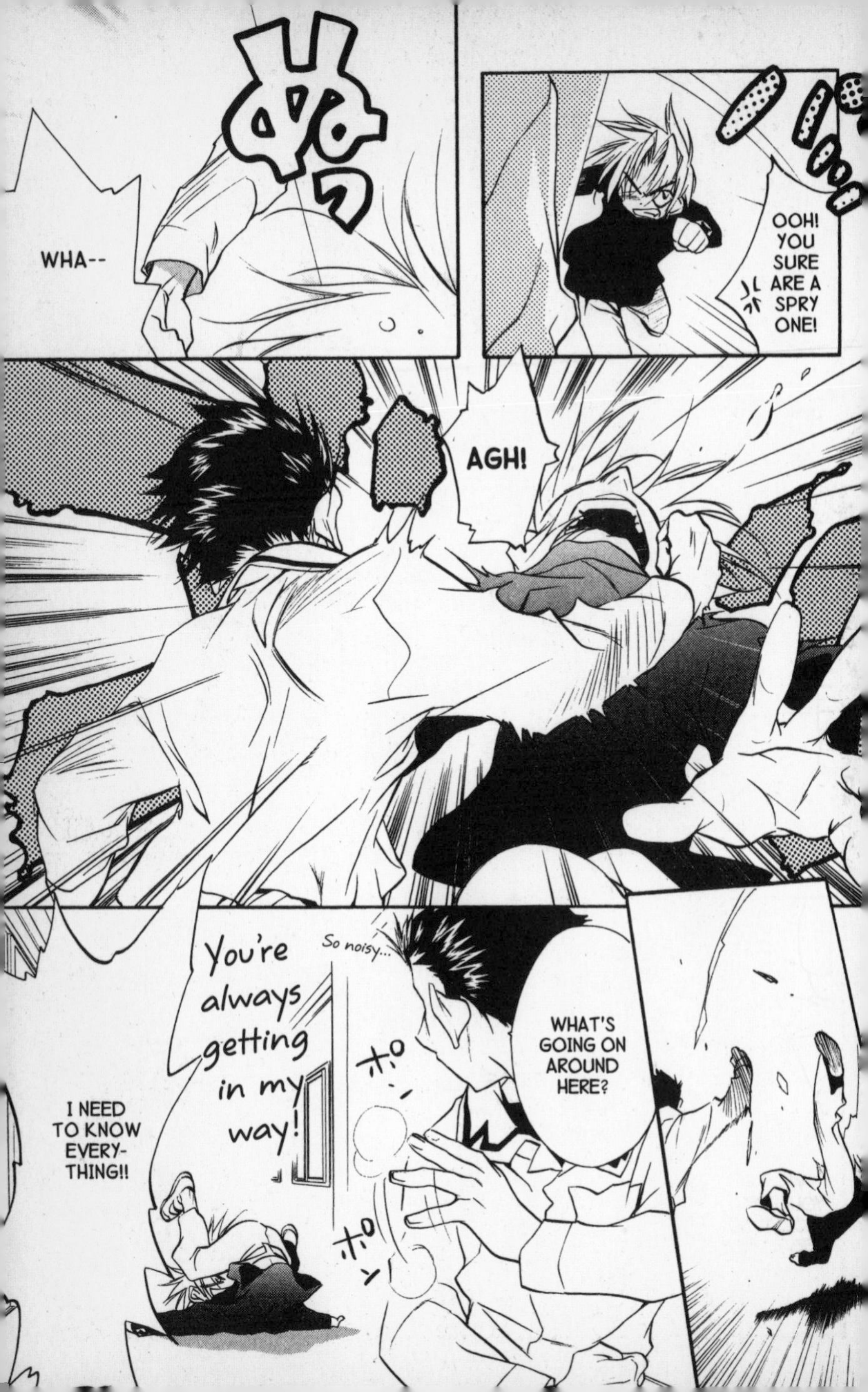
OOH! YOU SURE ARE A SPRY ONE!
WHA--
AGH!
WHAT'S GOING ON AROUND HERE?
So noisy...
You're always getting in my way!
I NEED TO KNOW EVERY-THING!!

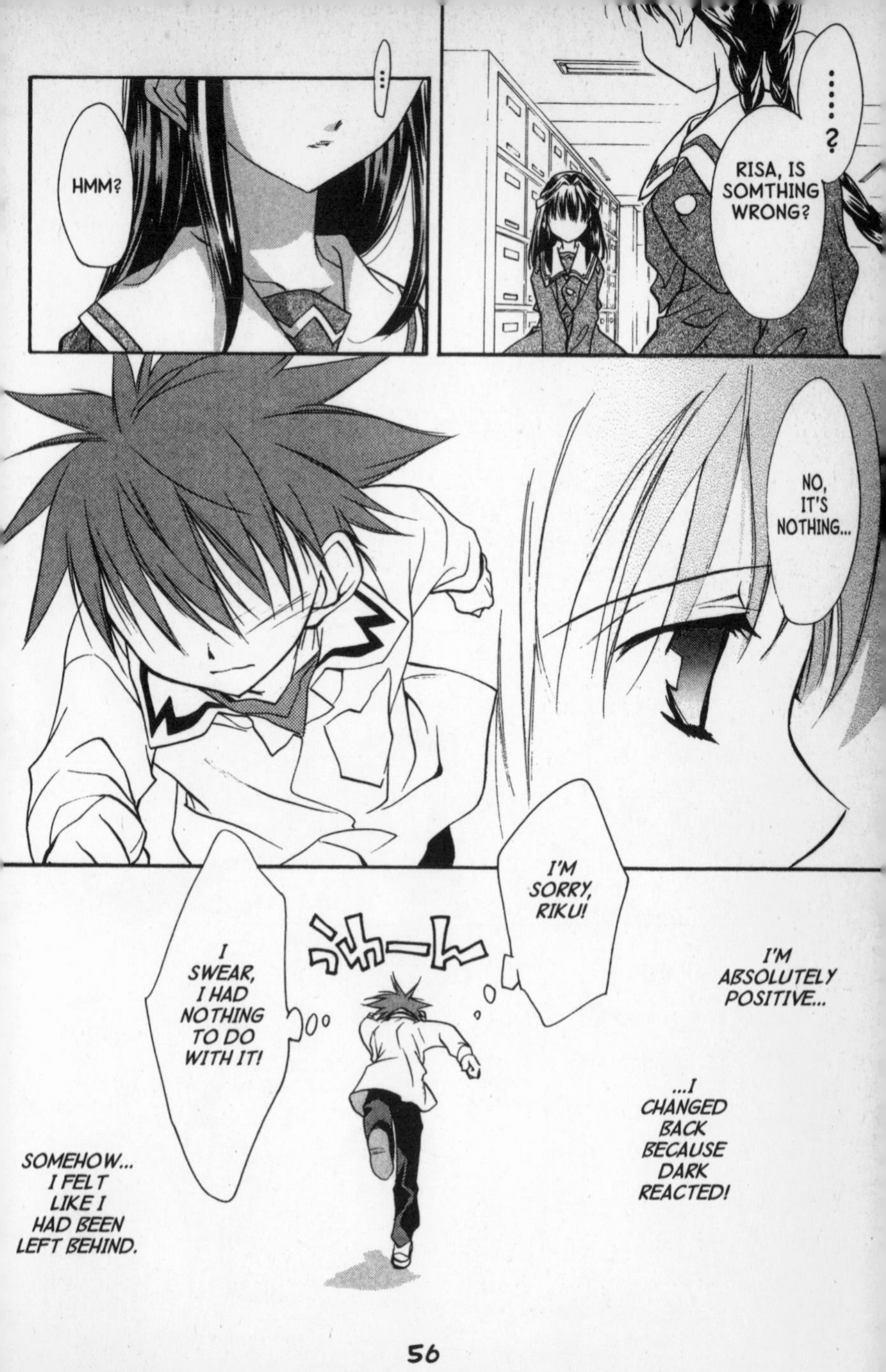
.....?
RISA, IS SOMTHING WRONG?
...
HMM?
NO, IT'S NOTHING...
I'M ABSOLUTELY POSITIVE...
...I CHANGED BACK BECAUSE DARK REACTED!
I'M SORRY, RIKU!
うわーん
I SWEAR, I HAD NOTHING TO DO WITH IT!
SOMEHOW... I FELT LIKE I HAD BEEN LEFT BEHIND.

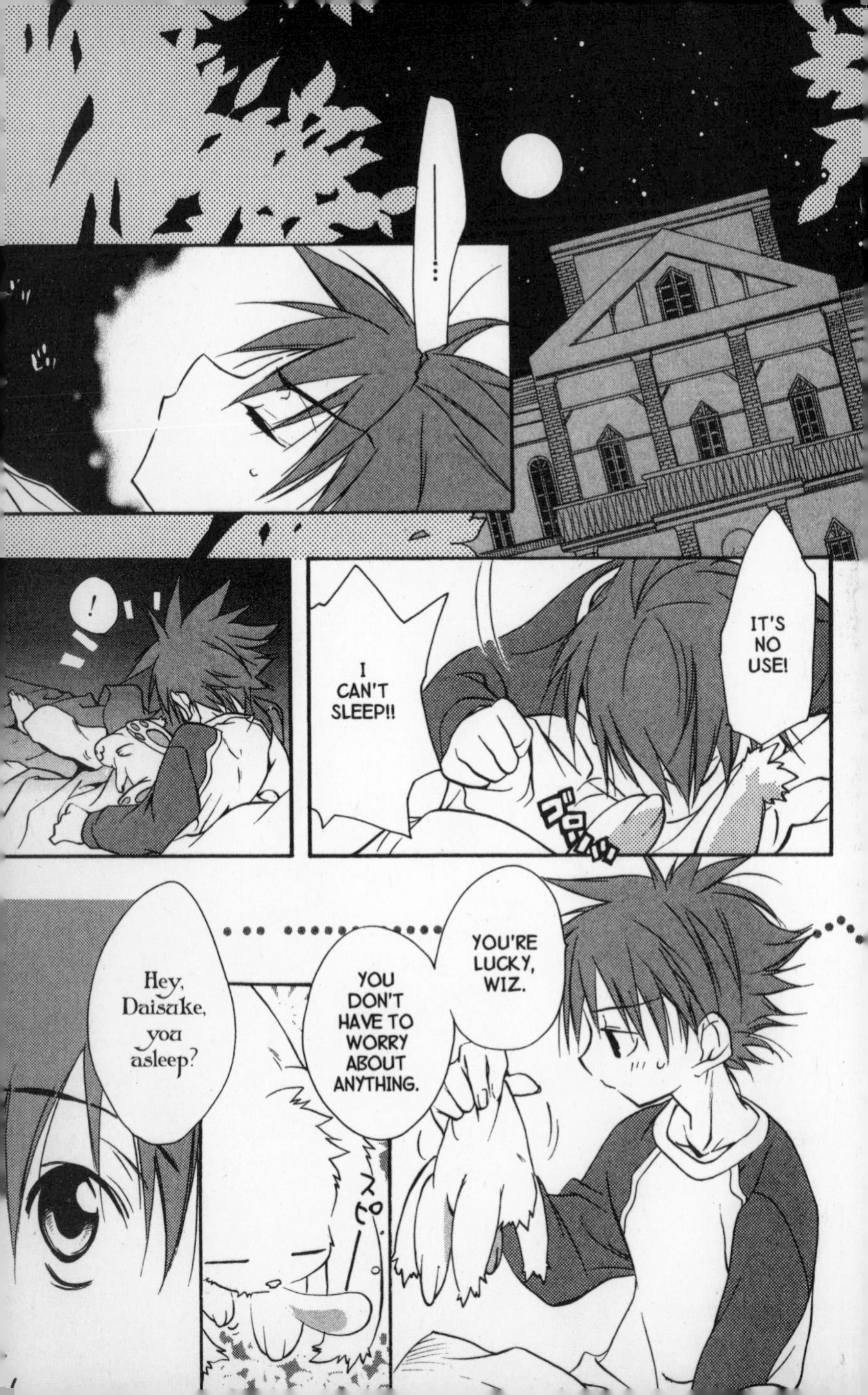

......
!
IT'S NO USE!
I CAN'T SLEEP!!
YOU'RE LUCKY, WIZ.
YOU DON'T HAVE TO WORRY ABOUT ANYTHING.
Hey, Daisuke, you asleep?

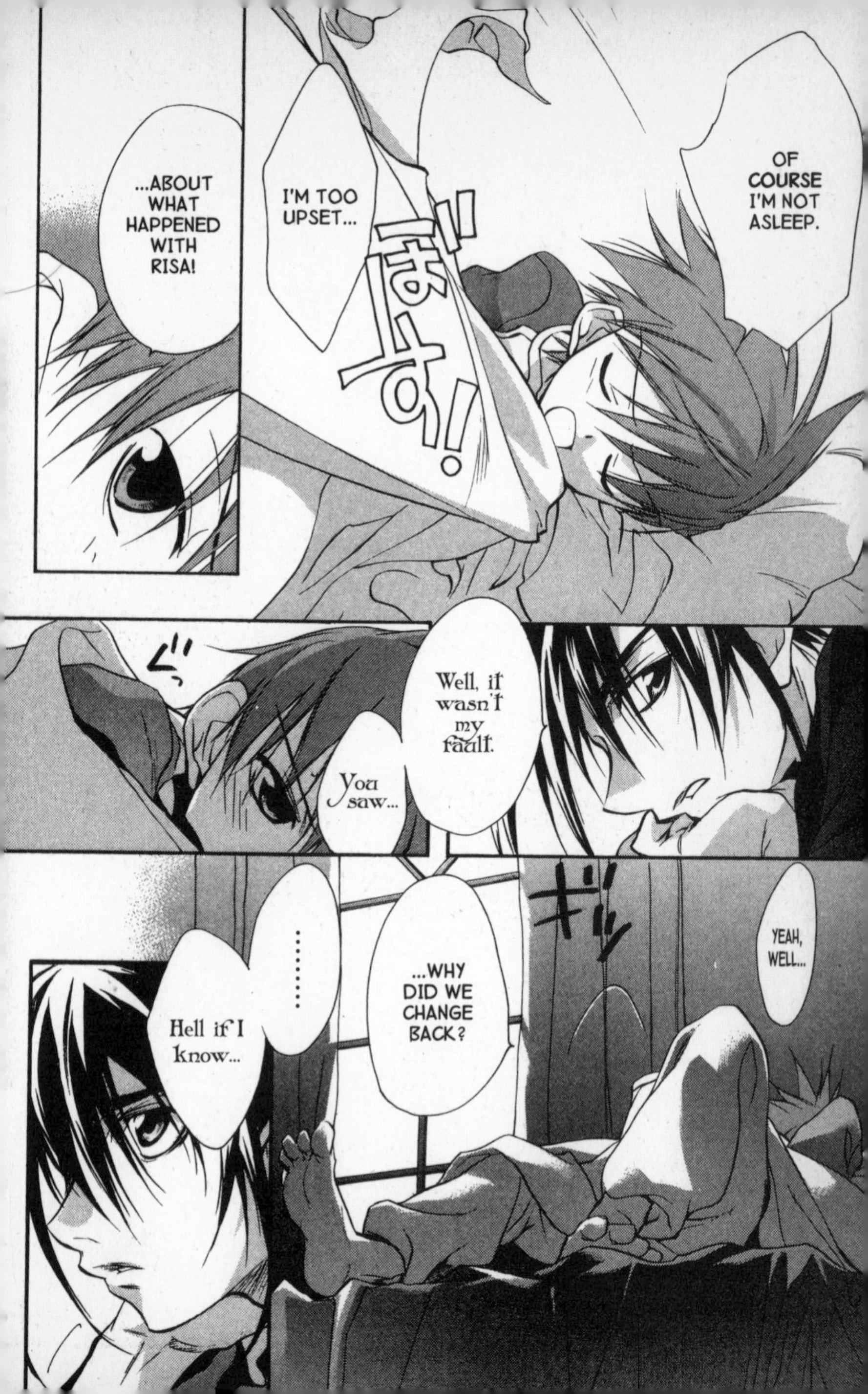
OF COURSE I'M NOT ASLEEP.
ぼすっ!
I'M TOO UPSET...
...ABOUT WHAT HAPPENED WITH RISA!
Well, it wasn't my fault.
You saw...
ぐっ
YEAH, WELL...
ギシ
...WHY DID WE CHANGE BACK?
....
Hell if I know...

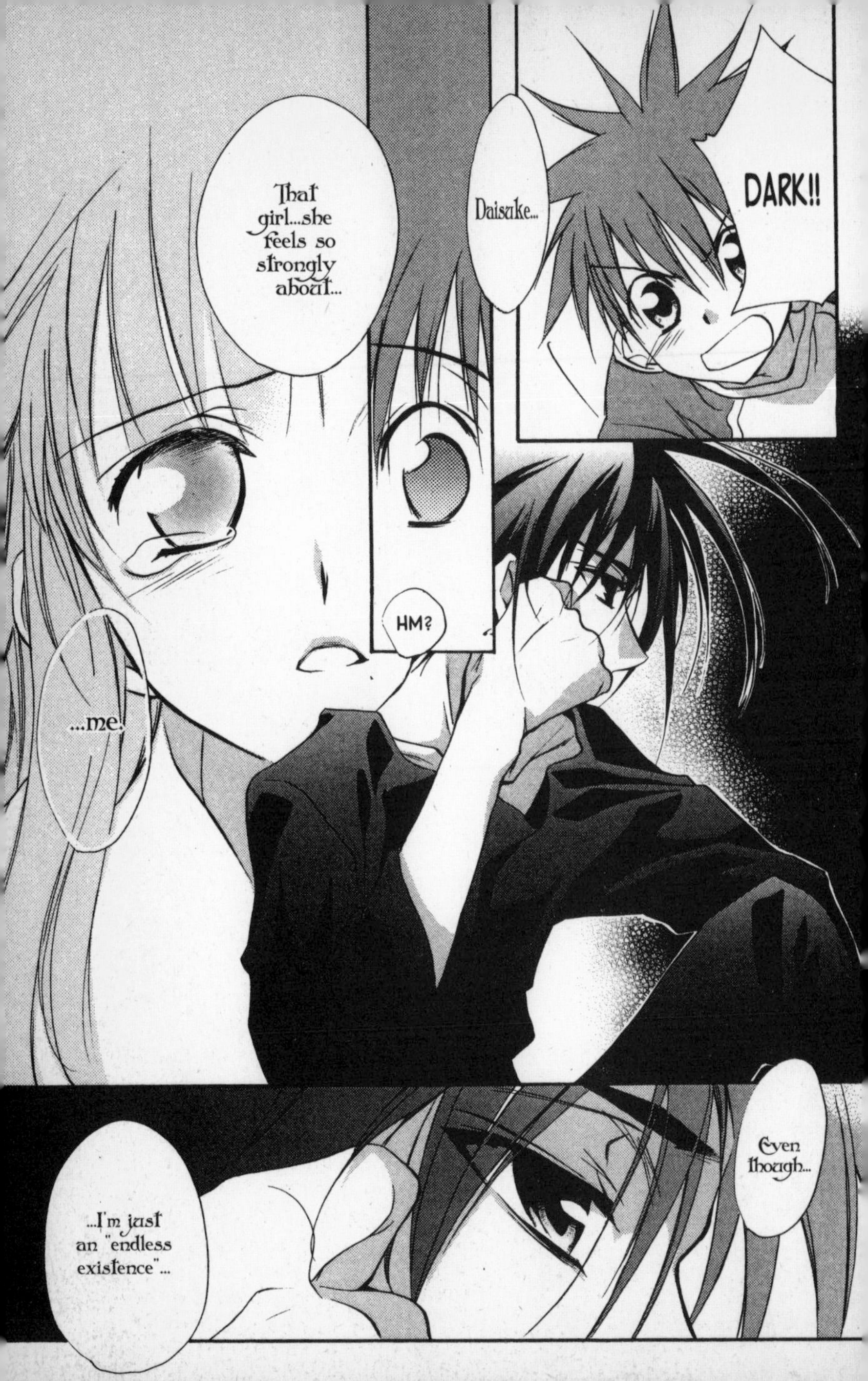
DARK!!
Daisuke...
That girl...she feels so strongly about...
HM?
...me.
Even though...
...I'm just an "endless existence"...

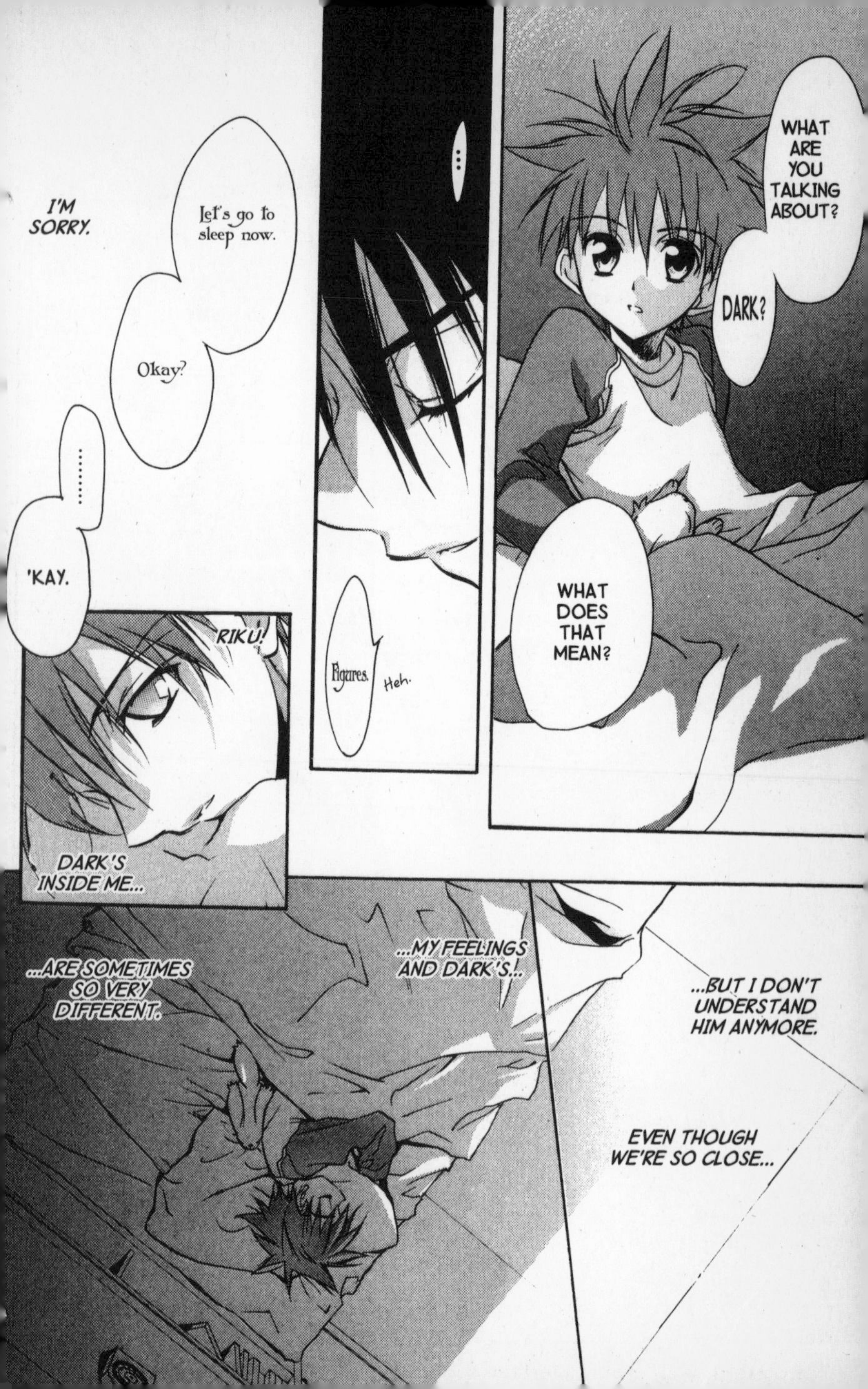
WHAT ARE YOU TALKING ABOUT?
DARK?
WHAT DOES THAT MEAN?
...
Figures.
Heh.
Let's go to sleep now.
Okay?
I'M SORRY.
....
'KAY.
RIKU!
DARK'S INSIDE ME...
...BUT I DON'T UNDERSTAND HIM ANYMORE.
EVEN THOUGH WE'RE SO CLOSE...
...MY FEELINGS AND DARK'S...
...ARE SOMETIMES SO VERY DIFFERENT.

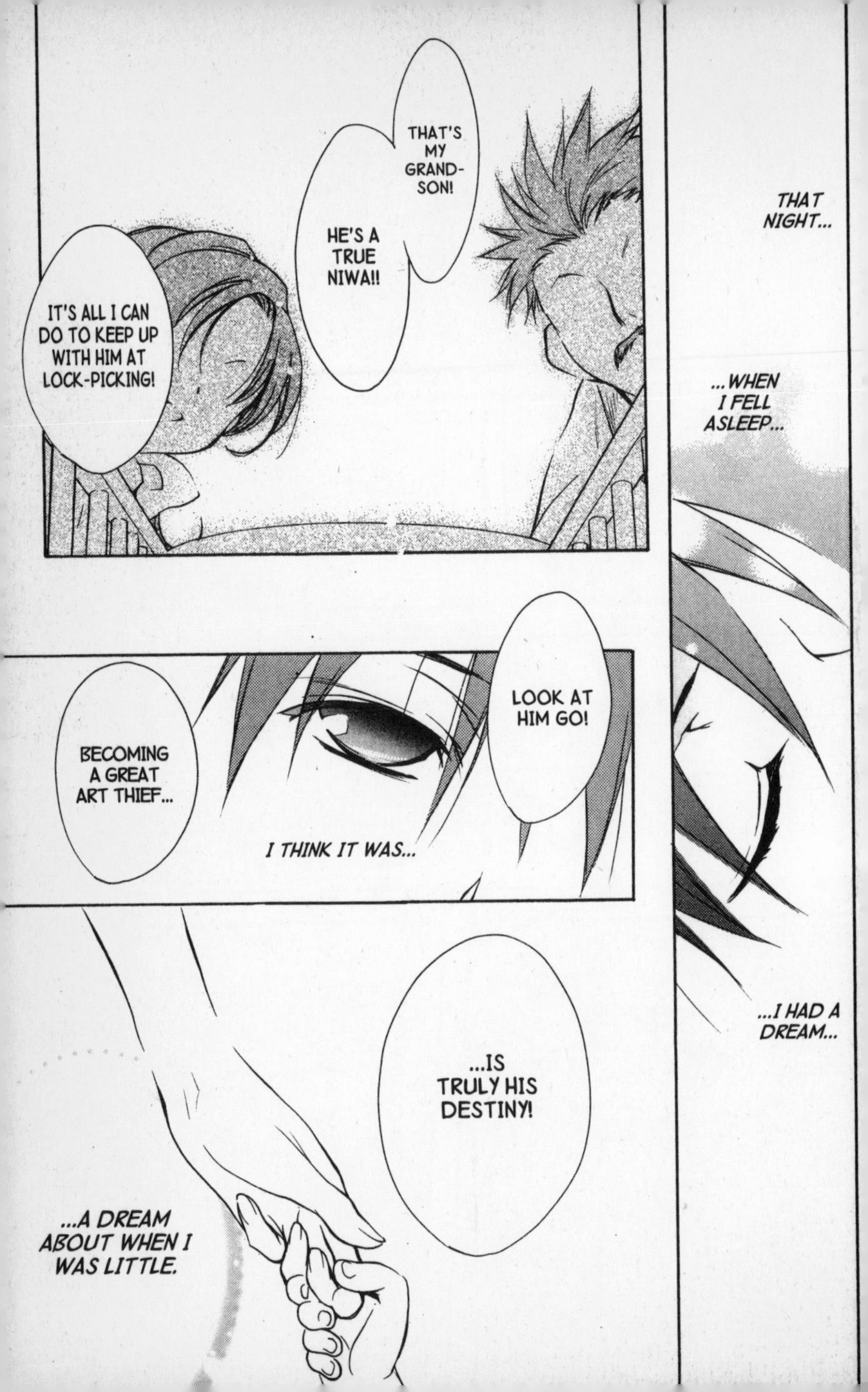
THAT NIGHT...
...WHEN I FELL ASLEEP...
...I HAD A DREAM...
THAT'S MY GRAND-SON!
HE'S A TRUE NIWA!!
IT'S ALL I CAN DO TO KEEP UP WITH HIM AT LOCK-PICKING!
LOOK AT HIM GO!
BECOMING A GREAT ART THIEF...
I THINK IT WAS...
...IS TRULY HIS DESTINY!
...A DREAM ABOUT WHEN I WAS LITTLE.

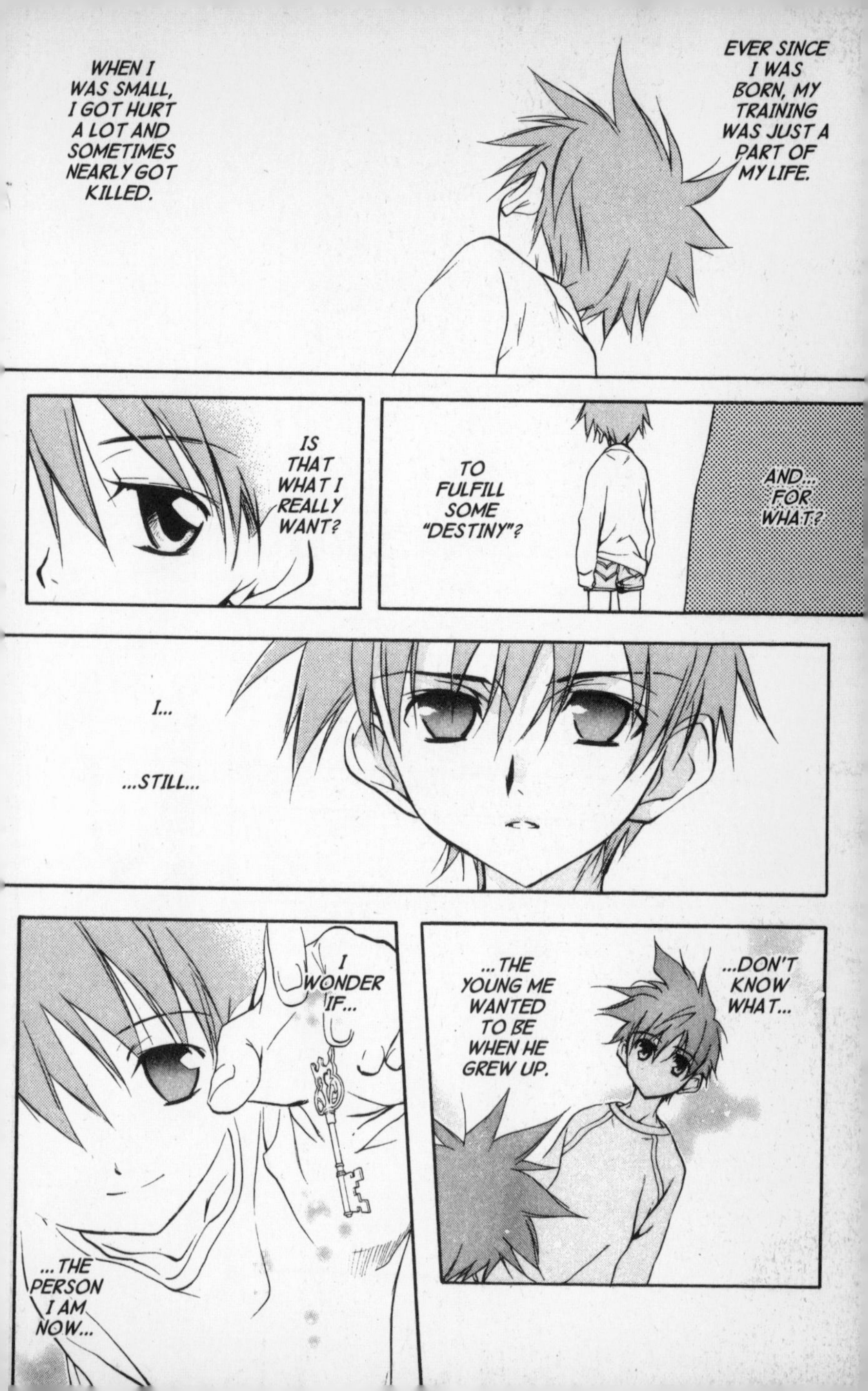
EVER SINCE I WAS BORN, MY TRAINING WAS JUST A PART OF MY LIFE.
WHEN I WAS SMALL, I GOT HURT A LOT AND SOMETIMES NEARLY GOT KILLED.
AND... FOR WHAT?
TO FULFILL SOME "DESTINY"?
IS THAT WHAT I REALLY WANT?
I...
...STILL...
...DON'T KNOW WHAT...
...THE YOUNG ME WANTED TO BE WHEN HE GREW UP.
I WONDER IF...
...THE PERSON I AM NOW...

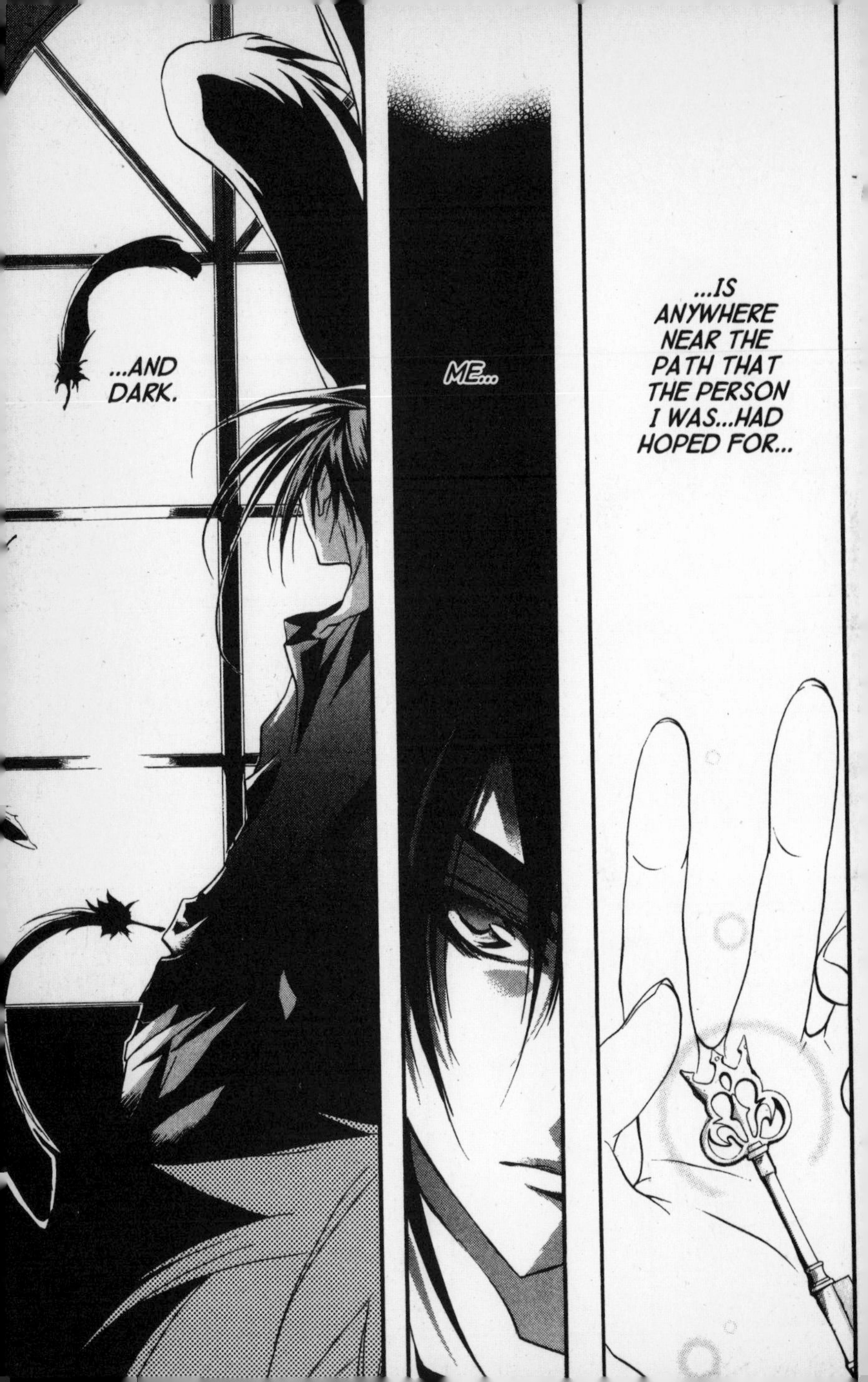
...IS ANYWHERE NEAR THE PATH THAT THE PERSON I WAS...HAD HOPED FOR...
ME...
...AND DARK.

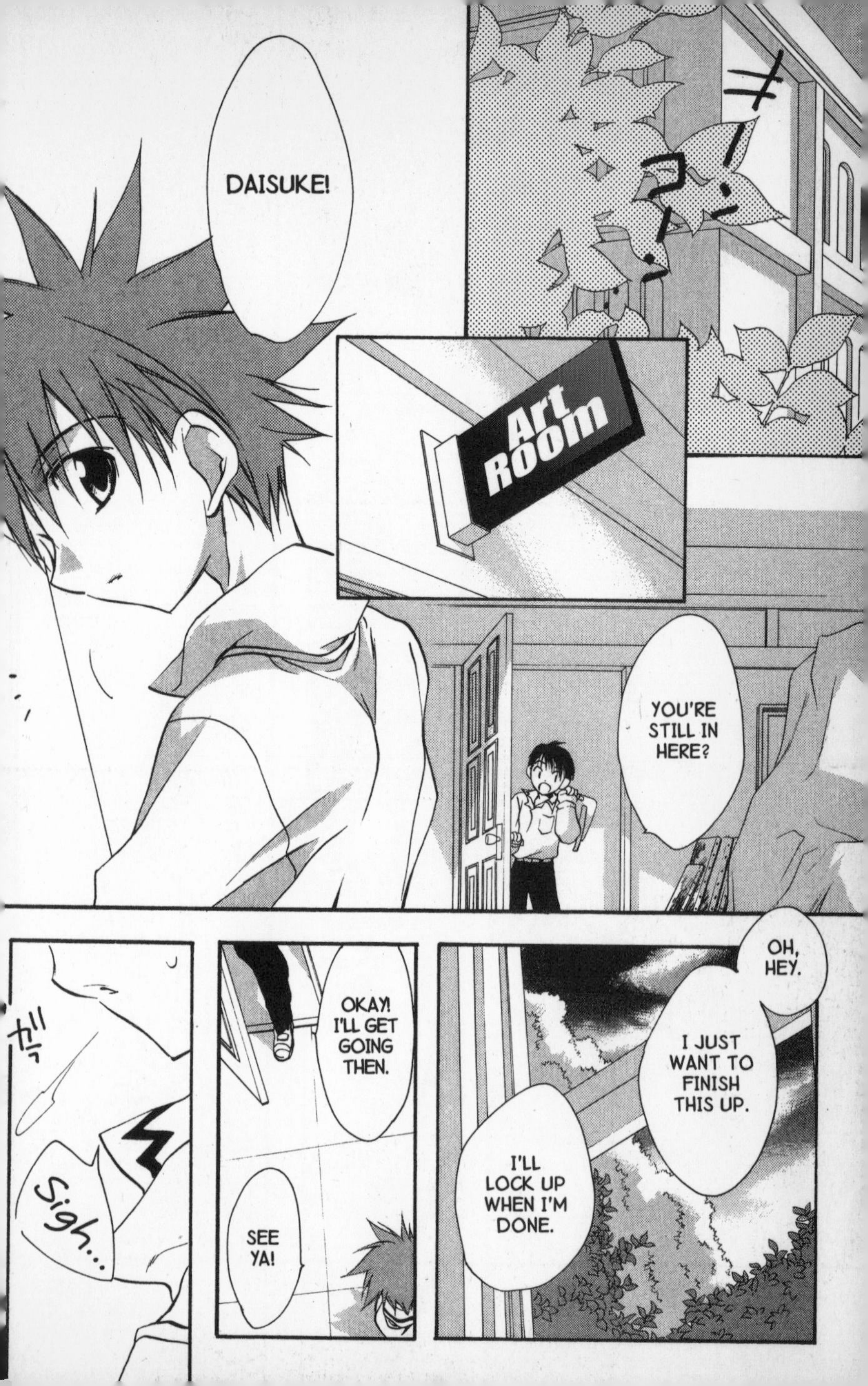
Art Room
DAISUKE!
YOU'RE STILL IN HERE?
OH, HEY.
I JUST WANT TO FINISH THIS UP.
I'LL LOCK UP WHEN I'M DONE.
OKAY! I'LL GET GOING THEN.
SEE YA!
Sigh...

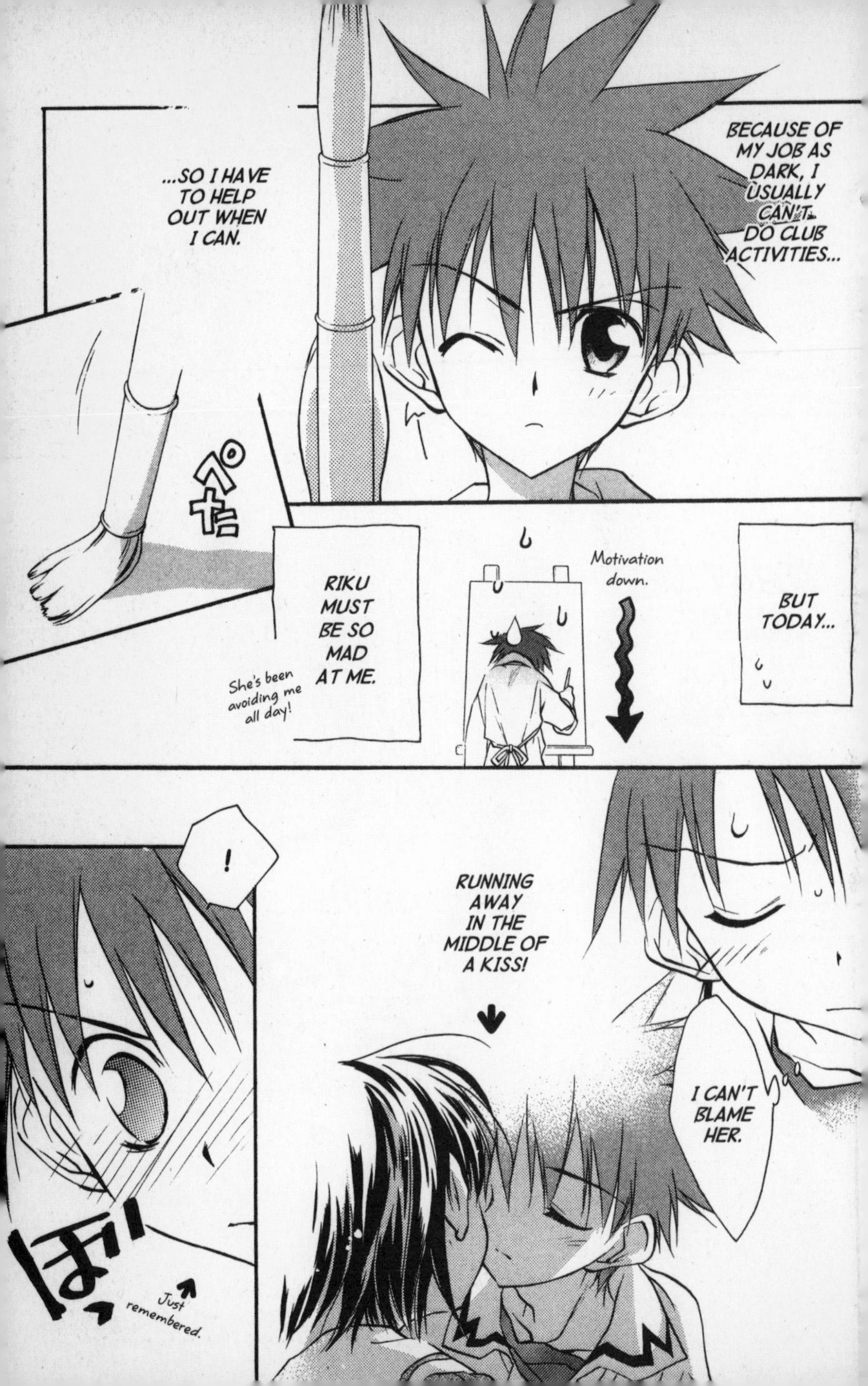
BECAUSE OF MY JOB AS DARK, I USUALLY CAN'T DO CLUB ACTIVITIES...
...SO I HAVE TO HELP OUT WHEN I CAN.
BUT TODAY...
Motivation down.
RIKU MUST BE SO MAD AT ME.
She's been avoiding me all day!
RUNNING AWAY IN THE MIDDLE OF A KISS!
I CAN'T BLAME HER.
!
Just remembered.

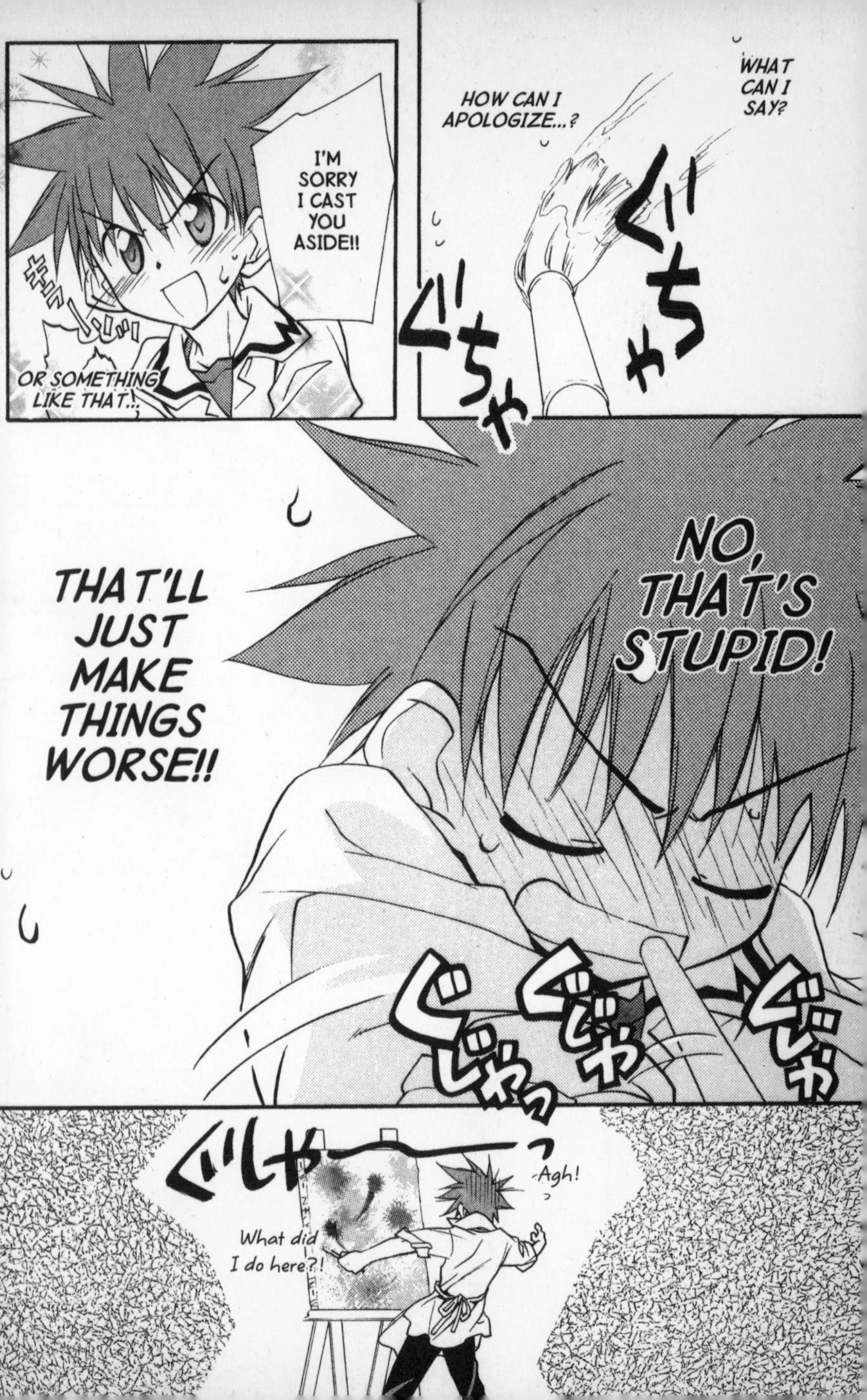

WHAT CAN I SAY?
HOW CAN I APOLOGIZE...?
ぐちゃ
ぐちゃ
I'M SORRY I CAST YOU ASIDE!!
OR SOMETHING LIKE THAT..
NO, THAT'S STUPID!
THAT'LL JUST MAKE THINGS WORSE!!
ぐじゃ
ぐじゃ
ぐじゃっ
ぐしゃーーっ
Agh!
What did I do here?!

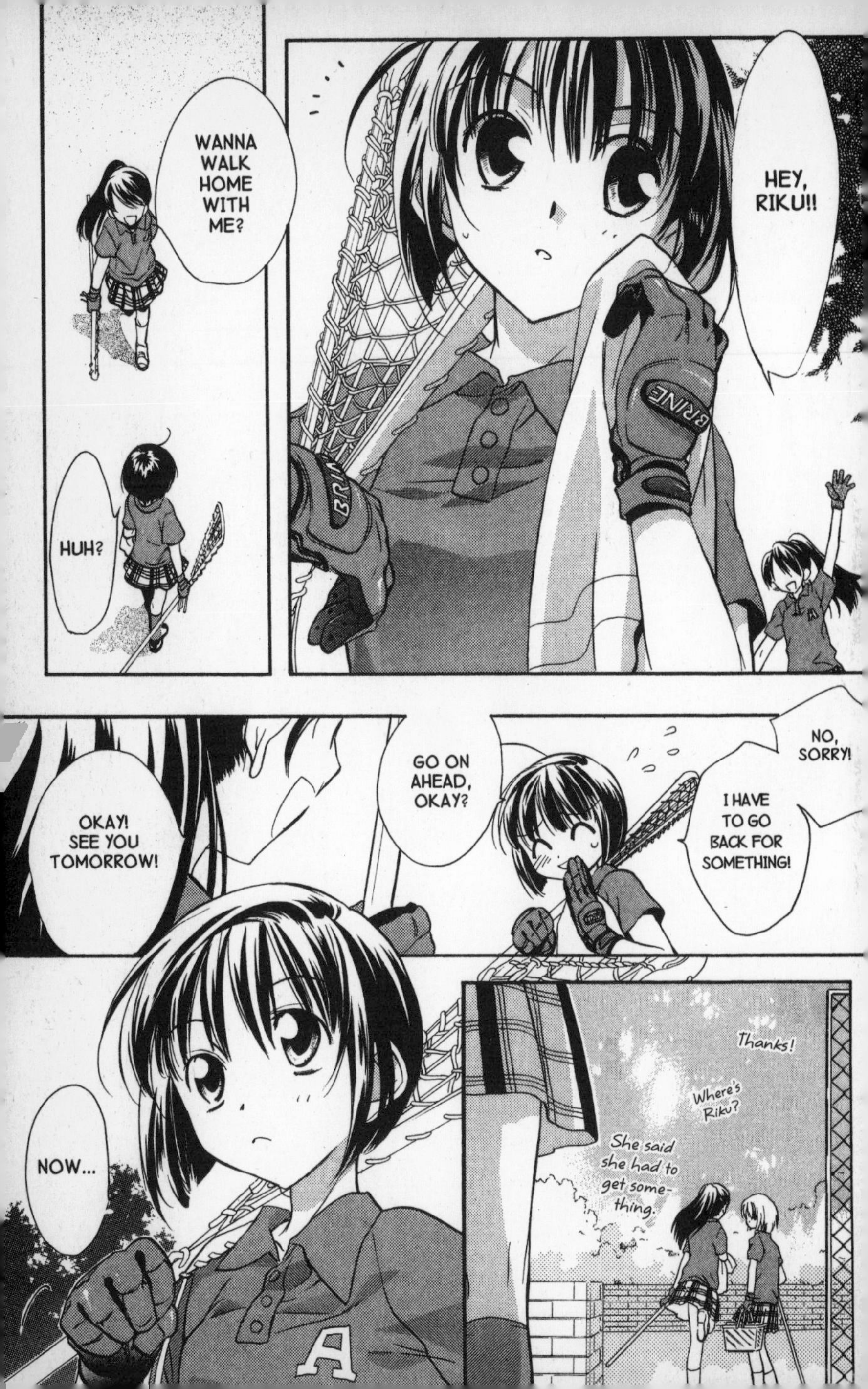

HEY, RIKU!!
BRINE
WANNA WALK HOME WITH ME?
HUH?
NO, SORRY!
I HAVE TO GO BACK FOR SOMETHING!
GO ON AHEAD, OKAY?
OKAY! SEE YOU TOMORROW!
Thanks!
Where's Riku?
She said she had to get some-thing.
NOW...

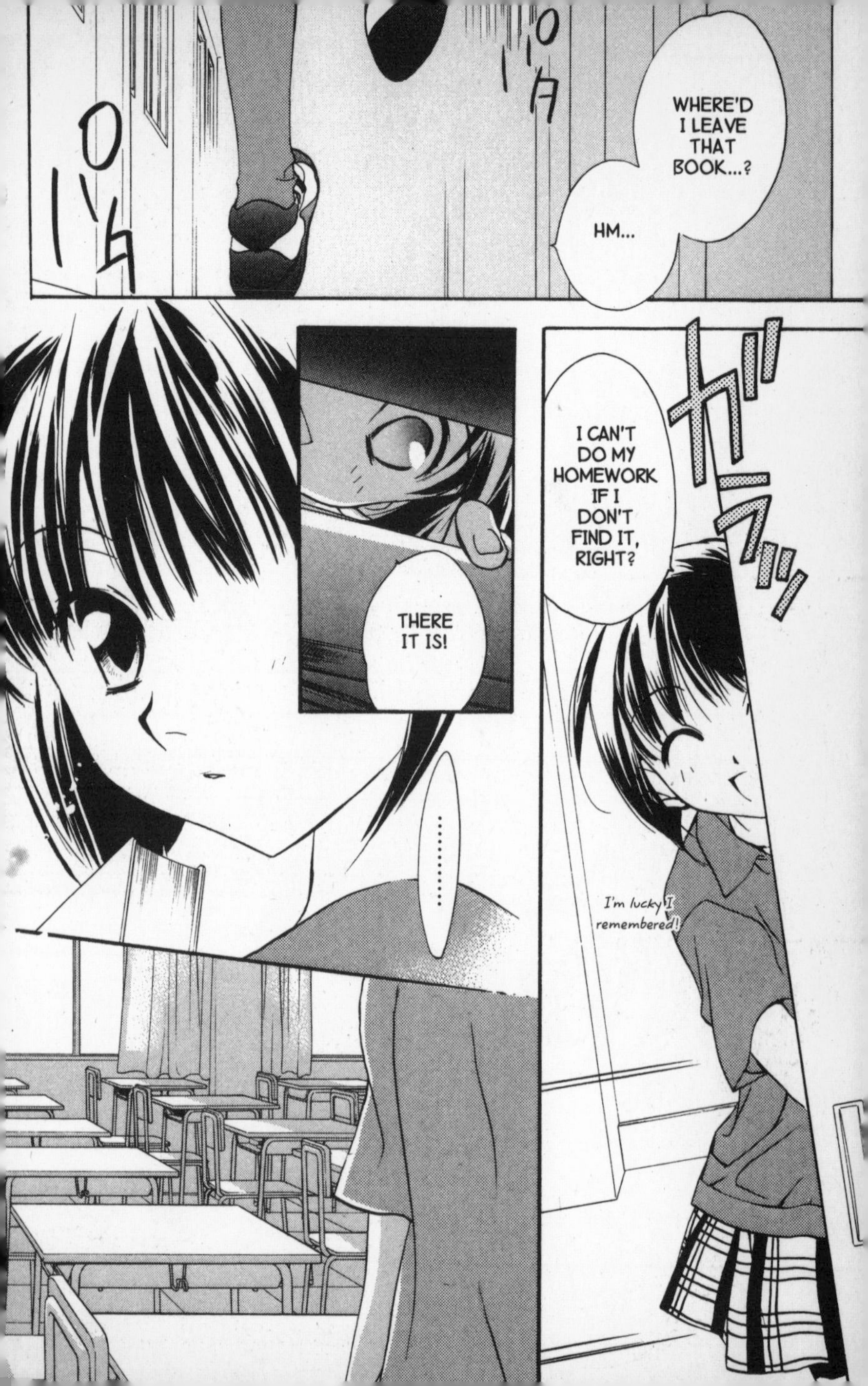
パタ
パタ
WHERE'D I LEAVE THAT BOOK...?
HM...
ガラッ
I CAN'T DO MY HOMEWORK IF I DON'T FIND IT, RIGHT?
I'm lucky I remembered!
THERE IT IS!
....

IT'S
DAISUKE'S
DESK...

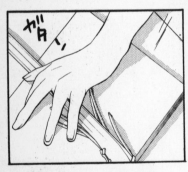

ガタ、

キョロ キョロ

I'm in
Daisuke's
seat...

おとん、...

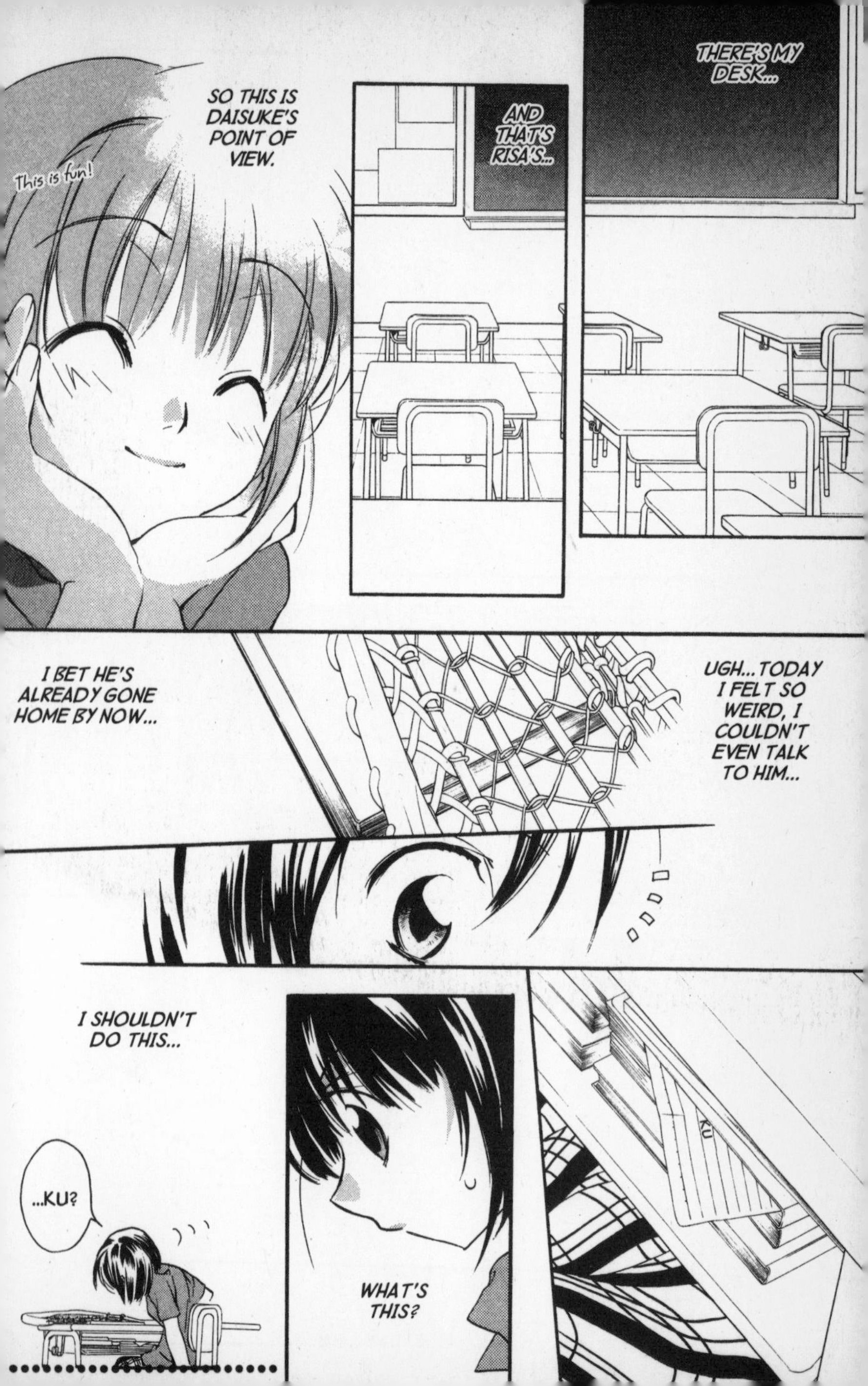
THERE'S MY DESK...
AND THAT'S RISA'S...
SO THIS IS DAISUKE'S POINT OF VIEW.
This is fun!
UGH...TODAY I FELT SO WEIRD, I COULDN'T EVEN TALK TO HIM...
I BET HE'S ALREADY GONE HOME BY NOW...
KU
WHAT'S THIS?
I SHOULDN'T DO THIS...
...KU?

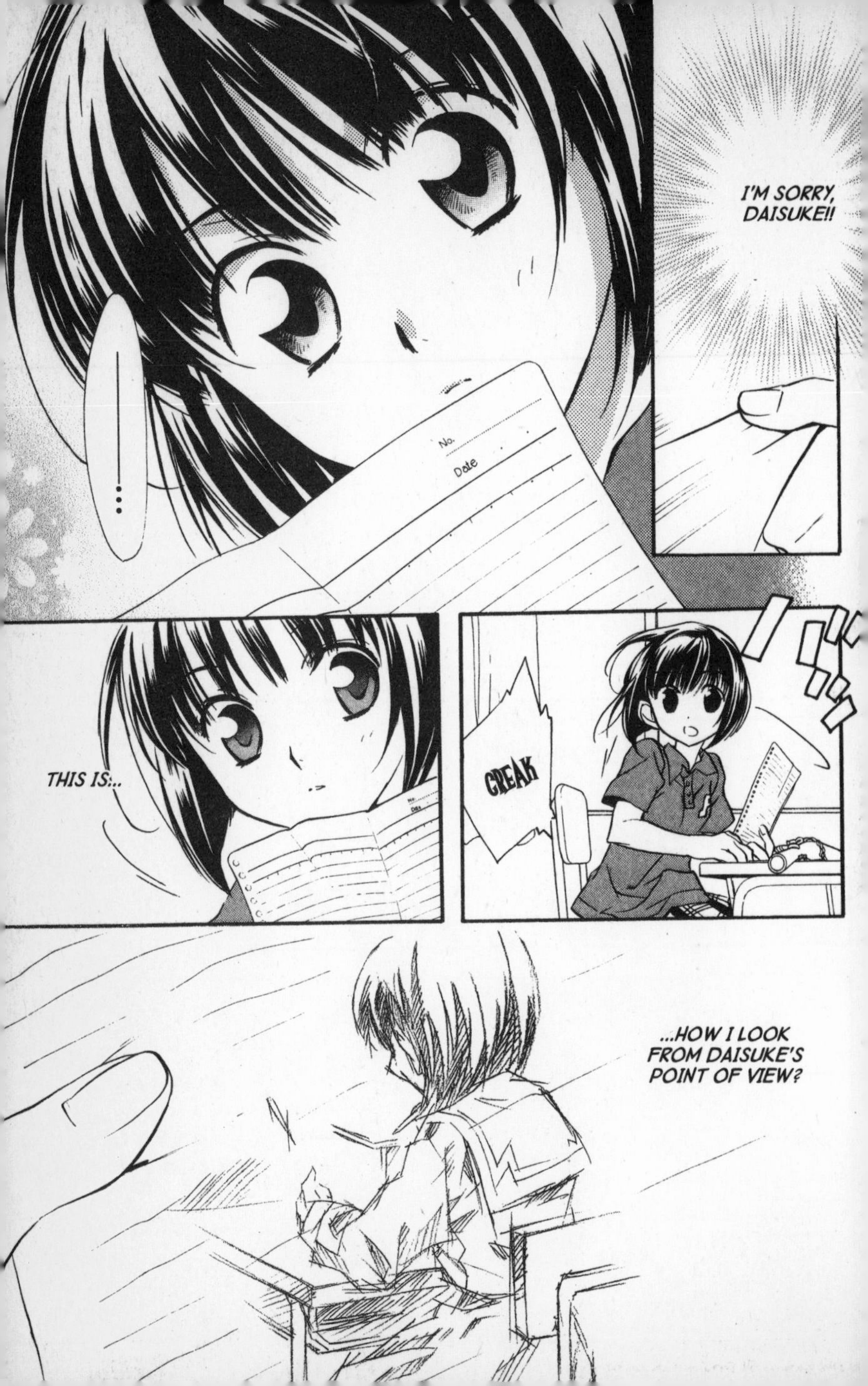
I'M SORRY, DAISUKE!!
...
No.
Date
CREAK
THIS IS...
...HOW I LOOK FROM DAISUKE'S POINT OF VIEW?

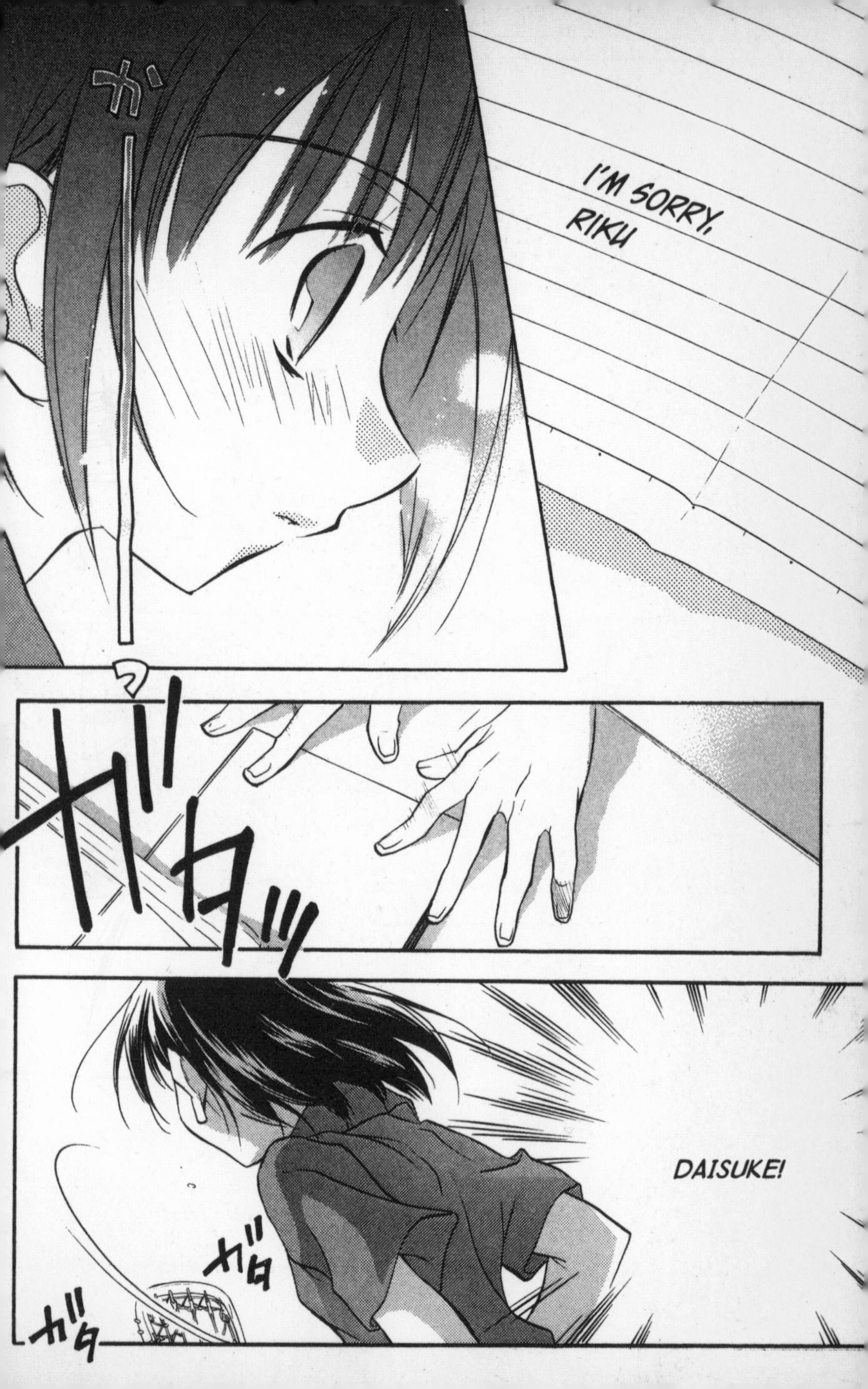
I'M SORRY, RIKU
ガーッ
ガタッ
DAISUKE!
ガタ
ガタ

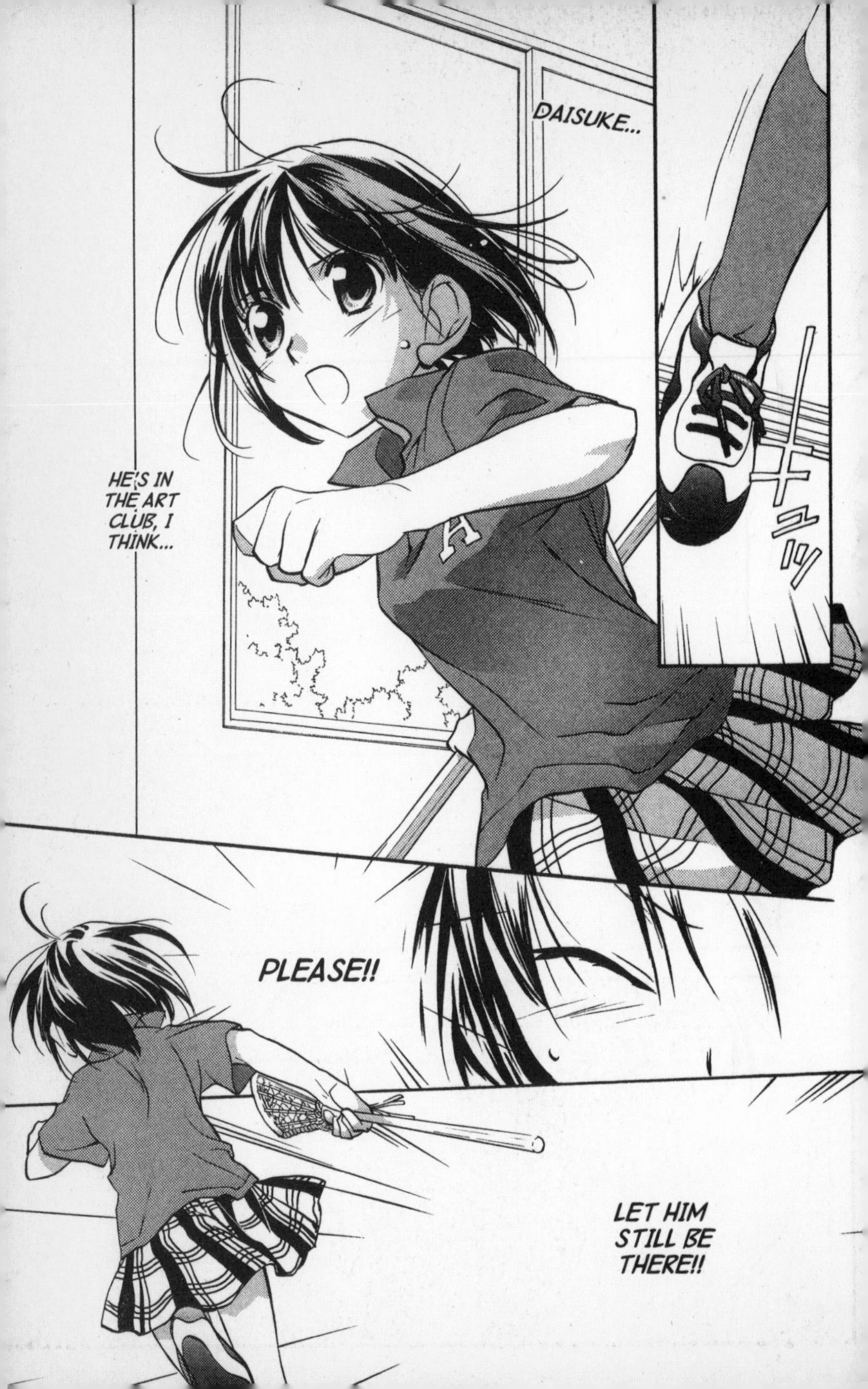
DAISUKE...
HE'S IN THE ART CLUB, I THINK...
キュッ
PLEASE!!
LET HIM STILL BE THERE!!

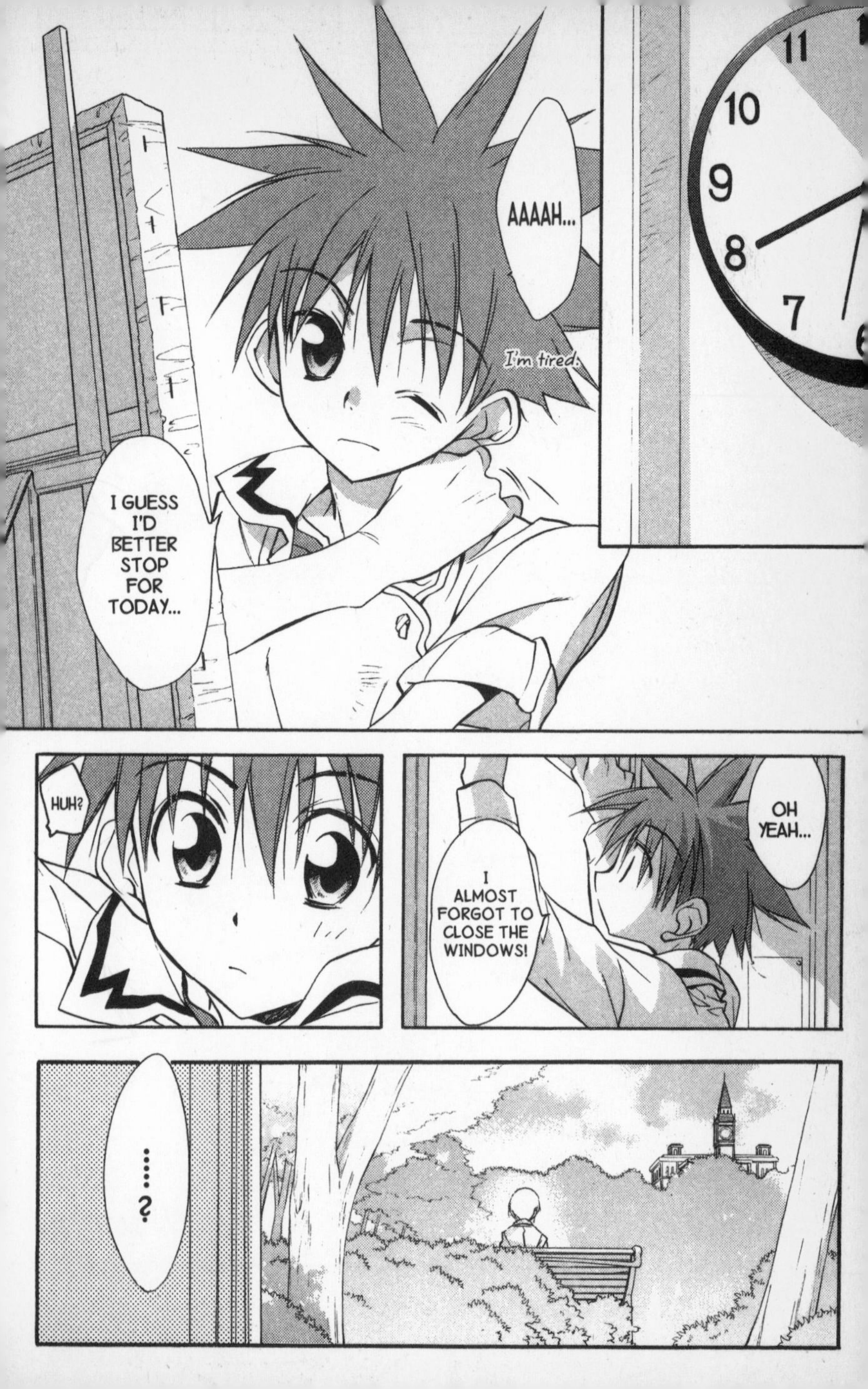
AAAAH...
I'm tired.
I GUESS I'D BETTER STOP FOR TODAY...
OH YEAH...
I ALMOST FORGOT TO CLOSE THE WINDOWS!
HUH?
.....?

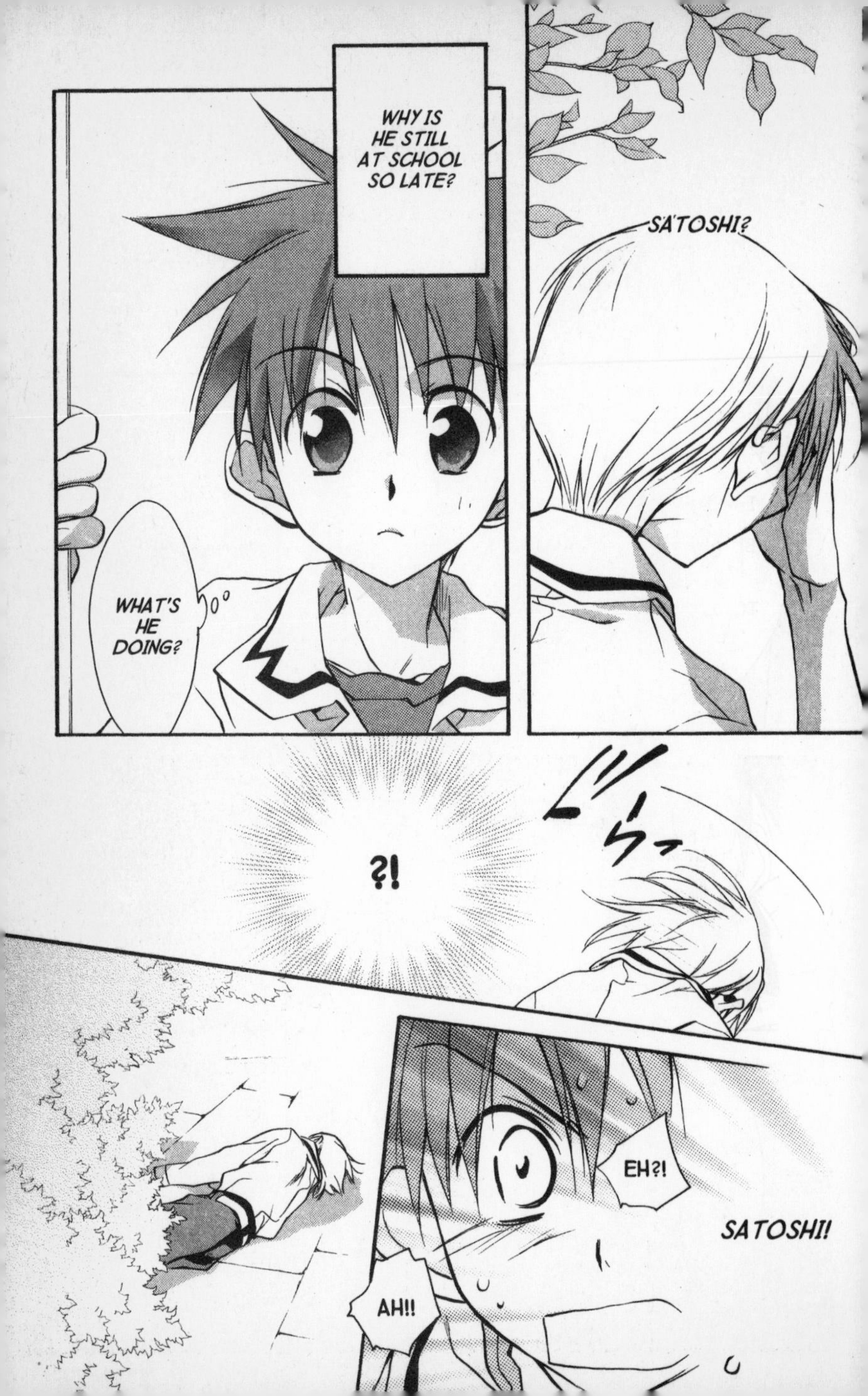
SATOSHI?
WHY IS HE STILL AT SCHOOL SO LATE?
WHAT'S HE DOING?
?!
SATOSHI!
EH?!
AH!!

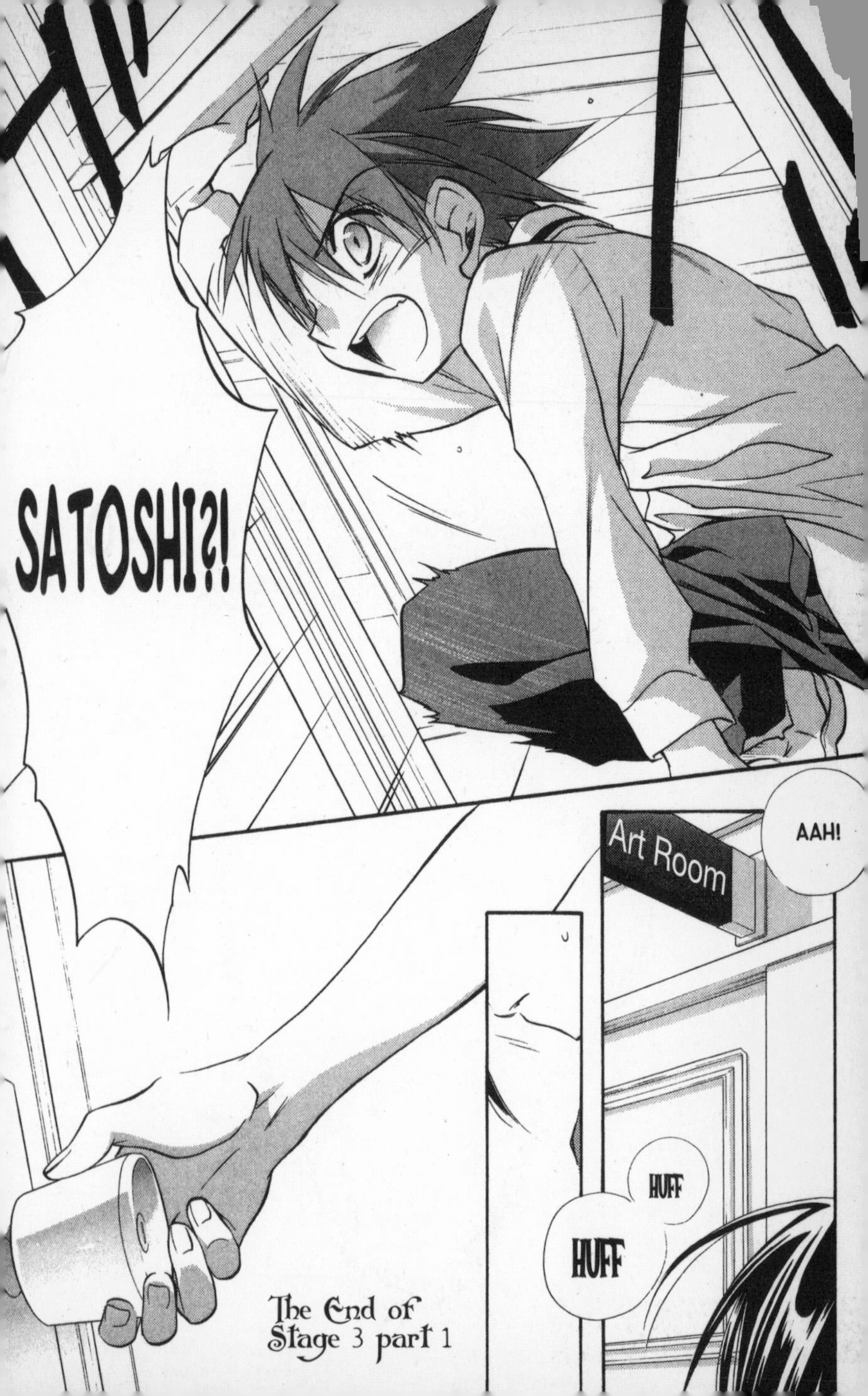
SATOSHI?!
Art Room
AAH!
HUFF
HUFF
The End of
Stage 3 part 1

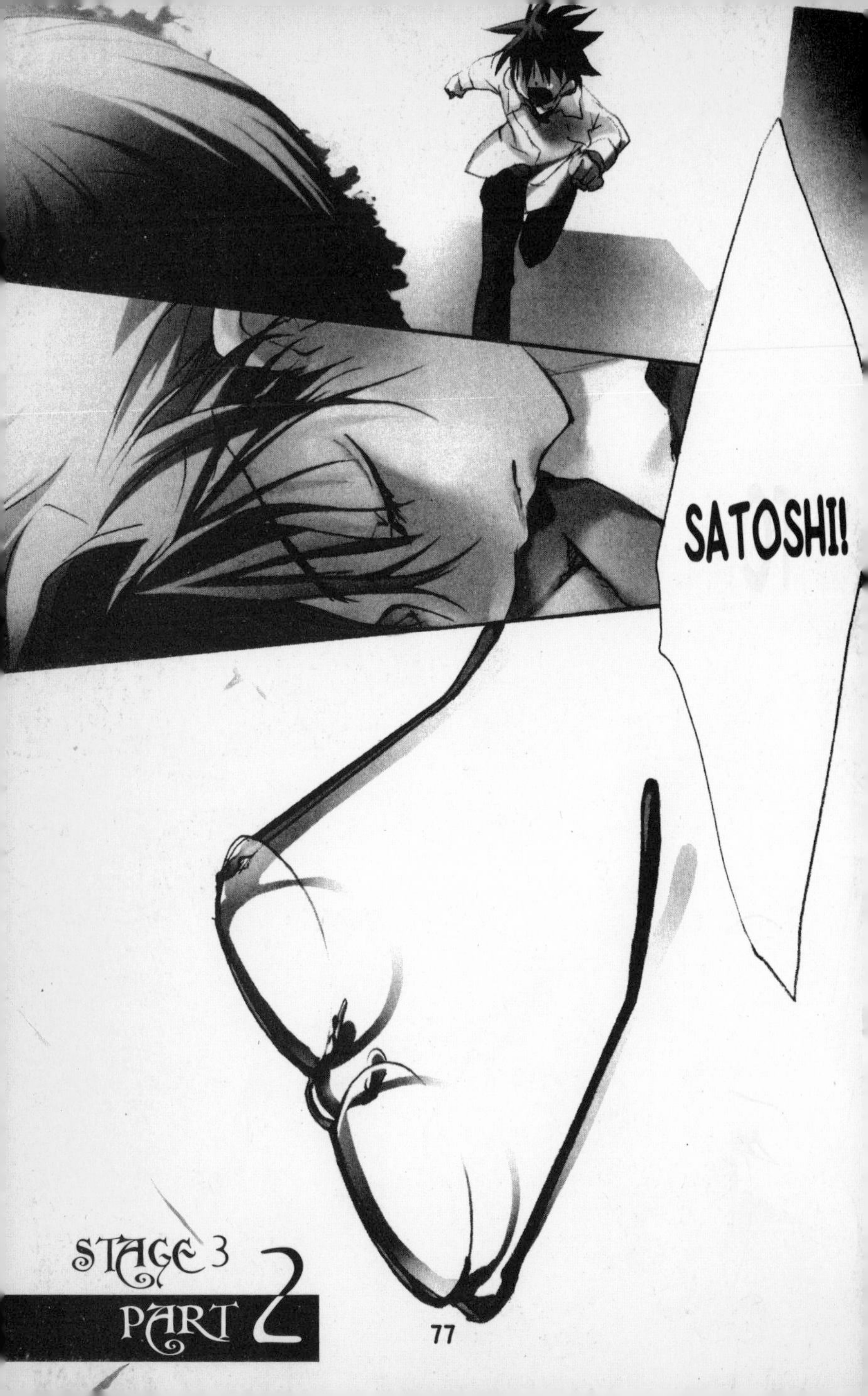
SATOSHI!
STAGE 3
PART 2

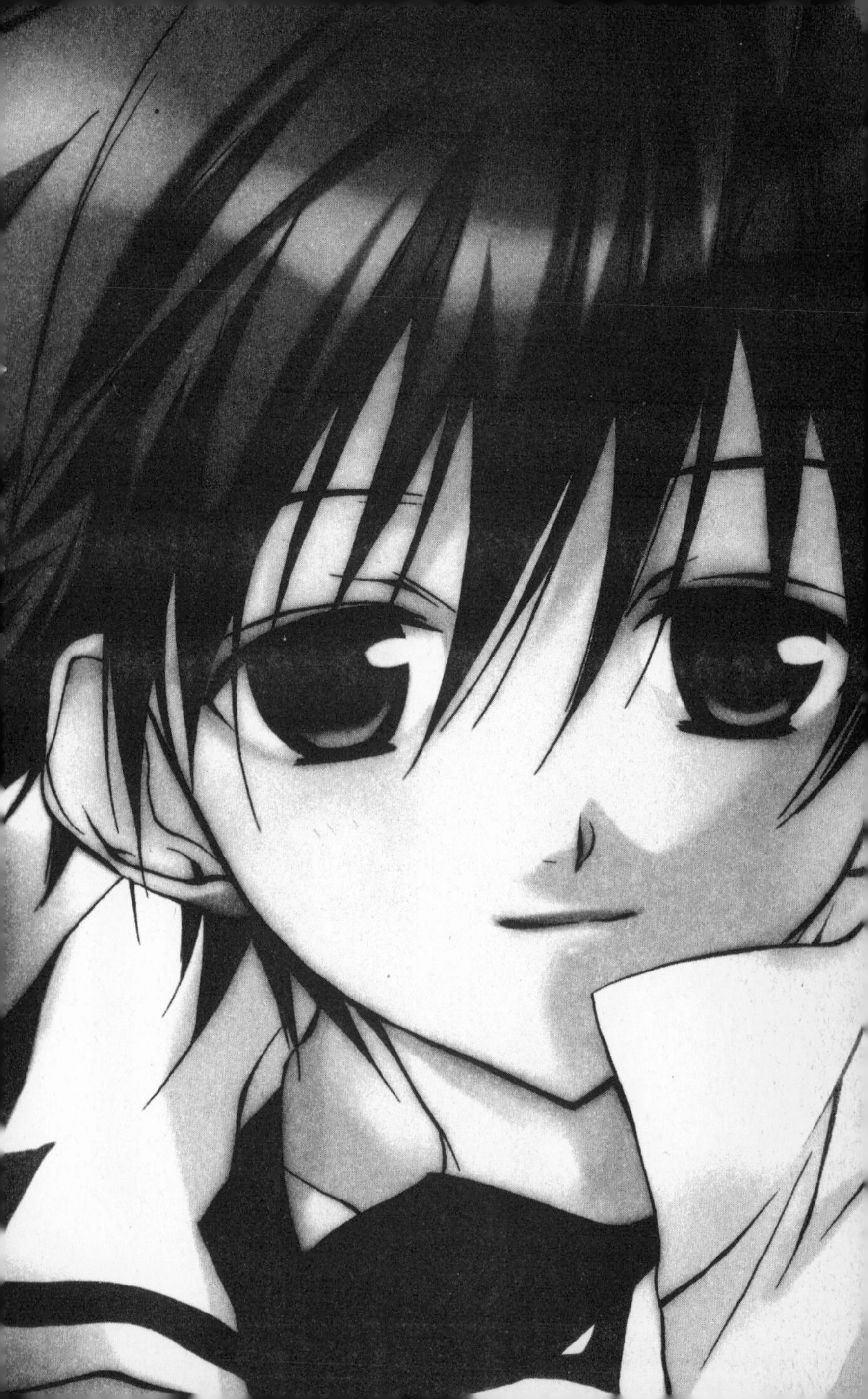

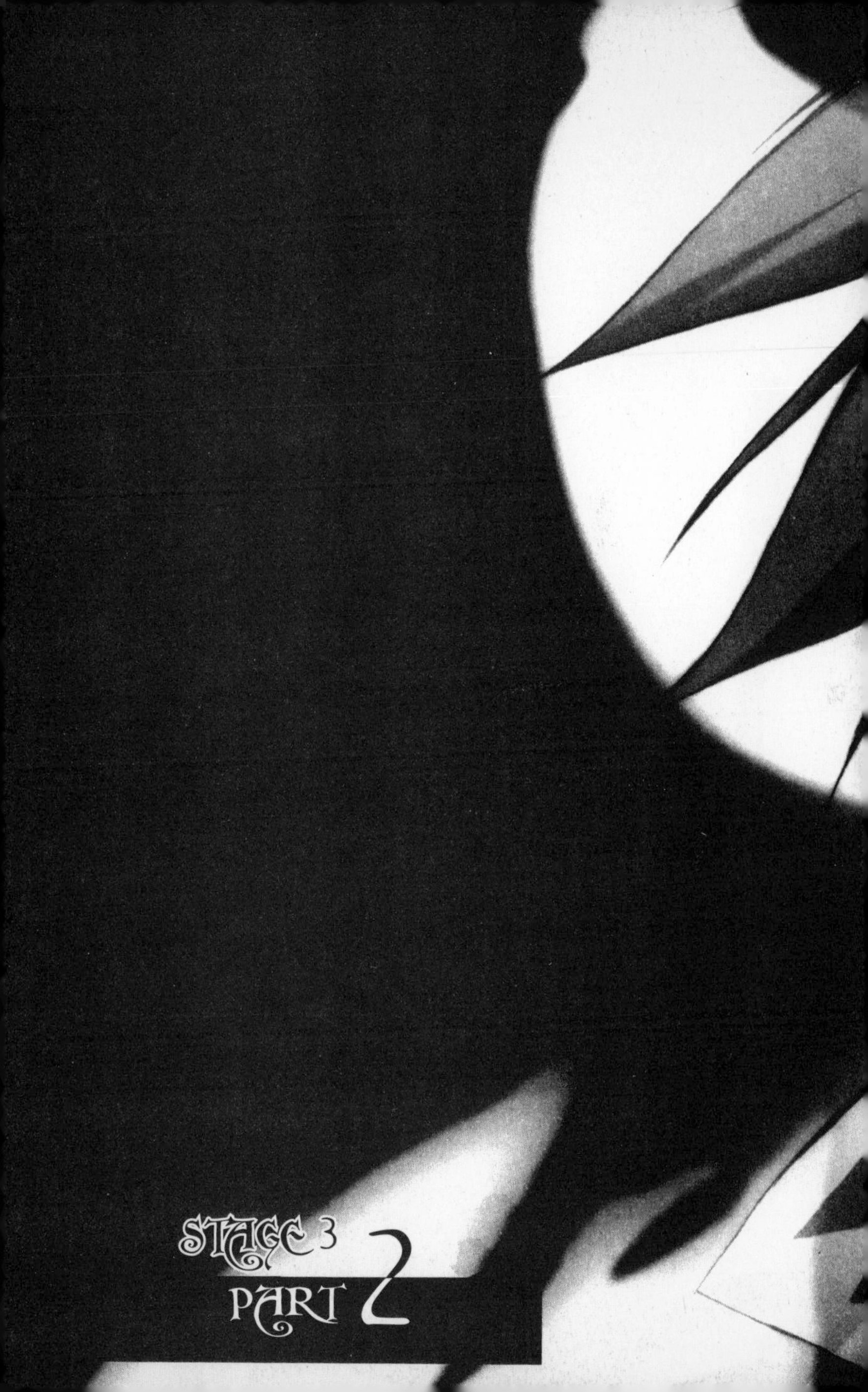
STAGE 3
PART 2

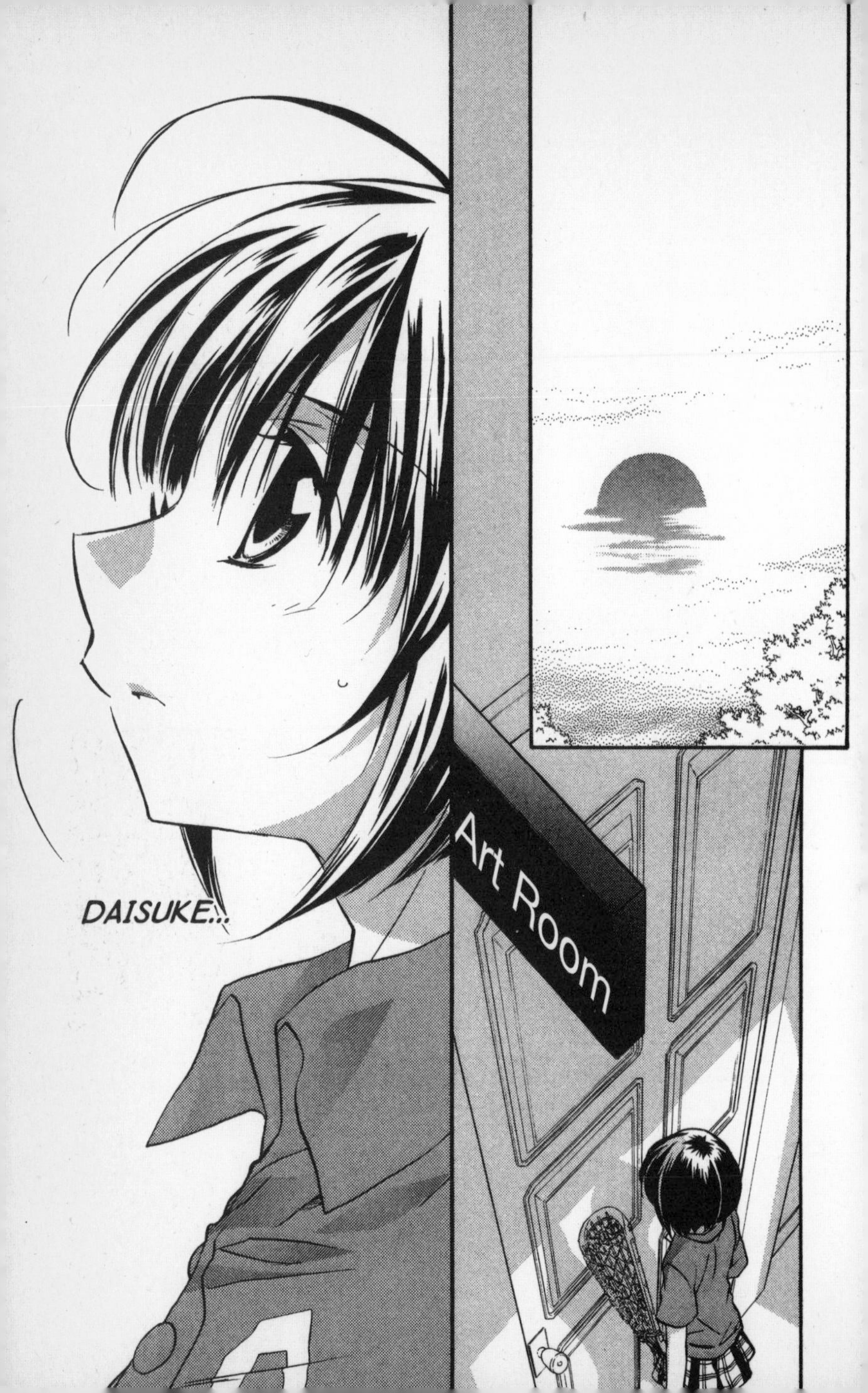
DAISUKE...
Art Room

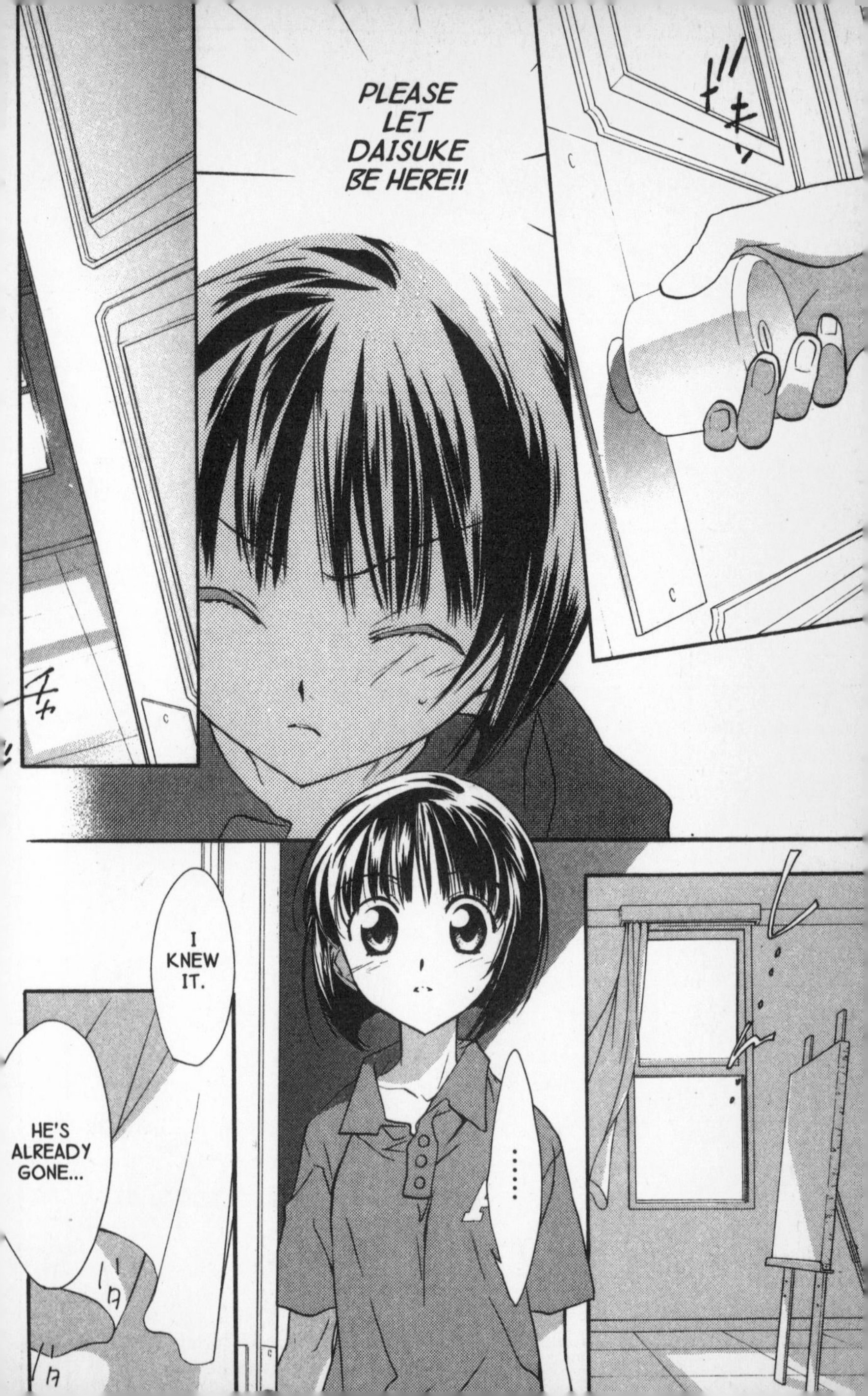
PLEASE LET DAISUKE BE HERE!!
......
I KNEW IT.
HE'S ALREADY GONE...

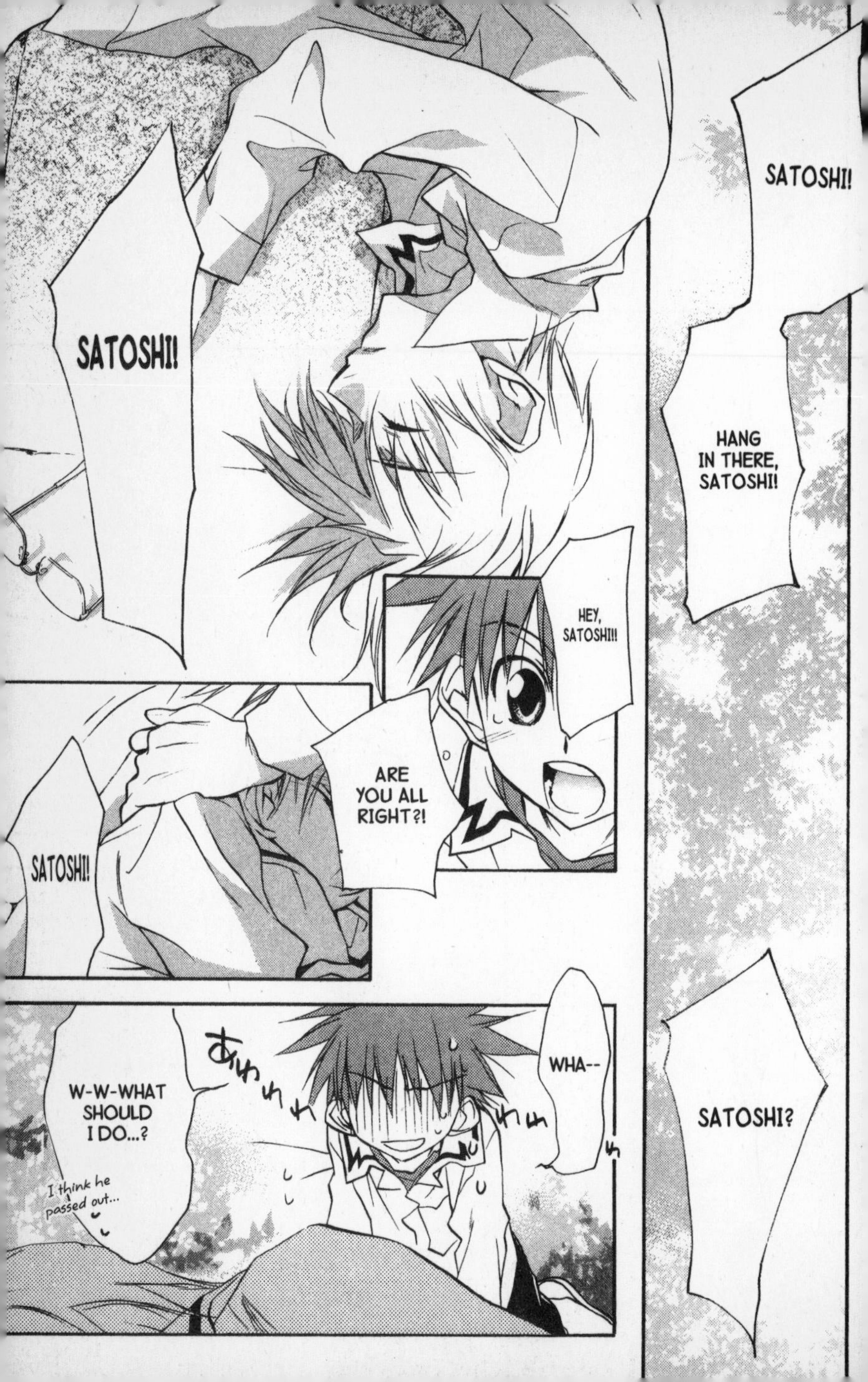
SATOSHI!
HANG IN THERE, SATOSHI!
SATOSHI?
SATOSHI!
HEY, SATOSHI!!
ARE YOU ALL RIGHT?!
SATOSHI!
WHA--
W-W-WHAT SHOULD I DO...?
I think he passed out...

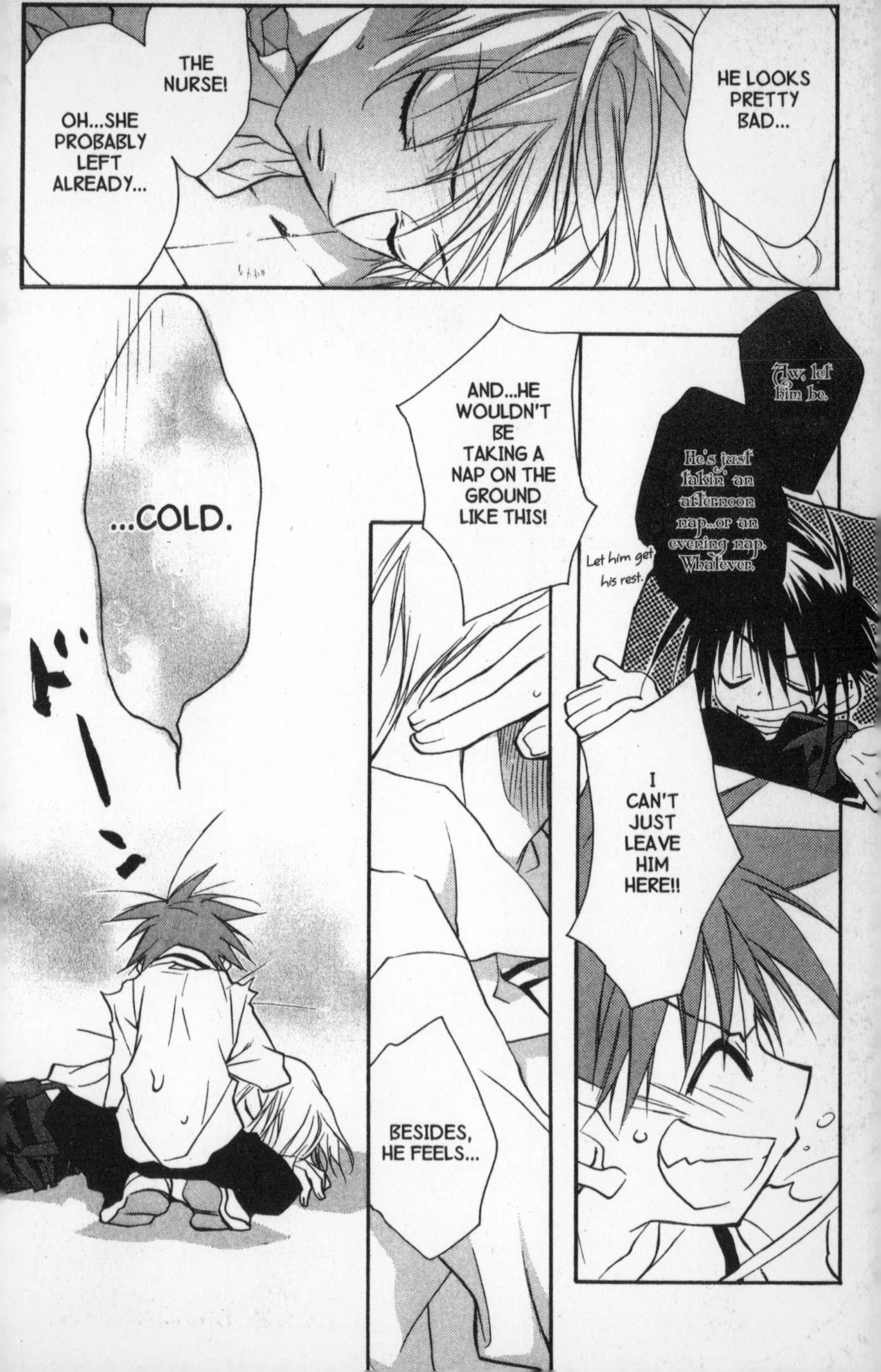
HE LOOKS PRETTY BAD...
THE NURSE!
OH...SHE PROBABLY LEFT ALREADY...
Aw, let him be.
He's just takin' an afternoon nap...or an evening nap. Whatever.
Let him get his rest.
AND...HE WOULDN'T BE TAKING A NAP ON THE GROUND LIKE THIS!
I CAN'T JUST LEAVE HIM HERE!!
BESIDES, HE FEELS...
...COLD.

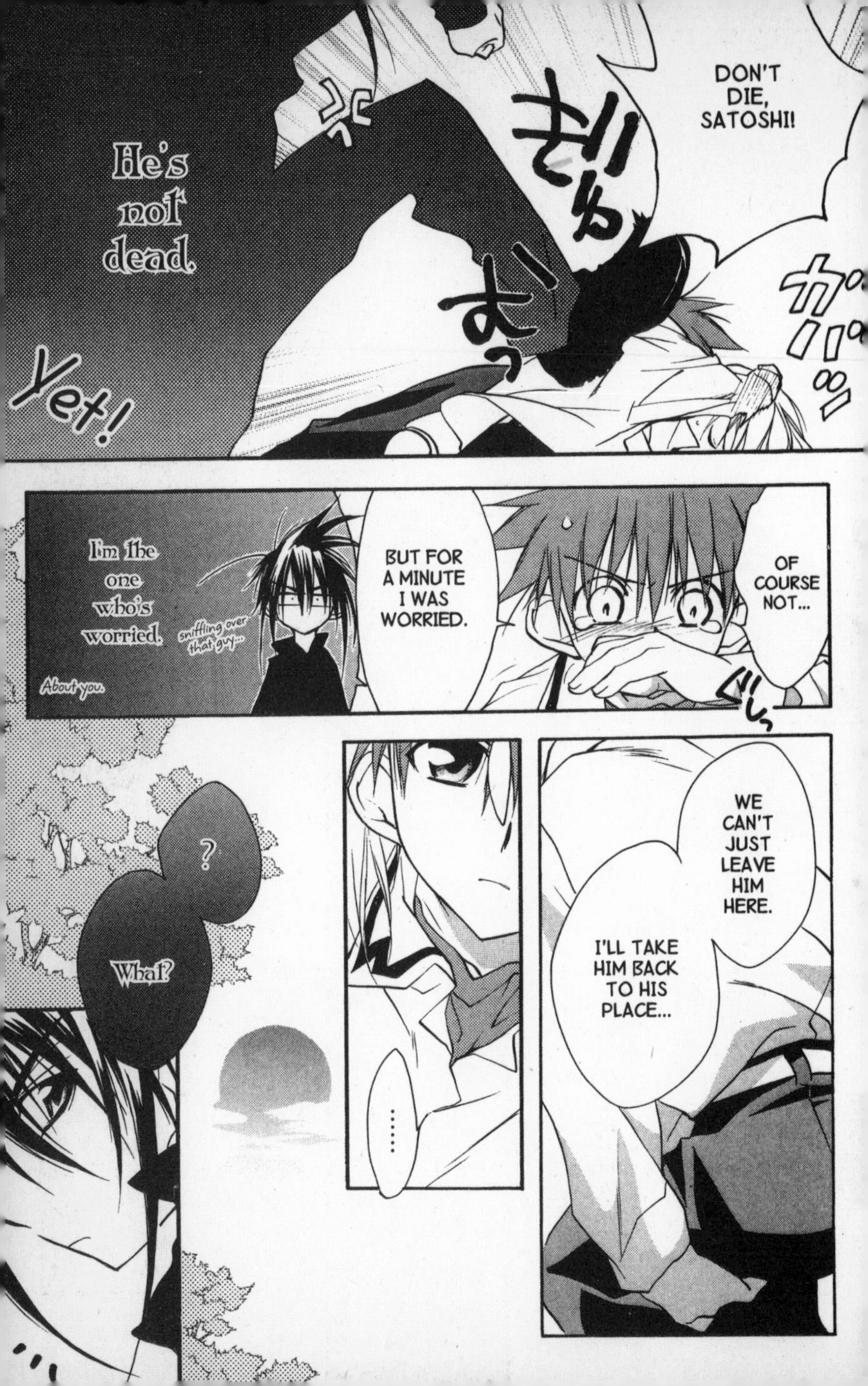
DON'T DIE, SATOSHI!
He's not dead.
Yet!
OF COURSE NOT...
BUT FOR A MINUTE I WAS WORRIED.
sniffling over that guy...
I'm the one who's worried.
About you.
WE CAN'T JUST LEAVE HIM HERE.
I'LL TAKE HIM BACK TO HIS PLACE...
......
?
What?
...

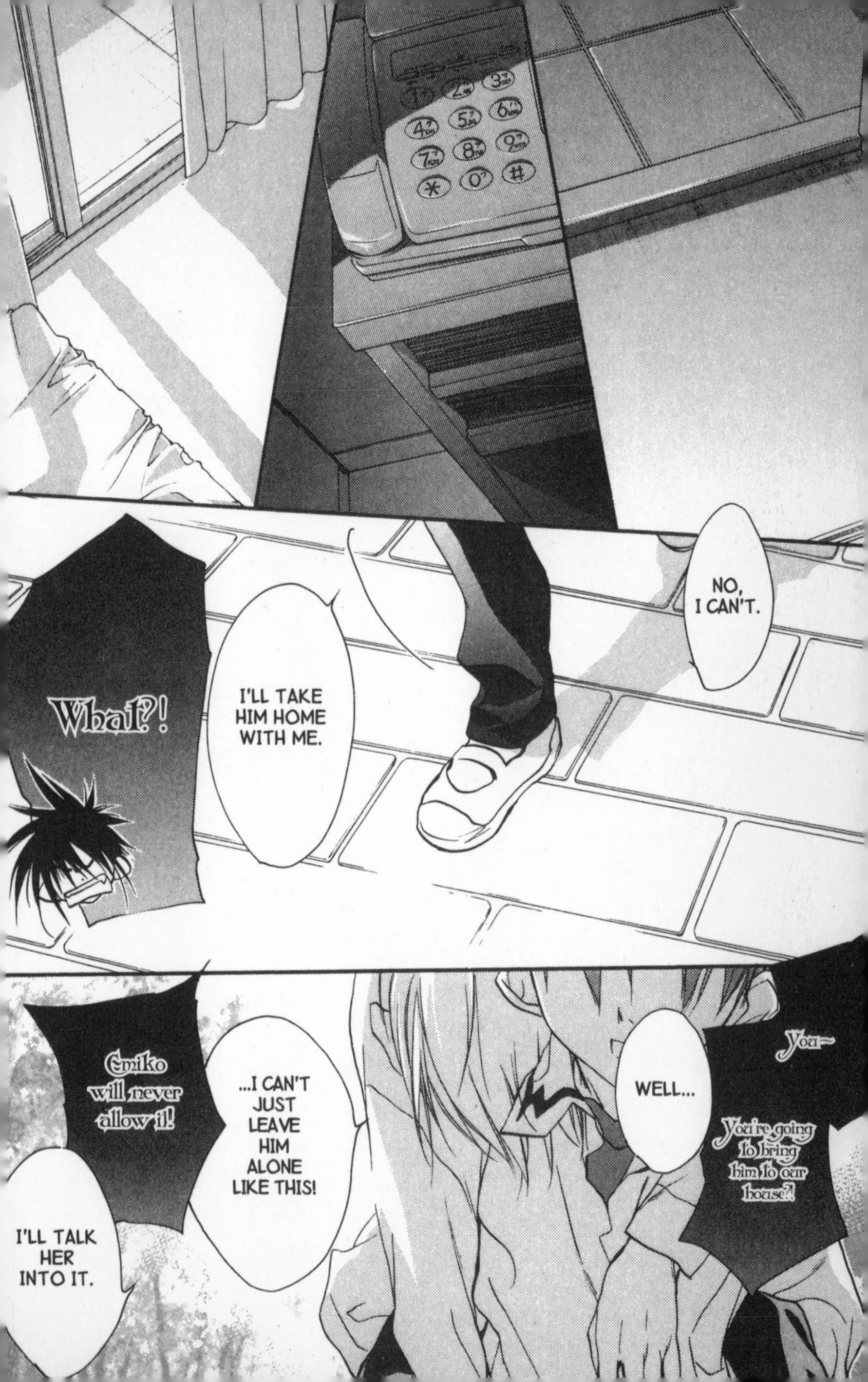
NO, I CAN'T.
I'LL TAKE HIM HOME WITH ME.
What?!
You—
You're going to bring him to our house?!
WELL...
...I CAN'T JUST LEAVE HIM ALONE LIKE THIS!
Emiko will never allow it!
I'LL TALK HER INTO IT.

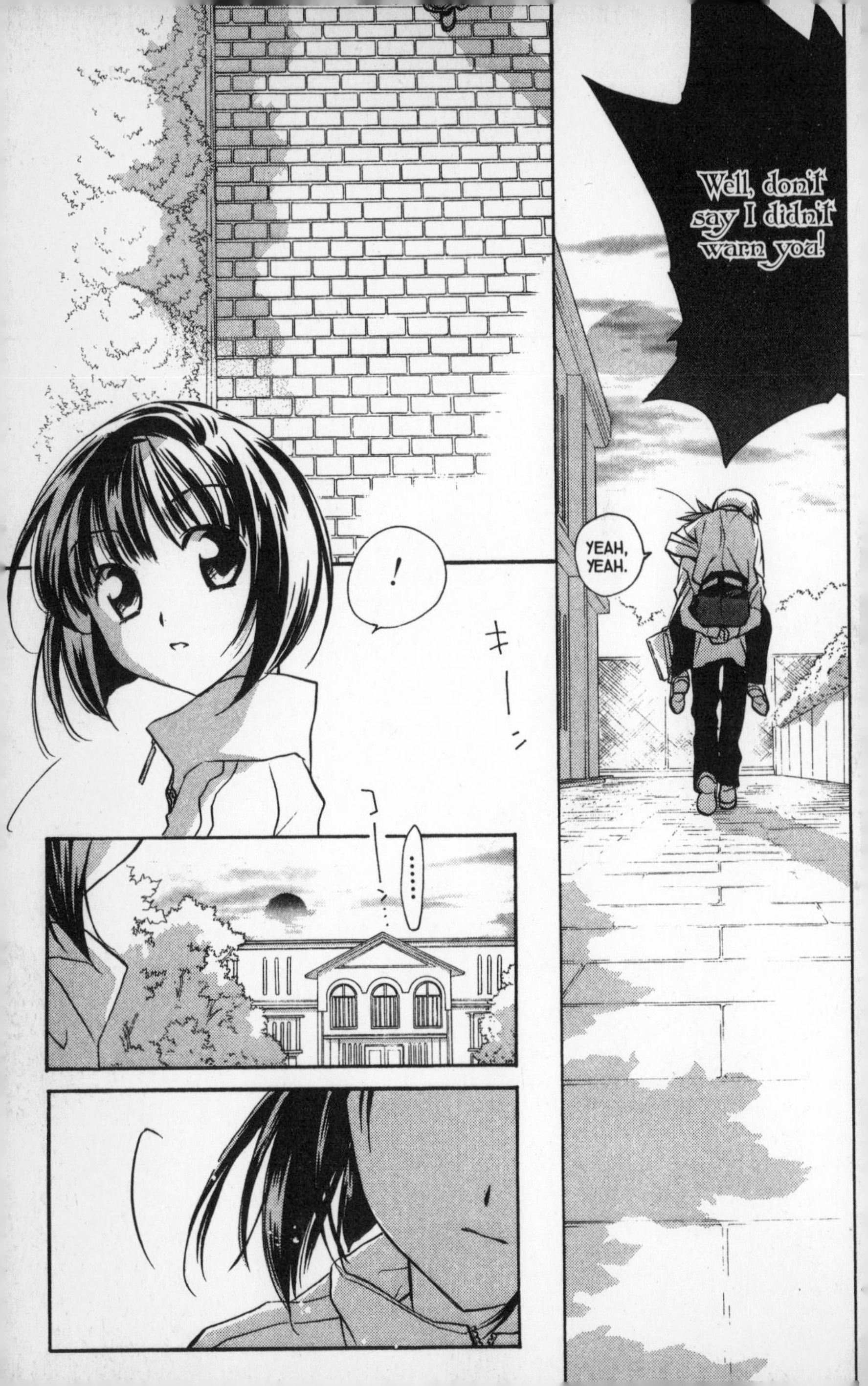
Well, don't say I didn't warn you!
YEAH, YEAH.
!
......

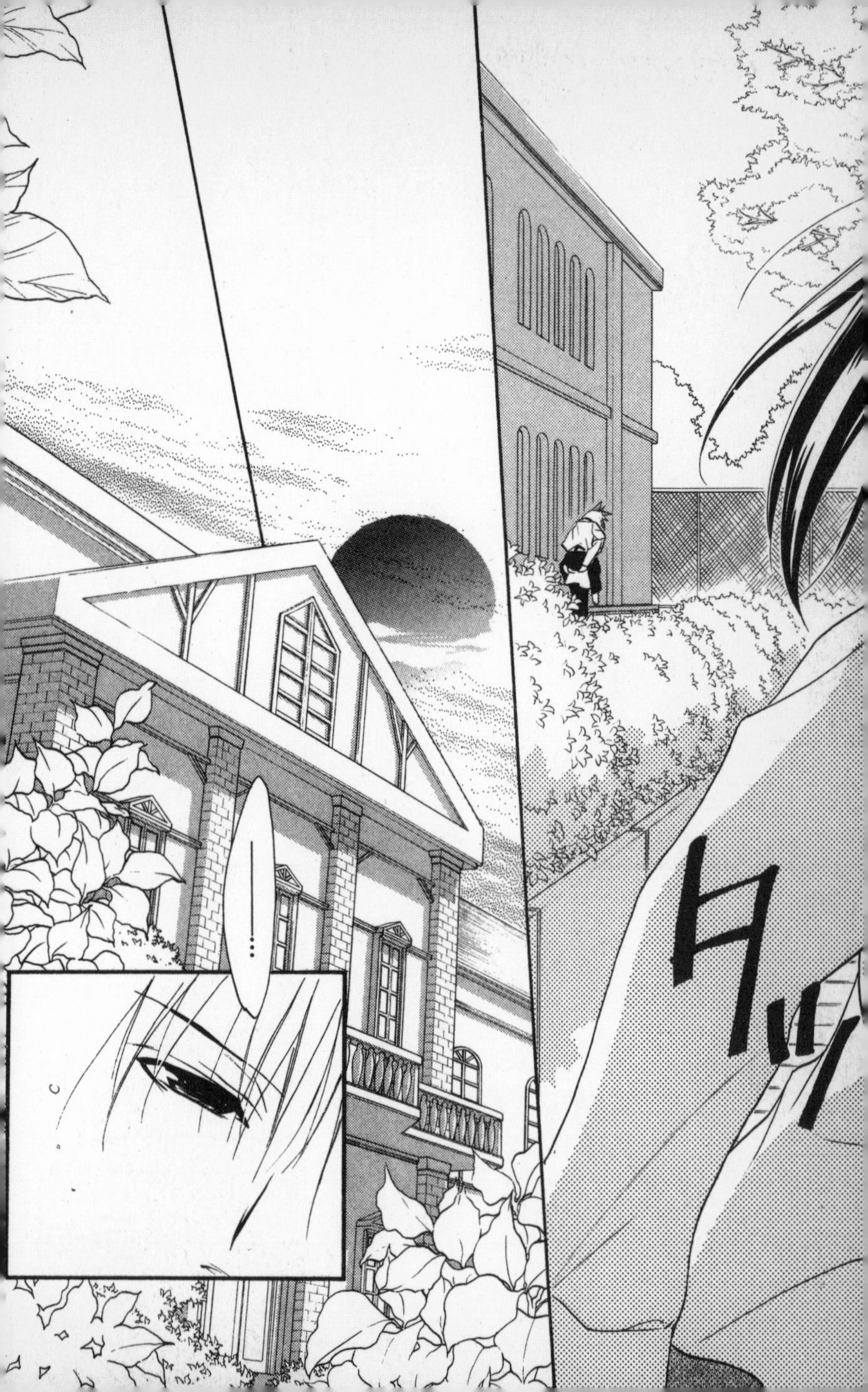
……
タッ

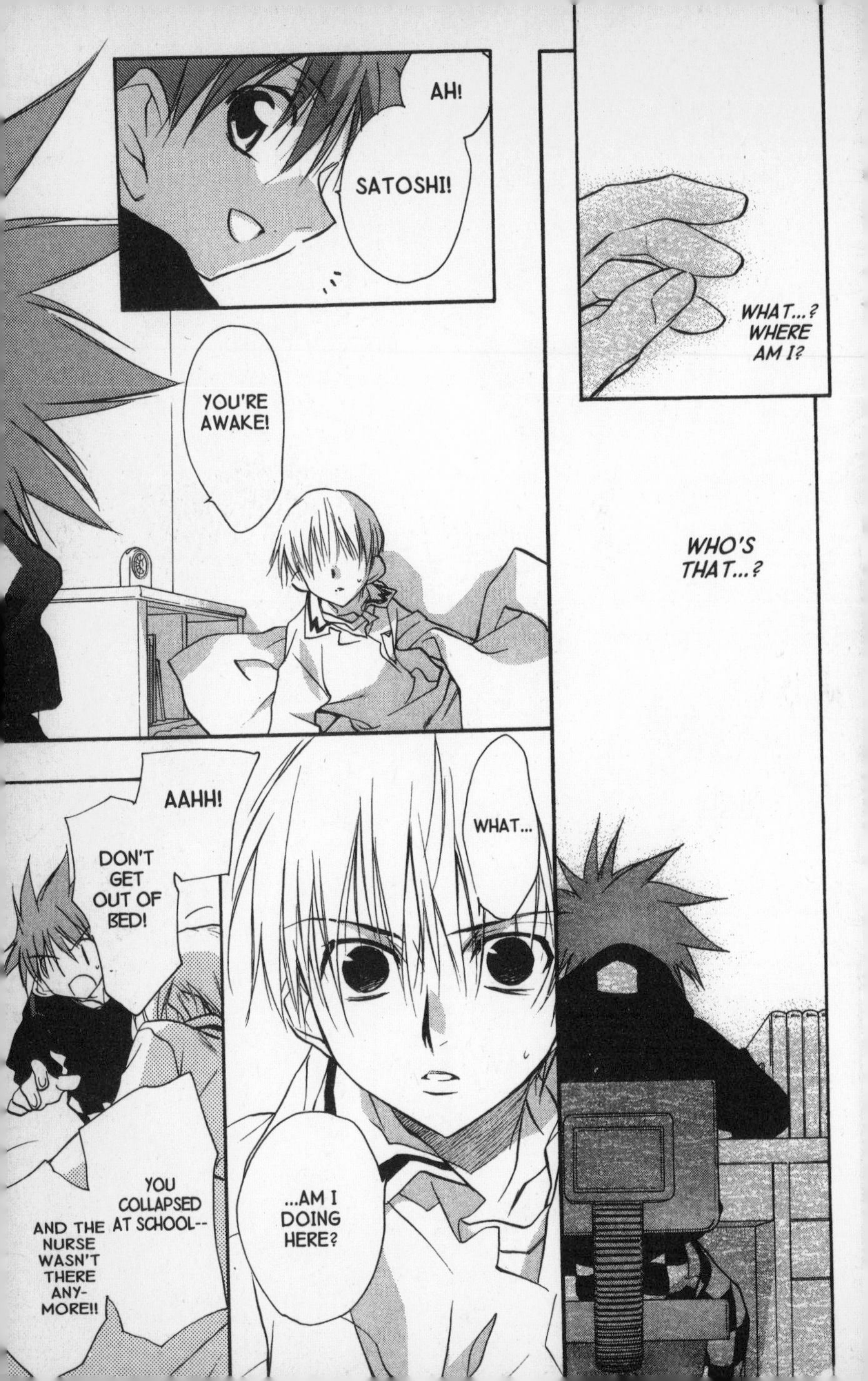
WHAT...? WHERE AM I?
AH!
SATOSHI!
YOU'RE AWAKE!
WHO'S THAT...?
WHAT...
...AM I DOING HERE?
AAHH!
DON'T GET OUT OF BED!
YOU COLLAPSED AT SCHOOL--
AND THE NURSE WASN'T THERE ANY-MORE!!

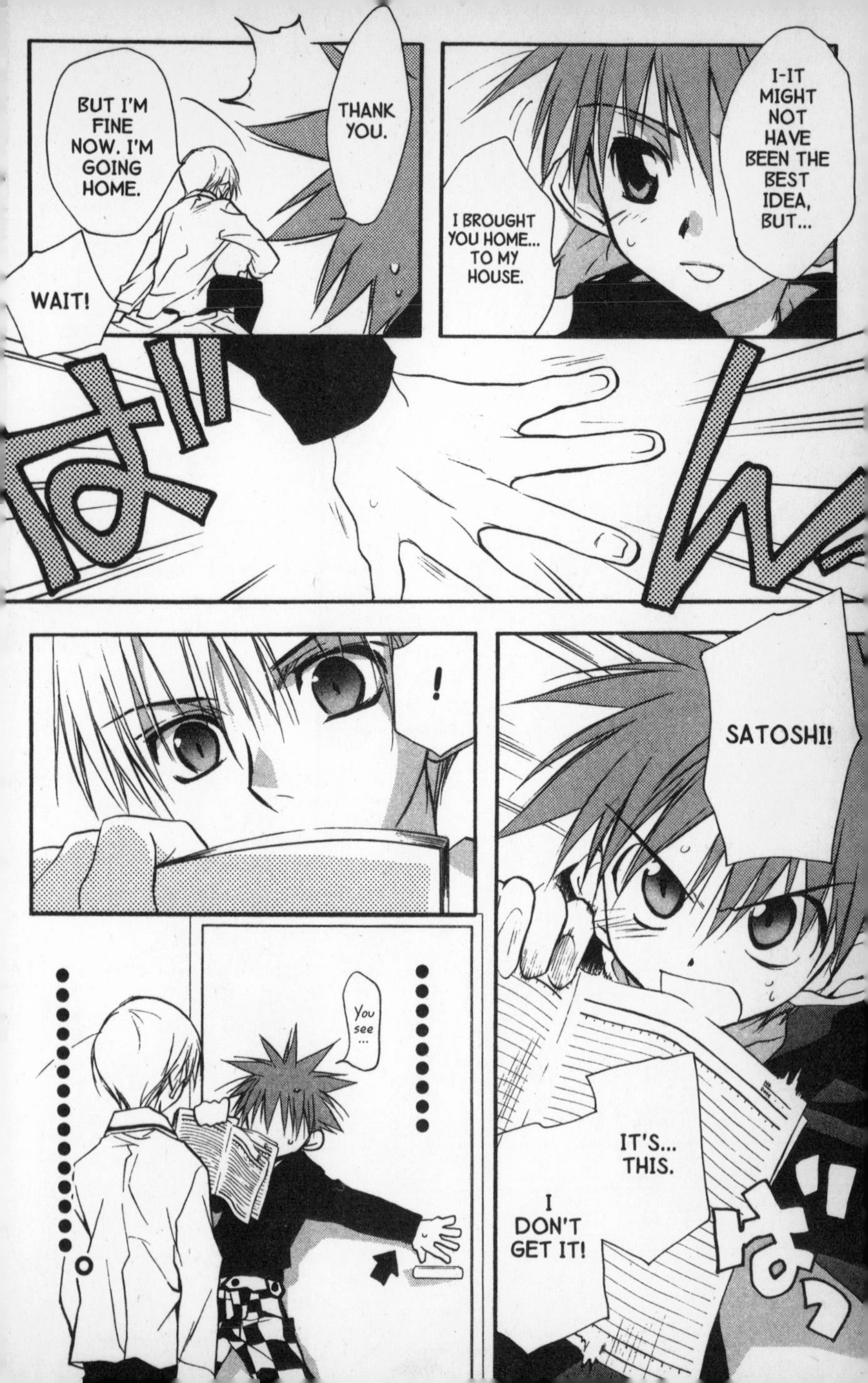

I-IT MIGHT NOT HAVE BEEN THE BEST IDEA, BUT...
I BROUGHT YOU HOME... TO MY HOUSE.
THANK YOU.
BUT I'M FINE NOW. I'M GOING HOME.
WAIT!
ばん
SATOSHI!
!
IT'S... THIS.
I DON'T GET IT!
ばっ
......
You see...
......。

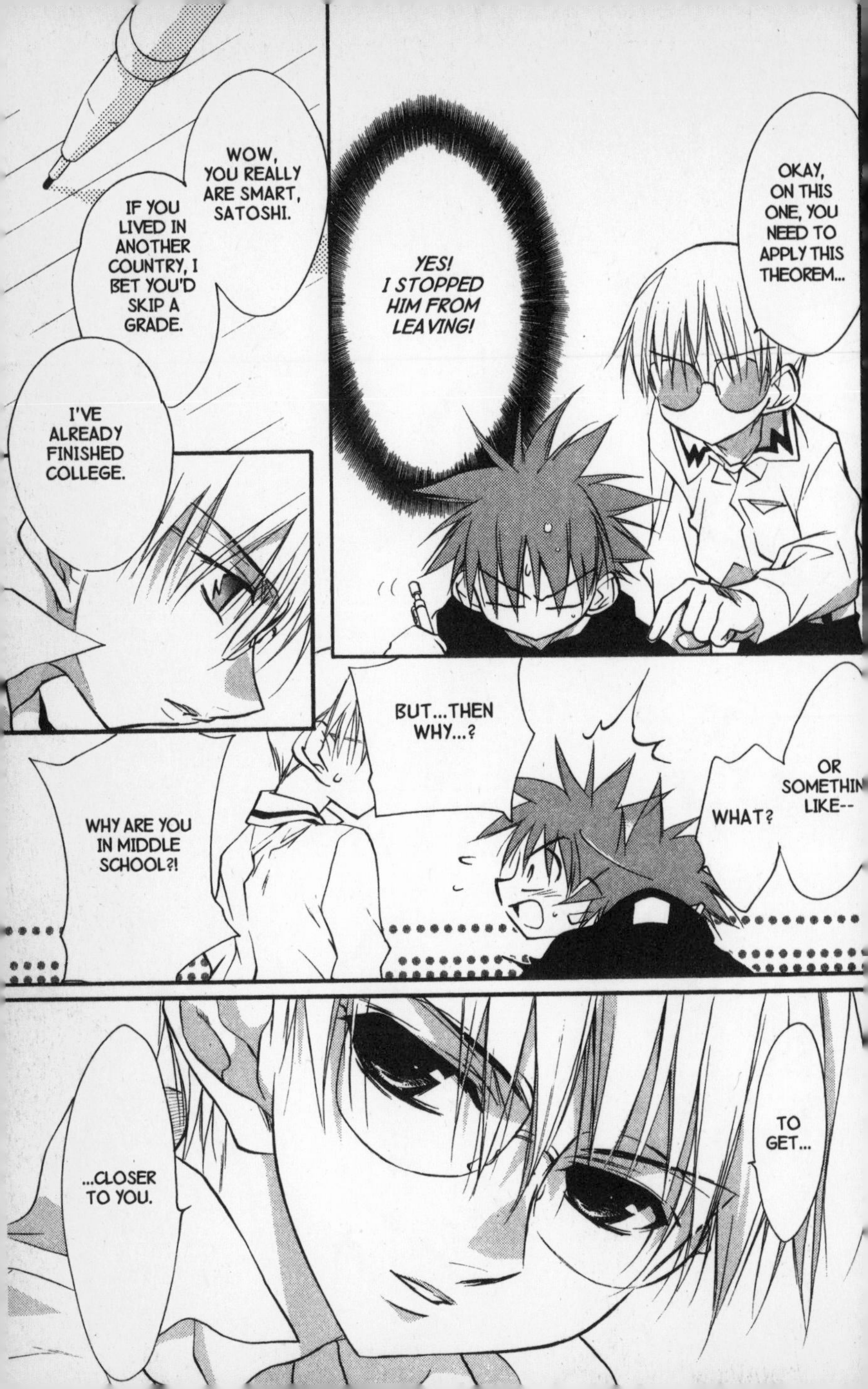
OKAY, ON THIS ONE, YOU NEED TO APPLY THIS THEOREM...
YES! I STOPPED HIM FROM LEAVING!
WOW, YOU REALLY ARE SMART, SATOSHI.
IF YOU LIVED IN ANOTHER COUNTRY, I BET YOU'D SKIP A GRADE.
OR SOMETHIN LIKE--
I'VE ALREADY FINISHED COLLEGE.
WHAT?
BUT...THEN WHY...?
WHY ARE YOU IN MIDDLE SCHOOL?!
TO GET...
...CLOSER TO YOU.

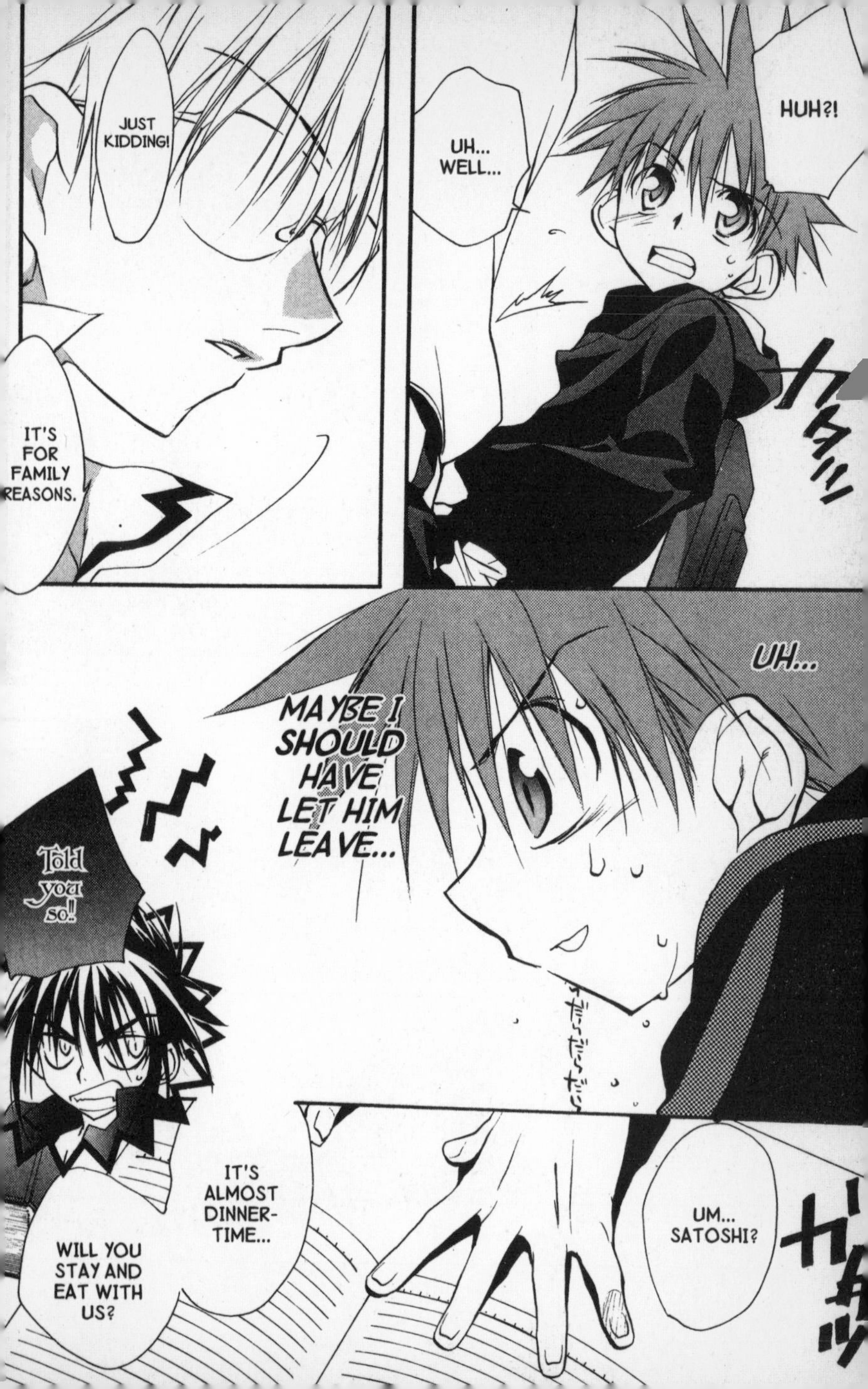
HUH?!
UH... WELL...
JUST KIDDING!
IT'S FOR FAMILY REASONS.
UH...
MAYBE I SHOULD HAVE LET HIM LEAVE...
Told you so!!
UM... SATOSHI?
IT'S ALMOST DINNER-TIME...
WILL YOU STAY AND EAT WITH US?

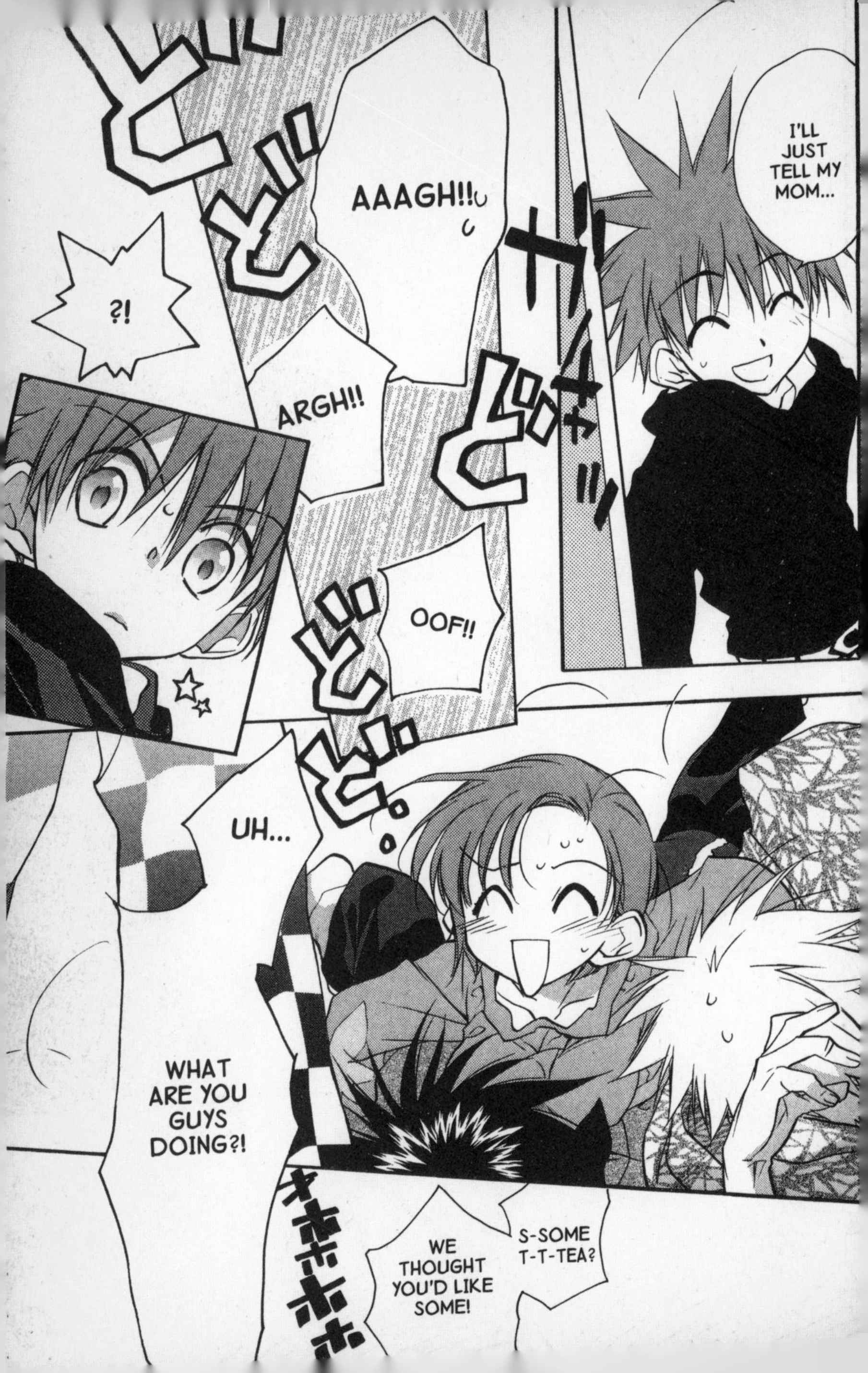
I'LL JUST TELL MY MOM...
AAAGH!!
ARGH!!
OOF!!
?!
UH...
WHAT ARE YOU GUYS DOING?!
S-SOME T-T-TEA?
WE THOUGHT YOU'D LIKE SOME!

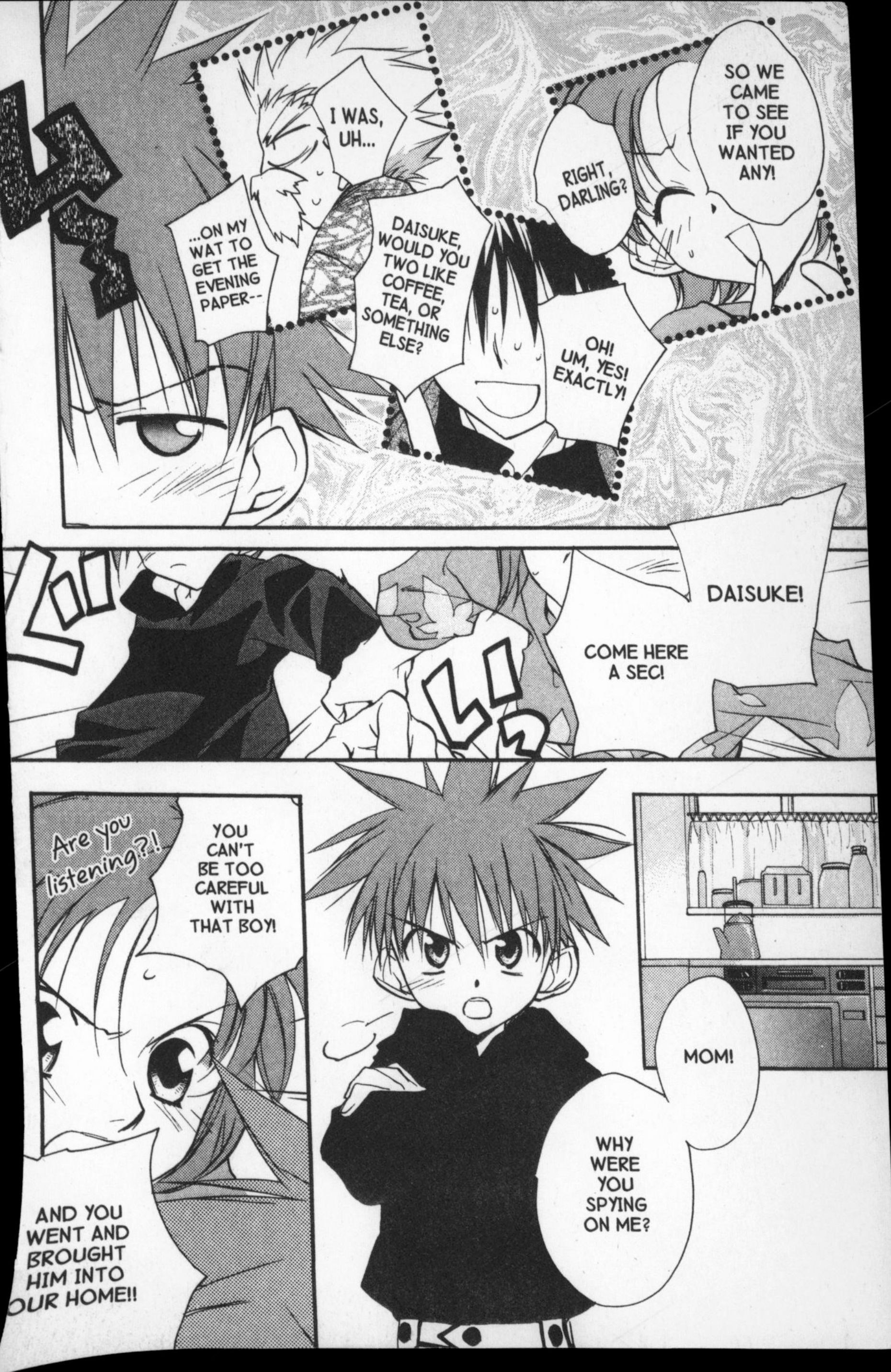
SO WE CAME TO SEE IF YOU WANTED ANY!
RIGHT, DARLING?
I WAS, UH...
...ON MY WAT TO GET THE EVENING PAPER--
DAISUKE, WOULD YOU TWO LIKE COFFEE, TEA, OR SOMETHING ELSE?
OH! UM, YES! EXACTLY!
DAISUKE!
COME HERE A SEC!
MOM!
WHY WERE YOU SPYING ON ME?
YOU CAN'T BE TOO CAREFUL WITH THAT BOY!
Are you listening?!
AND YOU WENT AND BROUGHT HIM INTO OUR HOME!!

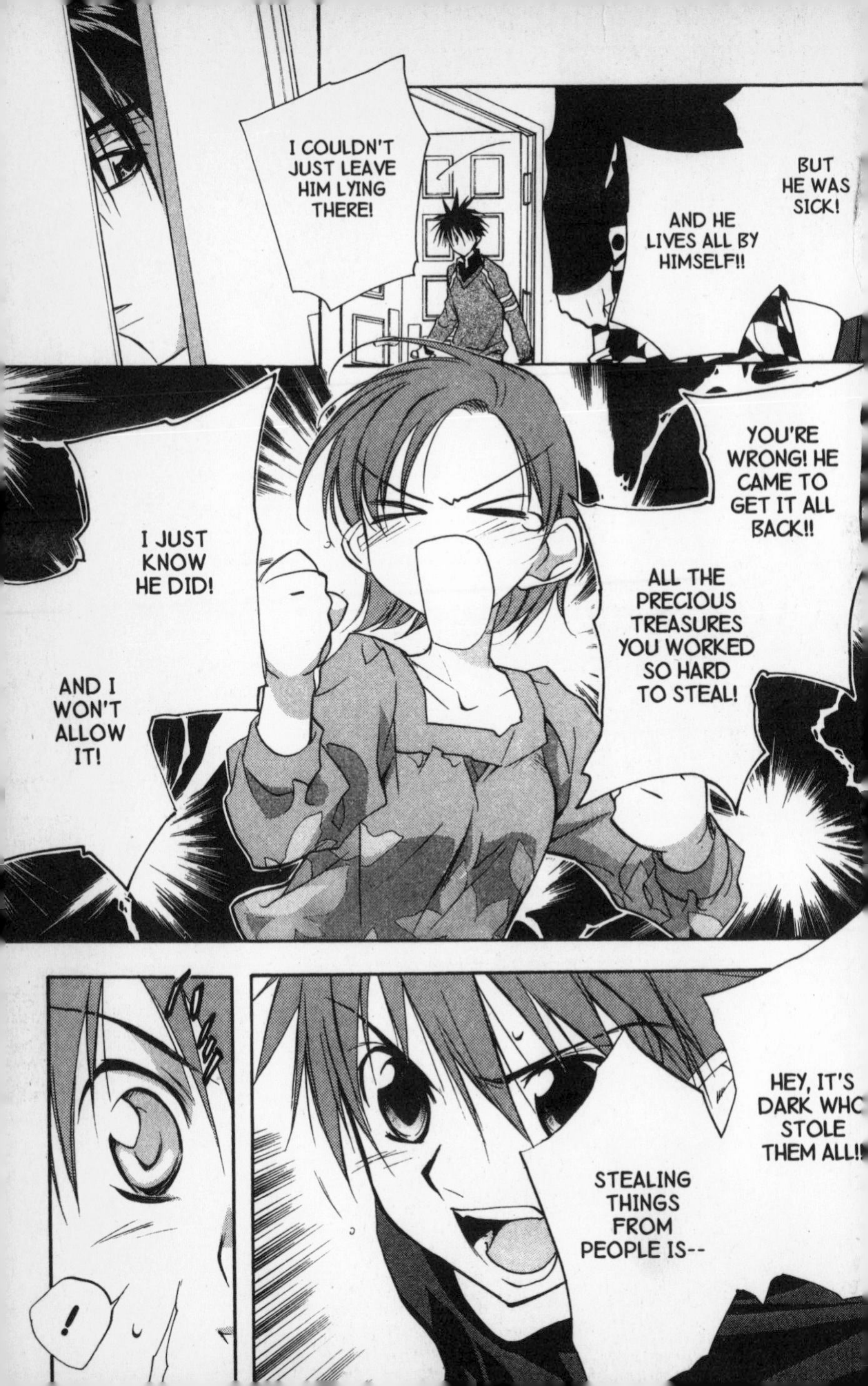
BUT HE WAS SICK!
AND HE LIVES ALL BY HIMSELF!!
I COULDN'T JUST LEAVE HIM LYING THERE!
YOU'RE WRONG! HE CAME TO GET IT ALL BACK!!
ALL THE PRECIOUS TREASURES YOU WORKED SO HARD TO STEAL!
I JUST KNOW HE DID!
AND I WON'T ALLOW IT!
HEY, IT'S DARK WHO STOLE THEM ALL!!
STEALING THINGS FROM PEOPLE IS--
!

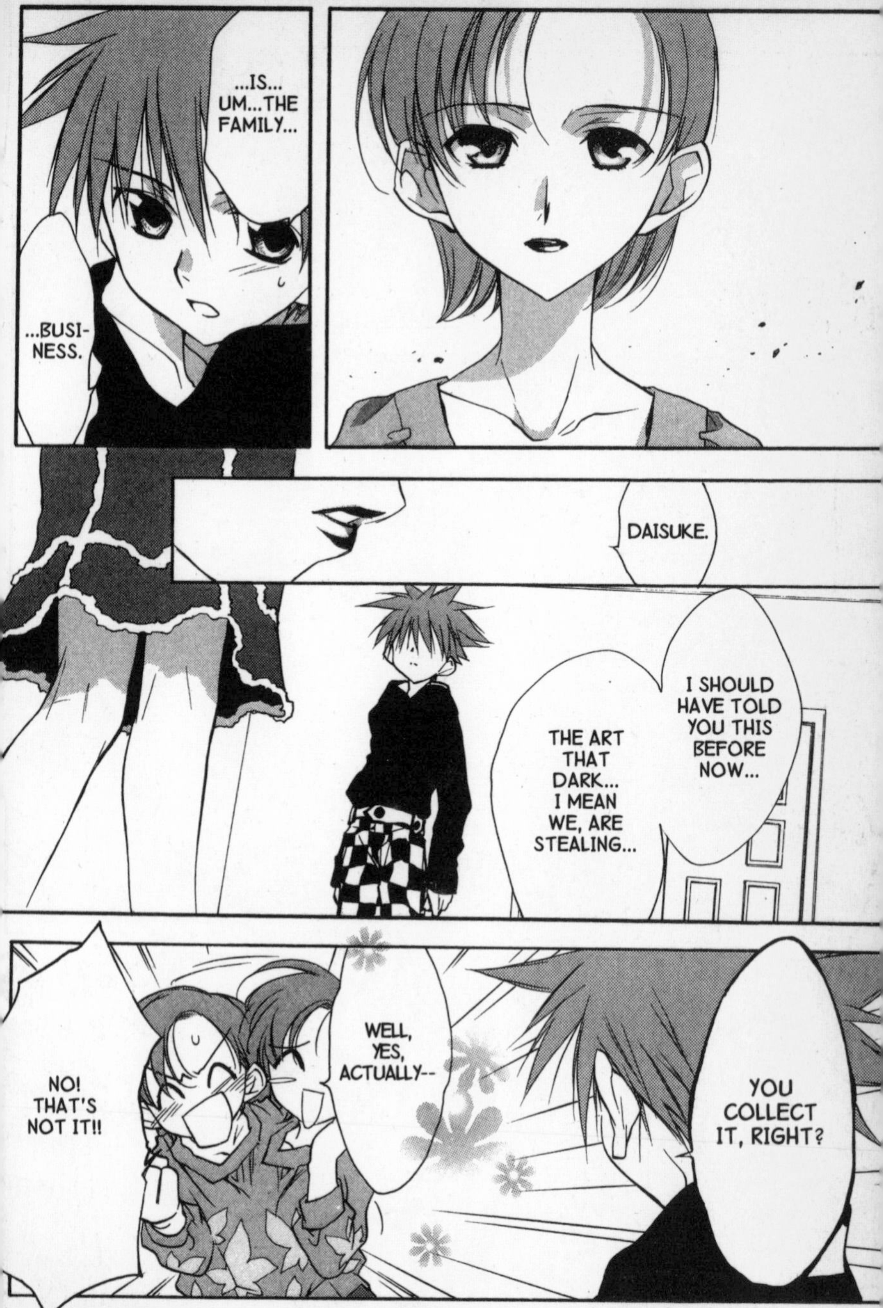
...IS... UM...THE FAMILY...
...BUSI-NESS.
DAISUKE.
I SHOULD HAVE TOLD YOU THIS BEFORE NOW...
THE ART THAT DARK... I MEAN WE, ARE STEALING...
YOU COLLECT IT, RIGHT?
WELL, YES, ACTUALLY--
NO! THAT'S NOT IT!!

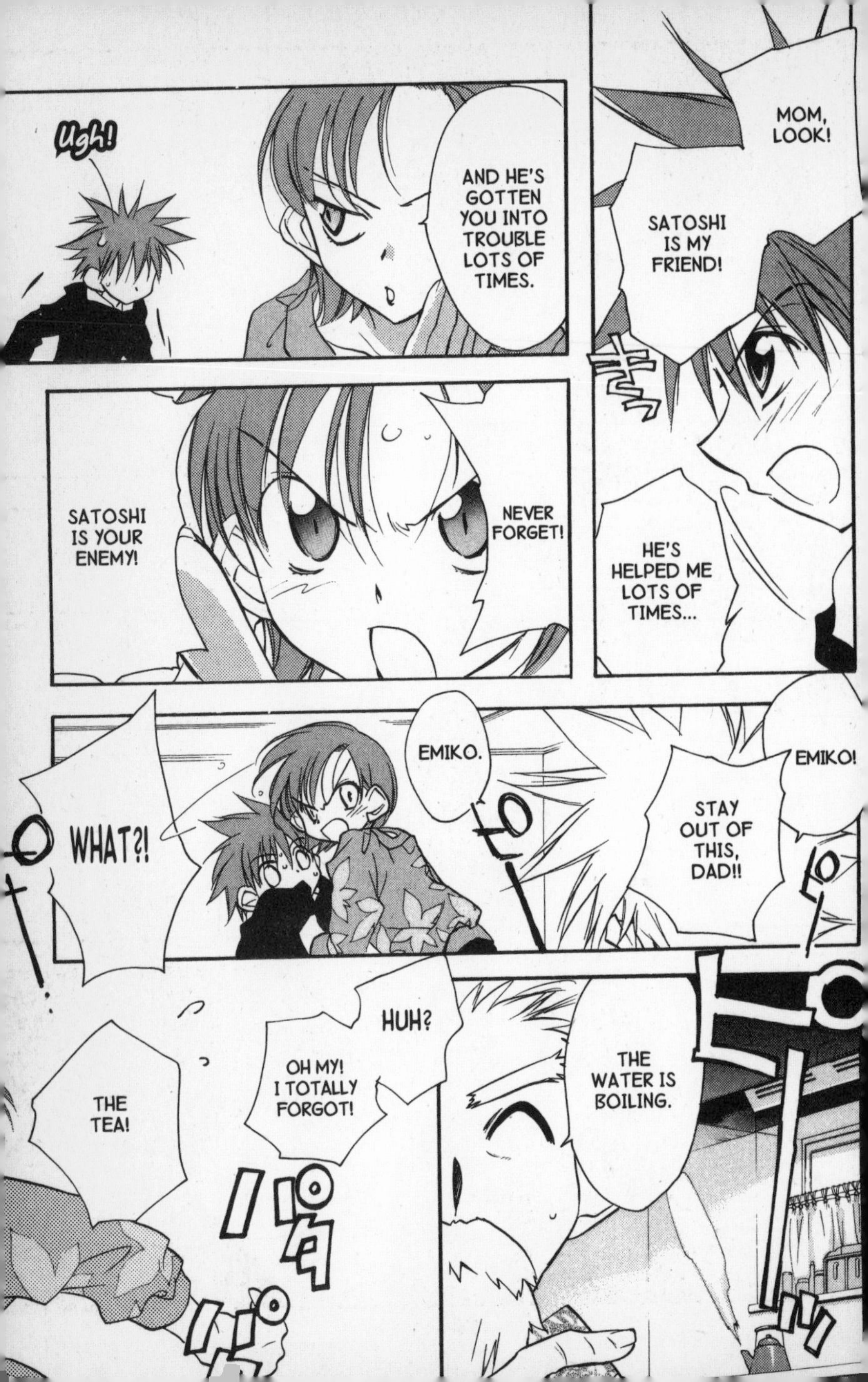
MOM, LOOK!
SATOSHI IS MY FRIEND!
HE'S HELPED ME LOTS OF TIMES...
AND HE'S GOTTEN YOU INTO TROUBLE LOTS OF TIMES.
Ugh!
NEVER FORGET!
SATOSHI IS YOUR ENEMY!
EMIKO!
STAY OUT OF THIS, DAD!!
EMIKO.
WHAT?!
THE WATER IS BOILING.
HUH?
OH MY! I TOTALLY FORGOT!
THE TEA!

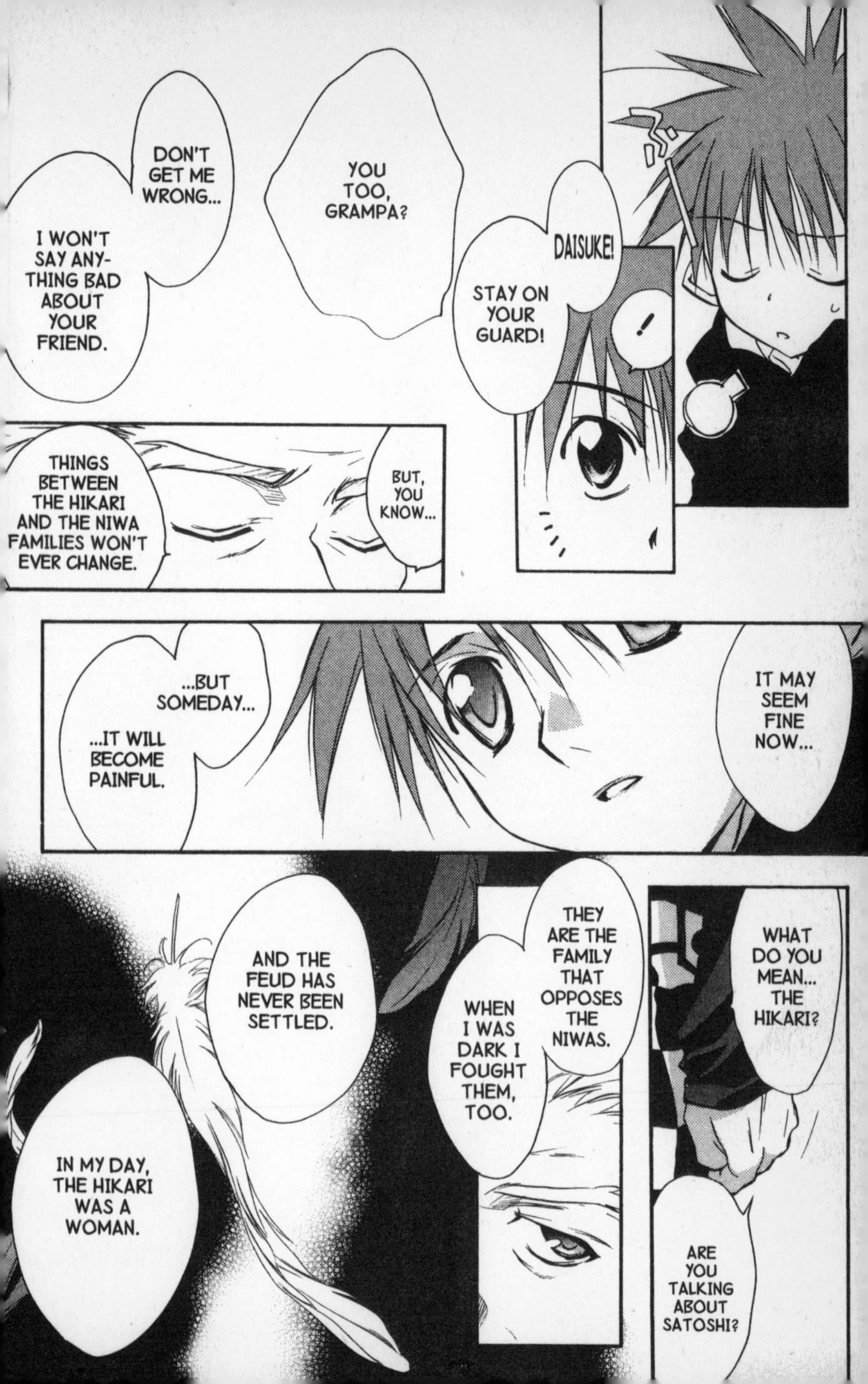
DAISUKE!
STAY ON YOUR GUARD!
!
YOU TOO, GRAMPA?
DON'T GET ME WRONG...
I WON'T SAY ANY-THING BAD ABOUT YOUR FRIEND.
BUT, YOU KNOW...
THINGS BETWEEN THE HIKARI AND THE NIWA FAMILIES WON'T EVER CHANGE.
IT MAY SEEM FINE NOW...
...BUT SOMEDAY...
...IT WILL BECOME PAINFUL.
WHAT DO YOU MEAN... THE HIKARI?
ARE YOU TALKING ABOUT SATOSHI?
THEY ARE THE FAMILY THAT OPPOSES THE NIWAS.
WHEN I WAS DARK I FOUGHT THEM, TOO.
AND THE FEUD HAS NEVER BEEN SETTLED.
IN MY DAY, THE HIKARI WAS A WOMAN.

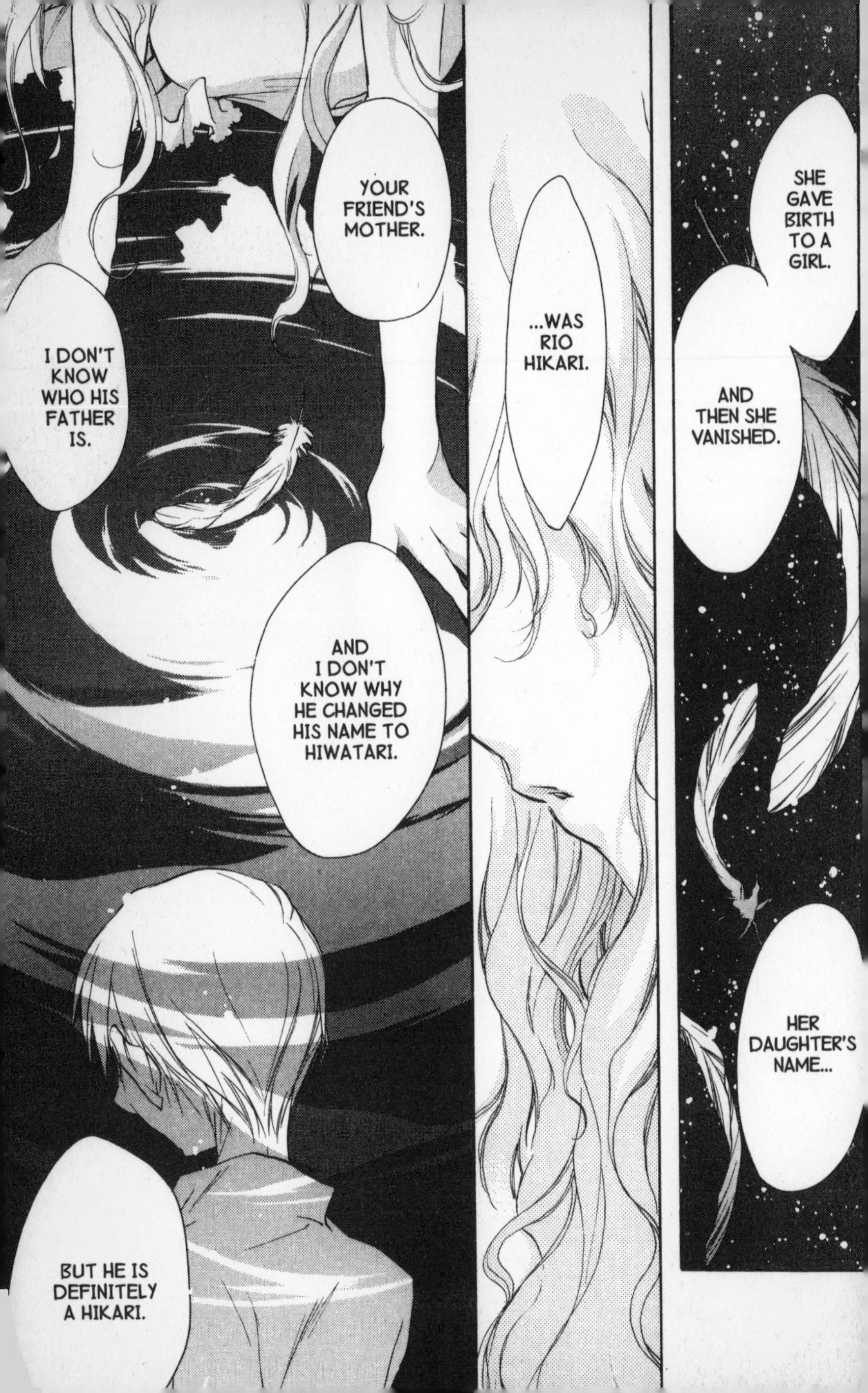
SHE GAVE BIRTH TO A GIRL.
AND THEN SHE VANISHED.
HER DAUGHTER'S NAME...
...WAS RIO HIKARI.
YOUR FRIEND'S MOTHER.
I DON'T KNOW WHO HIS FATHER IS.
AND I DON'T KNOW WHY HE CHANGED HIS NAME TO HIWATARI.
BUT HE IS DEFINITELY A HIKARI.

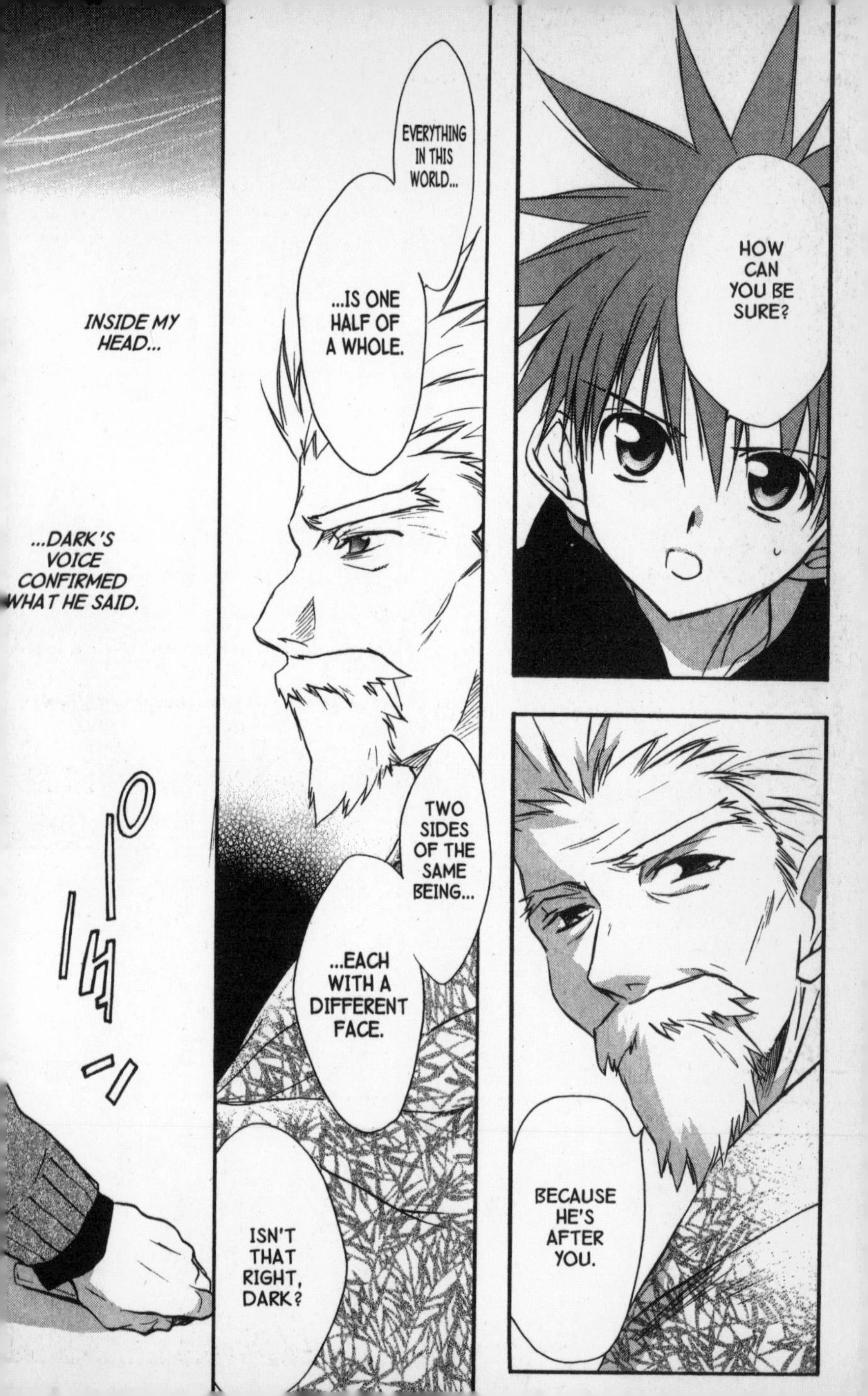

HOW CAN YOU BE SURE?
BECAUSE HE'S AFTER YOU.
EVERYTHING IN THIS WORLD...
...IS ONE HALF OF A WHOLE.
TWO SIDES OF THE SAME BEING...
...EACH WITH A DIFFERENT FACE.
ISN'T THAT RIGHT, DARK?
INSIDE MY HEAD...
...DARK'S VOICE CONFIRMED WHAT HE SAID.

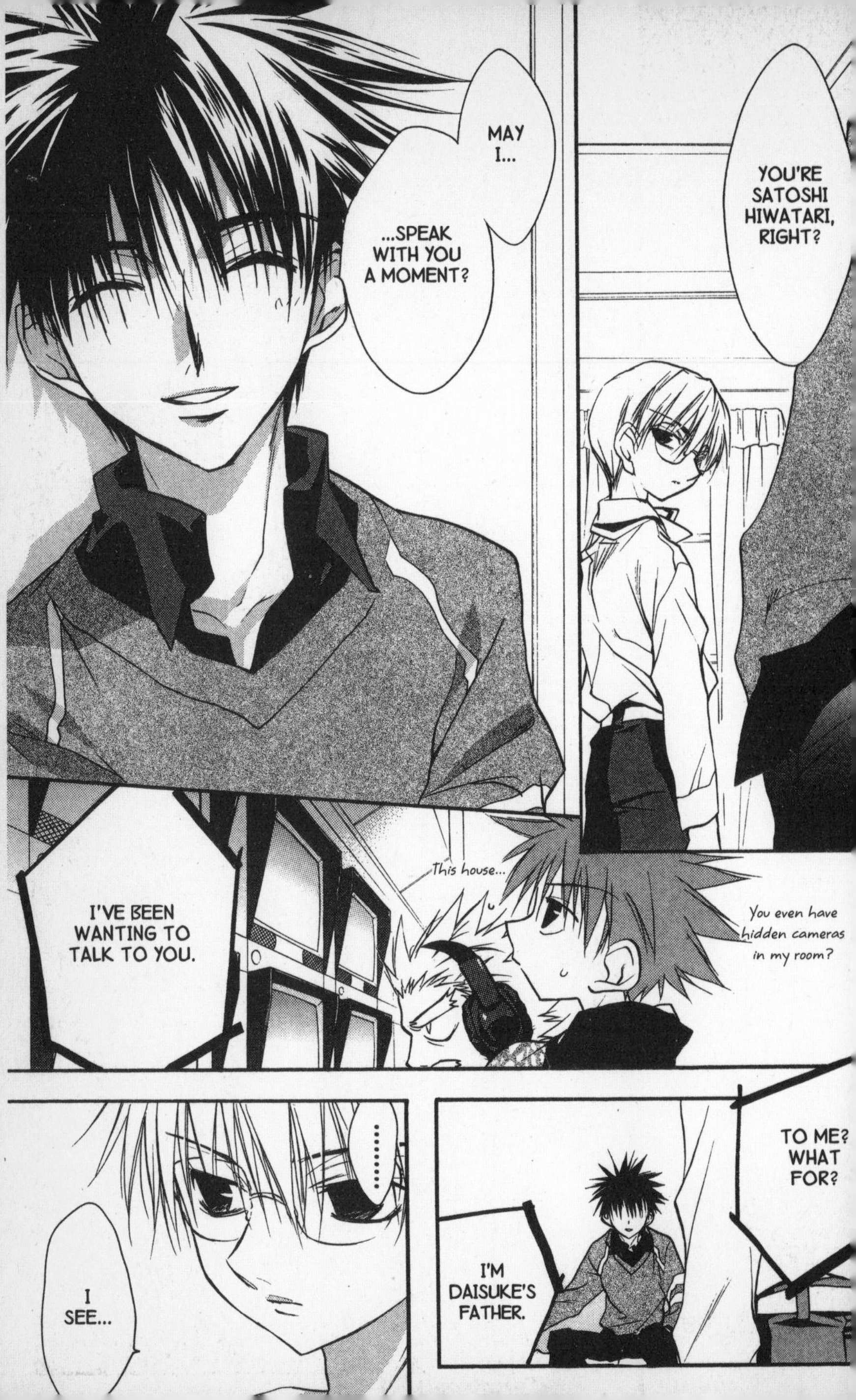
YOU'RE SATOSHI HIWATARI, RIGHT?
MAY I...
...SPEAK WITH YOU A MOMENT?
This house...
You even have hidden cameras in my room?
I'VE BEEN WANTING TO TALK TO YOU.
TO ME? WHAT FOR?
I'M DAISUKE'S FATHER.
....
I SEE...

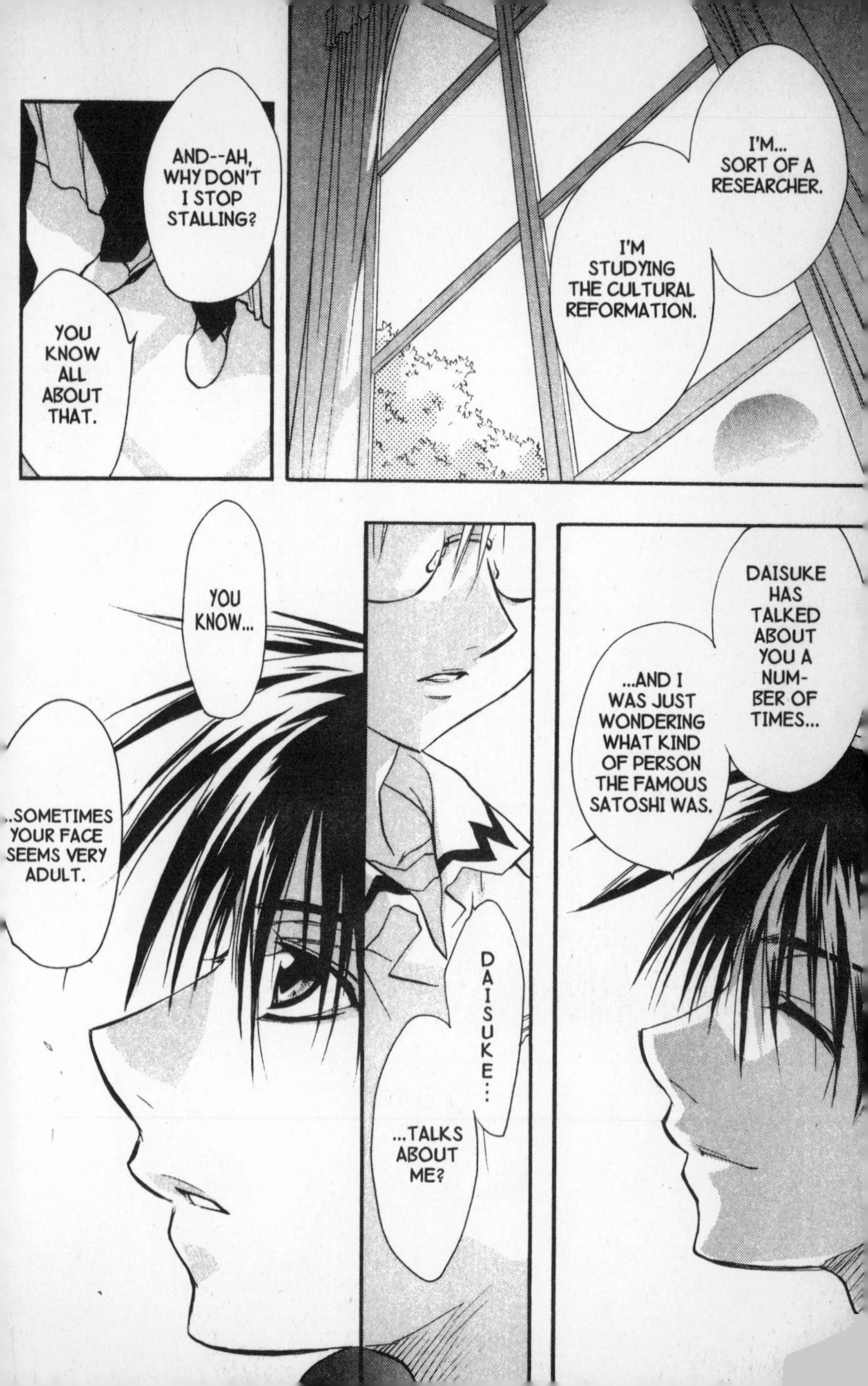
I'M... SORT OF A RESEARCHER.
I'M STUDYING THE CULTURAL REFORMATION.
AND--AH, WHY DON'T I STOP STALLING?
YOU KNOW ALL ABOUT THAT.
DAISUKE HAS TALKED ABOUT YOU A NUM-BER OF TIMES...
...AND I WAS JUST WONDERING WHAT KIND OF PERSON THE FAMOUS SATOSHI WAS.
DAISUKE...
...TALKS ABOUT ME?
YOU KNOW...
..SOMETIMES YOUR FACE SEEMS VERY ADULT.

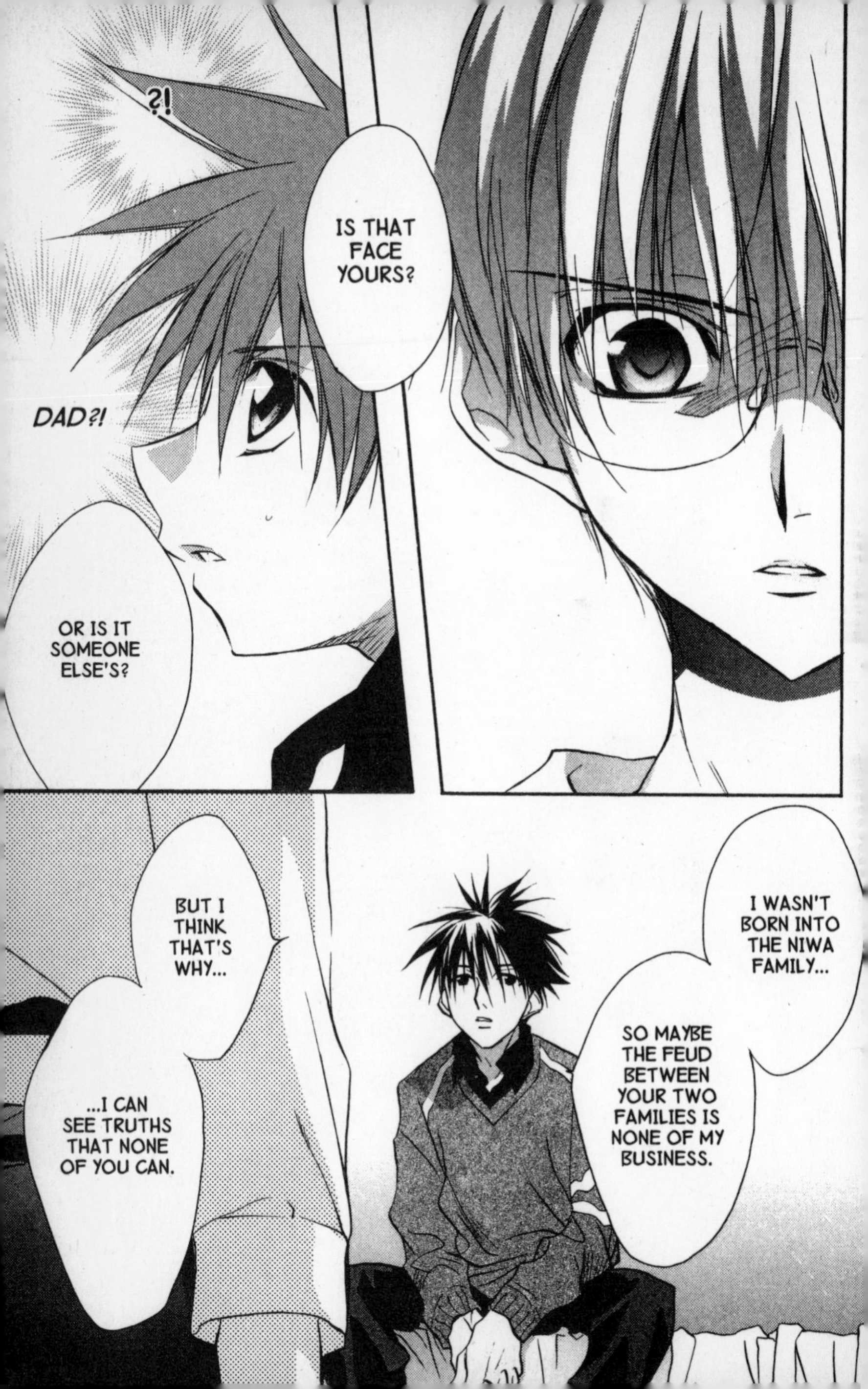
IS THAT FACE YOURS?
?!
DAD?!
OR IS IT SOMEONE ELSE'S?
I WASN'T BORN INTO THE NIWA FAMILY...
SO MAYBE THE FEUD BETWEEN YOUR TWO FAMILIES IS NONE OF MY BUSINESS.
BUT I THINK THAT'S WHY...
...I CAN SEE TRUTHS THAT NONE OF YOU CAN.

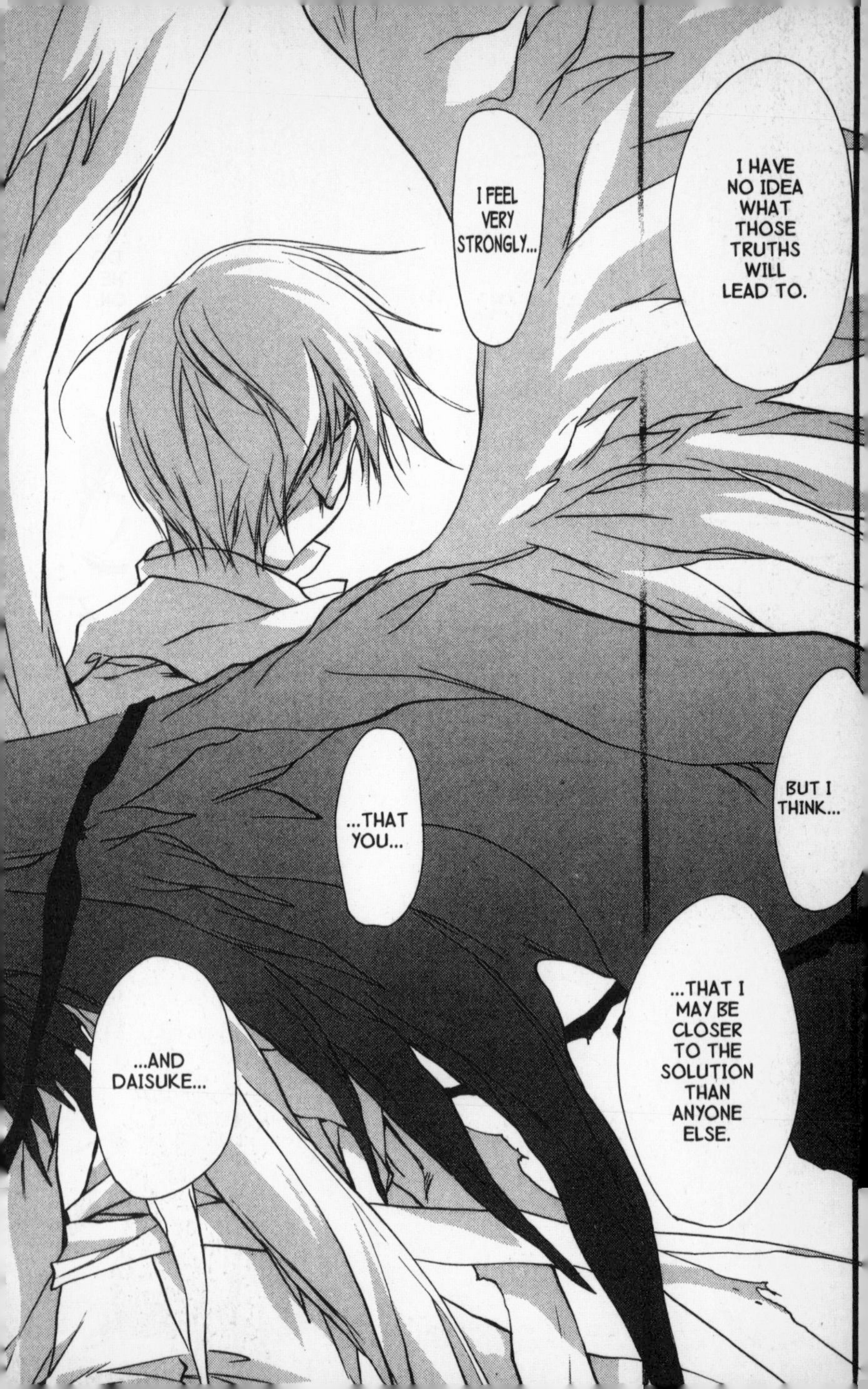
I HAVE NO IDEA WHAT THOSE TRUTHS WILL LEAD TO.
I FEEL VERY STRONGLY...
BUT I THINK...
...THAT YOU...
...THAT I MAY BE CLOSER TO THE SOLUTION THAN ANYONE ELSE.
...AND DAISUKE...

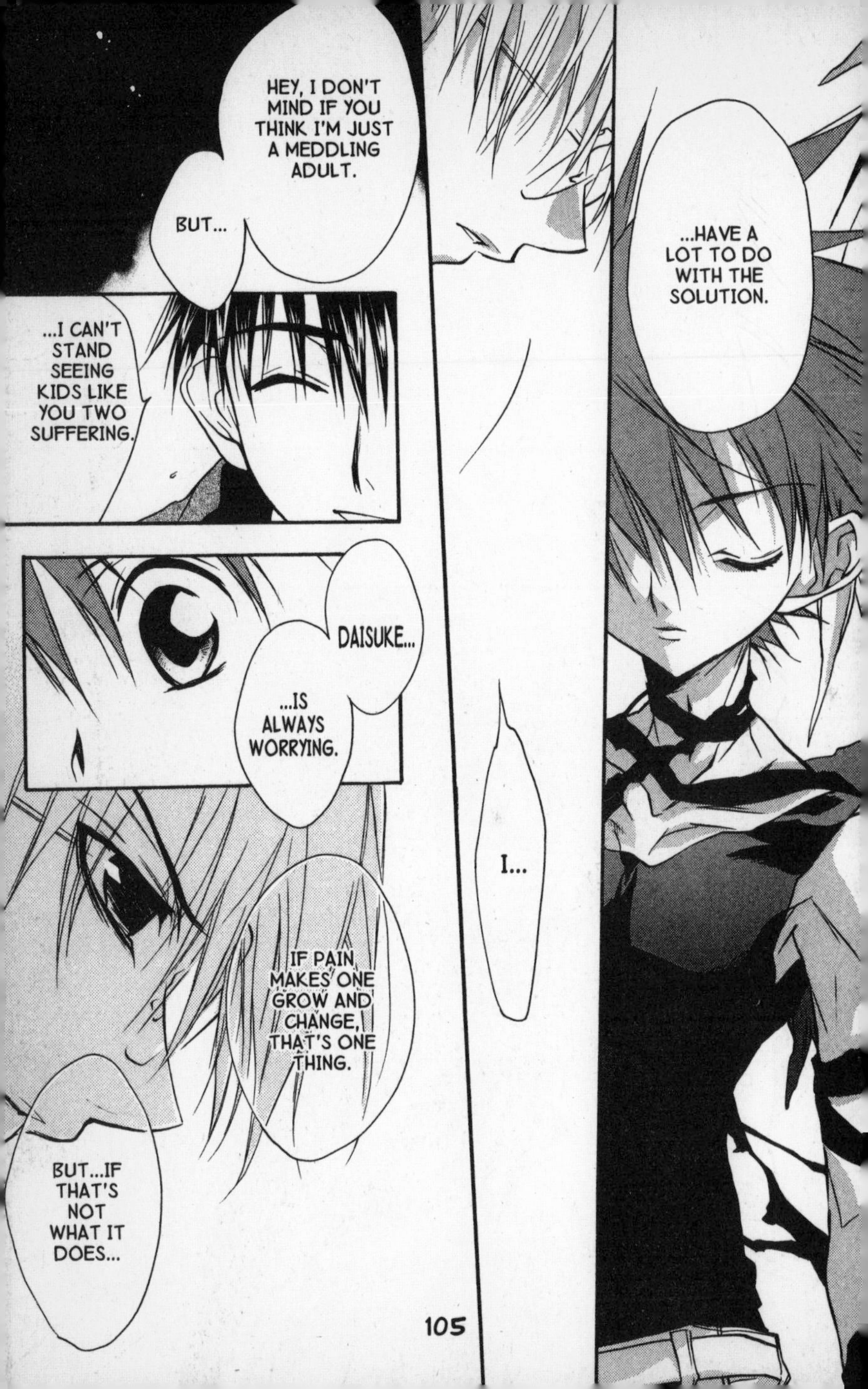
...HAVE A LOT TO DO WITH THE SOLUTION.
I...
HEY, I DON'T MIND IF YOU THINK I'M JUST A MEDDLING ADULT.
BUT...
...I CAN'T STAND SEEING KIDS LIKE YOU TWO SUFFERING.
DAISUKE...
...IS ALWAYS WORRYING.
IF PAIN MAKES ONE GROW AND CHANGE, THAT'S ONE THING.
BUT...IF THAT'S NOT WHAT IT DOES...

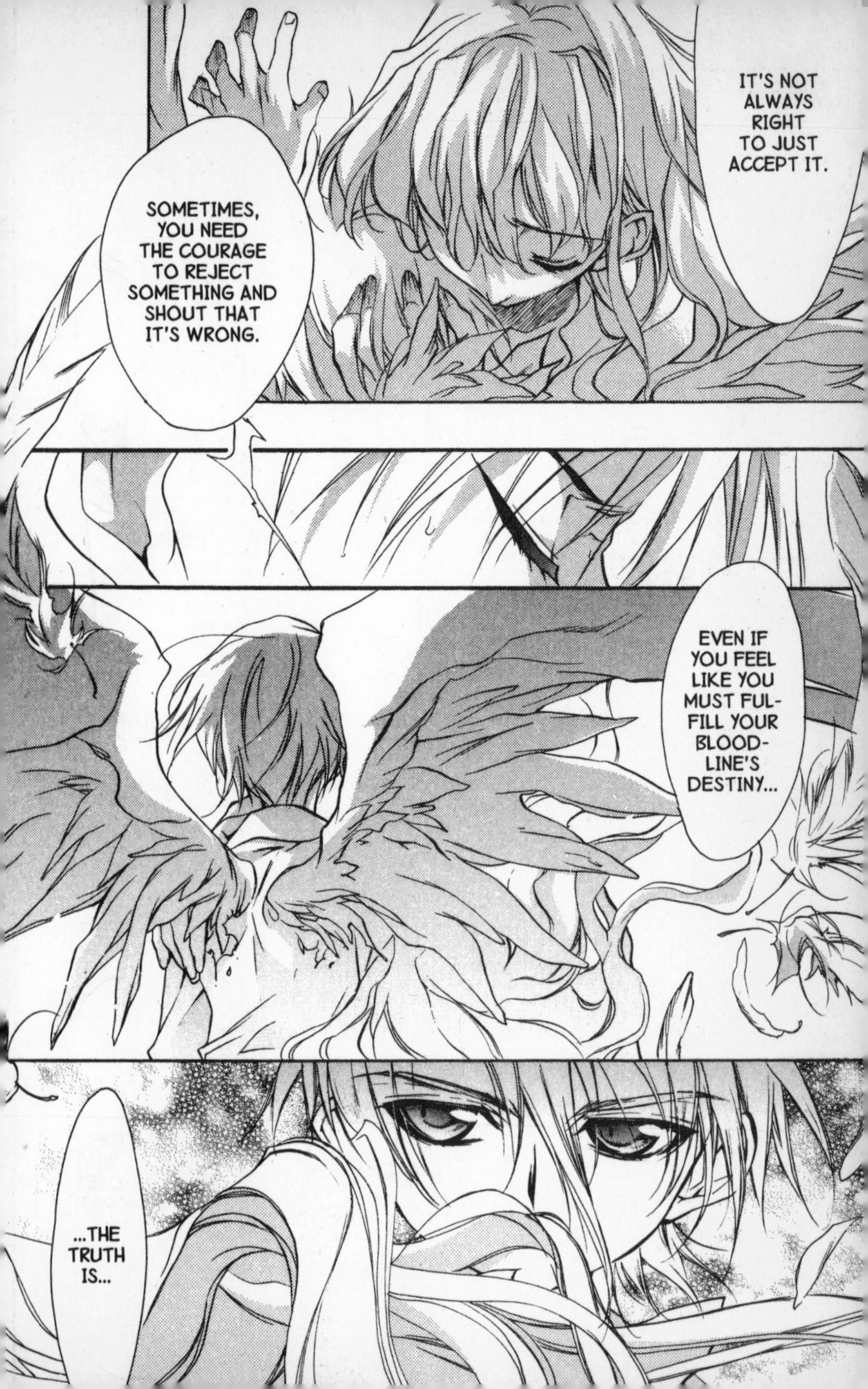
IT'S NOT ALWAYS RIGHT TO JUST ACCEPT IT.
SOMETIMES, YOU NEED THE COURAGE TO REJECT SOMETHING AND SHOUT THAT IT'S WRONG.
EVEN IF YOU FEEL LIKE YOU MUST FUL-FILL YOUR BLOOD-LINE'S DESTINY...
...THE TRUTH IS...

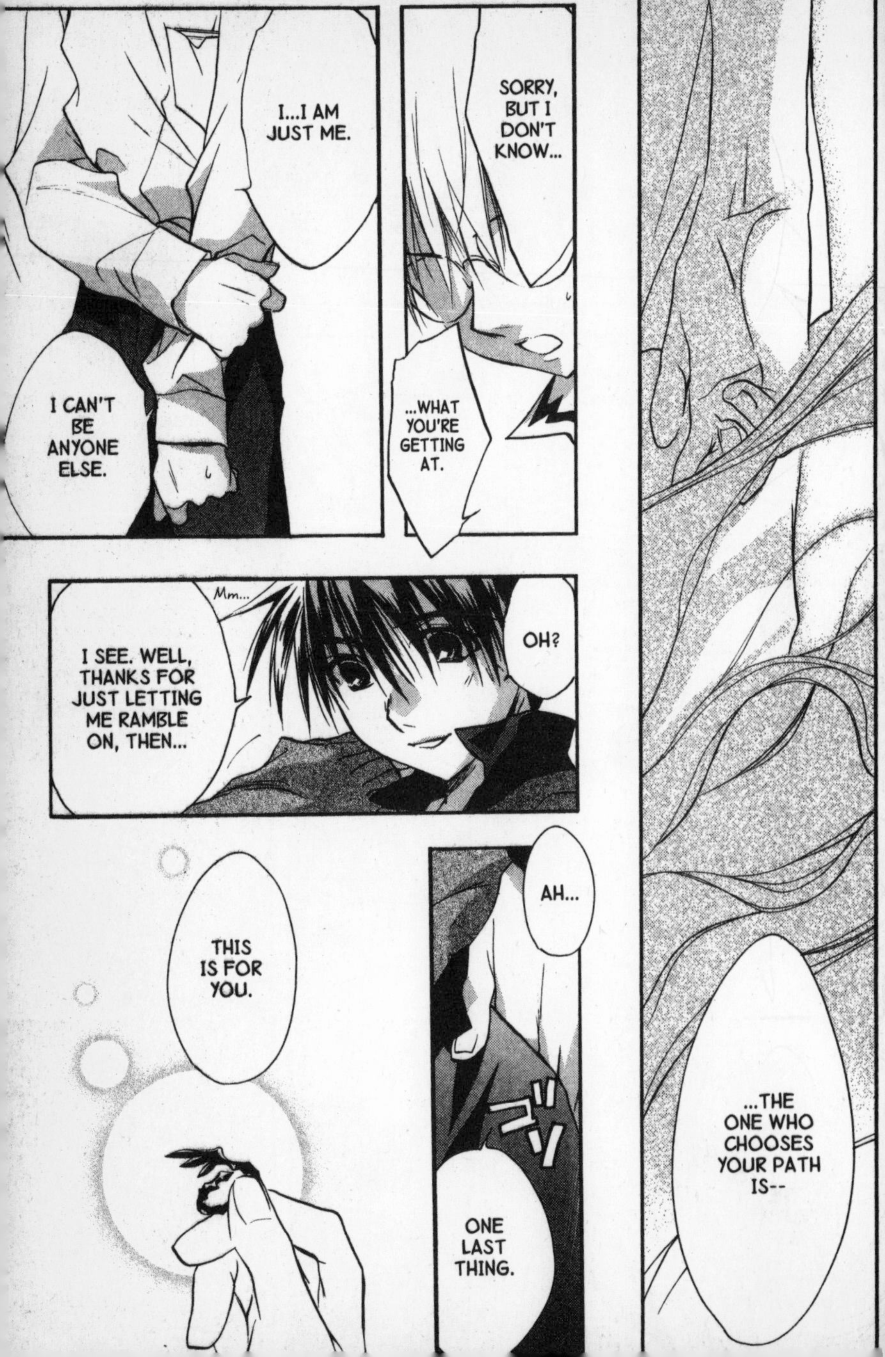
SORRY, BUT I DON'T KNOW...
...WHAT YOU'RE GETTING AT.
I...I AM JUST ME.
I CAN'T BE ANYONE ELSE.
OH?
Mm...
I SEE. WELL, THANKS FOR JUST LETTING ME RAMBLE ON, THEN...
AH...
ゴソ
ONE LAST THING.
THIS IS FOR YOU.
...THE ONE WHO CHOOSES YOUR PATH IS--

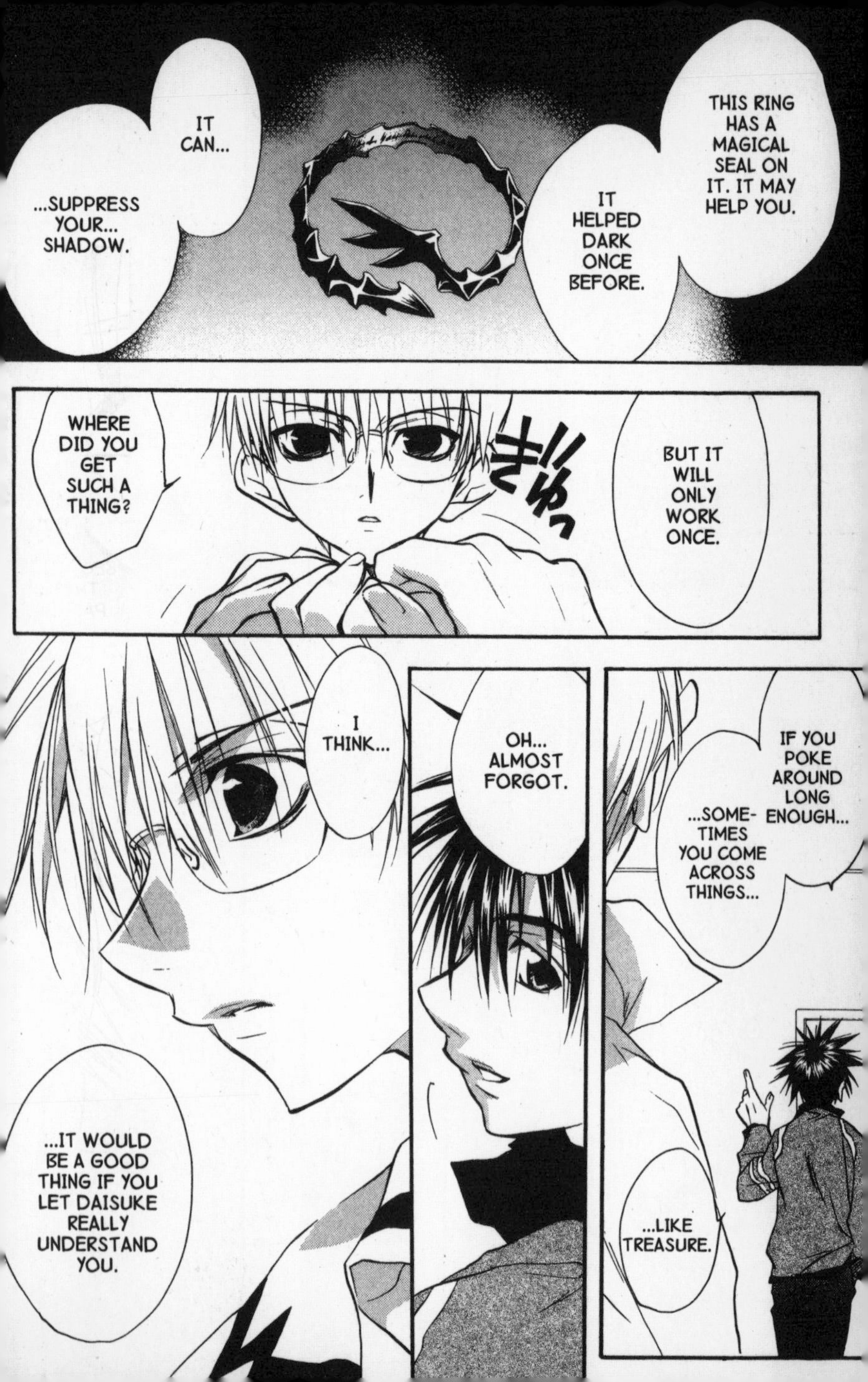
THIS RING HAS A MAGICAL SEAL ON IT. IT MAY HELP YOU.
IT HELPED DARK ONCE BEFORE.
IT CAN...
...SUPPRESS YOUR... SHADOW.
BUT IT WILL ONLY WORK ONCE.
WHERE DID YOU GET SUCH A THING?
IF YOU POKE AROUND LONG ENOUGH...
...SOME-TIMES YOU COME ACROSS THINGS...
...LIKE TREASURE.
OH... ALMOST FORGOT.
I THINK...
...IT WOULD BE A GOOD THING IF YOU LET DAISUKE REALLY UNDERSTAND YOU.

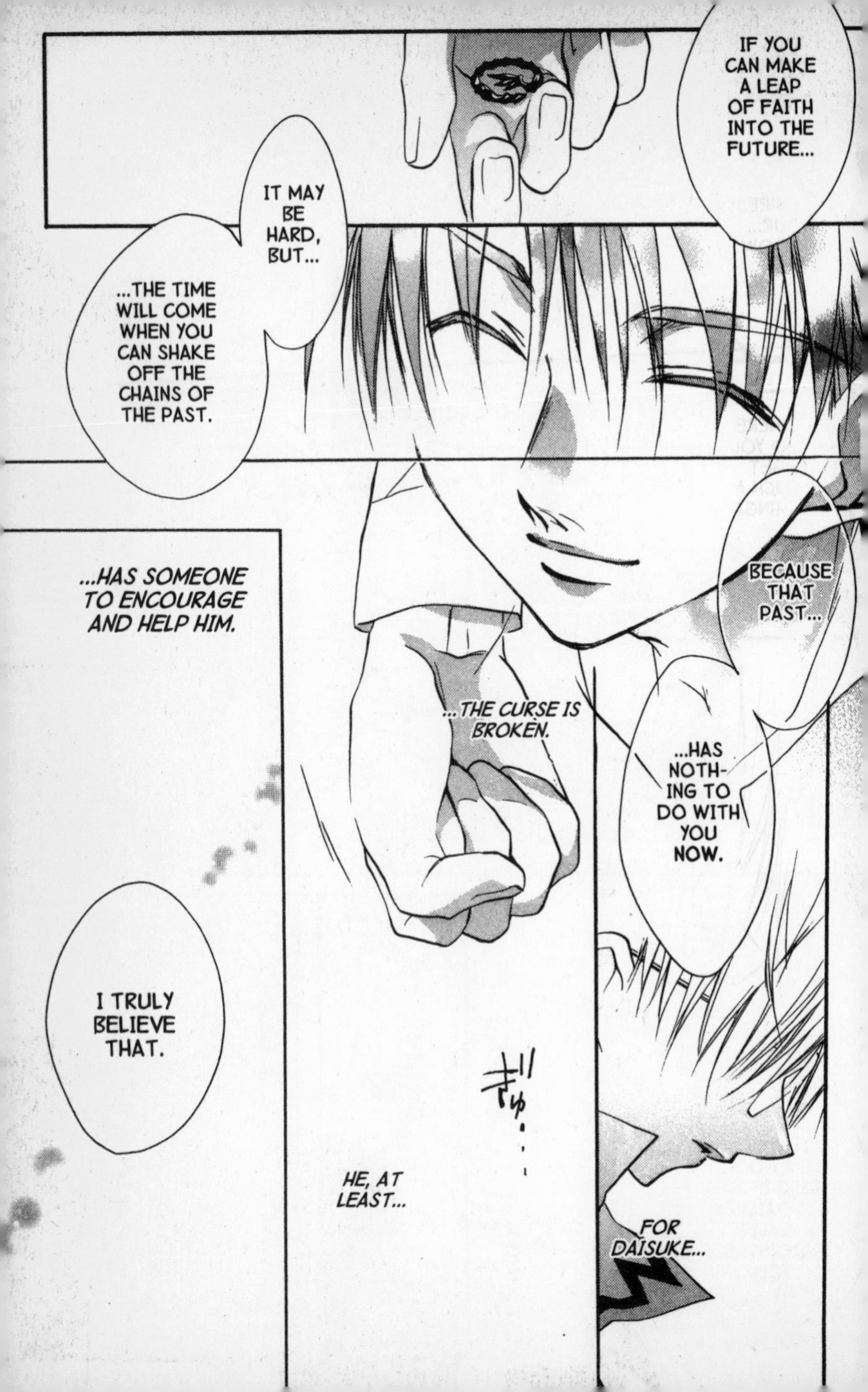
IF YOU CAN MAKE A LEAP OF FAITH INTO THE FUTURE...
IT MAY BE HARD, BUT...
...THE TIME WILL COME WHEN YOU CAN SHAKE OFF THE CHAINS OF THE PAST.
BECAUSE THAT PAST...
...HAS NOTH-ING TO DO WITH YOU NOW.
...THE CURSE IS BROKEN.
FOR DAISUKE...
HE, AT LEAST...
...HAS SOMEONE TO ENCOURAGE AND HELP HIM.
I TRULY BELIEVE THAT.

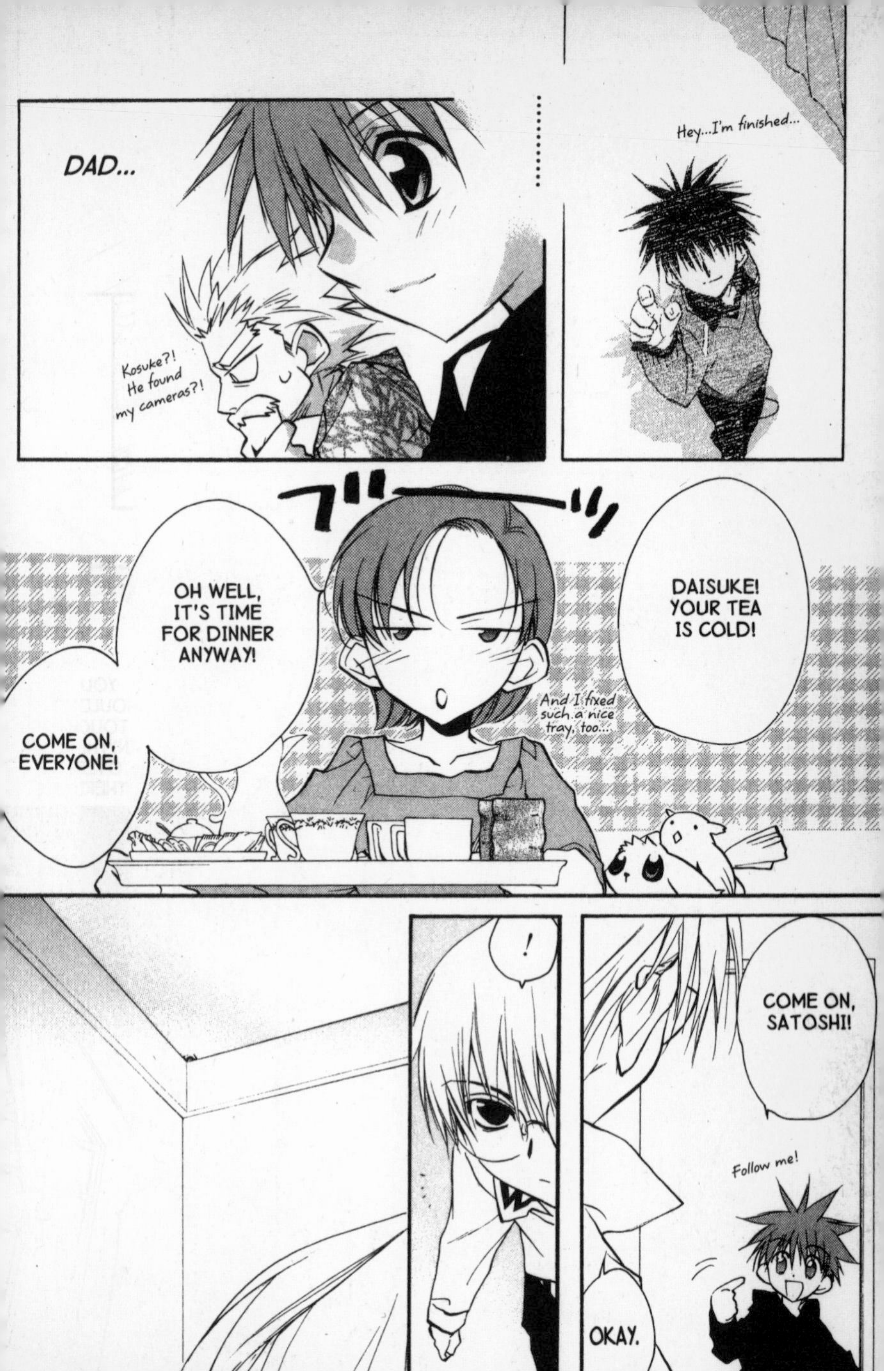
Hey...I'm finished...
DAD...
Kosuke?! He found my cameras?!
DAISUKE! YOUR TEA IS COLD!
And I fixed such a nice tray, too...
OH WELL, IT'S TIME FOR DINNER ANYWAY!
COME ON, EVERYONE!
COME ON, SATOSHI!
Follow me!
OKAY.
!

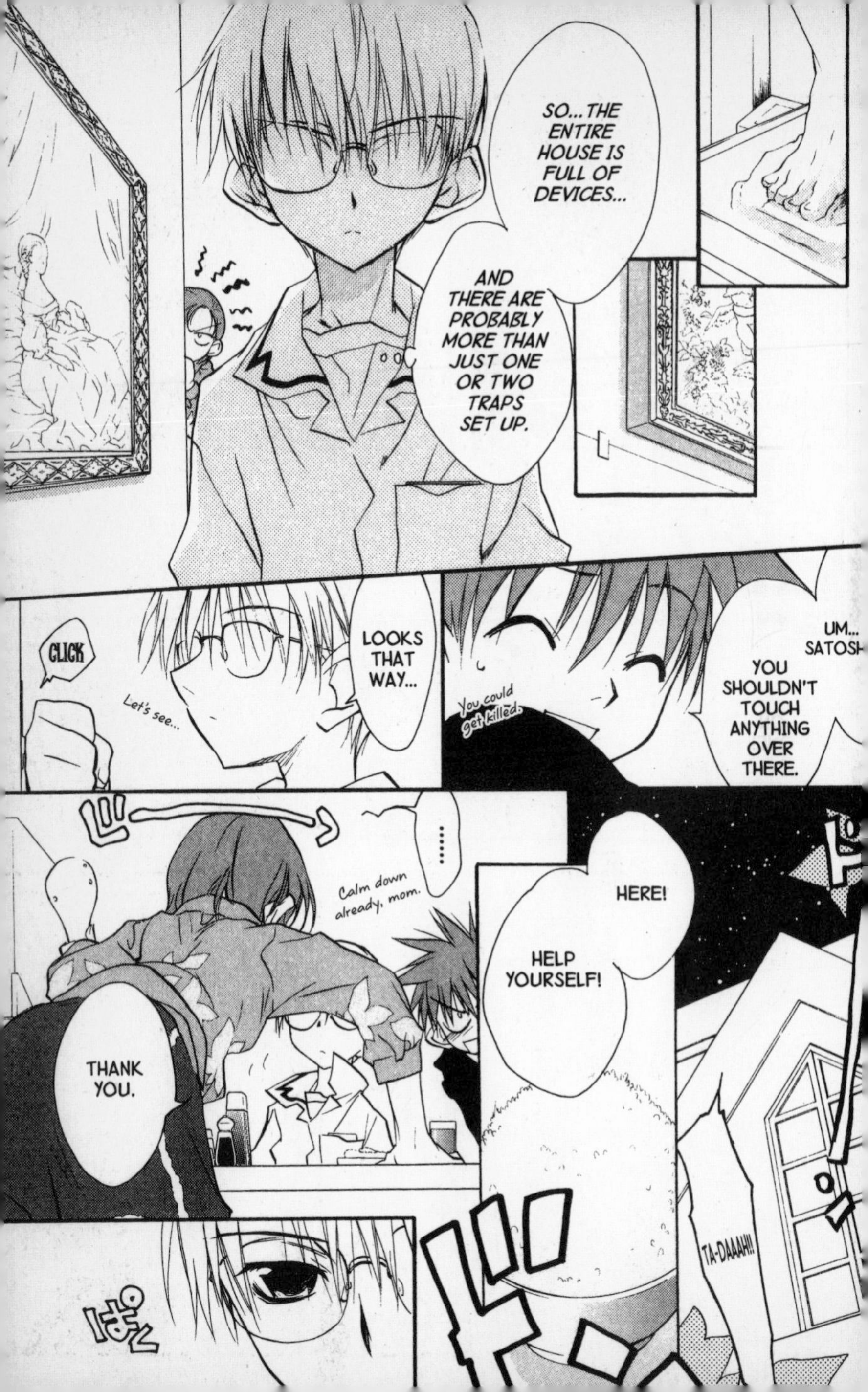
SO...THE ENTIRE HOUSE IS FULL OF DEVICES...
AND THERE ARE PROBABLY MORE THAN JUST ONE OR TWO TRAPS SET UP.
UM... SATOSH
YOU SHOULDN'T TOUCH ANYTHING OVER THERE.
You could get killed.
LOOKS THAT WAY...
Let's see...
CLICK
HERE!
HELP YOURSELF!
TA-DAAAH!!
......
Calm down already, mom.
THANK YOU.

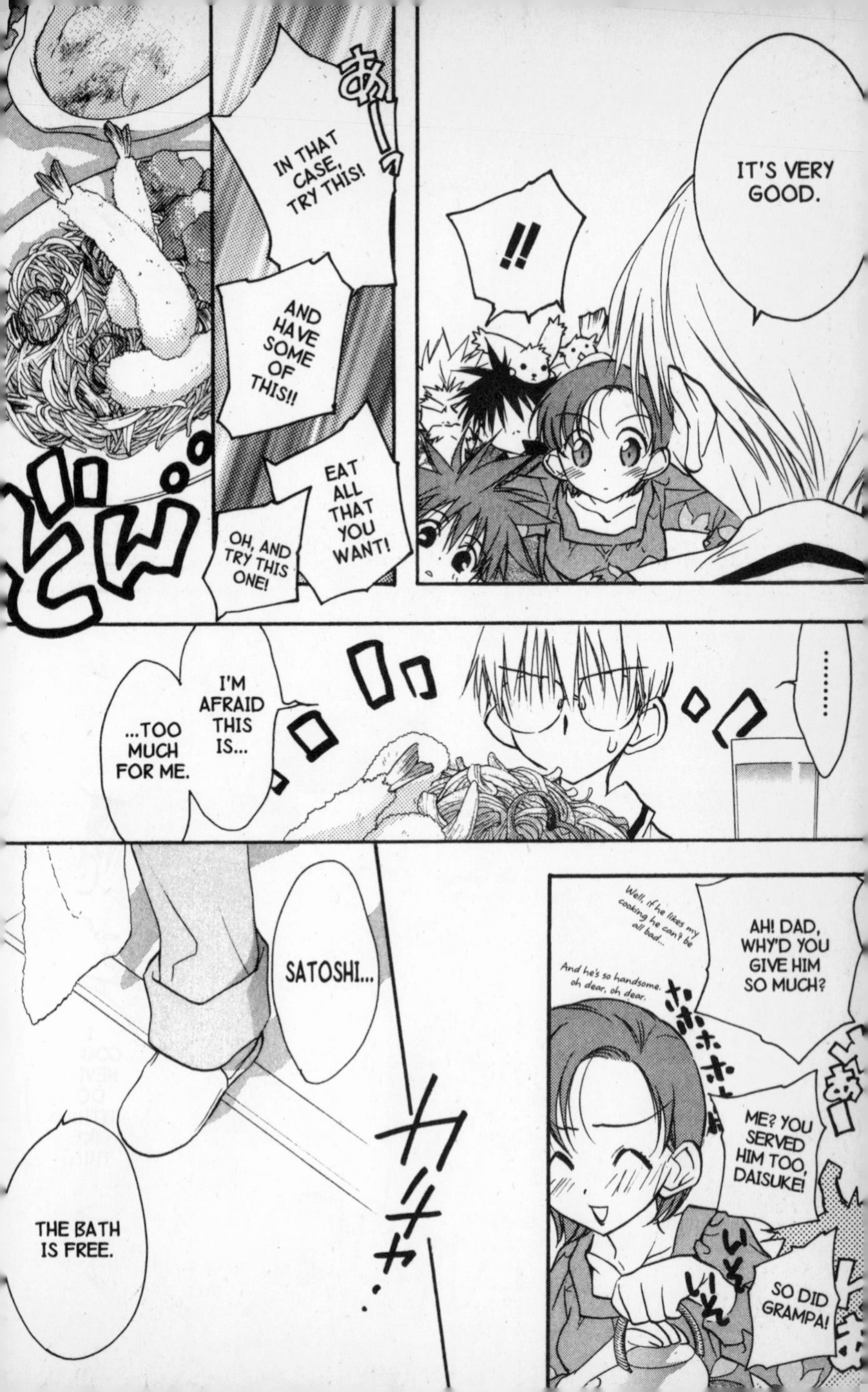
IT'S VERY GOOD.
!!
IN THAT CASE, TRY THIS!
AND HAVE SOME OF THIS!!
EAT ALL THAT YOU WANT!
OH, AND TRY THIS ONE!
......
I'M AFRAID THIS IS...
...TOO MUCH FOR ME.
AH! DAD, WHY'D YOU GIVE HIM SO MUCH?
Well, if he likes my cooking he can't be all bad...
And he's so handsome. oh dear, oh dear.
ME? YOU SERVED HIM TOO, DAISUKE!
SO DID GRAMPA!
SATOSHI...
THE BATH IS FREE.

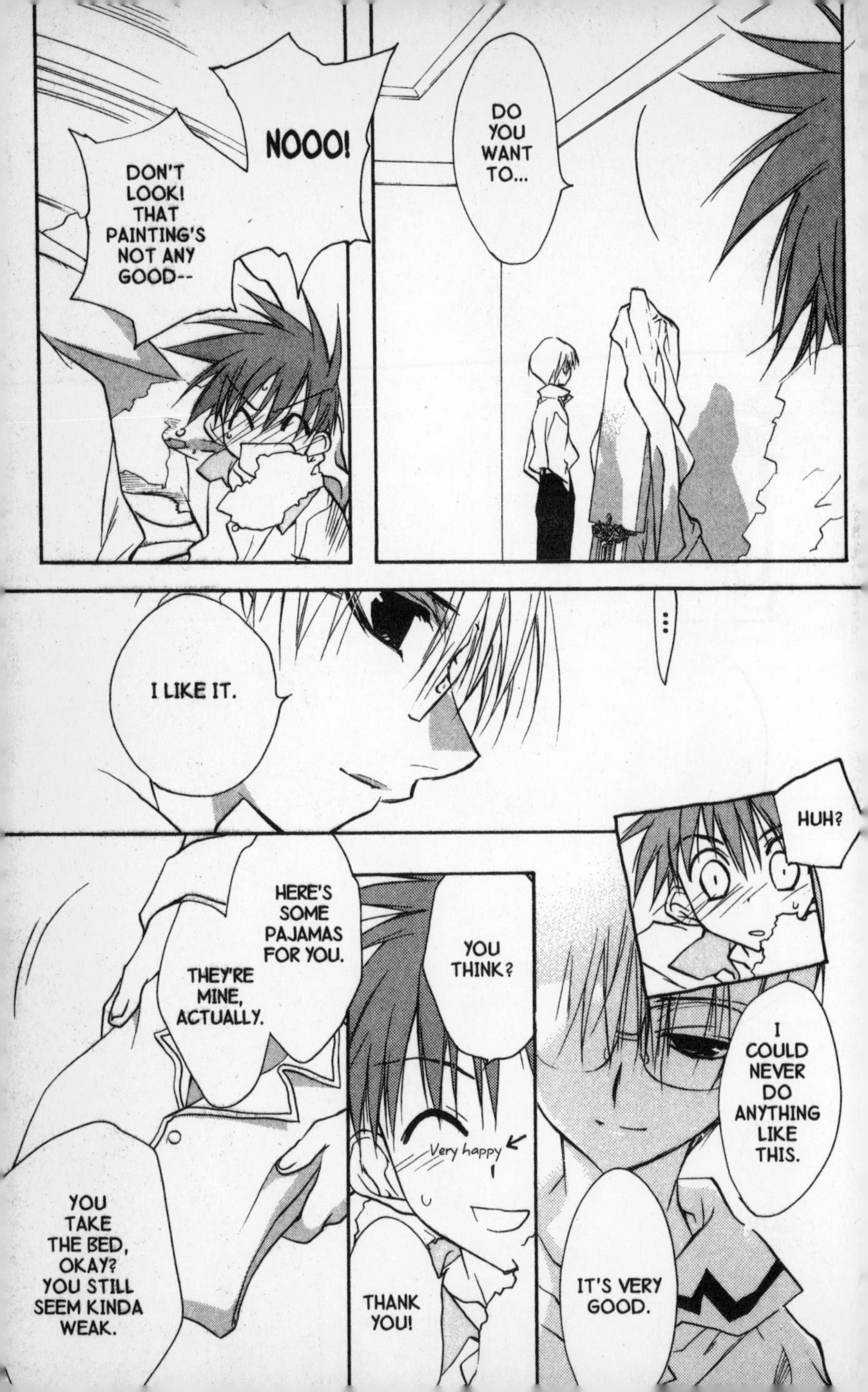
DO YOU WANT TO...
NOOO!
DON'T LOOK! THAT PAINTING'S NOT ANY GOOD--
...
I LIKE IT.
HUH?
I COULD NEVER DO ANYTHING LIKE THIS.
IT'S VERY GOOD.
YOU THINK?
Very happy
THANK YOU!
HERE'S SOME PAJAMAS FOR YOU.
THEY'RE MINE, ACTUALLY.
YOU TAKE THE BED, OKAY? YOU STILL SEEM KINDA WEAK.

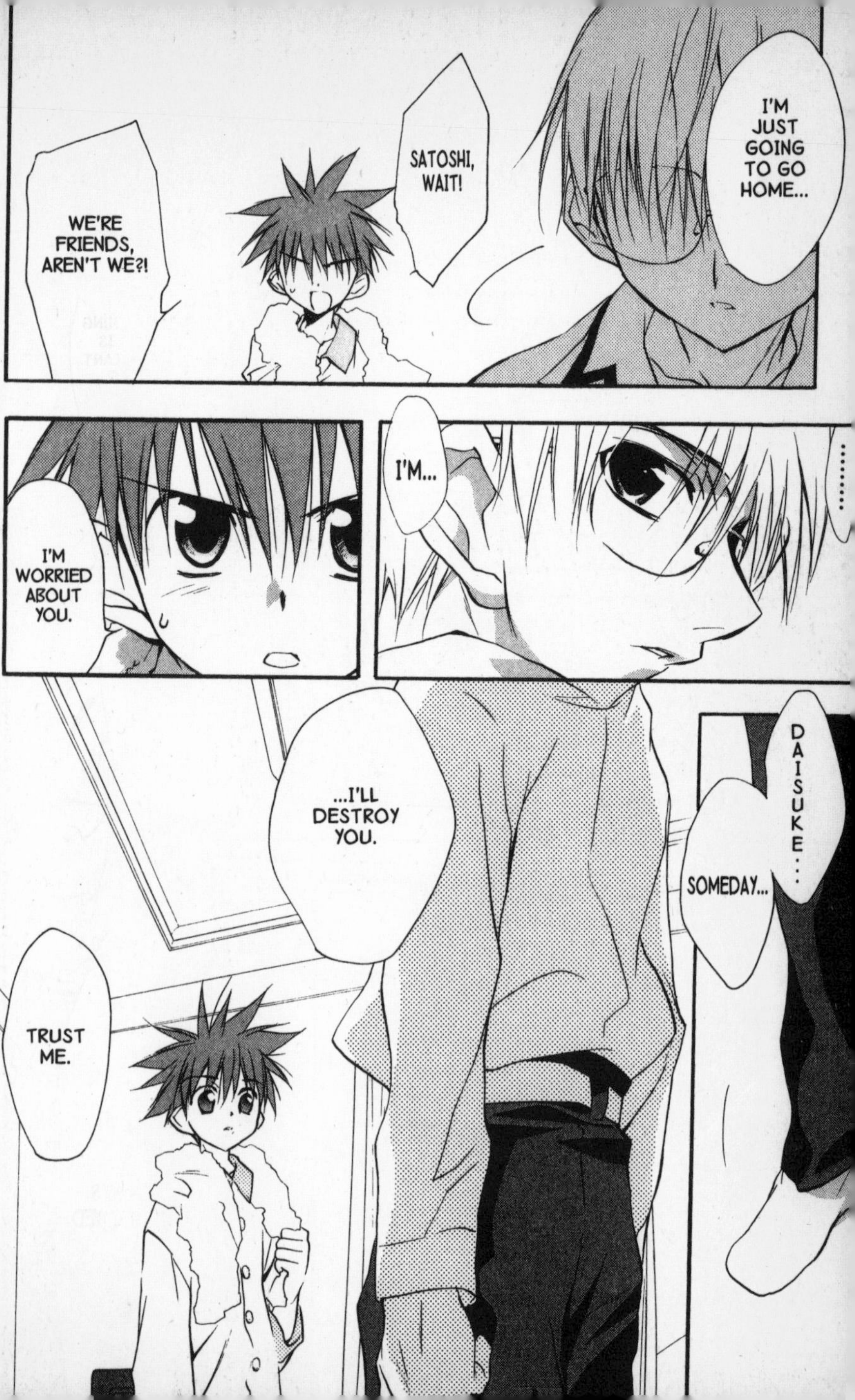
I'M JUST GOING TO GO HOME...
SATOSHI, WAIT!
WE'RE FRIENDS, AREN'T WE?!
I'M...
I'M WORRIED ABOUT YOU.
DAISUKE...
SOMEDAY...
...I'LL DESTROY YOU.
TRUST ME.

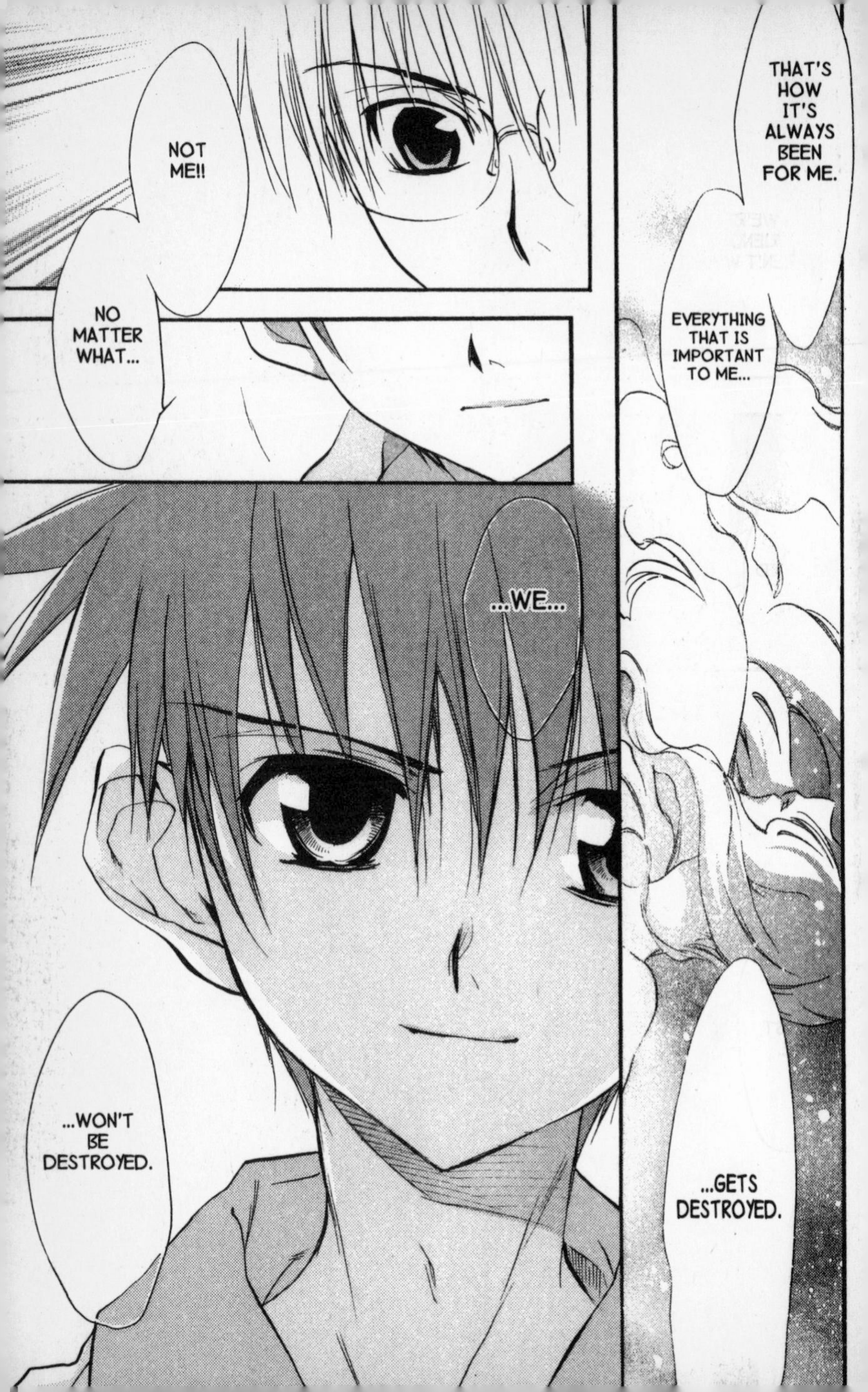
THAT'S HOW IT'S ALWAYS BEEN FOR ME.
EVERYTHING THAT IS IMPORTANT TO ME...
...GETS DESTROYED.
NOT ME!!
NO MATTER WHAT...
...WE...
...WON'T BE DESTROYED.

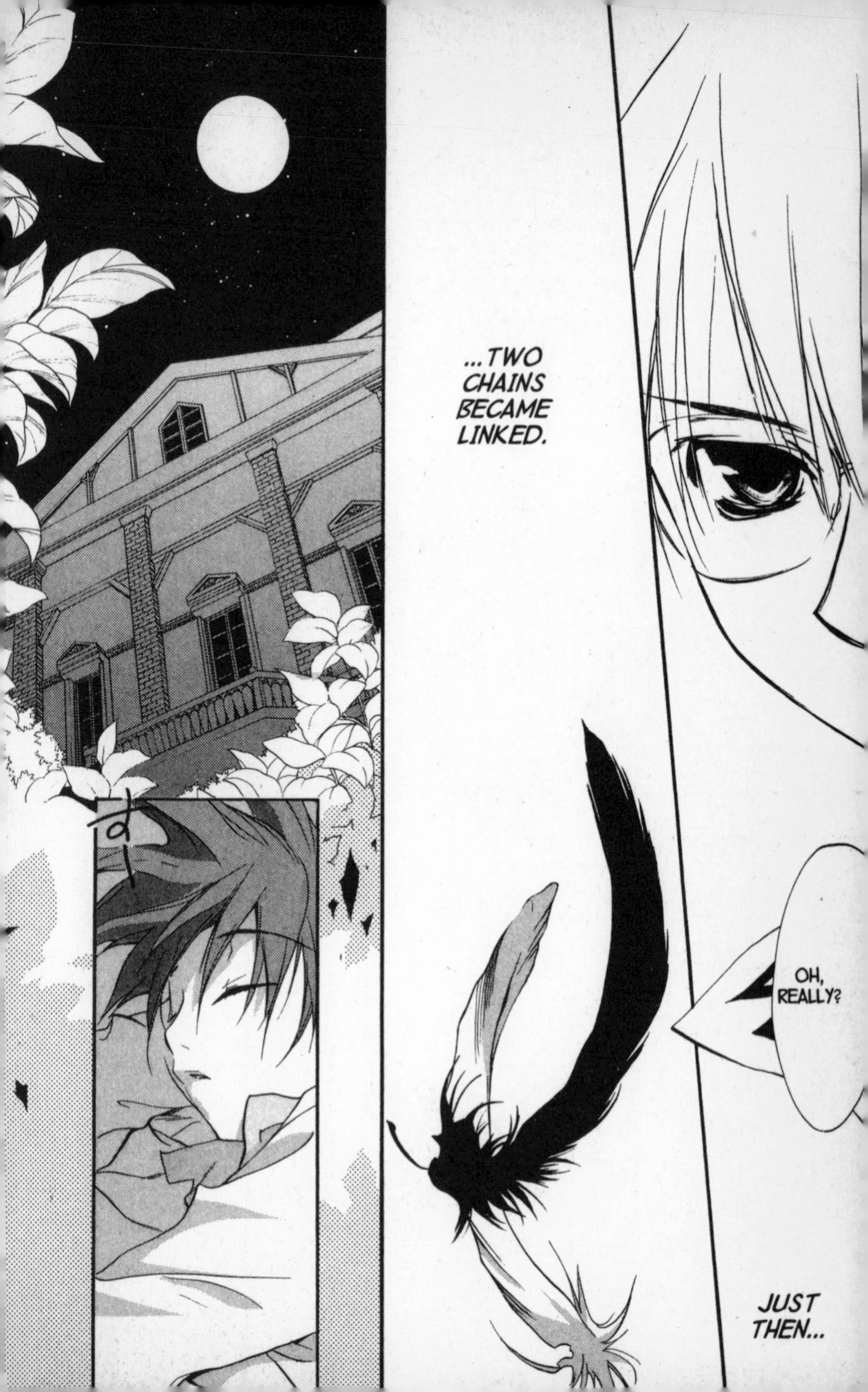
...TWO CHAINS BECAME LINKED.
OH, REALLY?
JUST THEN...

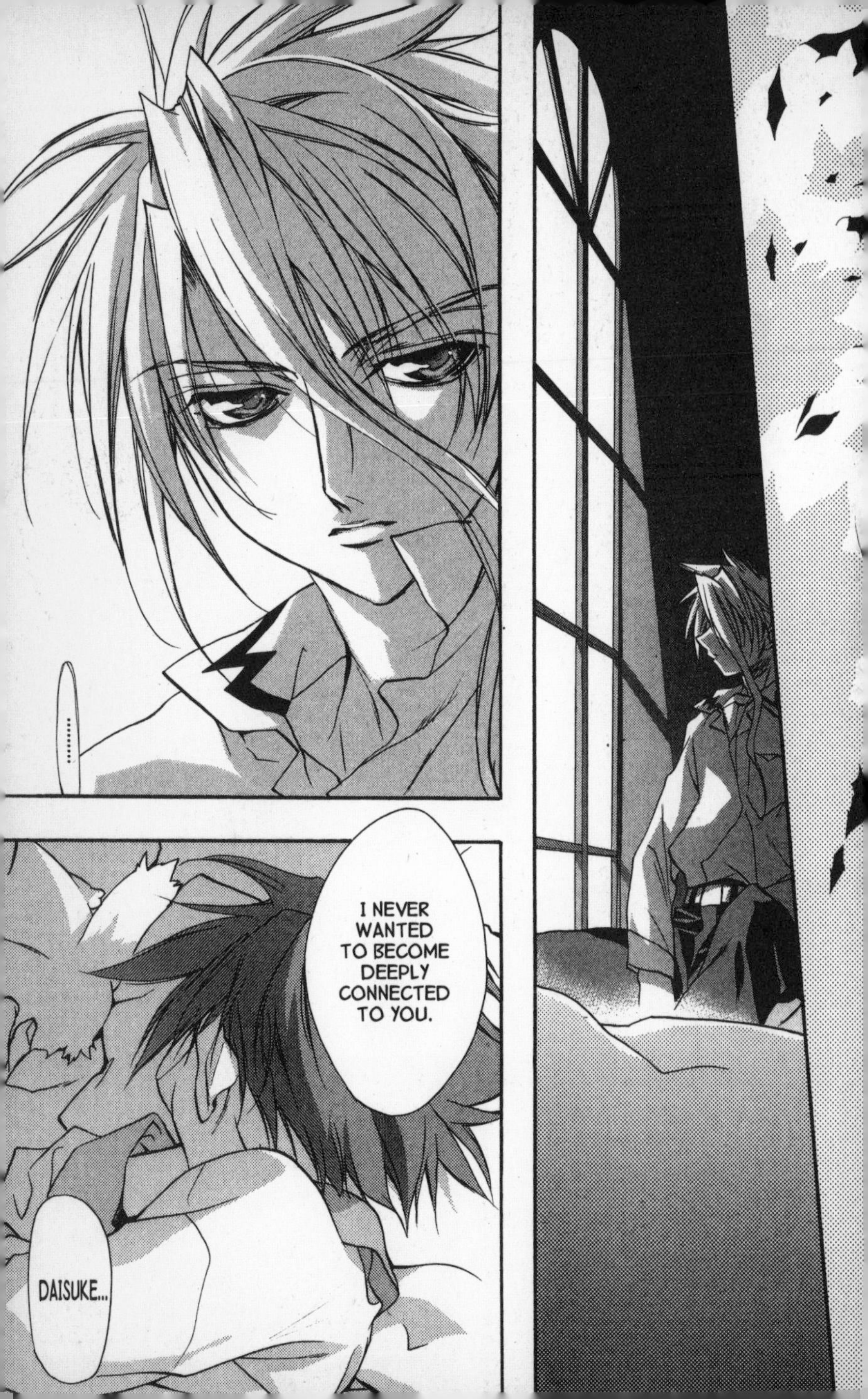

....
I NEVER WANTED TO BECOME DEEPLY CONNECTED TO YOU.
DAISUKE...

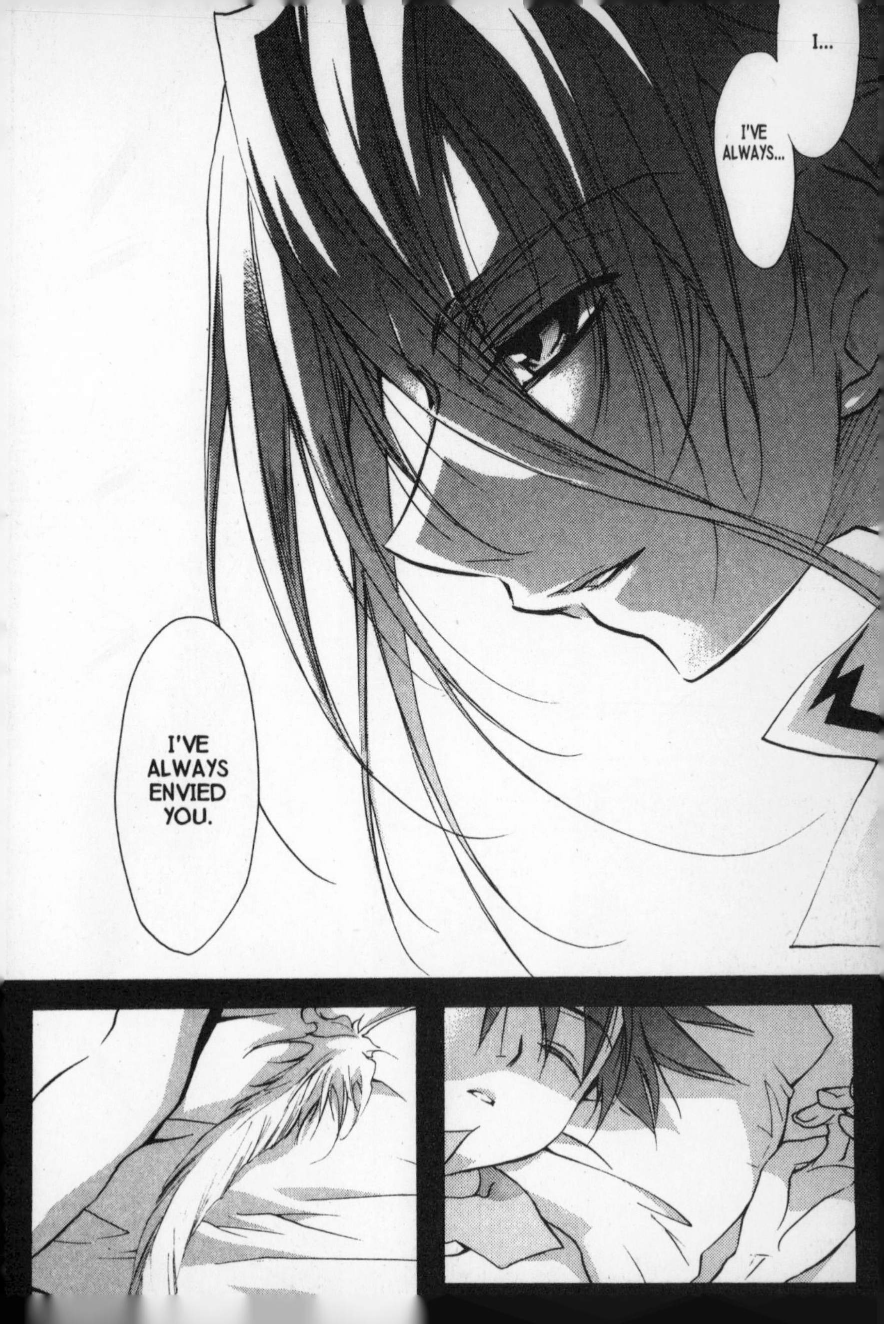
I...
I'VE ALWAYS...
I'VE ALWAYS ENVIED YOU.

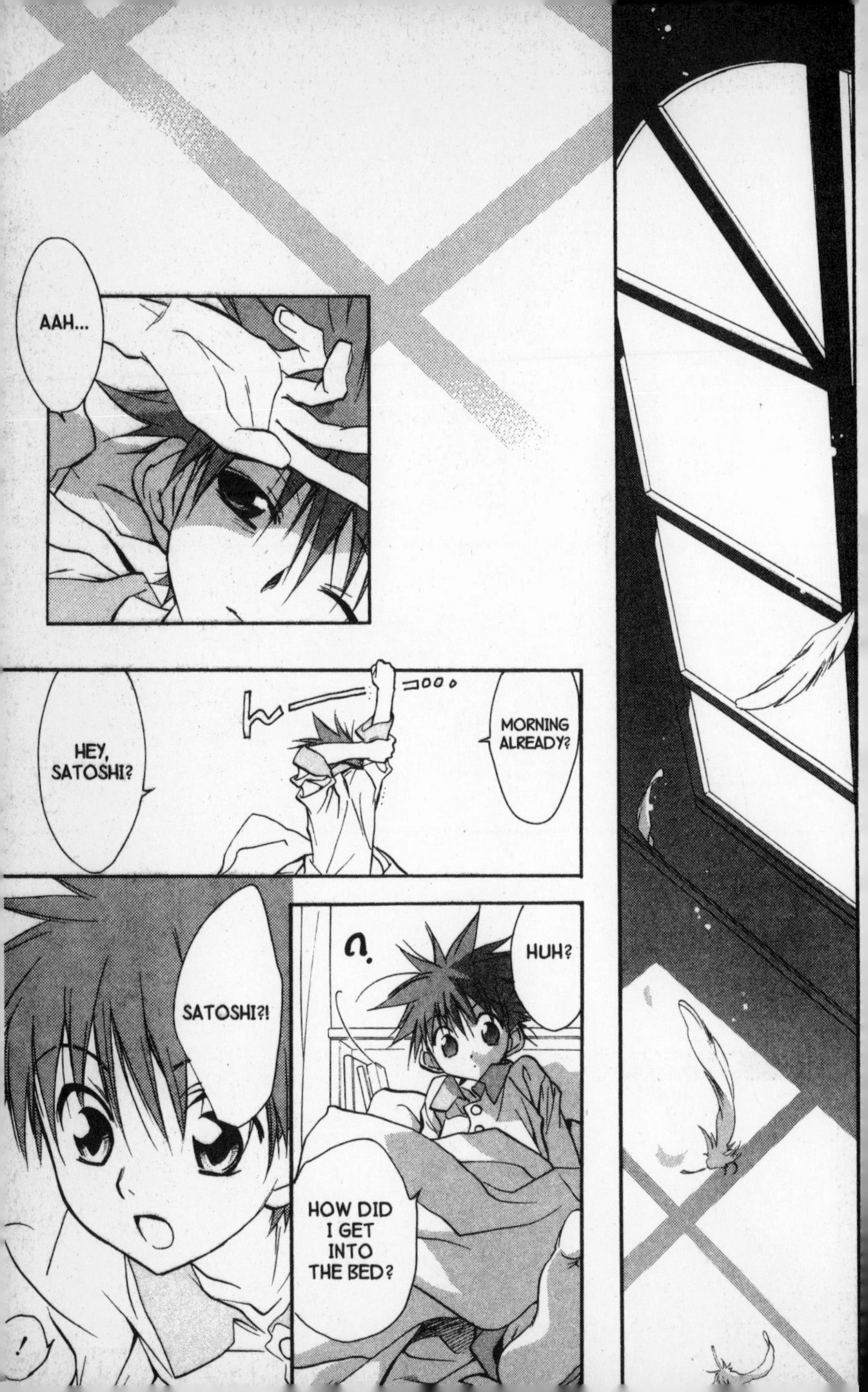
AAH...
MORNING ALREADY?
HEY, SATOSHI?
HUH?
HOW DID I GET INTO THE BED?
SATOSHI?!

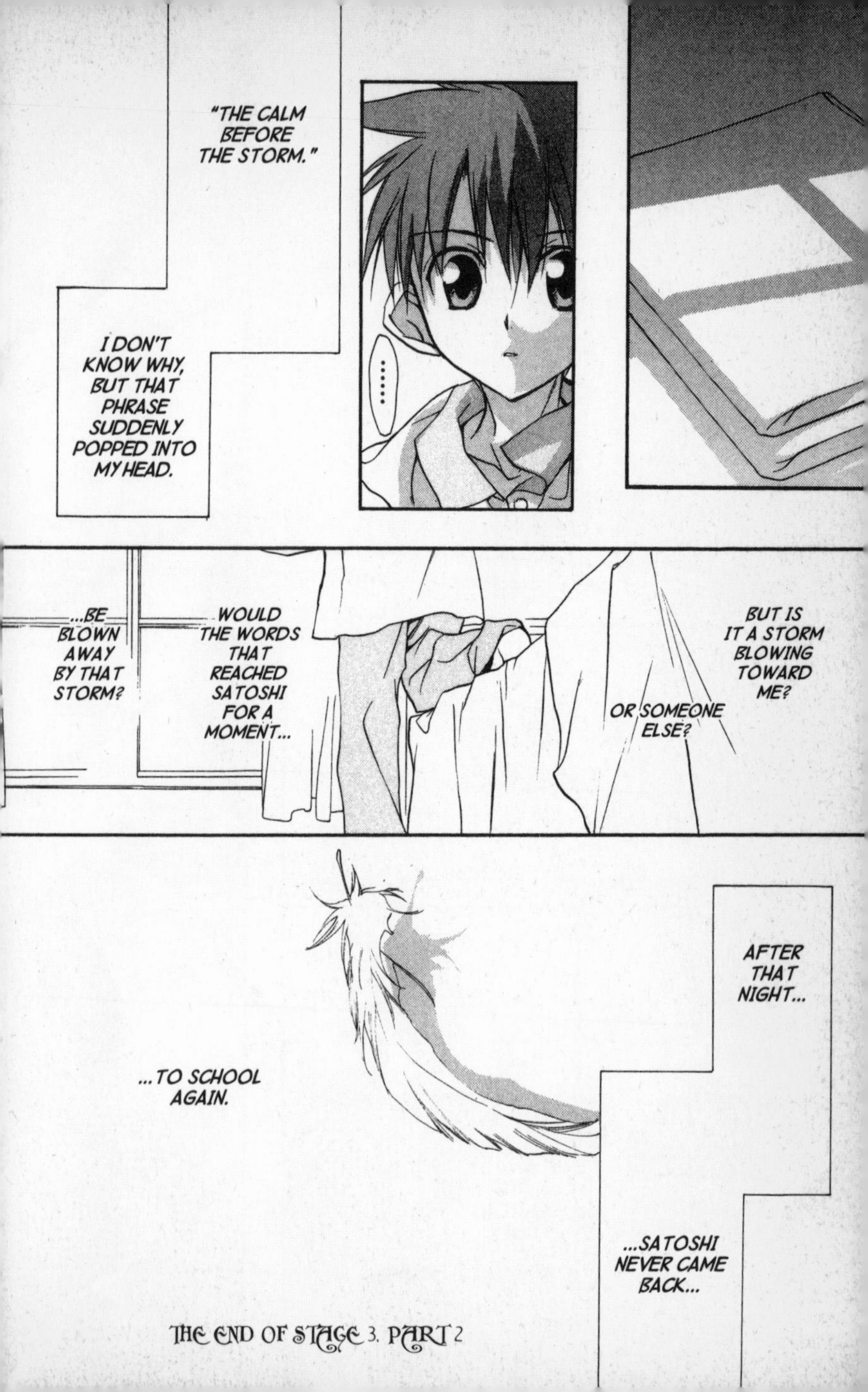
......
"THE CALM BEFORE THE STORM."
I DON'T KNOW WHY, BUT THAT PHRASE SUDDENLY POPPED INTO MY HEAD.
BUT IS IT A STORM BLOWING TOWARD ME?
OR SOMEONE ELSE?
WOULD THE WORDS THAT REACHED SATOSHI FOR A MOMENT...
...BE BLOWN AWAY BY THAT STORM?
AFTER THAT NIGHT...
...SATOSHI NEVER CAME BACK...
...TO SCHOOL AGAIN.
THE END OF STAGE 3, PART 2

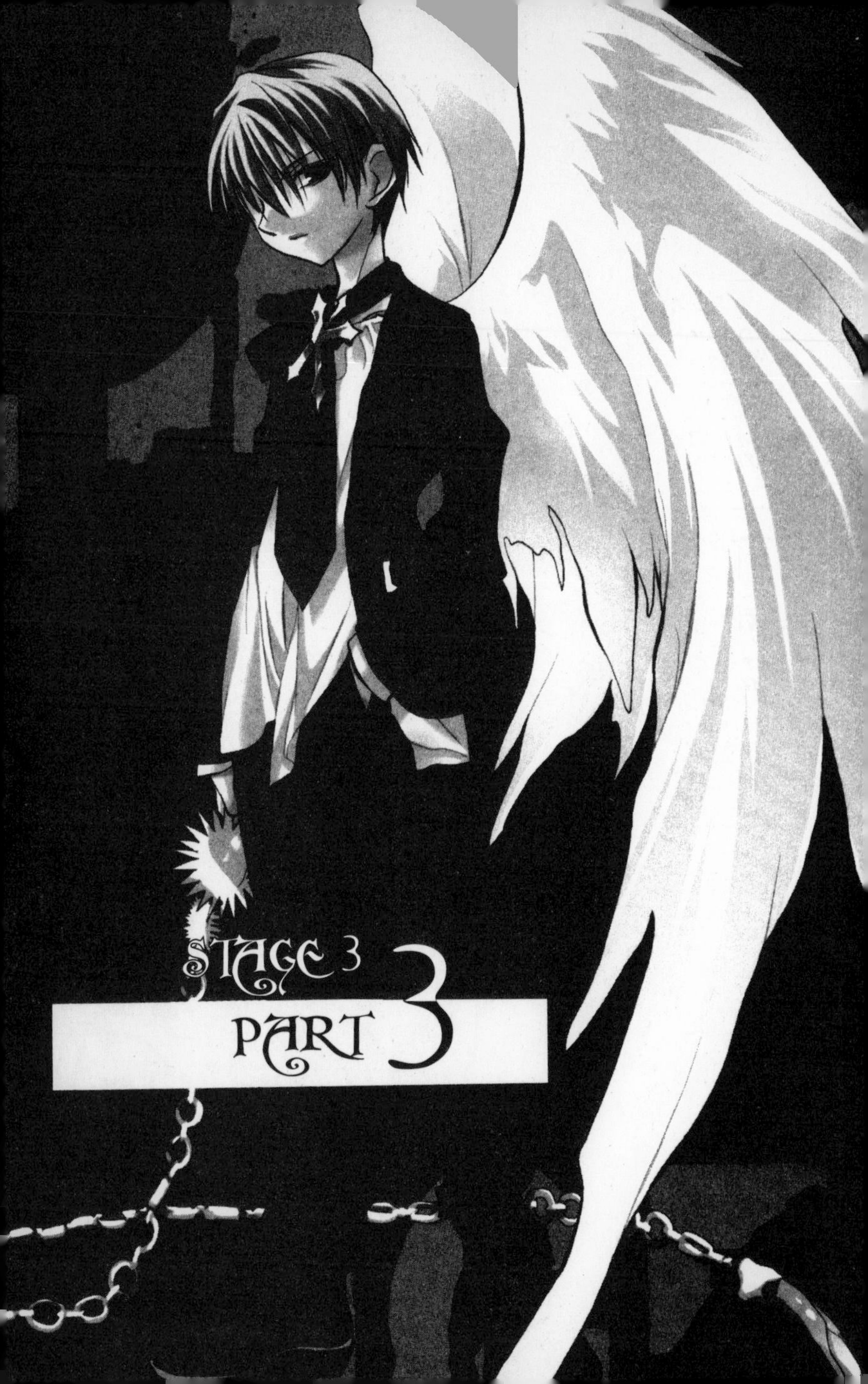
STAGE 3
PART 3

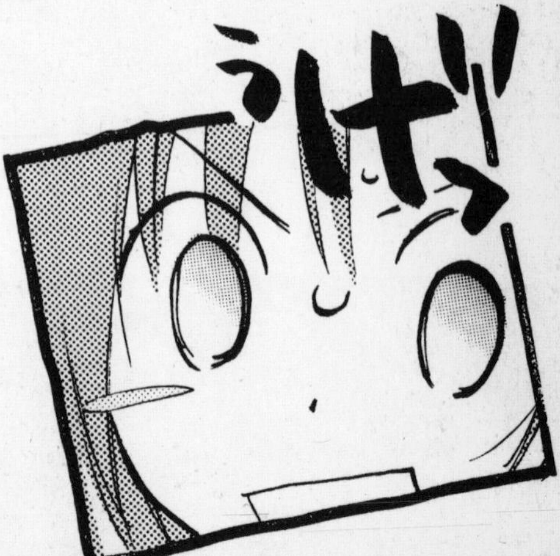
うげっ

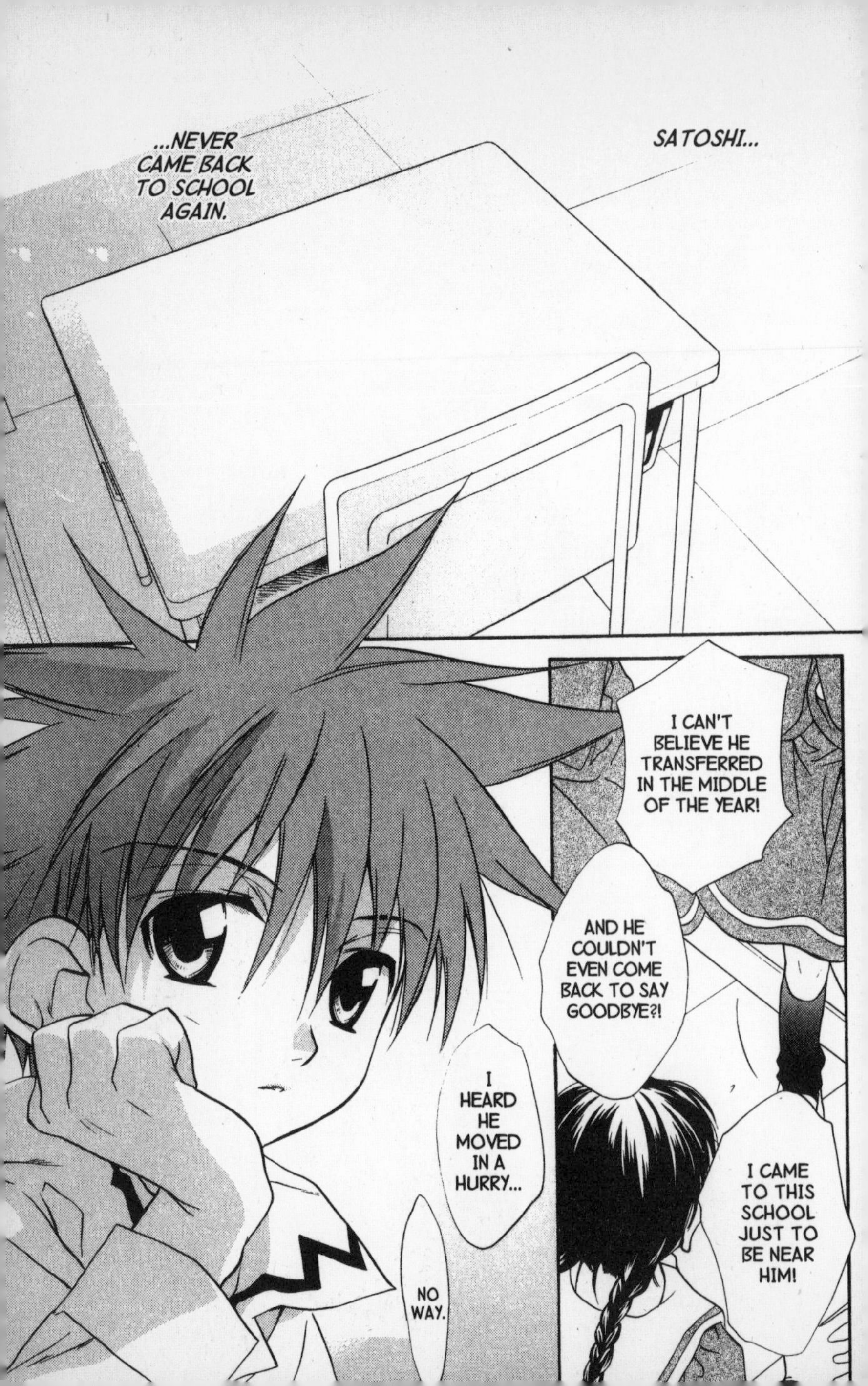
SATOSHI...
...NEVER CAME BACK TO SCHOOL AGAIN.
I CAN'T BELIEVE HE TRANSFERRED IN THE MIDDLE OF THE YEAR!
AND HE COULDN'T EVEN COME BACK TO SAY GOODBYE?!
I CAME TO THIS SCHOOL JUST TO BE NEAR HIM!
I HEARD HE MOVED IN A HURRY...
NO WAY.

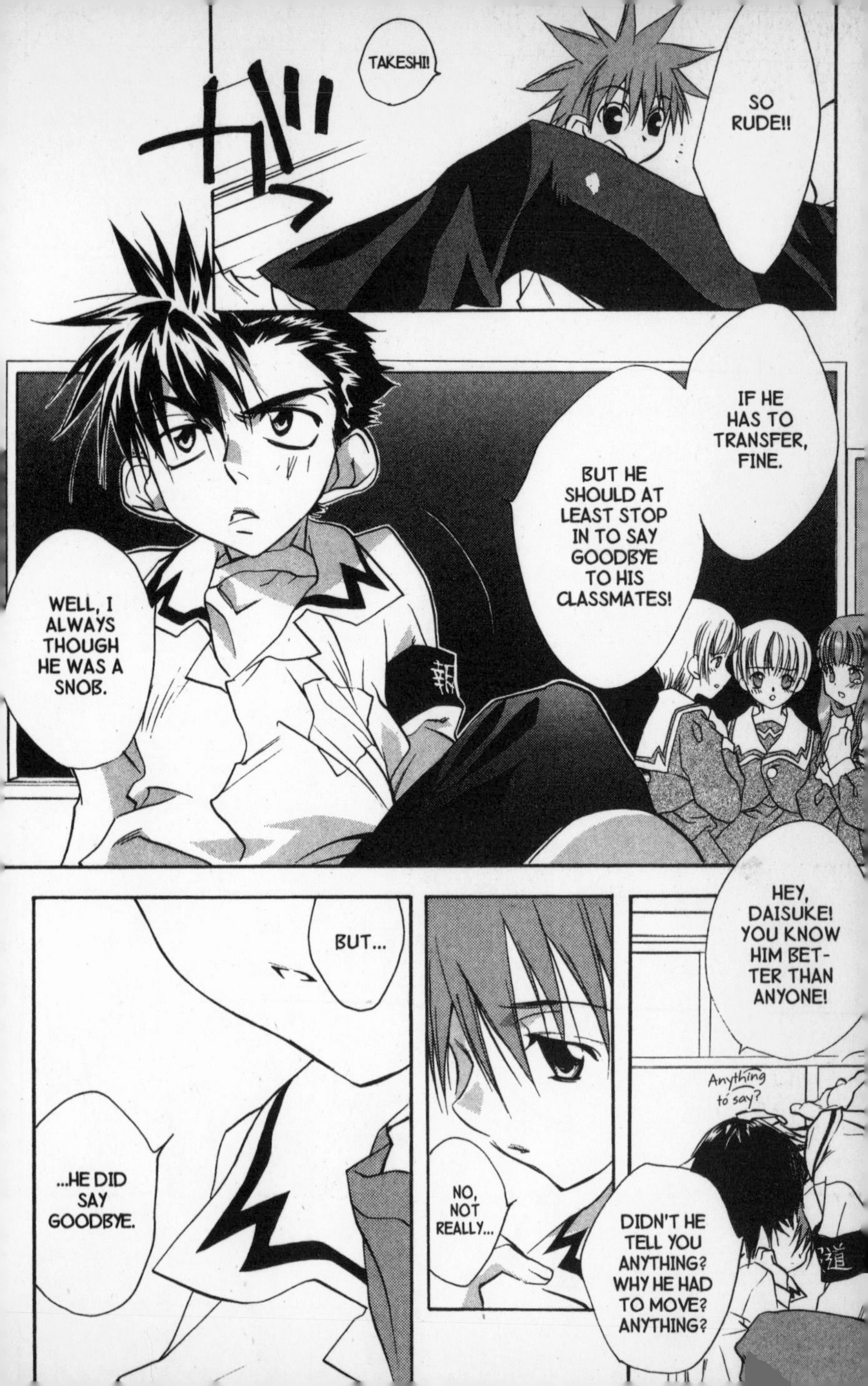
SO RUDE!!
TAKESHI!
ガッ
IF HE HAS TO TRANSFER, FINE.
BUT HE SHOULD AT LEAST STOP IN TO SAY GOODBYE TO HIS CLASSMATES!
WELL, I ALWAYS THOUGH HE WAS A SNOB.
HEY, DAISUKE! YOU KNOW HIM BET-TER THAN ANYONE!
Anything to say?
DIDN'T HE TELL YOU ANYTHING? WHY HE HAD TO MOVE? ANYTHING?
NO, NOT REALLY...
BUT...
...HE DID SAY GOODBYE.

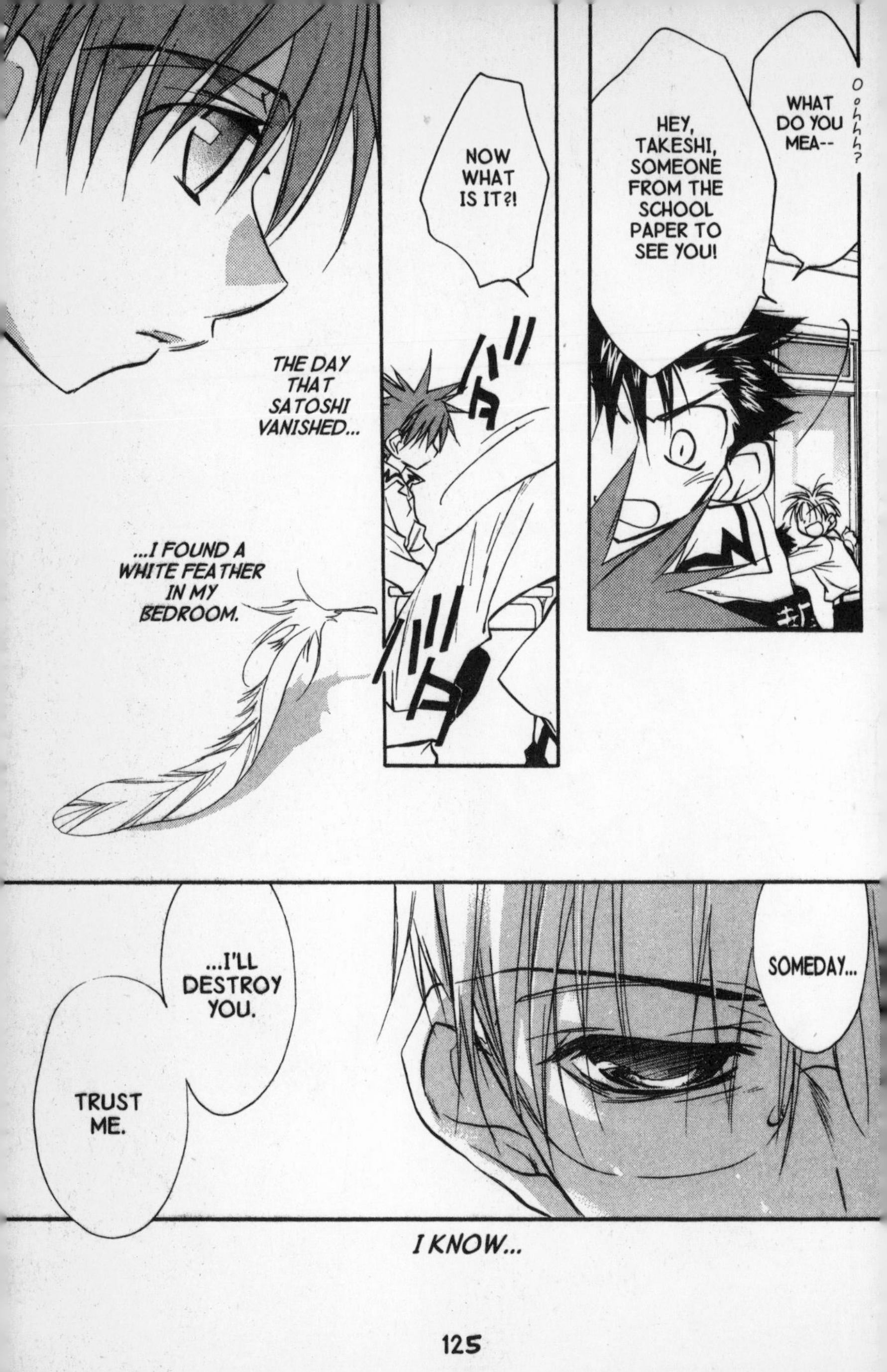
WHAT DO YOU MEA--
Oohhh?
HEY, TAKESHI, SOMEONE FROM THE SCHOOL PAPER TO SEE YOU!
NOW WHAT IS IT?!
THE DAY THAT SATOSHI VANISHED...
...I FOUND A WHITE FEATHER IN MY BEDROOM.
SOMEDAY...
...I'LL DESTROY YOU.
TRUST ME.
I KNOW...

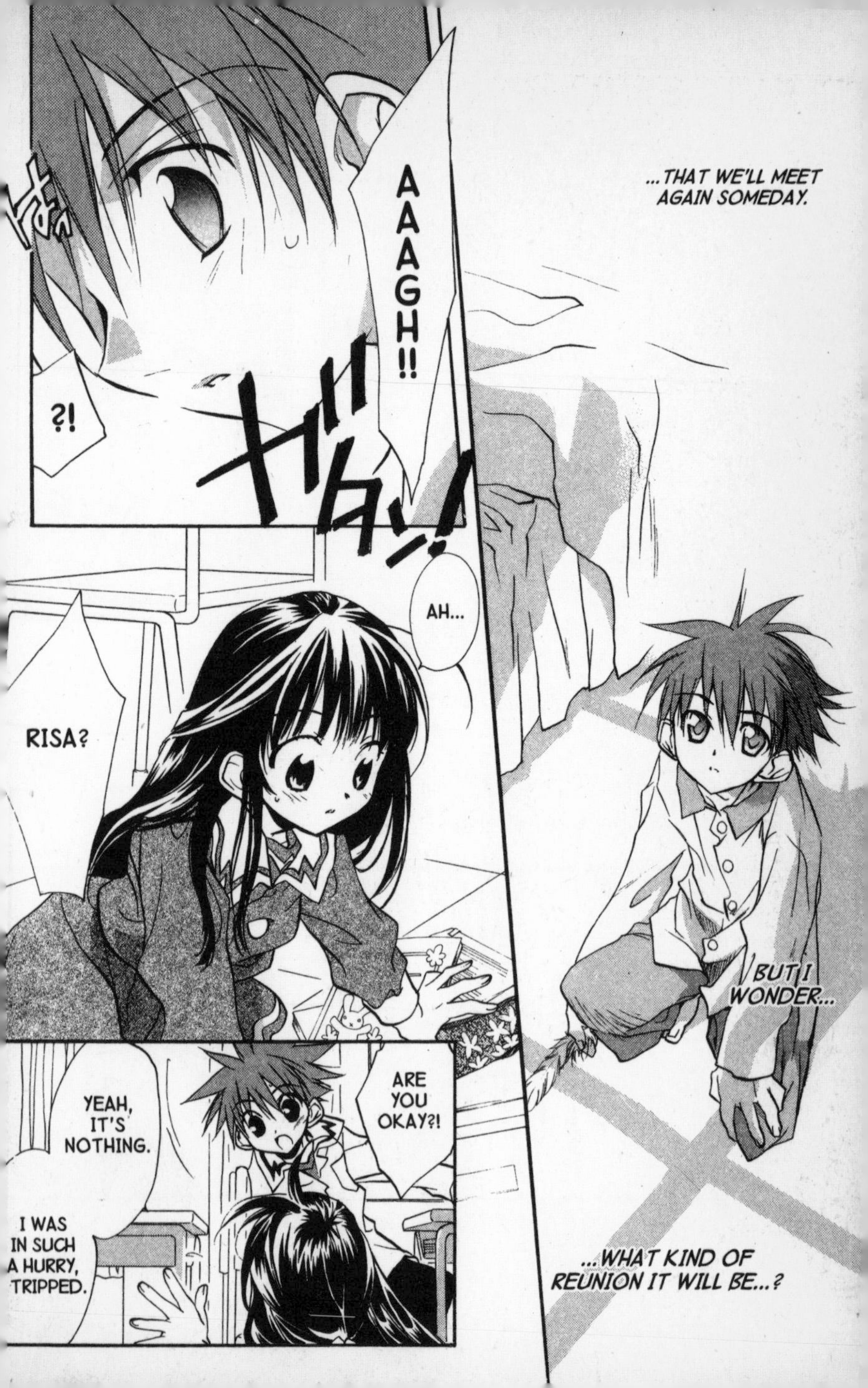

...THAT WE'LL MEET AGAIN SOMEDAY.
BUT I WONDER...
...WHAT KIND OF REUNION IT WILL BE...?
AAAAGH!!
?!
ガタッ!
AH...
RISA?
ARE YOU OKAY?!
YEAH, IT'S NOTHING.
I WAS IN SUCH A HURRY, TRIPPED.

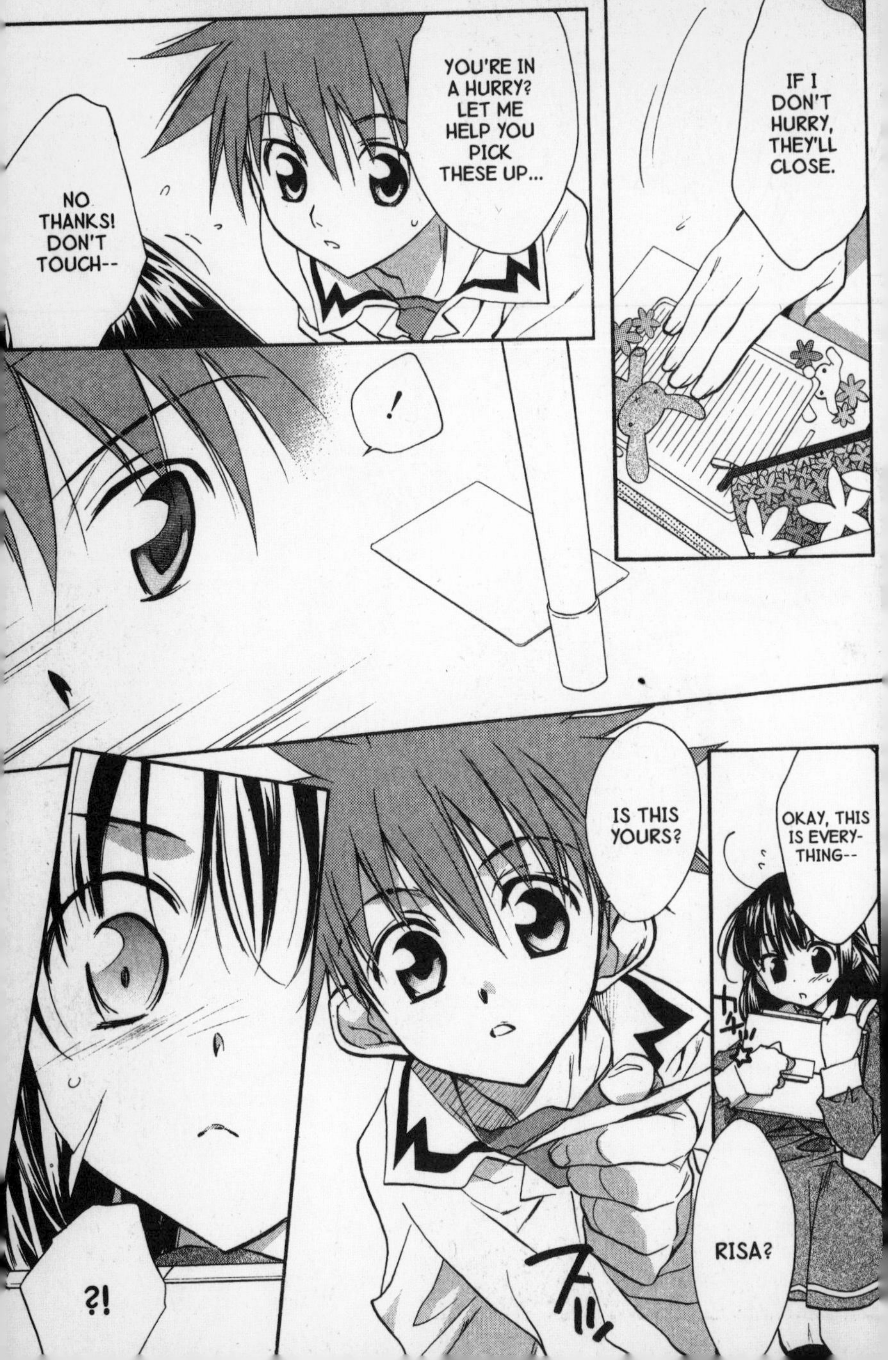
IF I DON'T HURRY, THEY'LL CLOSE.
YOU'RE IN A HURRY? LET ME HELP YOU PICK THESE UP...
NO THANKS! DON'T TOUCH--
!
OKAY, THIS IS EVERY-THING--
IS THIS YOURS?
RISA?
?!

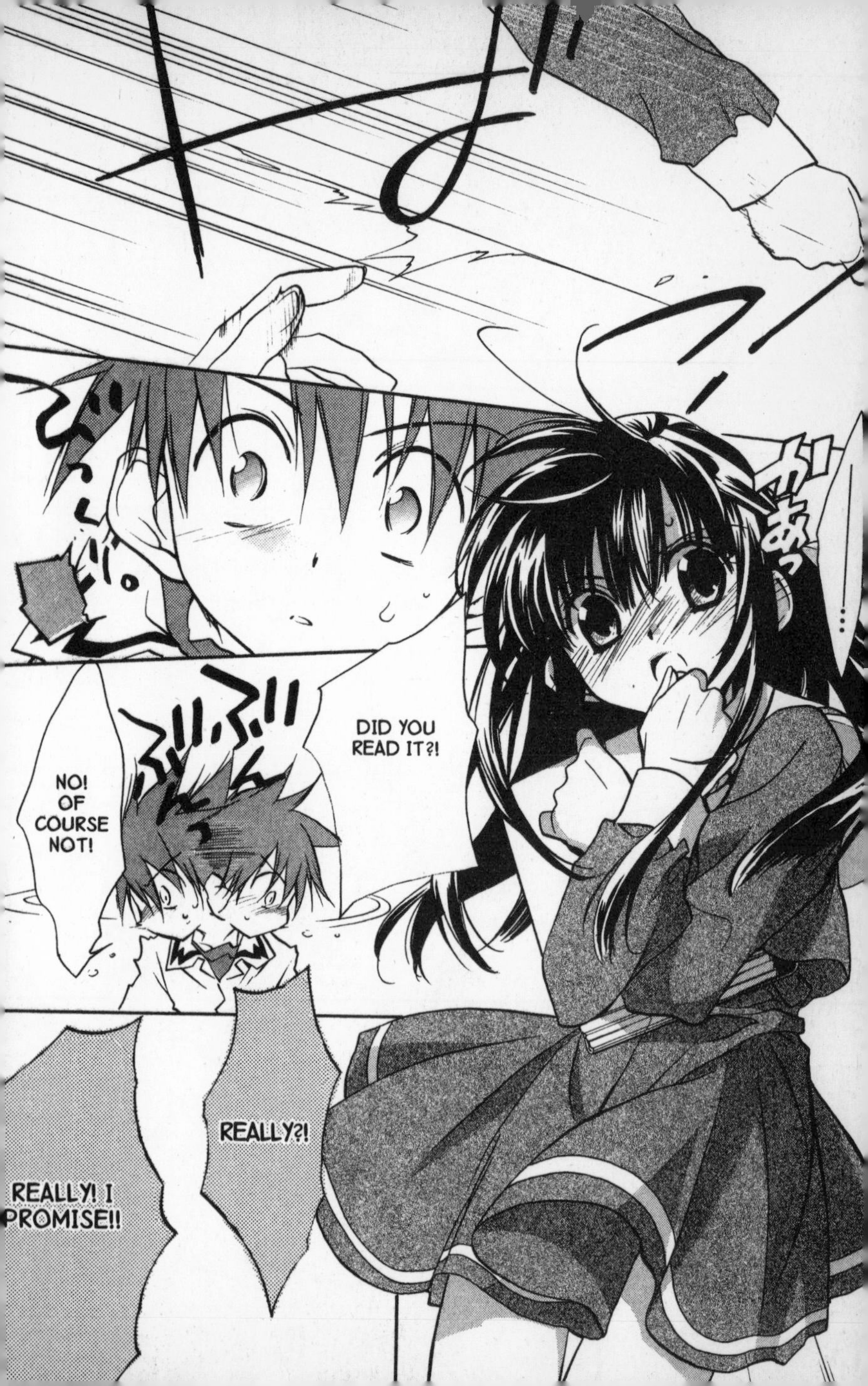
DID YOU READ IT?!
NO! OF COURSE NOT!
REALLY?!
REALLY! I PROMISE!!

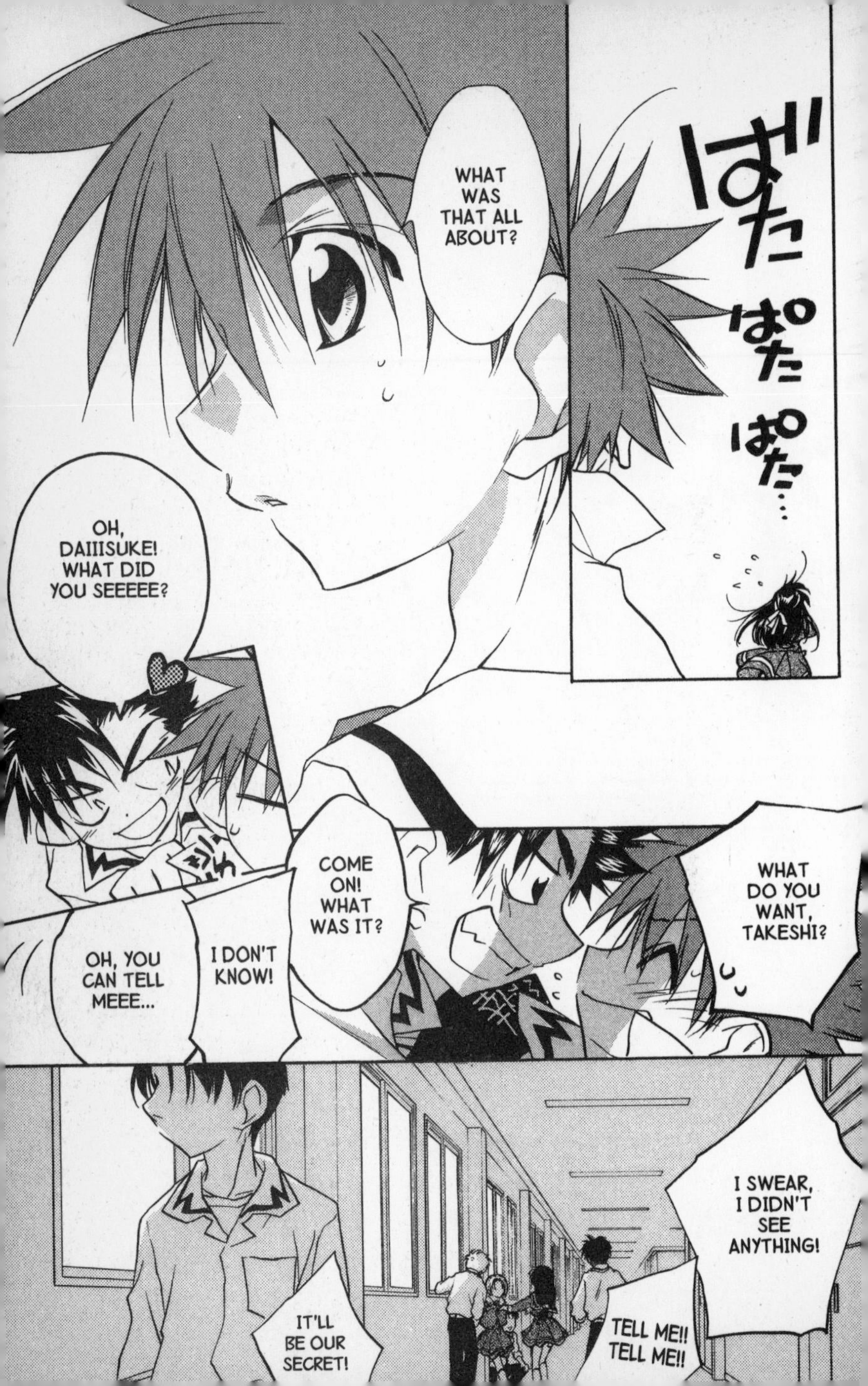

ぱた ぱた ぱた…
WHAT WAS THAT ALL ABOUT?
OH, DAIIISUKE! WHAT DID YOU SEEEEE?
WHAT DO YOU WANT, TAKESHI?
COME ON! WHAT WAS IT?
I DON'T KNOW!
OH, YOU CAN TELL MEEE...
I SWEAR, I DIDN'T SEE ANYTHING!
TELL ME!! TELL ME!!
IT'LL BE OUR SECRET!

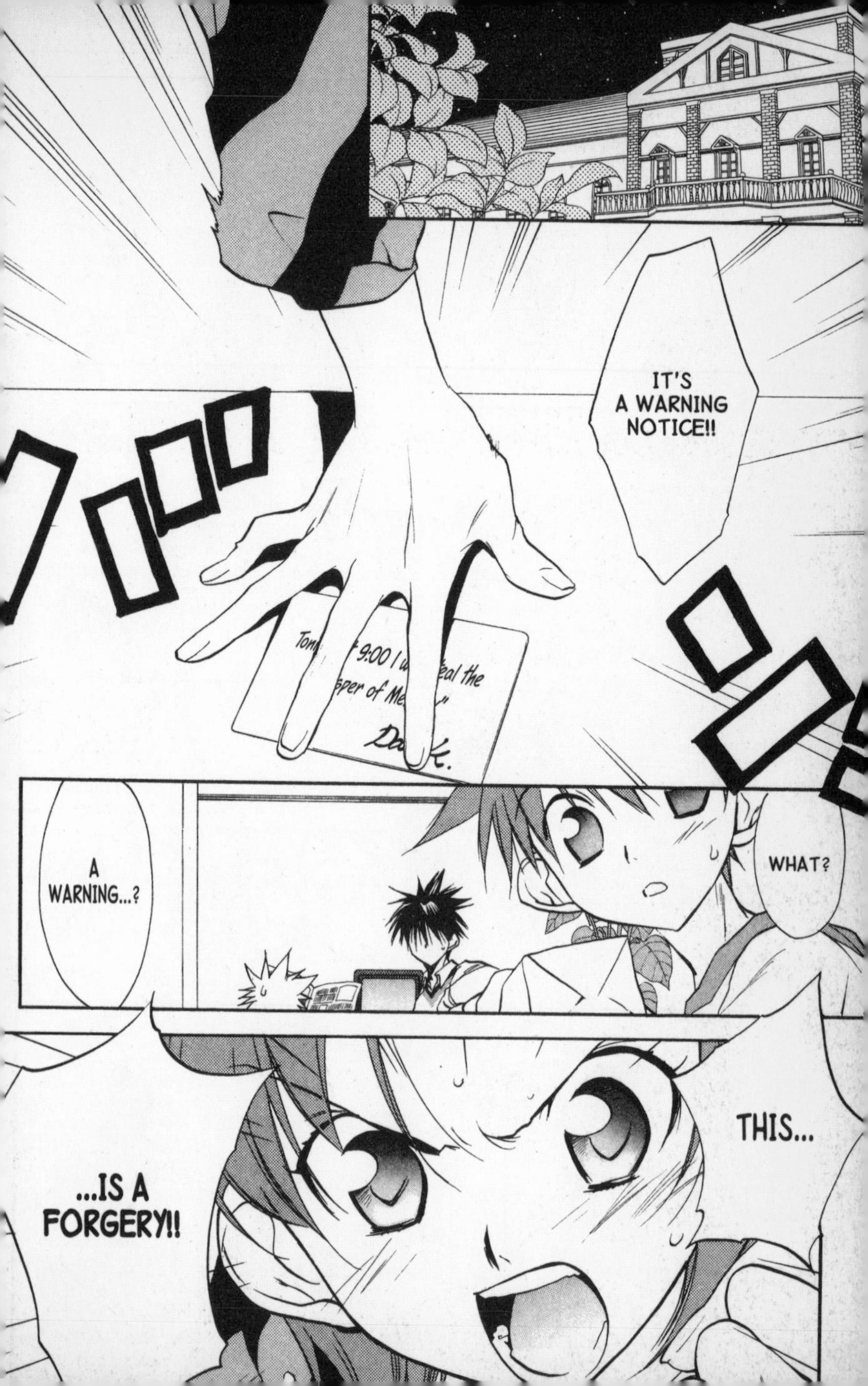
IT'S A WARNING NOTICE!!
WHAT?
A WARNING...?
THIS...
...IS A FORGERY!!

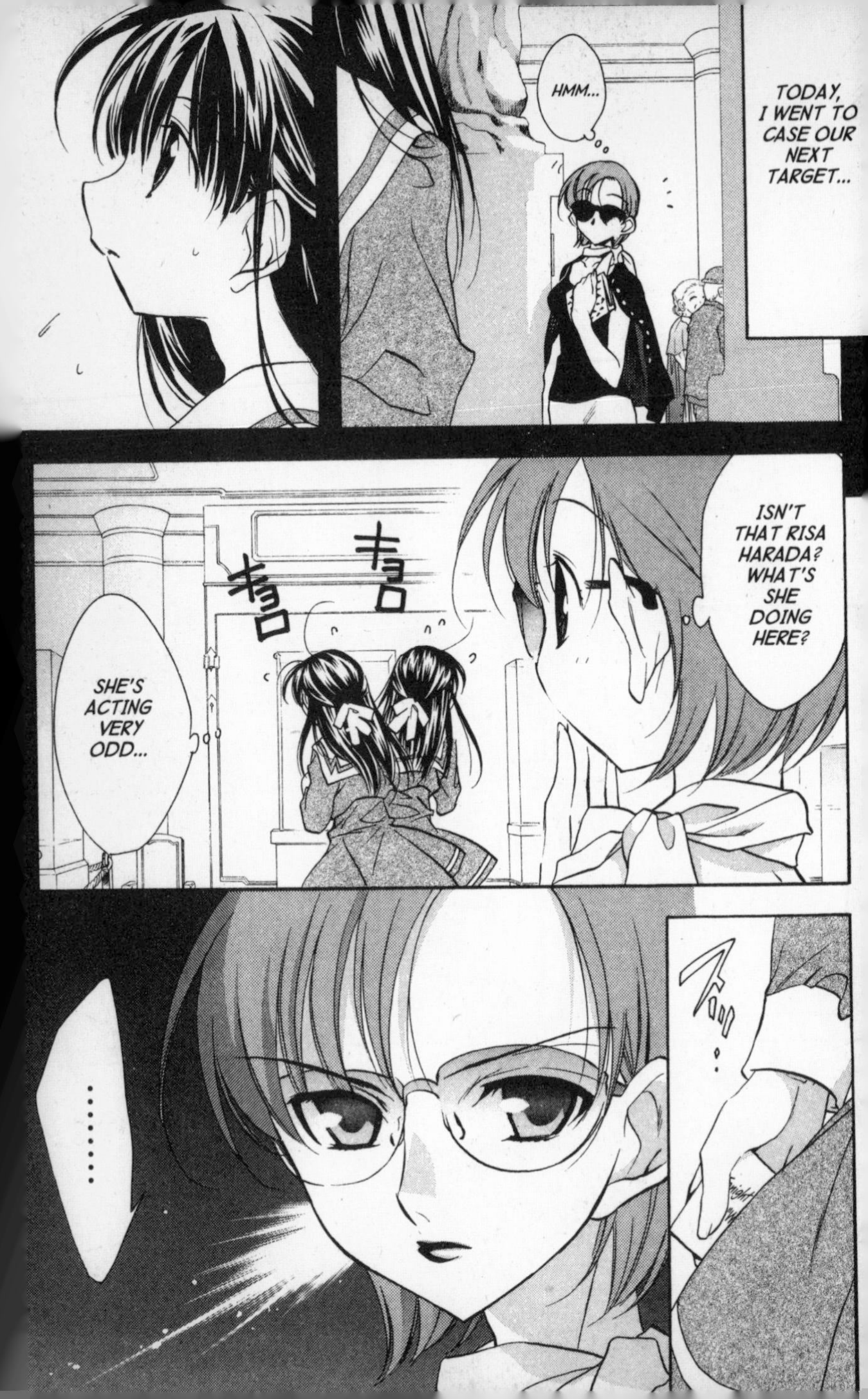
TODAY, I WENT TO CASE OUR NEXT TARGET...
HMM...
ISN'T THAT RISA HARADA? WHAT'S SHE DOING HERE?
SHE'S ACTING VERY ODD...
....

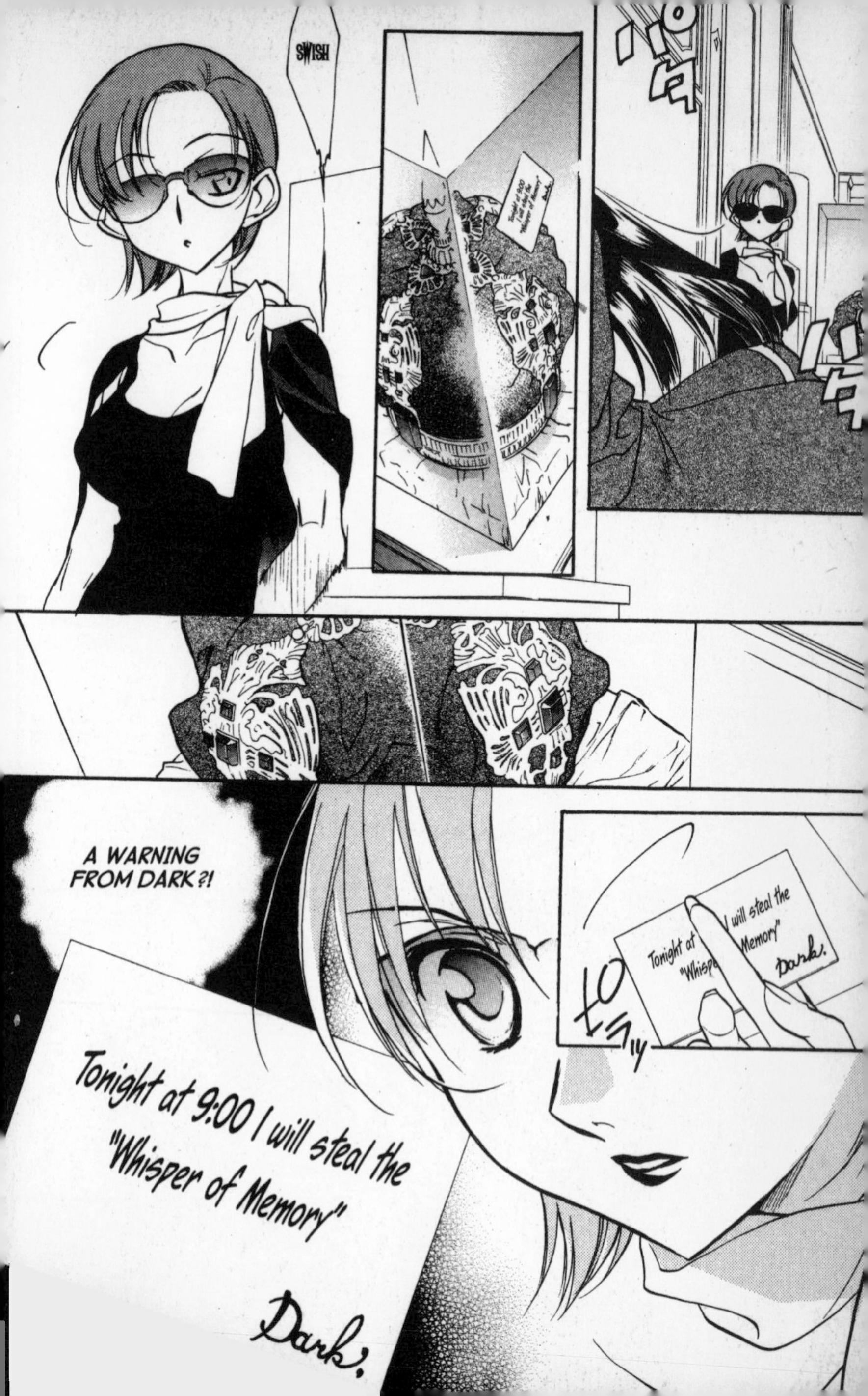
SWISH
A WARNING FROM DARK?!
Tonight at 9:00 I will steal the "Whisper of Memory"
Dark.

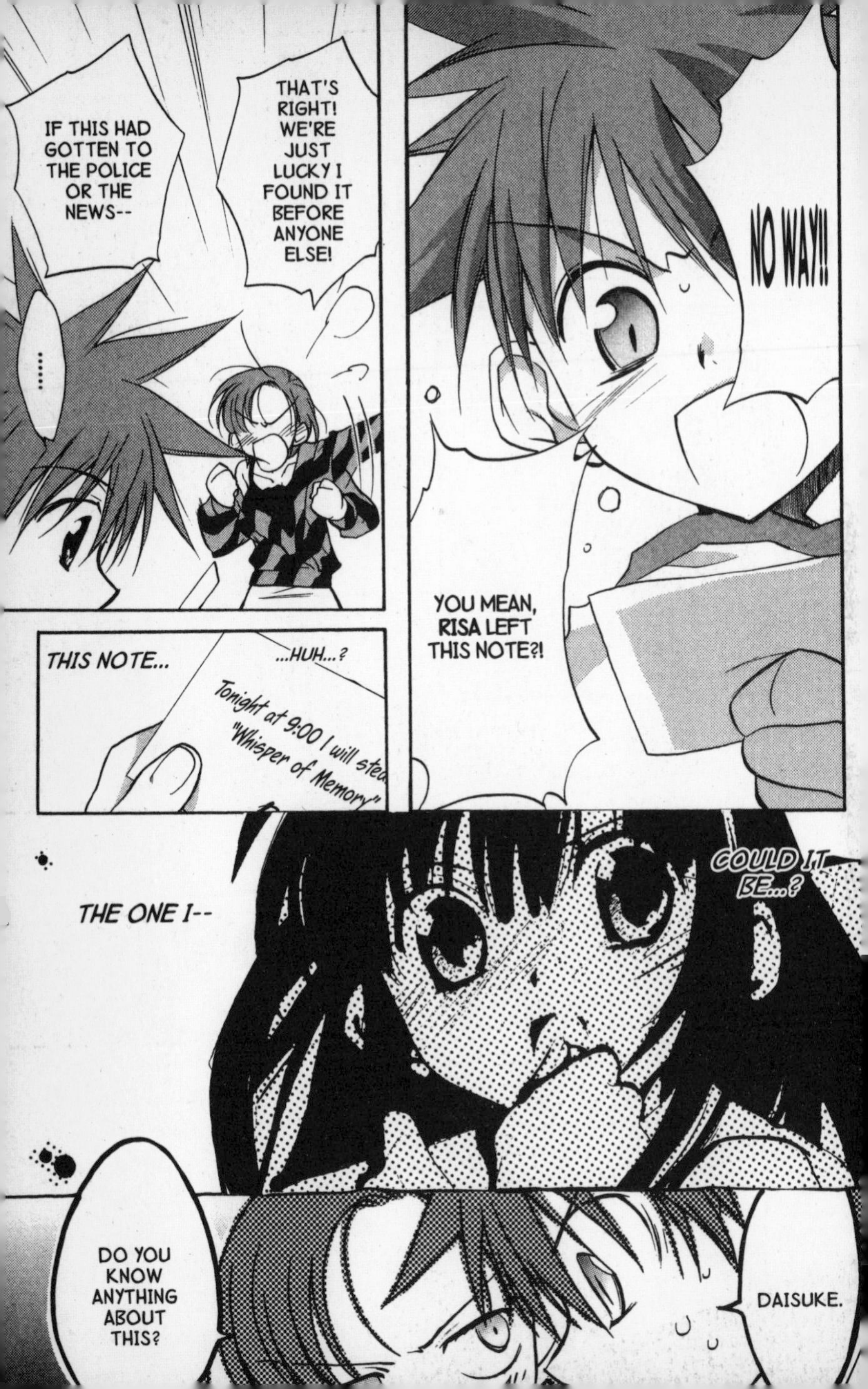
THAT'S RIGHT! WE'RE JUST LUCKY I FOUND IT BEFORE ANYONE ELSE!
IF THIS HAD GOTTEN TO THE POLICE OR THE NEWS--
......
...HUH...?
THIS NOTE...
Tonight at 9:00 I will stea
"Whisper of Memory"
NO WAY!!
YOU MEAN, RISA LEFT THIS NOTE?!
COULD IT BE...?
THE ONE I--
DAISUKE.
DO YOU KNOW ANYTHING ABOUT THIS?

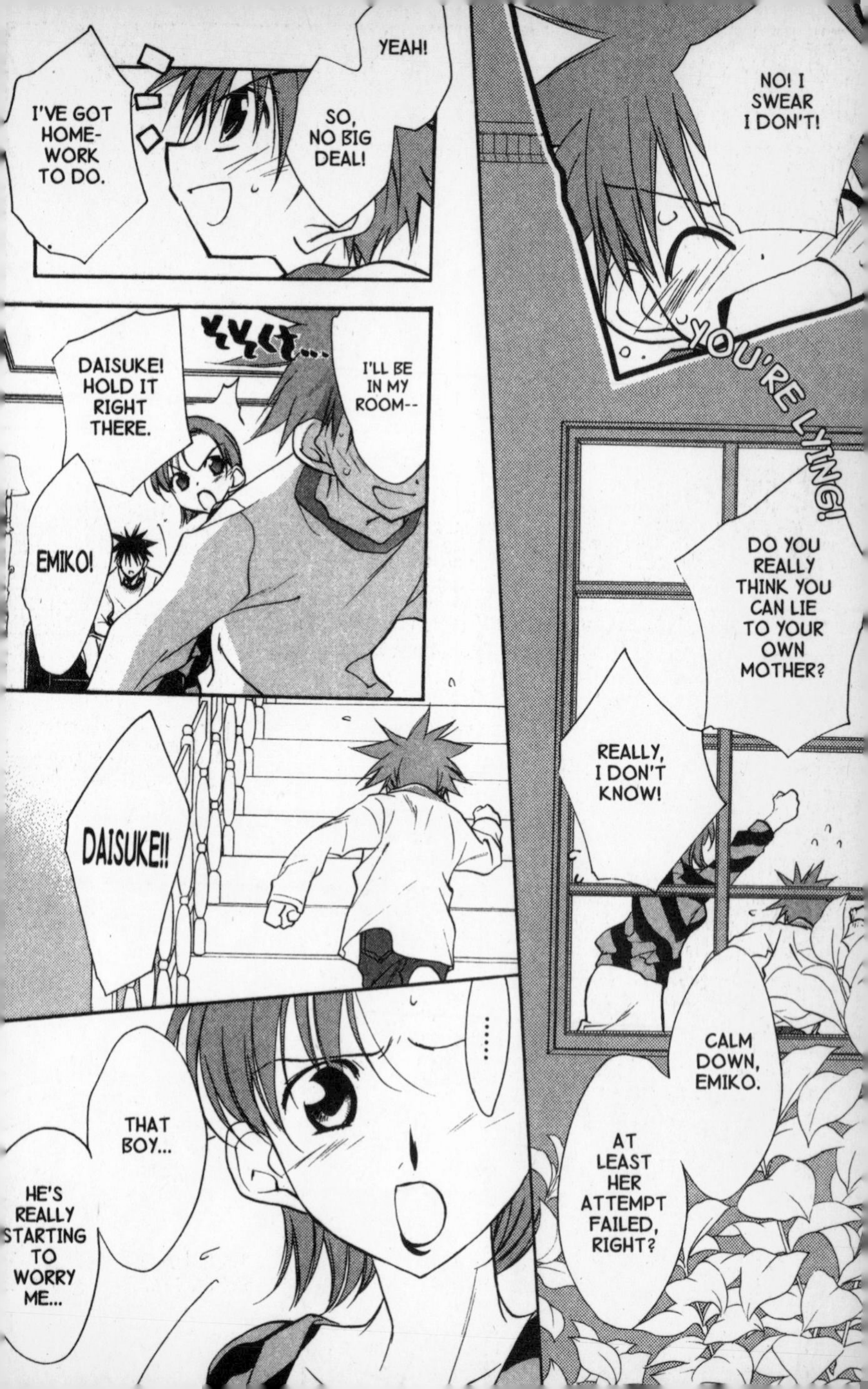

NO! I SWEAR I DON'T!
YOU'RE LYING!
DO YOU REALLY THINK YOU CAN LIE TO YOUR OWN MOTHER?
REALLY, I DON'T KNOW!
CALM DOWN, EMIKO.
AT LEAST HER ATTEMPT FAILED, RIGHT?
YEAH!
SO, NO BIG DEAL!
I'VE GOT HOMEWORK TO DO.
I'LL BE IN MY ROOM--
DAISUKE! HOLD IT RIGHT THERE.
EMIKO!
DAISUKE!!
......
THAT BOY...
HE'S REALLY STARTING TO WORRY ME...

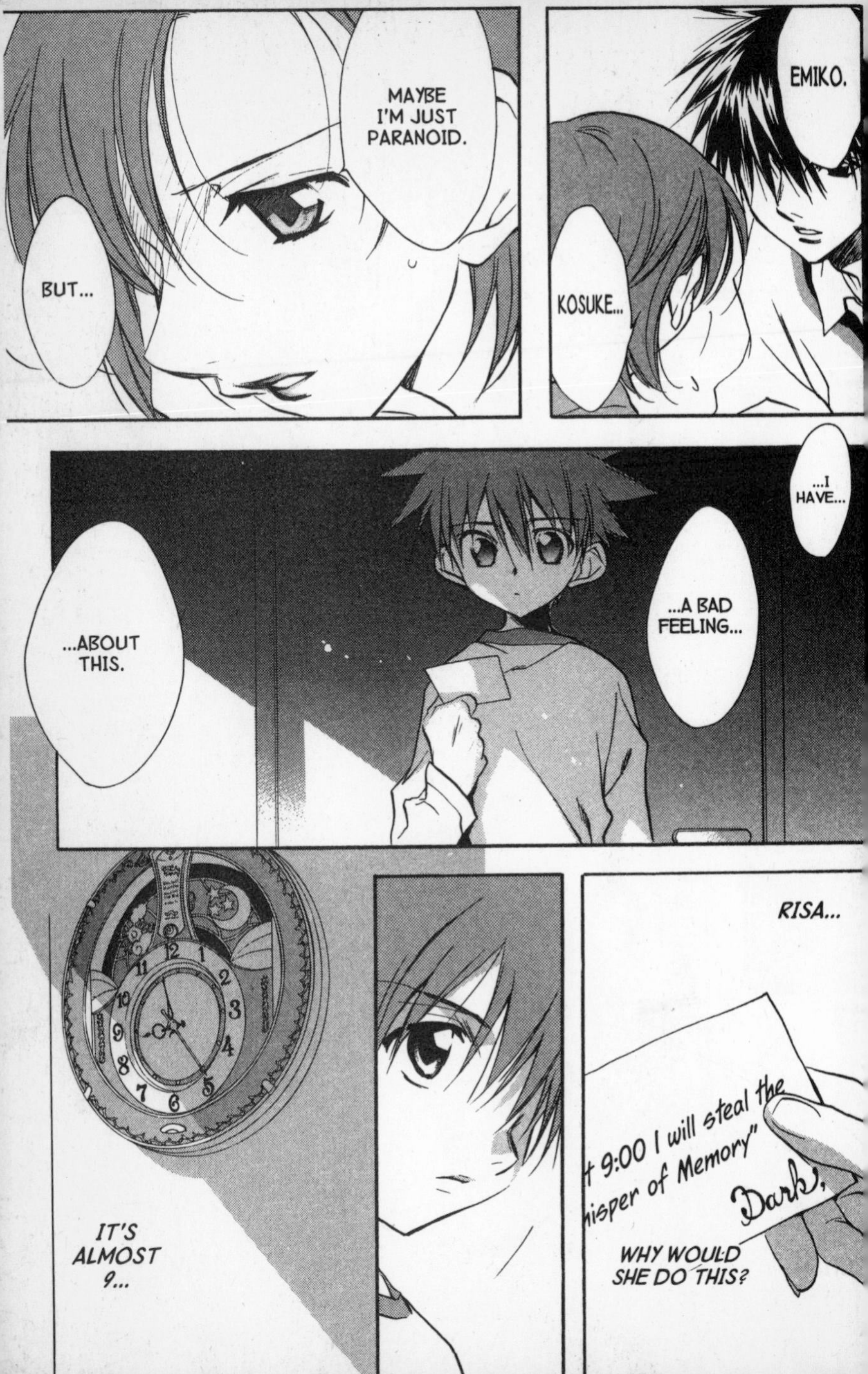
EMIKO.
KOSUKE...
MAYBE I'M JUST PARANOID.
BUT...
...I HAVE...
...A BAD FEELING...
...ABOUT THIS.
RISA...
t 9:00 I will steal the
hisper of Memory"
Dark,
WHY WOULD SHE DO THIS?
IT'S ALMOST 9...

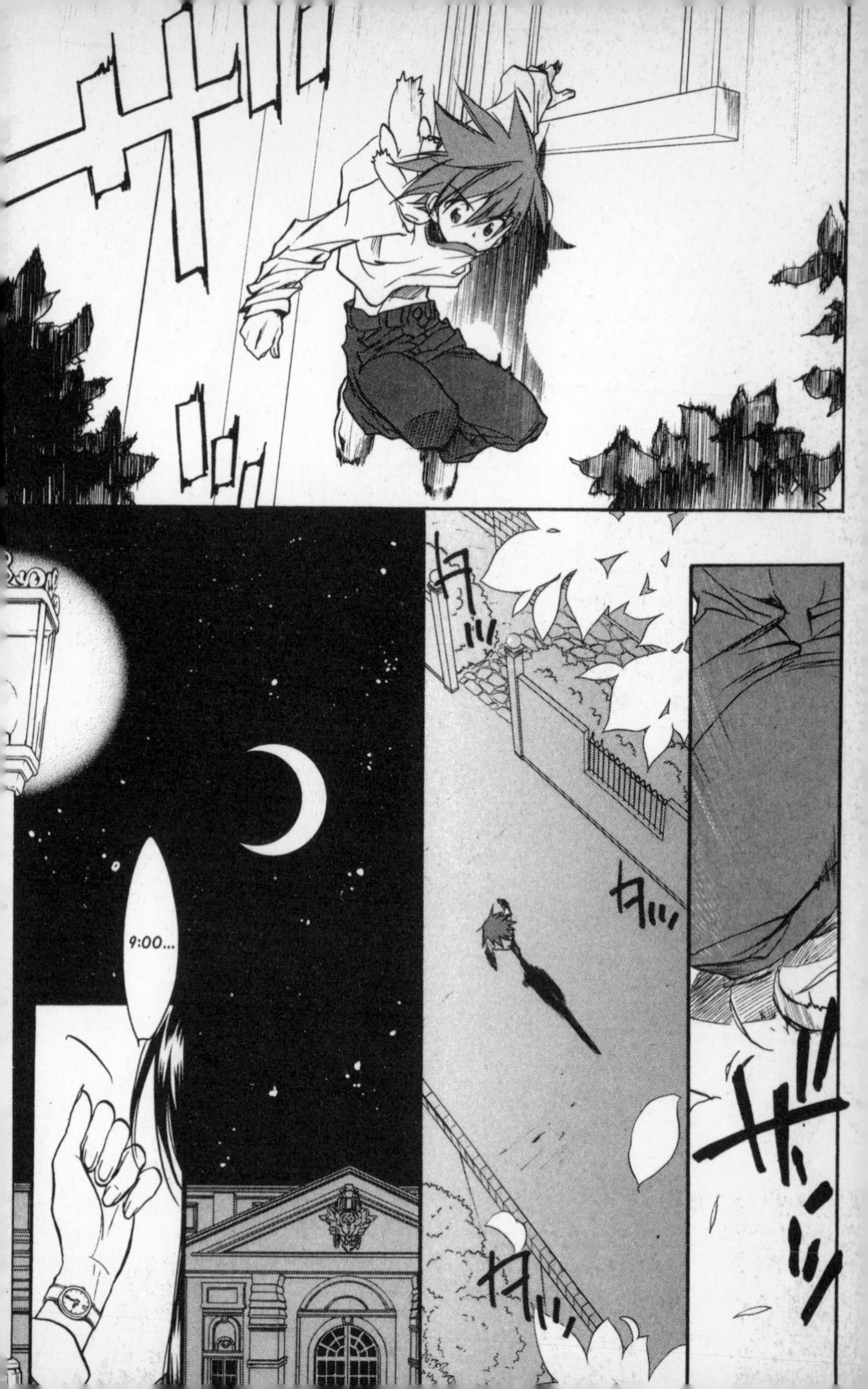

タッ
タッ
タッ
9:00...

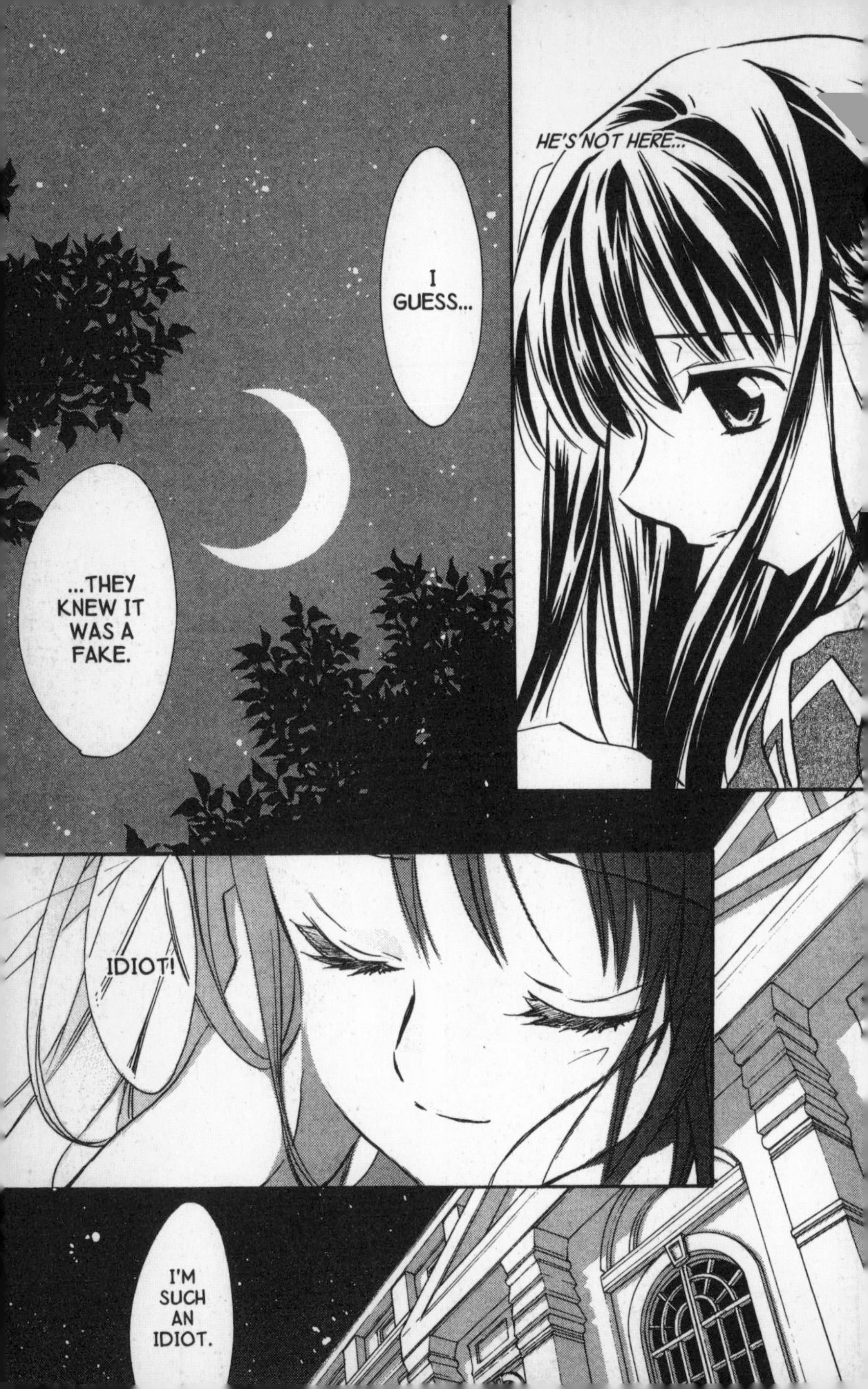
HE'S NOT HERE...
I GUESS...
...THEY KNEW IT WAS A FAKE.
IDIOT!
I'M SUCH AN IDIOT.

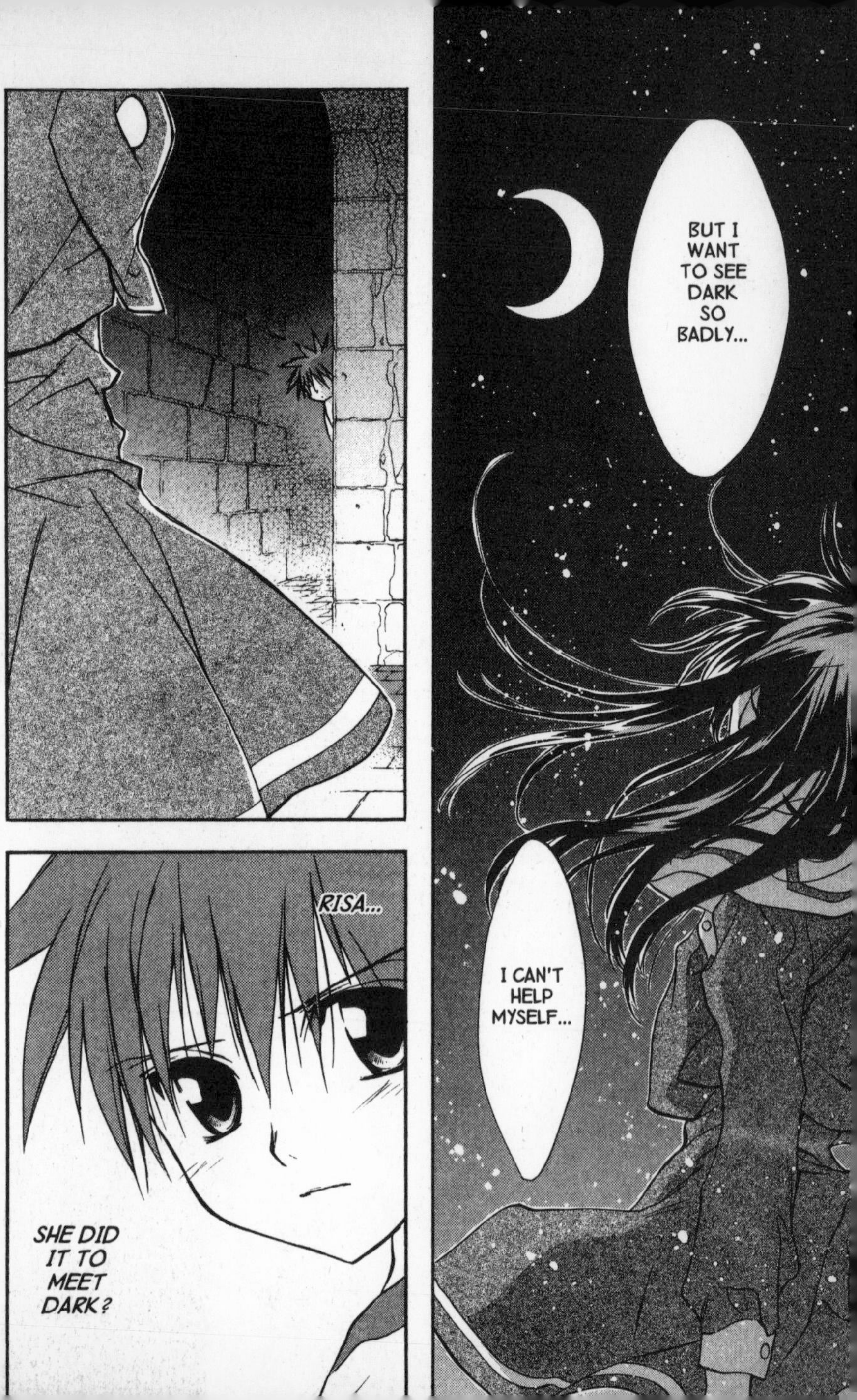
BUT I WANT TO SEE DARK SO BADLY...
I CAN'T HELP MYSELF...
RISA...
SHE DID IT TO MEET DARK?

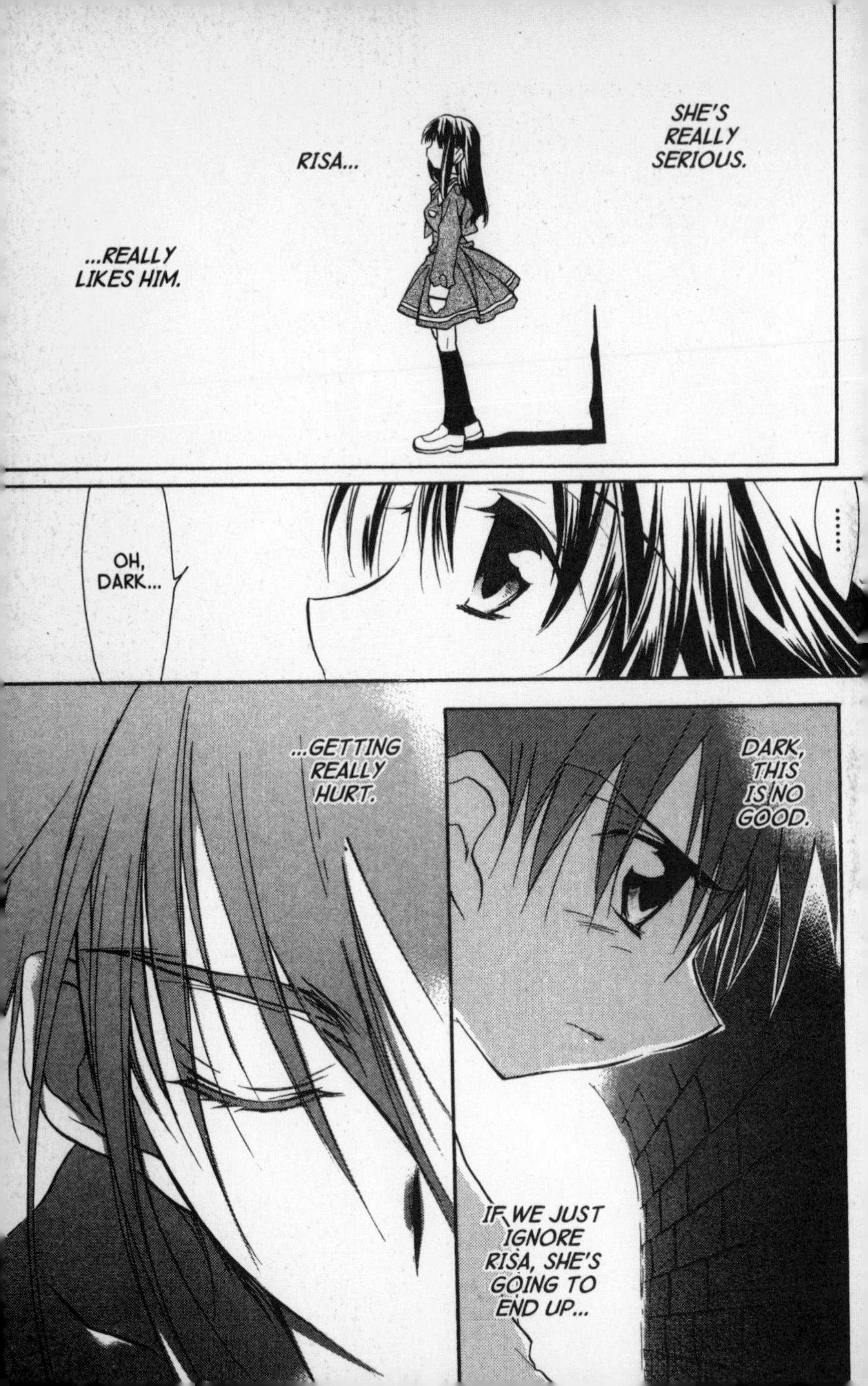
SHE'S REALLY SERIOUS.
RISA...
...REALLY LIKES HIM.
......
OH, DARK...
DARK, THIS IS NO GOOD.
IF WE JUST IGNORE RISA, SHE'S GOING TO END UP...
...GETTING REALLY HURT.

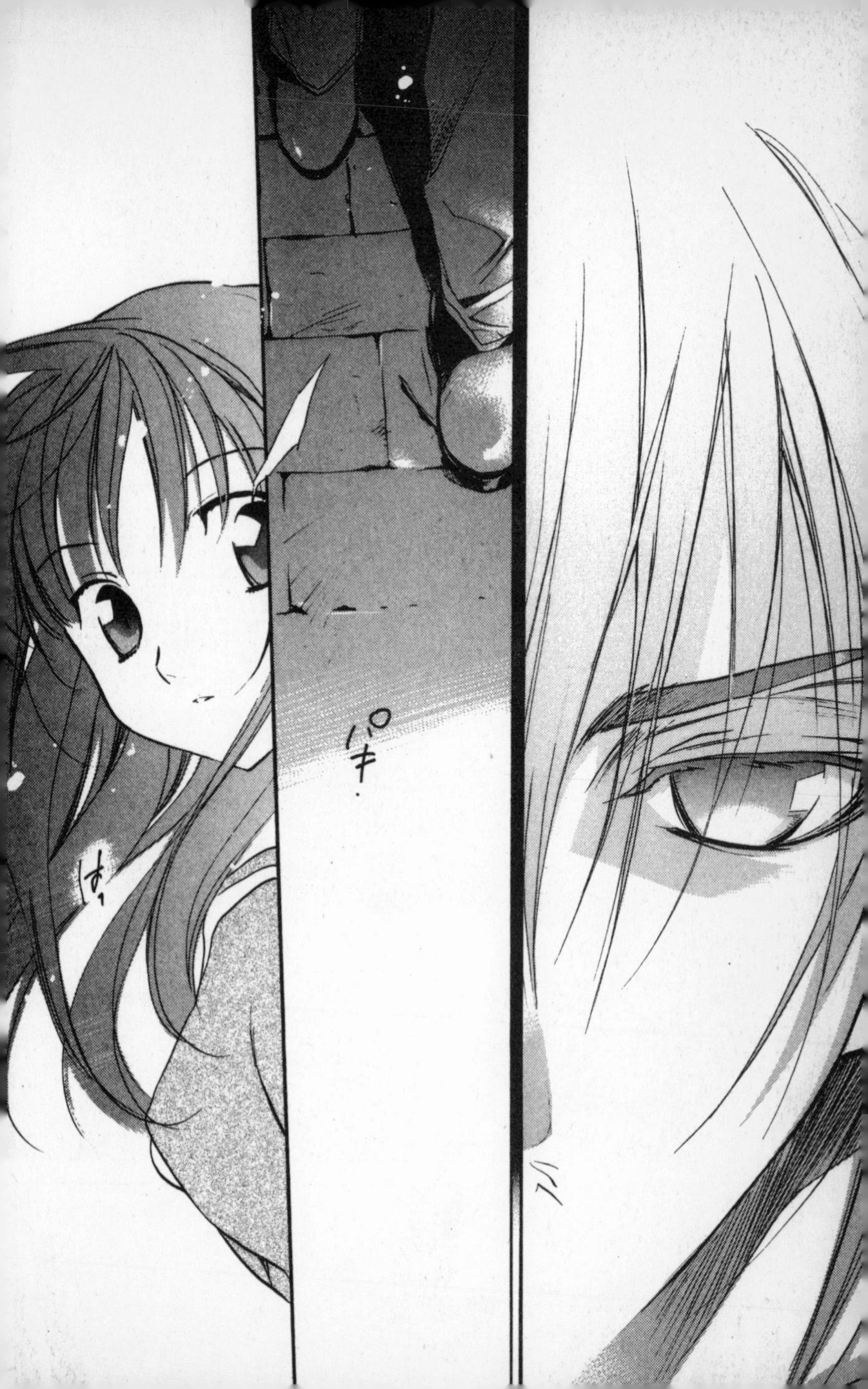
パキ.
す,

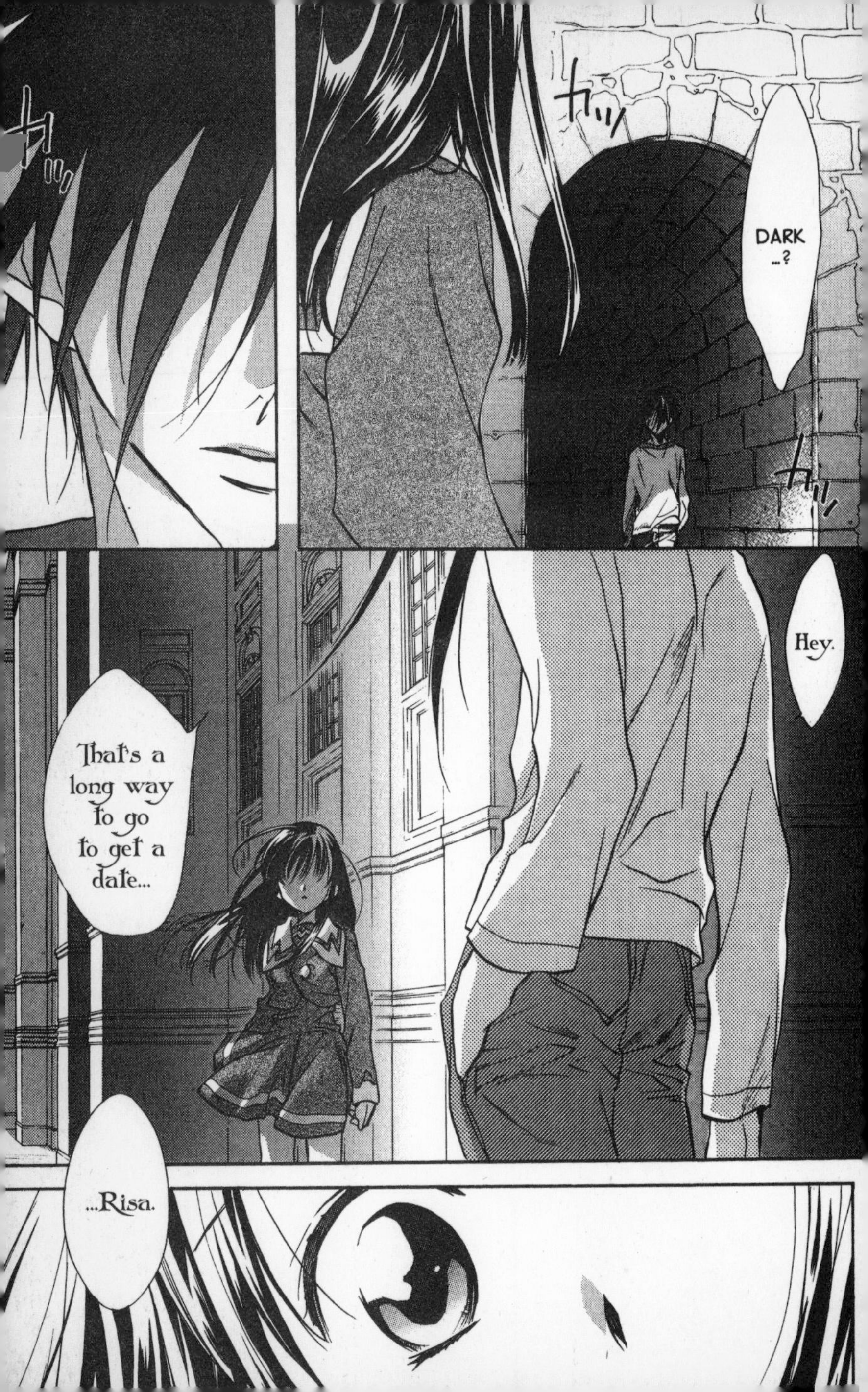
カッ
DARK ...?
カッ
カッ
Hey.
That's a long way to go to get a date...
...Risa.

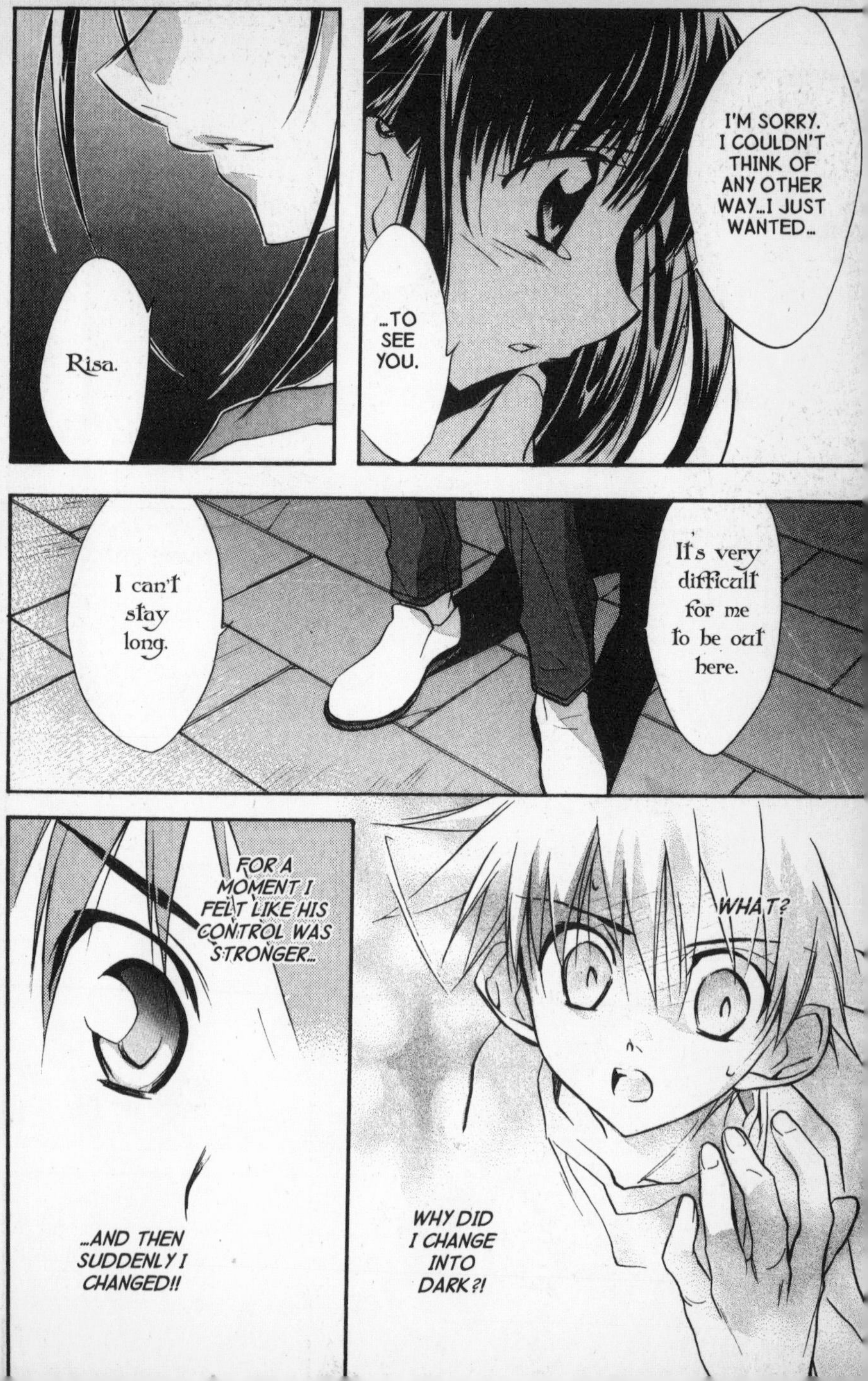

I'M SORRY. I COULDN'T THINK OF ANY OTHER WAY...I JUST WANTED...
...TO SEE YOU.
Risa.
It's very difficult for me to be out here.
I can't stay long.
WHAT?
WHY DID I CHANGE INTO DARK?!
FOR A MOMENT I FELT LIKE HIS CONTROL WAS STRONGER...
...AND THEN SUDDENLY I CHANGED!!

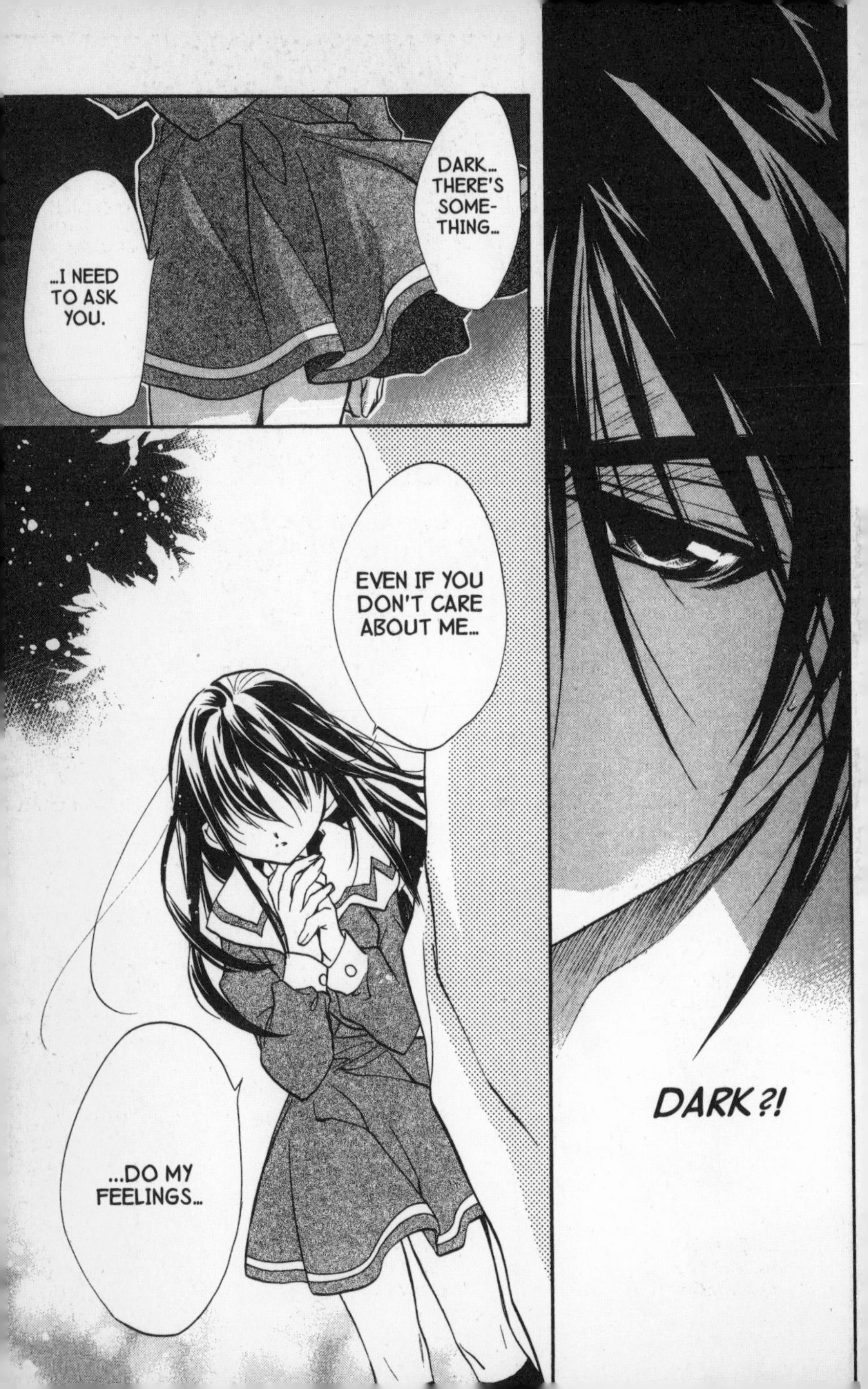
DARK... THERE'S SOMETHING...
...I NEED TO ASK YOU.
EVEN IF YOU DON'T CARE ABOUT ME...
...DO MY FEELINGS...
DARK?!

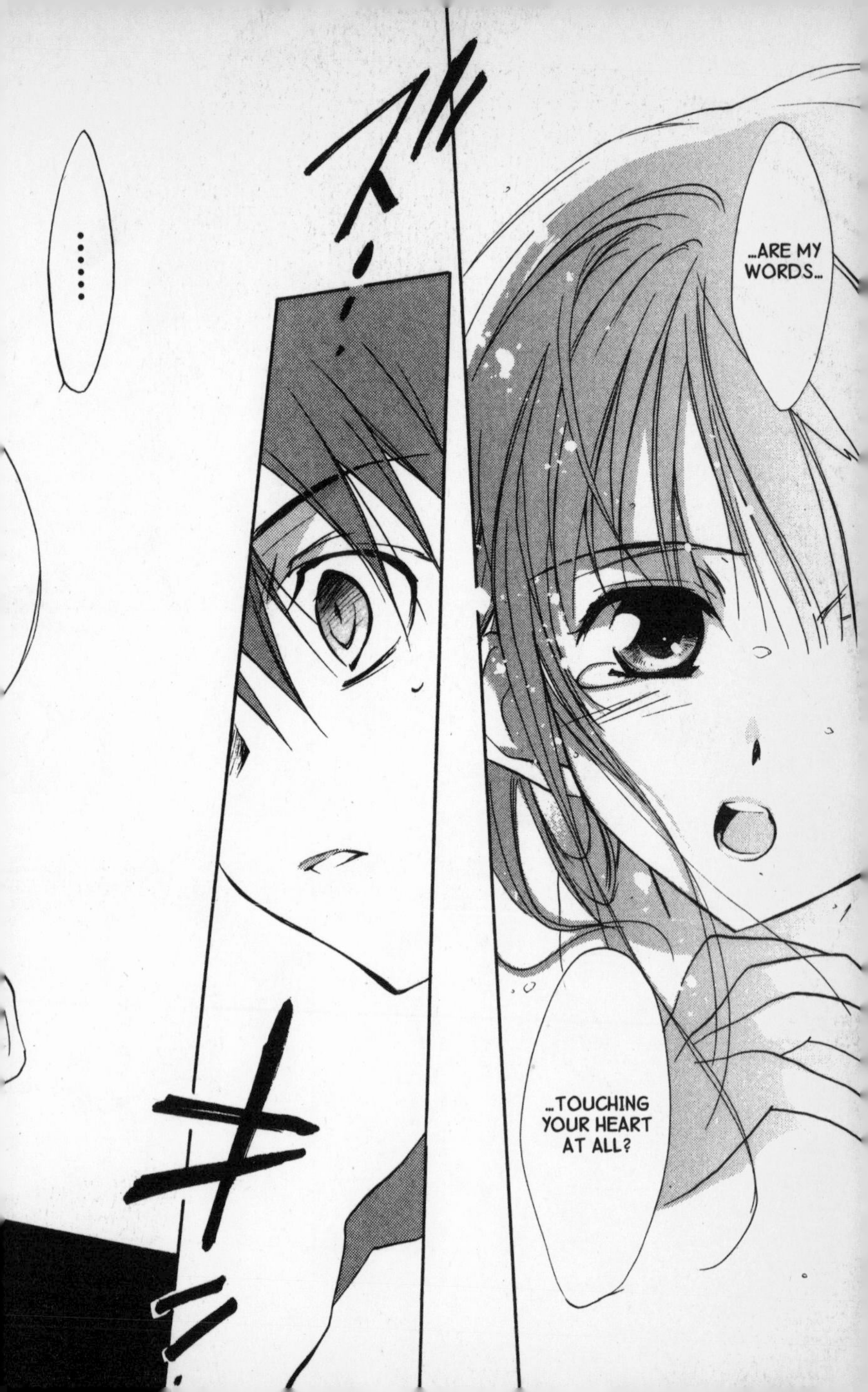
...ARE MY WORDS...
...TOUCHING YOUR HEART AT ALL?
......

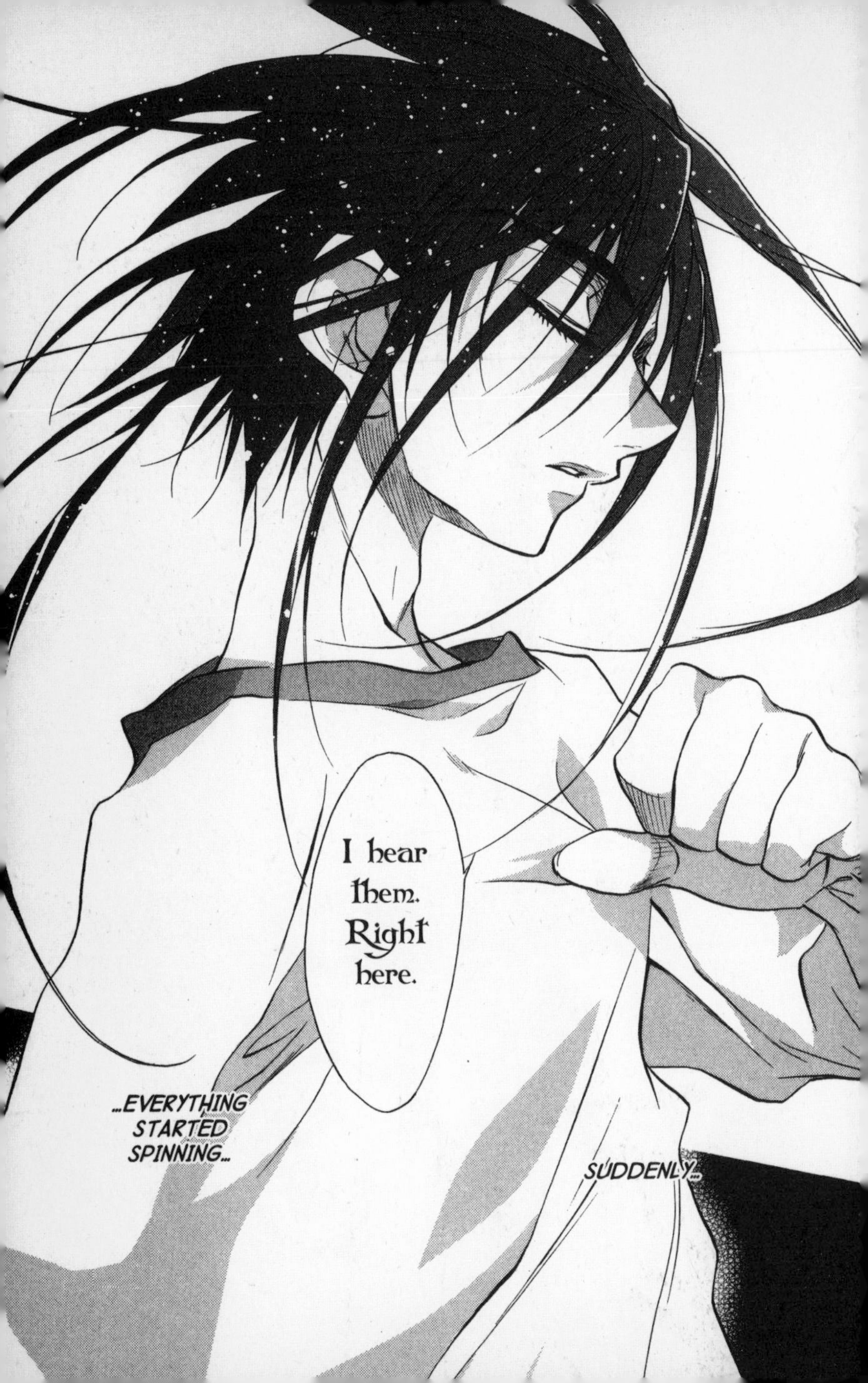
I hear them. Right here.
SUDDENLY...
...EVERYTHING STARTED SPINNING...

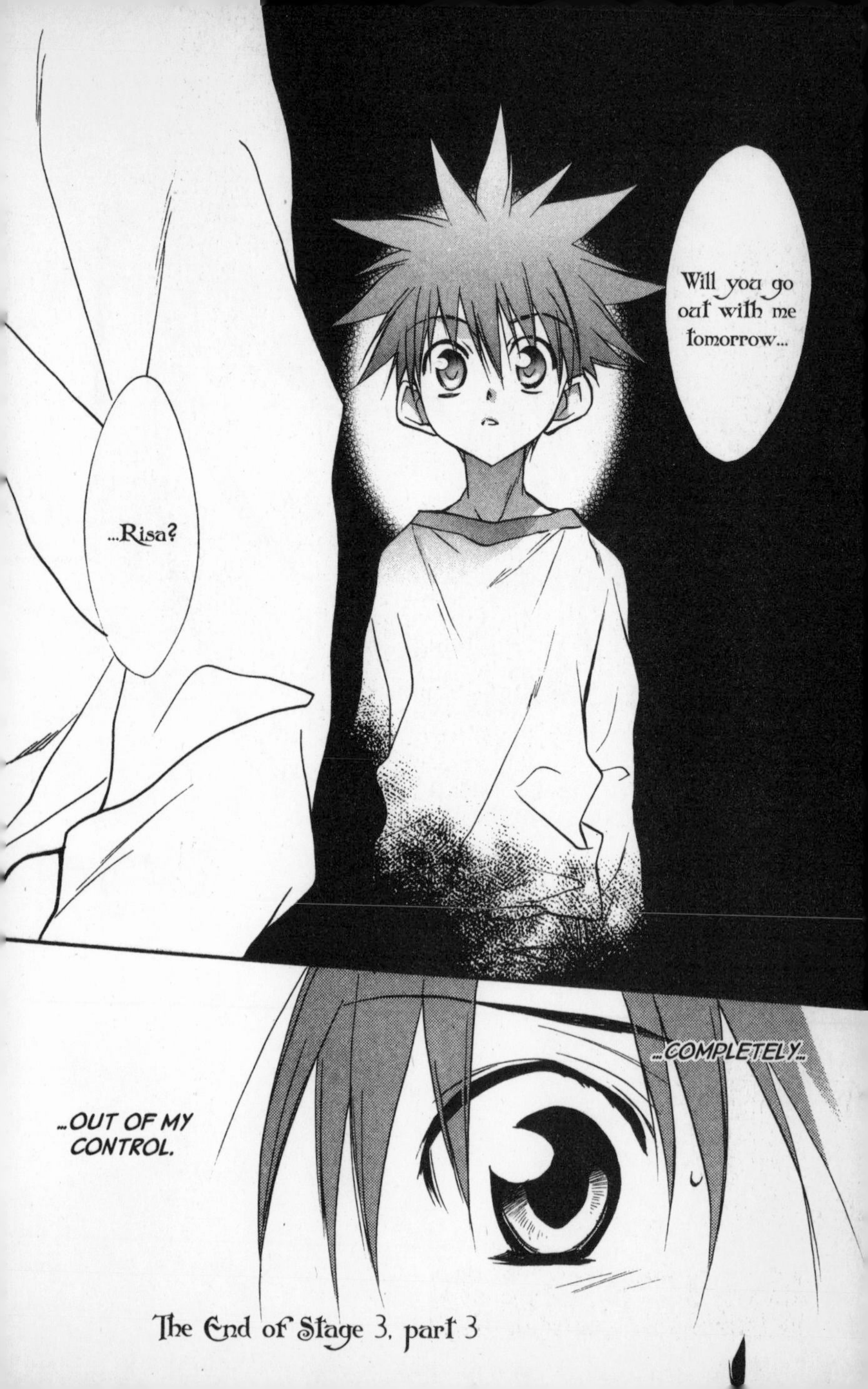
Will you go out with me tomorrow...
...Risa?
...COMPLETELY...
...OUT OF MY CONTROL.
The End of Stage 3, part 3

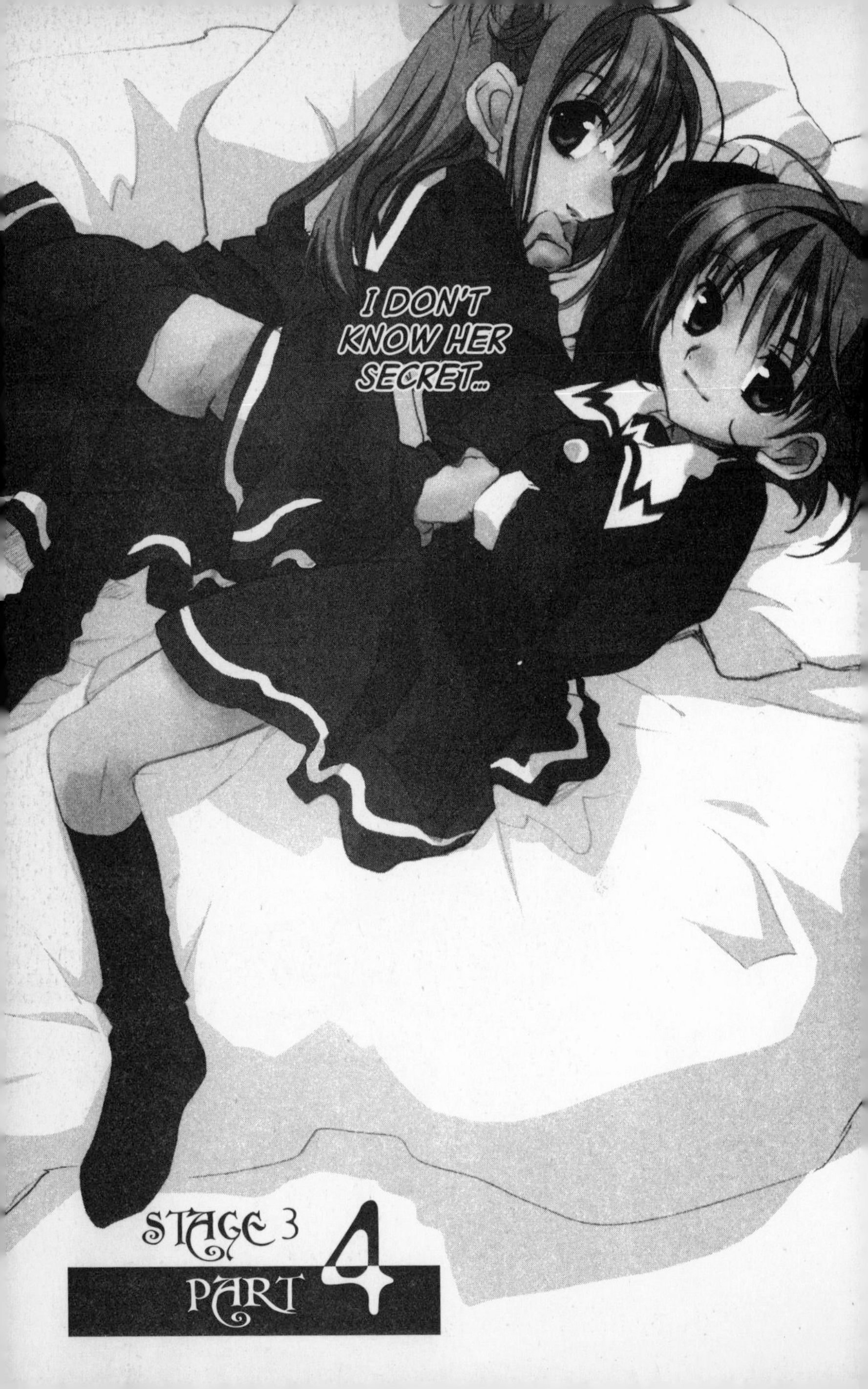
I DON'T KNOW HER SECRET...
STAGE 3
PART 4

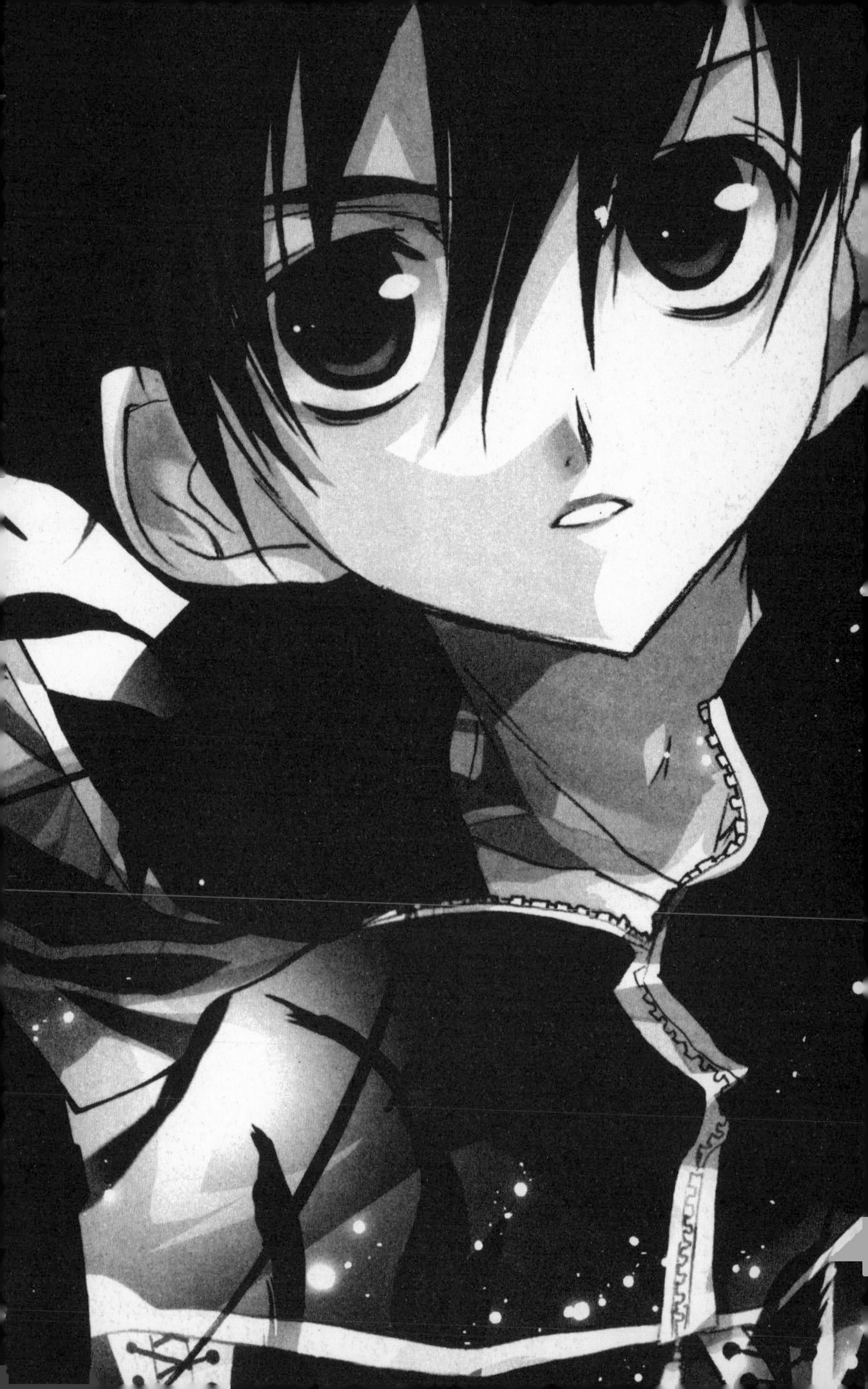

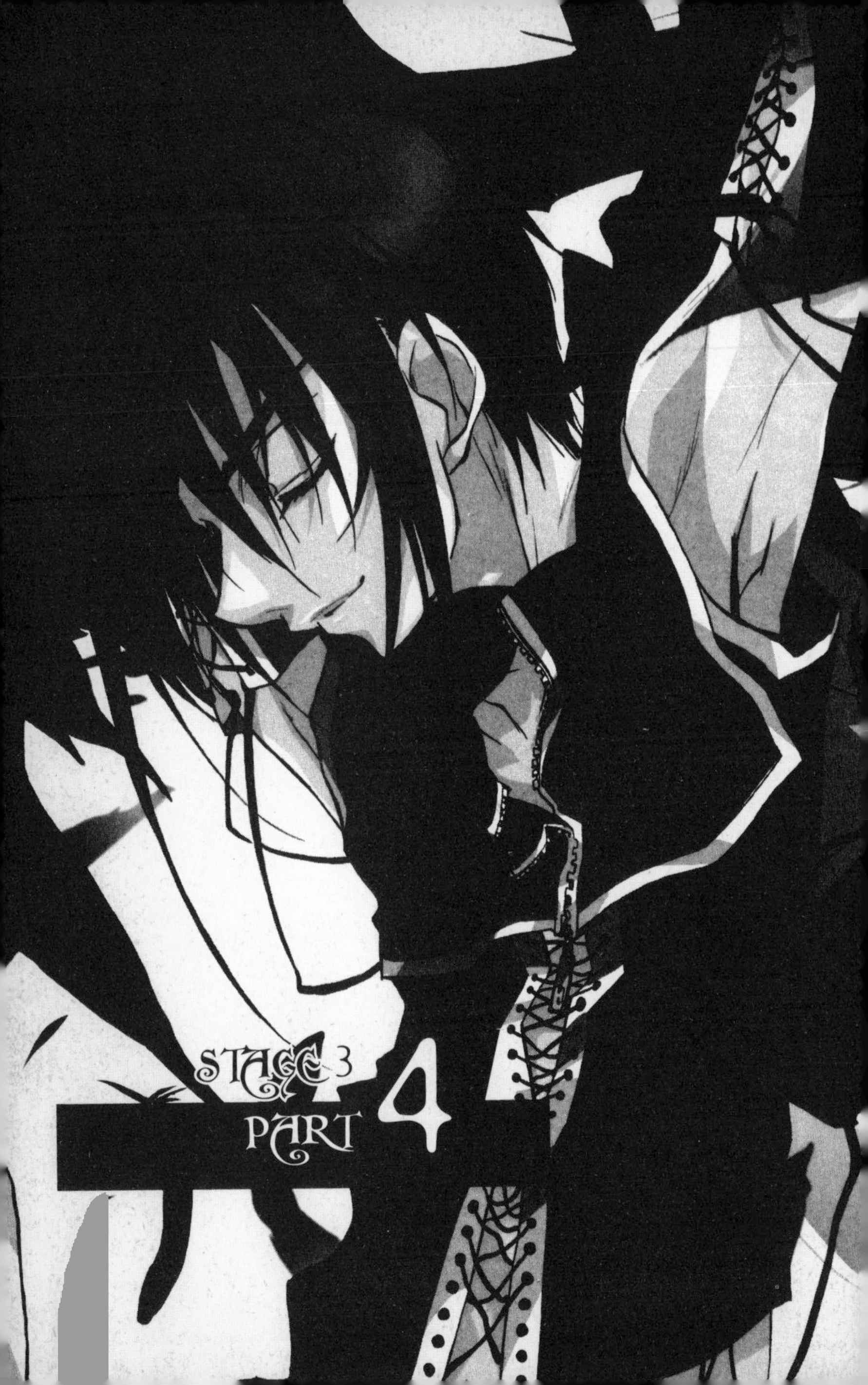
STAGE 3
PART 4

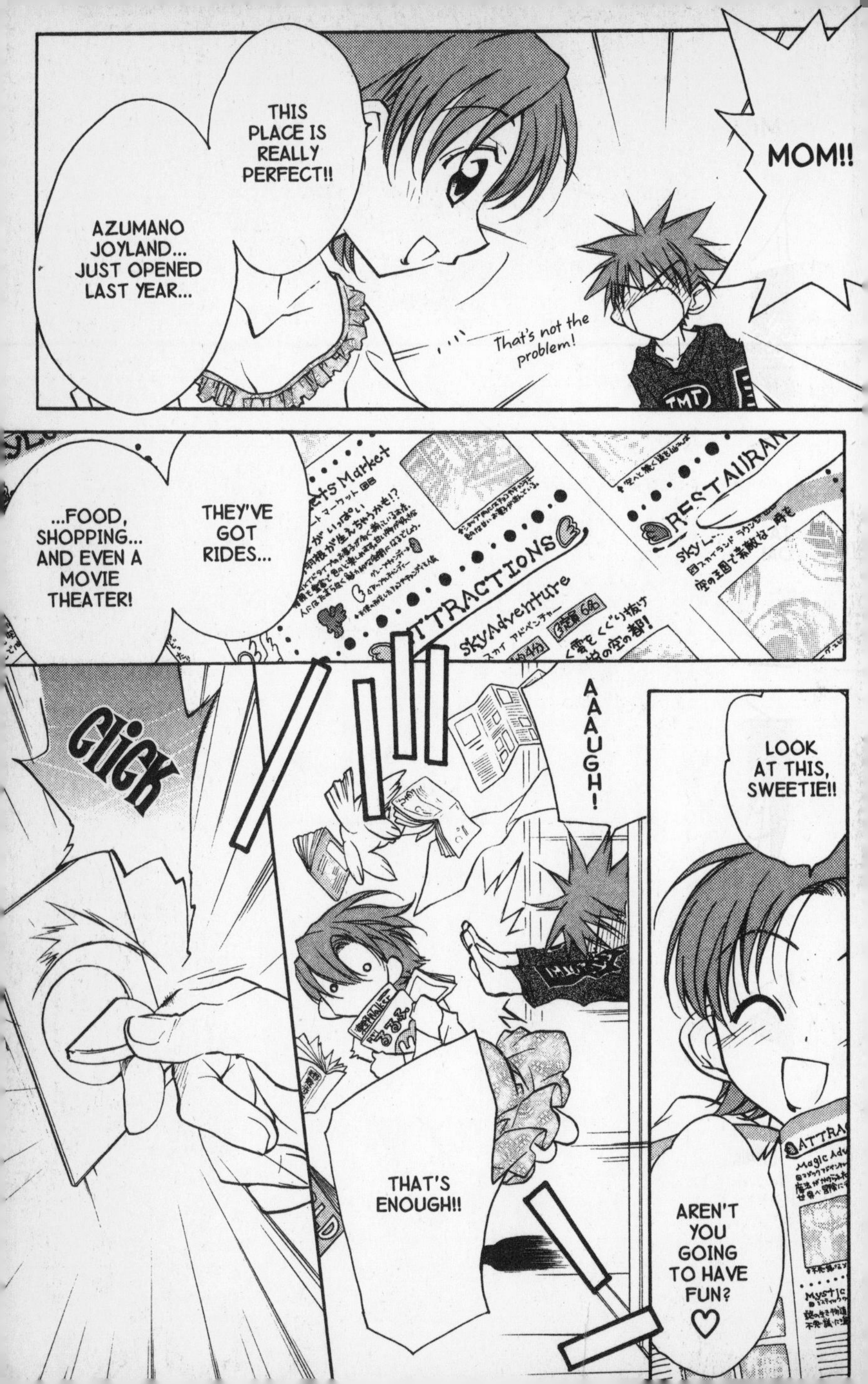
MOM!!
That's not the problem!
THIS PLACE IS REALLY PERFECT!!
AZUMANO JOYLAND... JUST OPENED LAST YEAR...
THEY'VE GOT RIDES...
...FOOD, SHOPPING... AND EVEN A MOVIE THEATER!
LOOK AT THIS, SWEETIE!!
AREN'T YOU GOING TO HAVE FUN? ♡
AAAUGH!
THAT'S ENOUGH!!
CLICK

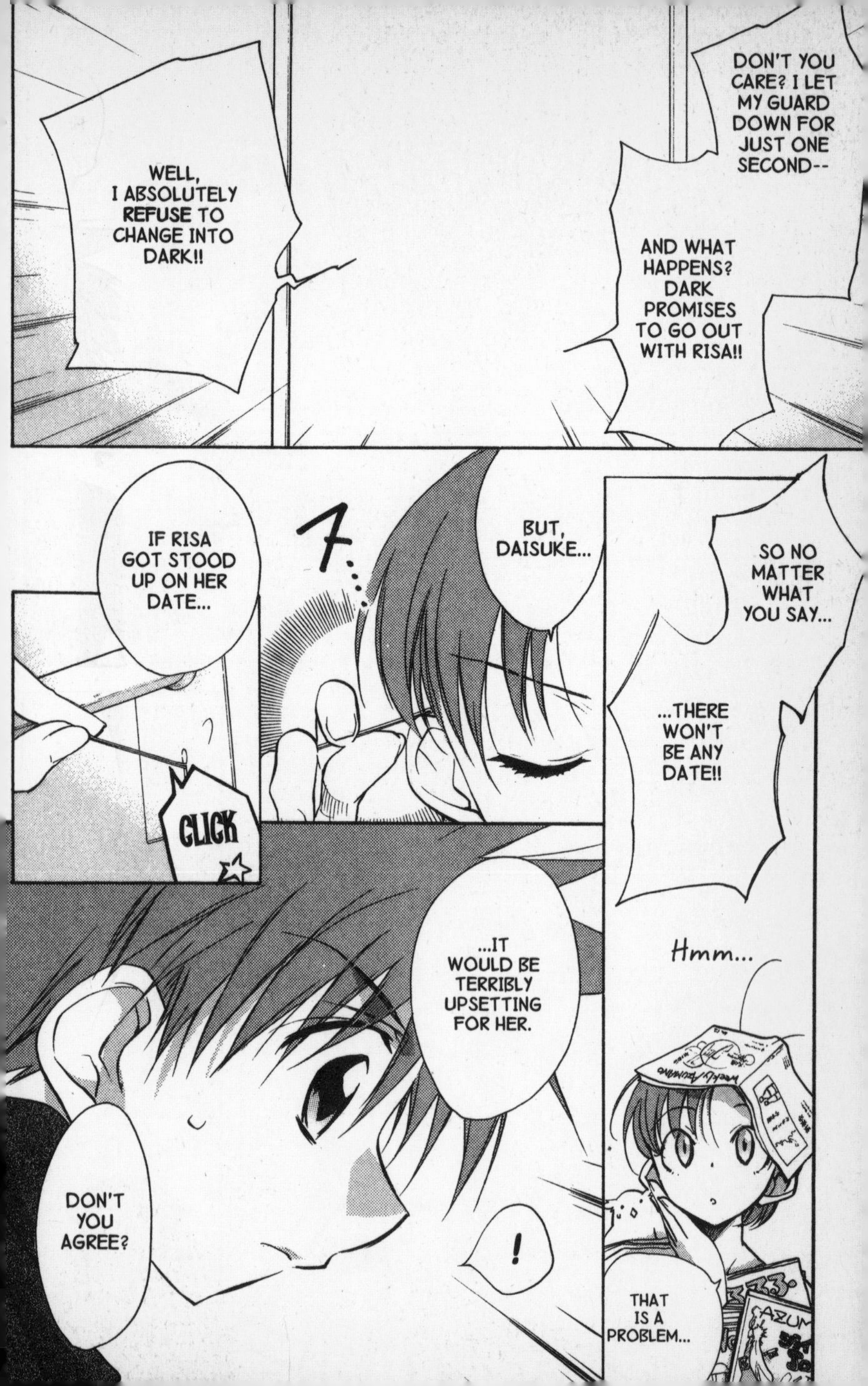
DON'T YOU CARE? I LET MY GUARD DOWN FOR JUST ONE SECOND--
AND WHAT HAPPENS? DARK PROMISES TO GO OUT WITH RISA!!
WELL, I ABSOLUTELY REFUSE TO CHANGE INTO DARK!!
SO NO MATTER WHAT YOU SAY...
...THERE WON'T BE ANY DATE!!
BUT, DAISUKE...
IF RISA GOT STOOD UP ON HER DATE...
CLICK
Hmm...
THAT IS A PROBLEM...
...IT WOULD BE TERRIBLY UPSETTING FOR HER.
!
DON'T YOU AGREE?

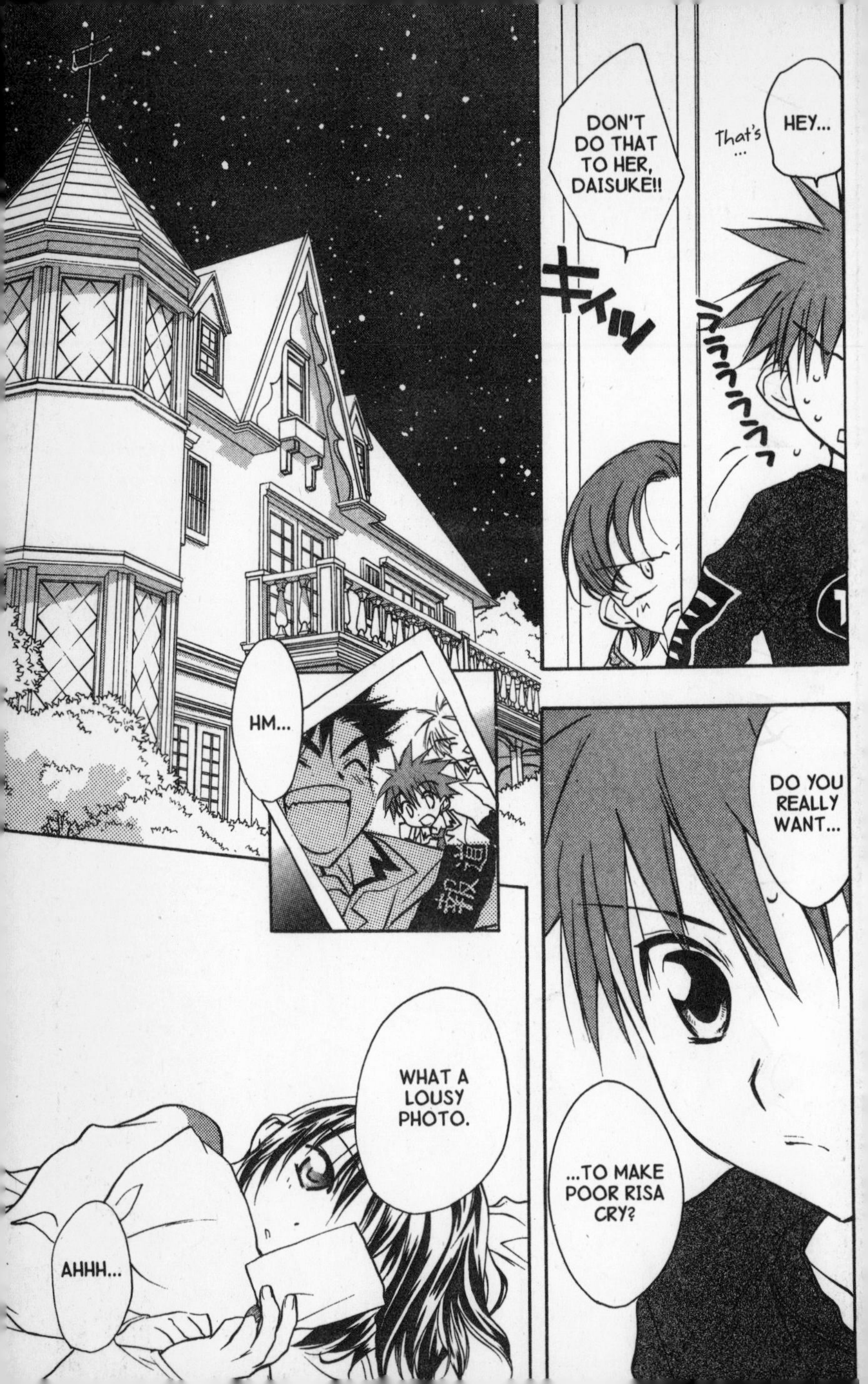
HEY...
That's ...
DON'T DO THAT TO HER, DAISUKE!!
DO YOU REALLY WANT...
...TO MAKE POOR RISA CRY?
HM...
WHAT A LOUSY PHOTO.
AHHH...

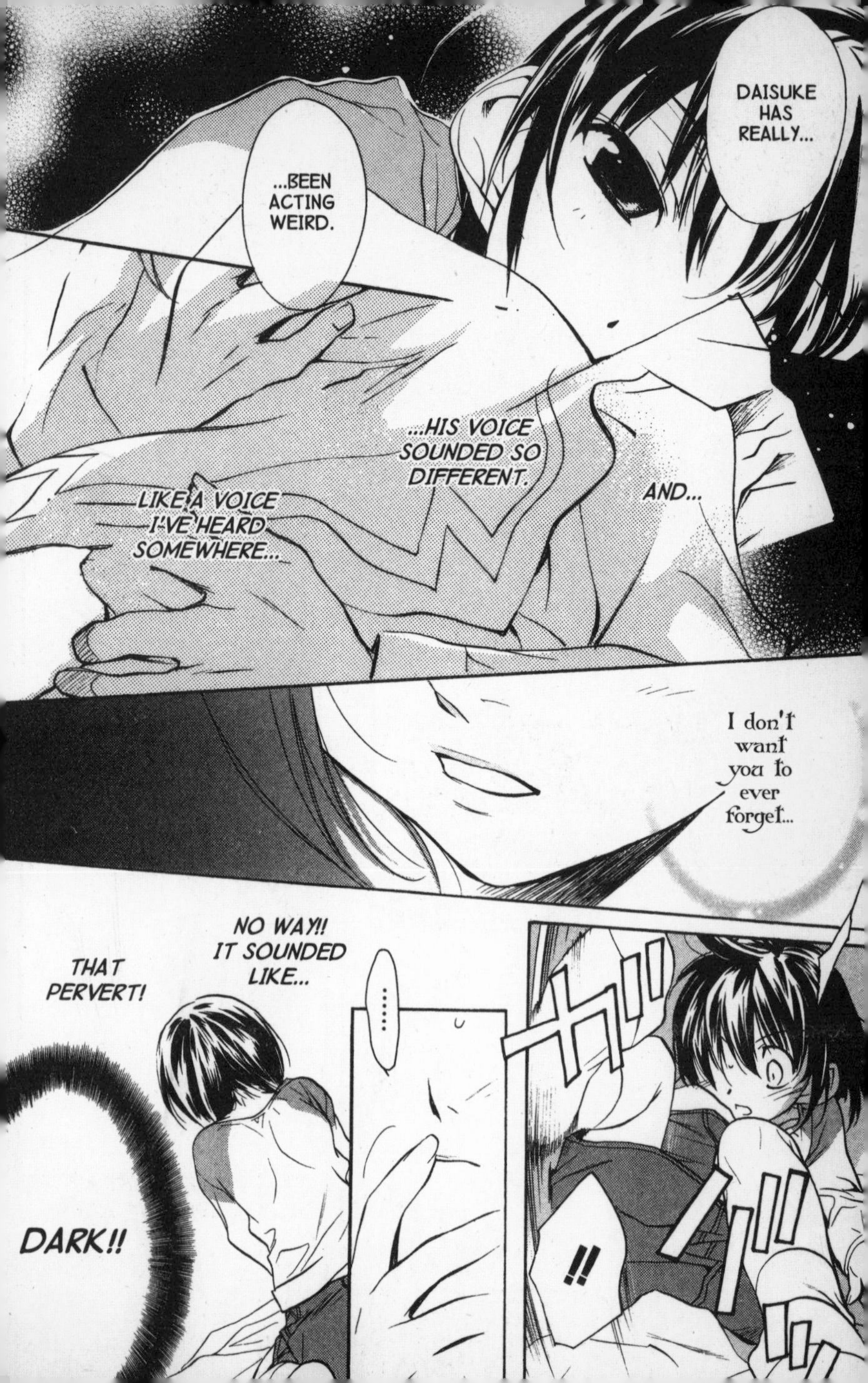
DAISUKE HAS REALLY...
...BEEN ACTING WEIRD.
AND...
...HIS VOICE SOUNDED SO DIFFERENT.
LIKE A VOICE I'VE HEARD SOMEWHERE...
I don't want you to ever forget...
!!
......
NO WAY!! IT SOUNDED LIKE...
THAT PERVERT!
DARK!!

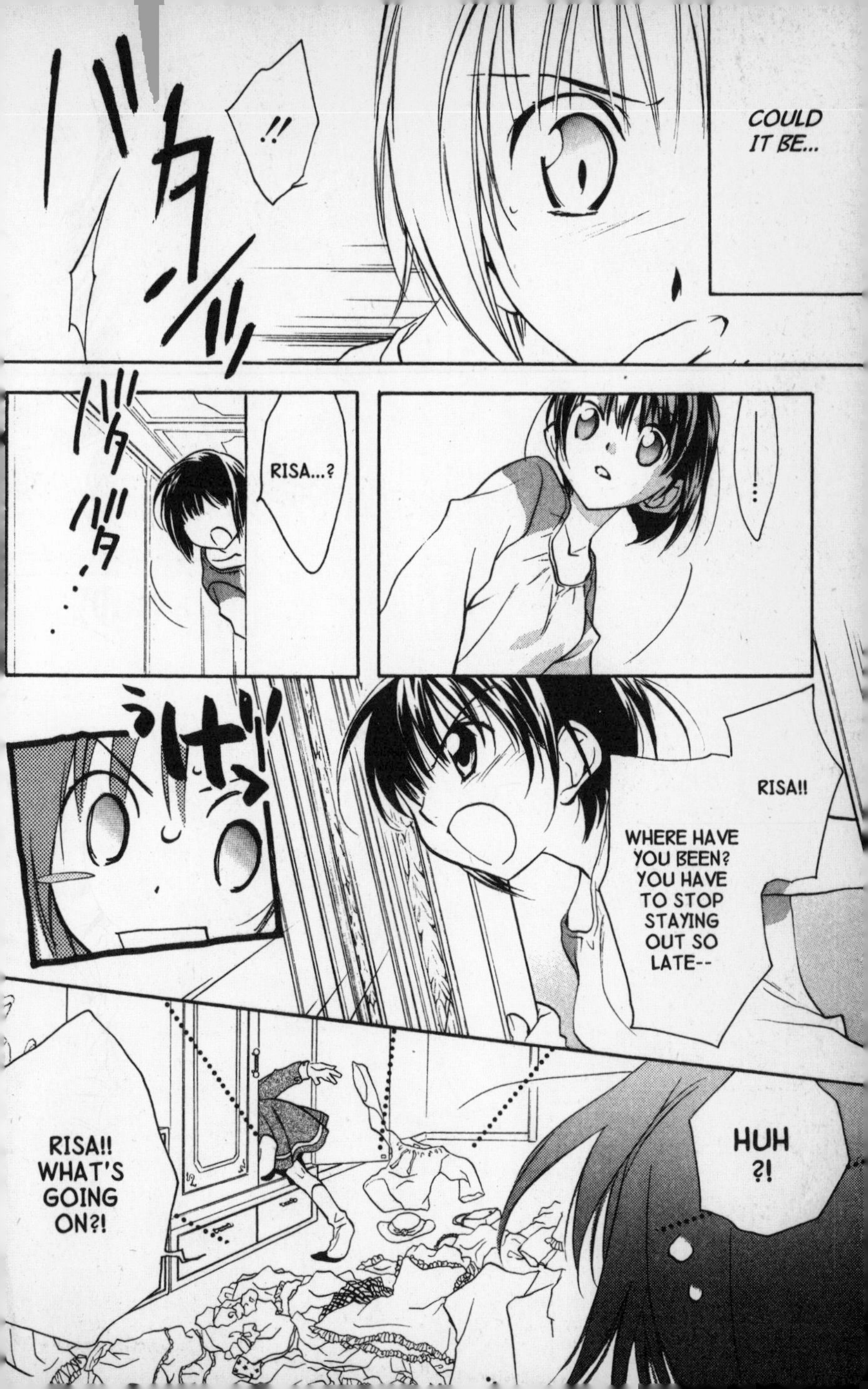
COULD IT BE...
!!
バタンッ
バタバタ...
......
RISA...?
RISA!!
WHERE HAVE YOU BEEN? YOU HAVE TO STOP STAYING OUT SO LATE--
うげッ
HUH ?!
RISA!! WHAT'S GOING ON?!

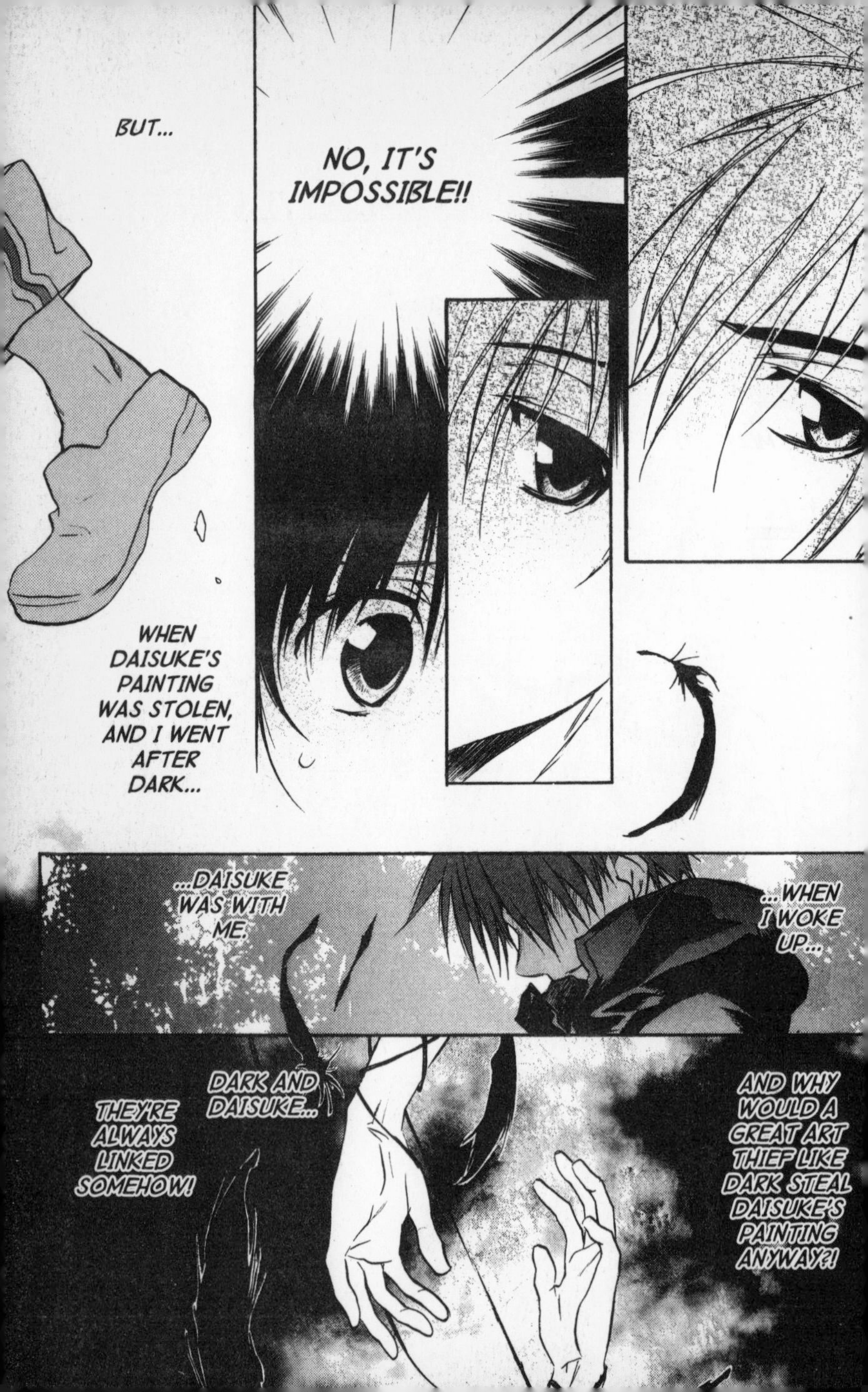
NO, IT'S IMPOSSIBLE!!
BUT...
WHEN DAISUKE'S PAINTING WAS STOLEN, AND I WENT AFTER DARK...
...WHEN I WOKE UP...
...DAISUKE WAS WITH ME.
AND WHY WOULD A GREAT ART THIEF LIKE DARK STEAL DAISUKE'S PAINTING ANYWAY?!
DARK AND DAISUKE...
THEY'RE ALWAYS LINKED SOMEHOW!

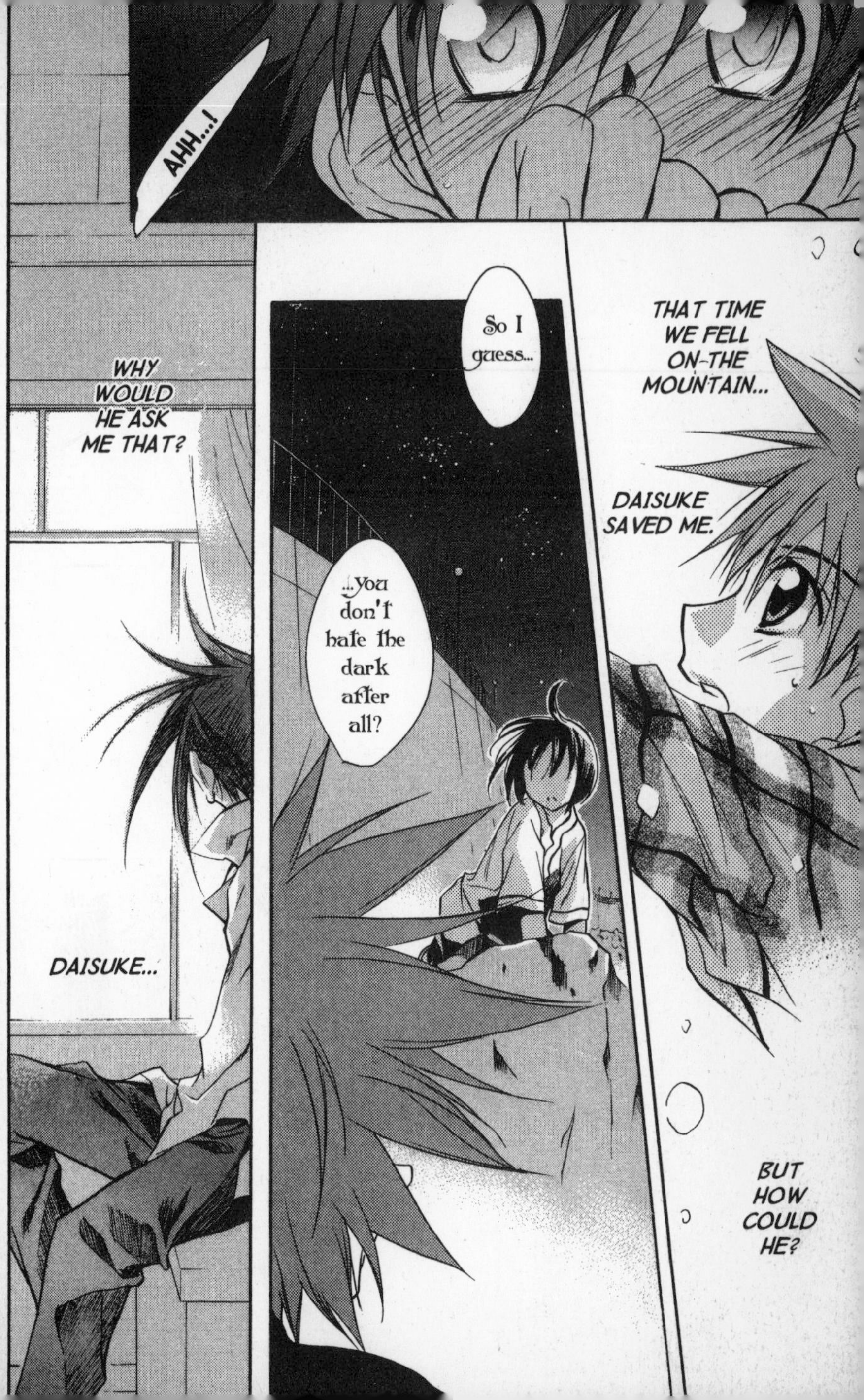
AHH...!
THAT TIME WE FELL ON-THE MOUNTAIN...
DAISUKE SAVED ME.
BUT HOW COULD HE?
So I guess...
...you don't hate the dark after all?
WHY WOULD HE ASK ME THAT?
DAISUKE...

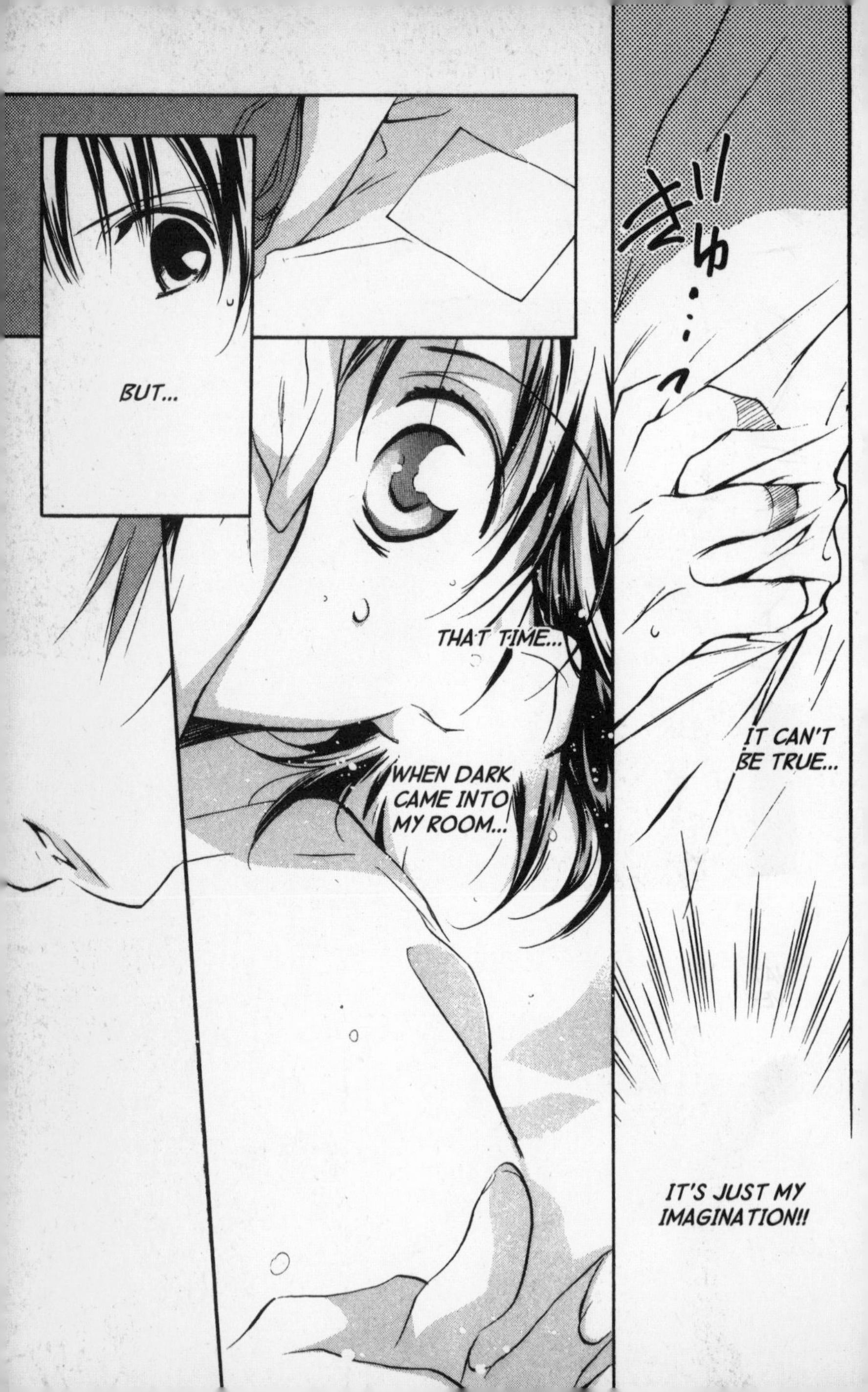

きゅ…っ
IT CAN'T BE TRUE...
IT'S JUST MY IMAGINATION!!
BUT...
THAT TIME...
WHEN DARK CAME INTO MY ROOM...

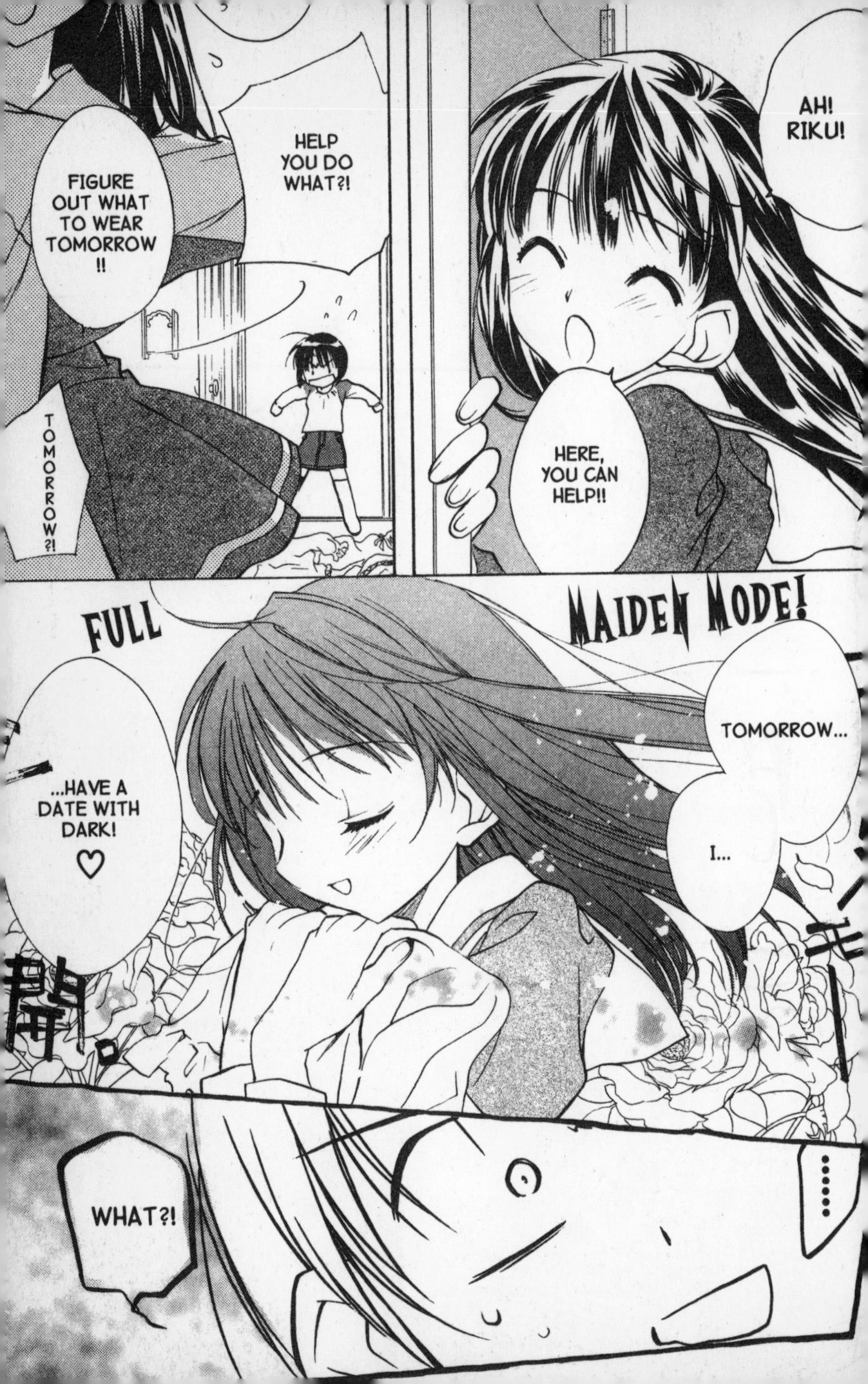

AH! RIKU!
HERE, YOU CAN HELP!!
HELP YOU DO WHAT?!
FIGURE OUT WHAT TO WEAR TOMORROW !!
TOMORROW?!
FULL MAIDEN MODE!
TOMORROW...
I...
...HAVE A DATE WITH DARK! ♡
......
WHAT?!

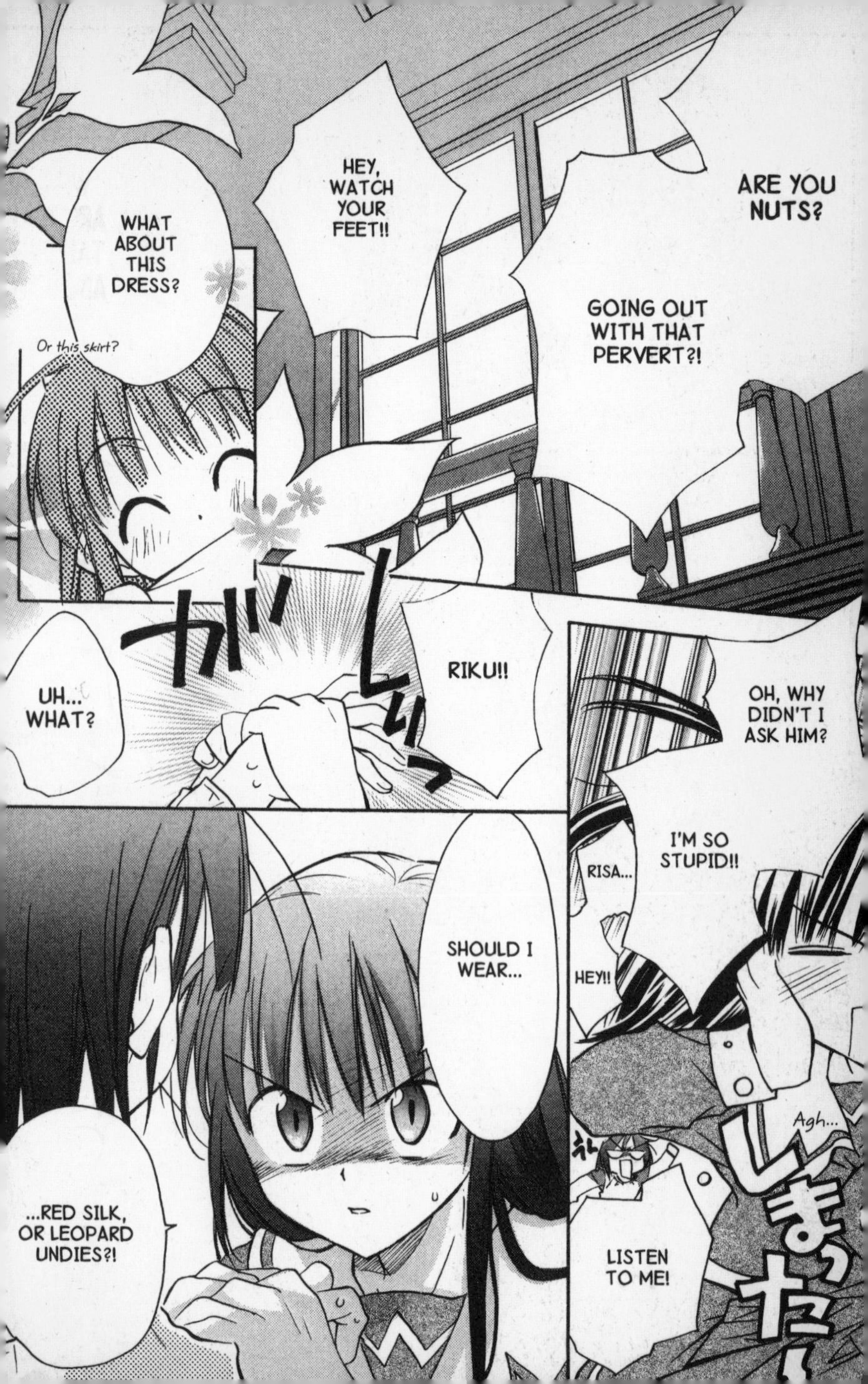
ARE YOU NUTS?
GOING OUT WITH THAT PERVERT?!
HEY, WATCH YOUR FEET!!
WHAT ABOUT THIS DRESS?
Or this skirt?
OH, WHY DIDN'T I ASK HIM?
I'M SO STUPID!!
RISA...
HEY!!
Agh...
LISTEN TO ME!
しまった
RIKU!!
UH... WHAT?
SHOULD I WEAR...
...RED SILK, OR LEOPARD UNDIES?!

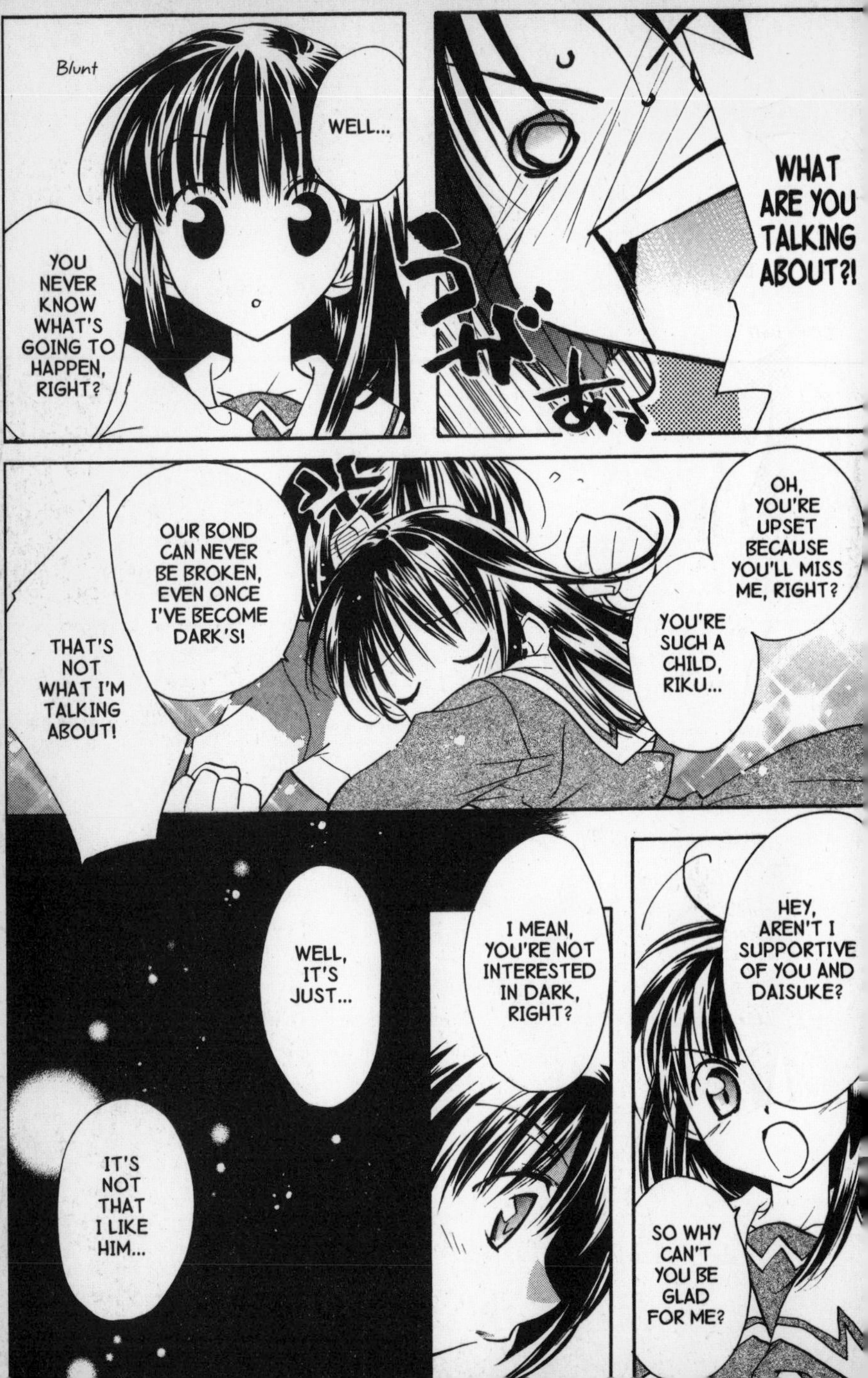
WHAT ARE YOU TALKING ABOUT?!
Blunt
WELL...
YOU NEVER KNOW WHAT'S GOING TO HAPPEN, RIGHT?
OH, YOU'RE UPSET BECAUSE YOU'LL MISS ME, RIGHT?
YOU'RE SUCH A CHILD, RIKU...
OUR BOND CAN NEVER BE BROKEN, EVEN ONCE I'VE BECOME DARK'S!
THAT'S NOT WHAT I'M TALKING ABOUT!
HEY, AREN'T I SUPPORTIVE OF YOU AND DAISUKE?
SO WHY CAN'T YOU BE GLAD FOR ME?
I MEAN, YOU'RE NOT INTERESTED IN DARK, RIGHT?
WELL, IT'S JUST...
IT'S NOT THAT I LIKE HIM...

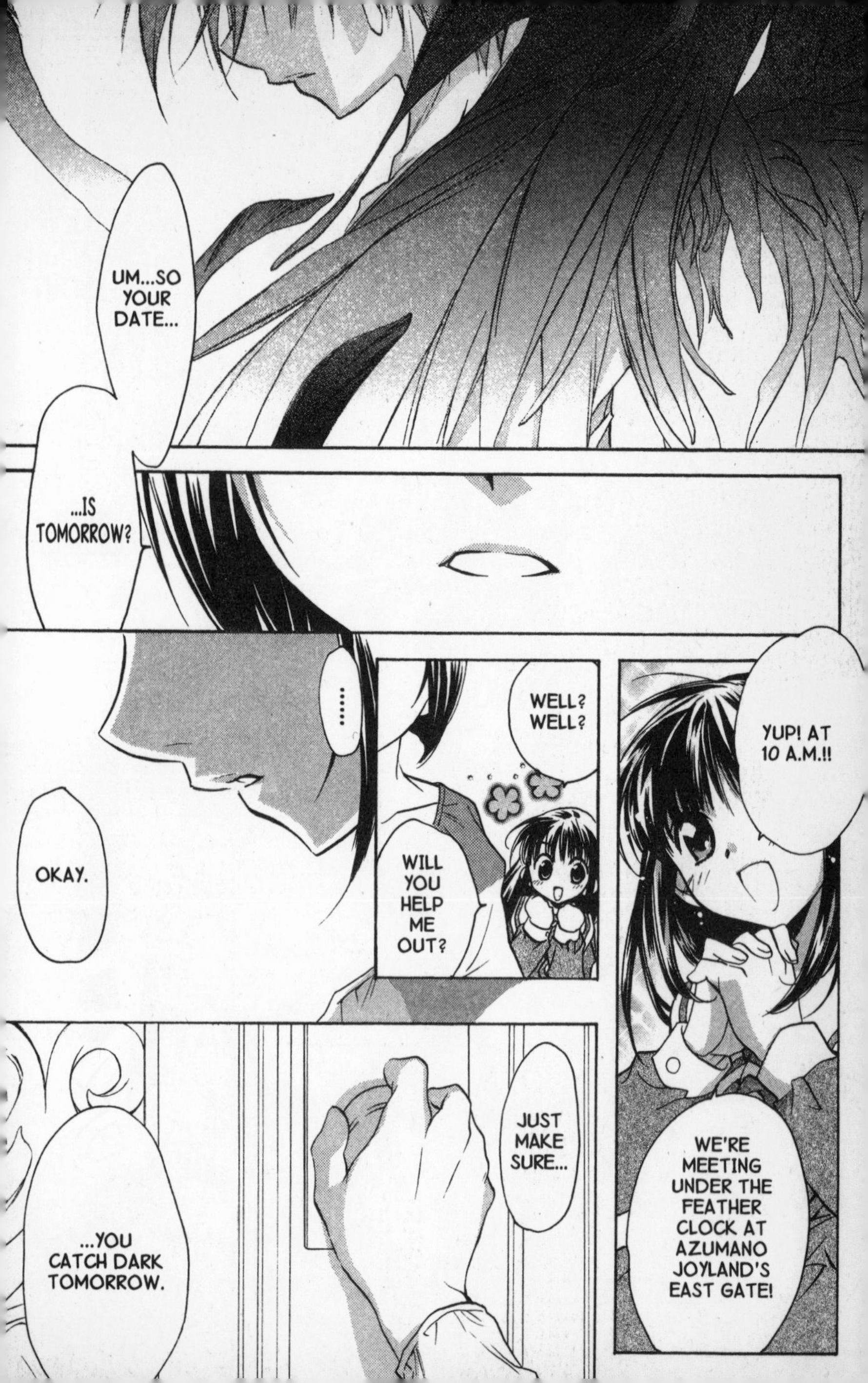
UM...SO YOUR DATE...
...IS TOMORROW?
YUP! AT 10 A.M.!!
WE'RE MEETING UNDER THE FEATHER CLOCK AT AZUMANO JOYLAND'S EAST GATE!
WELL? WELL?
WILL YOU HELP ME OUT?
......
OKAY.
JUST MAKE SURE...
...YOU CATCH DARK TOMORROW.

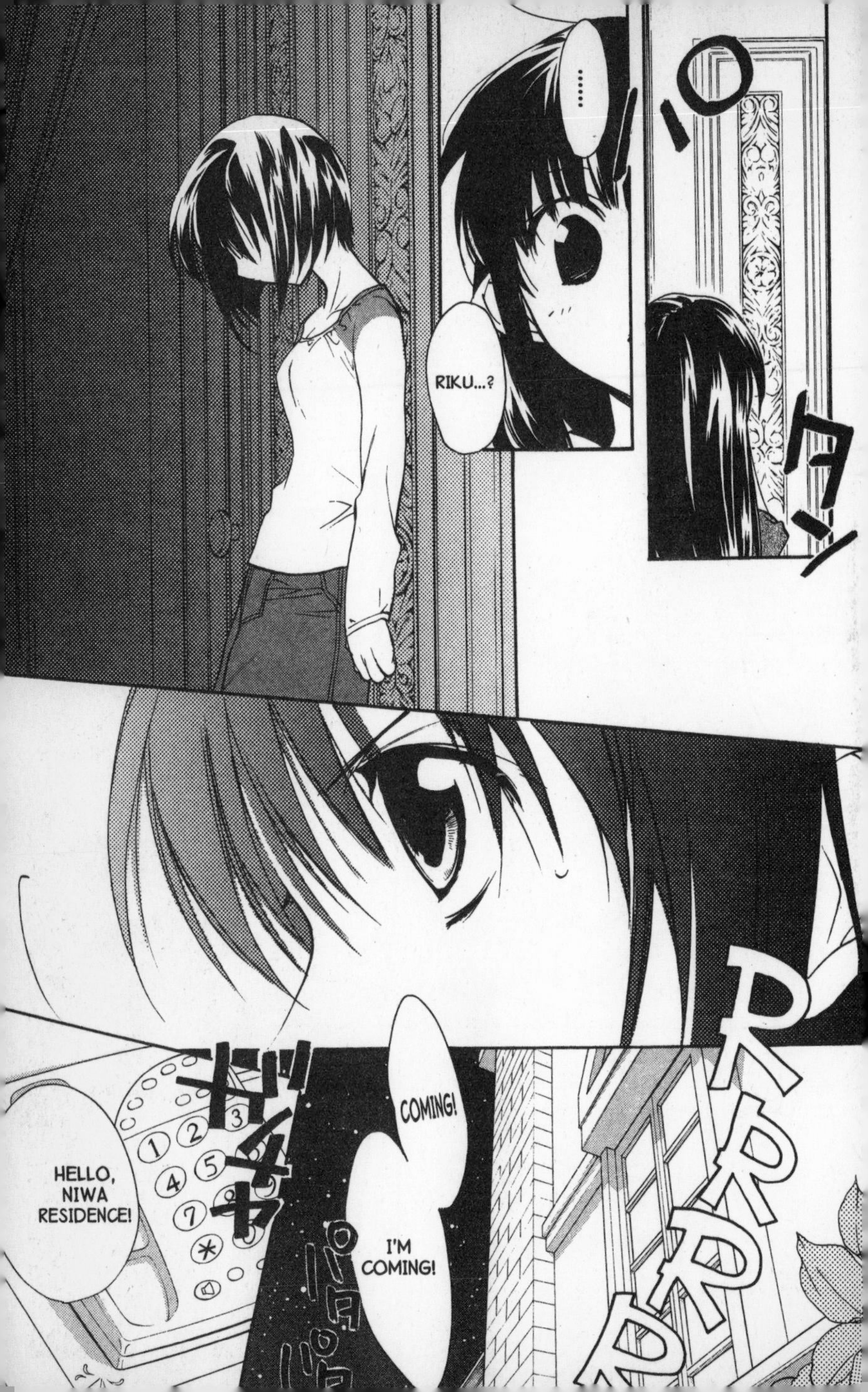
......
RIKU...?
RRRR
COMING!
I'M COMING!
HELLO, NIWA RESIDENCE!

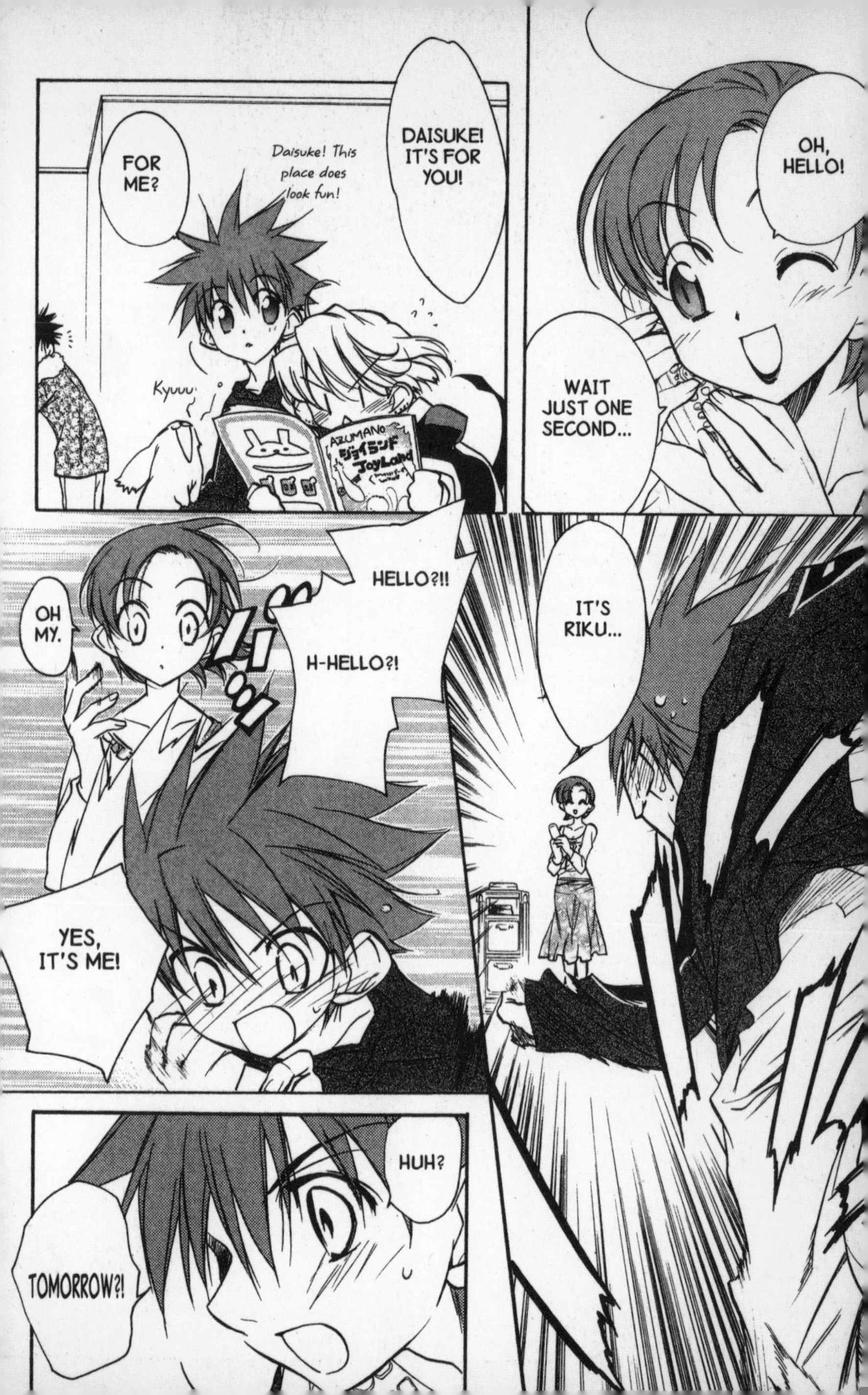
OH, HELLO!
WAIT JUST ONE SECOND...
DAISUKE! IT'S FOR YOU!
Daisuke! This place does look fun!
FOR ME?
Kyuuu
AZUMANO
ジョイランド
JoyLand
IT'S RIKU...
HELLO?!!
H-HELLO?!
OH MY.
YES, IT'S ME!
HUH?
TOMORROW?!

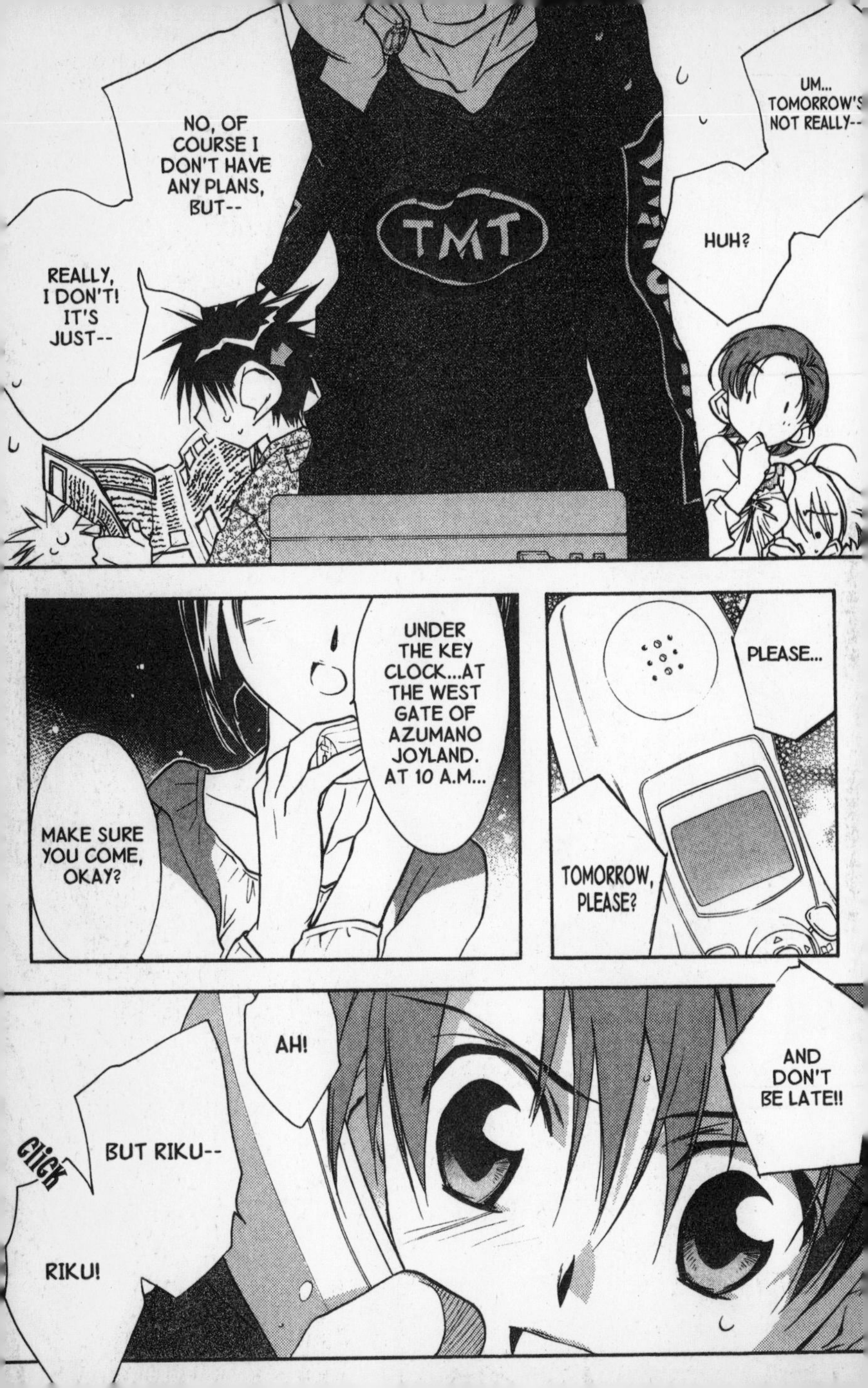
UM... TOMORROW'S NOT REALLY--
NO, OF COURSE I DON'T HAVE ANY PLANS, BUT--
HUH?
REALLY, I DON'T! IT'S JUST--
PLEASE...
TOMORROW, PLEASE?
UNDER THE KEY CLOCK...AT THE WEST GATE OF AZUMANO JOYLAND. AT 10 A.M...
MAKE SURE YOU COME, OKAY?
AND DON'T BE LATE!!
AH!
BUT RIKU--
CLICK
RIKU!

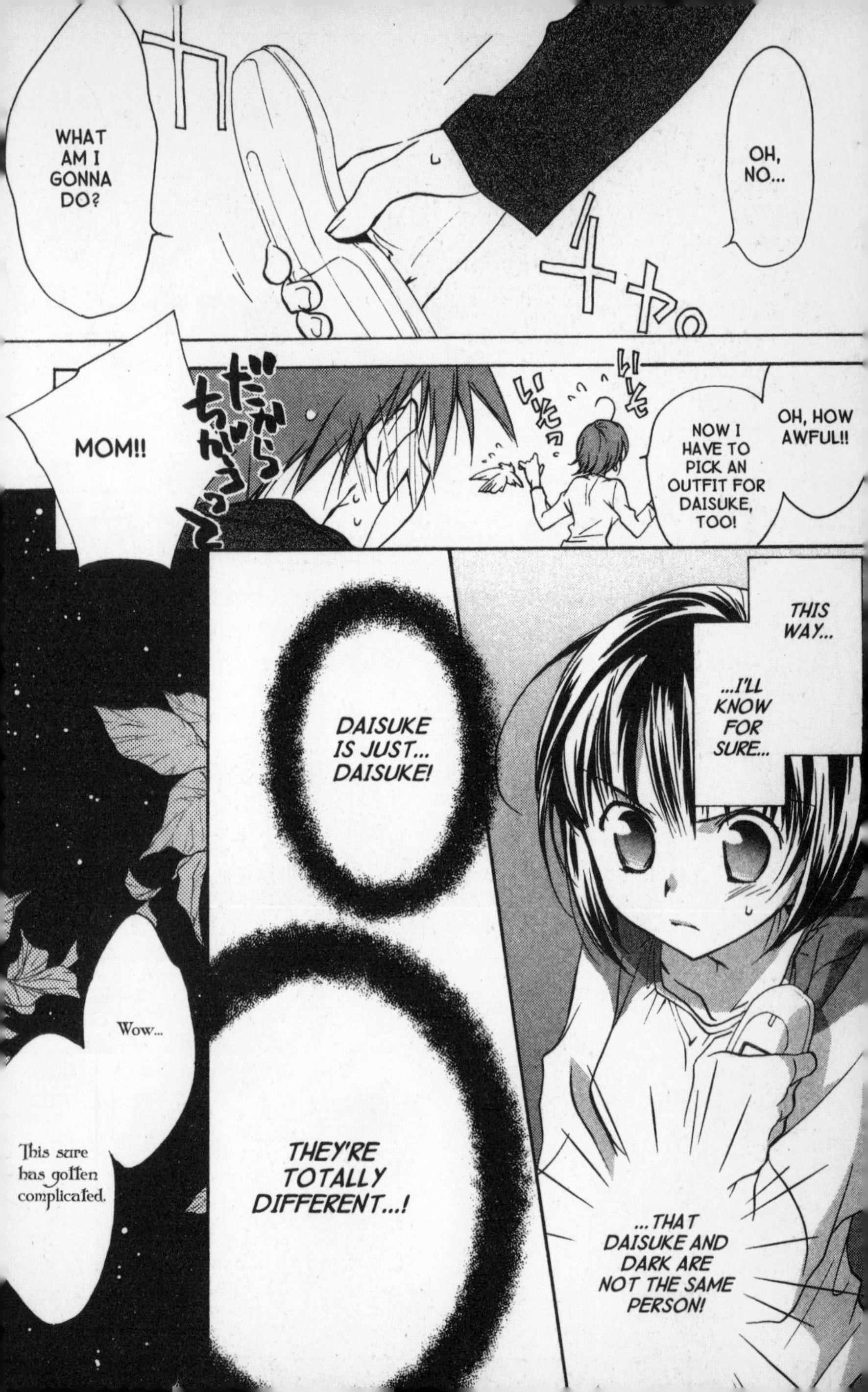
OH, NO...
WHAT AM I GONNA DO?
OH, HOW AWFUL!!
NOW I HAVE TO PICK AN OUTFIT FOR DAISUKE, TOO!
MOM!!
THIS WAY...
...I'LL KNOW FOR SURE...
...THAT DAISUKE AND DARK ARE NOT THE SAME PERSON!
DAISUKE IS JUST... DAISUKE!
THEY'RE TOTALLY DIFFERENT...!
Wow...
This sure has gotten complicated.

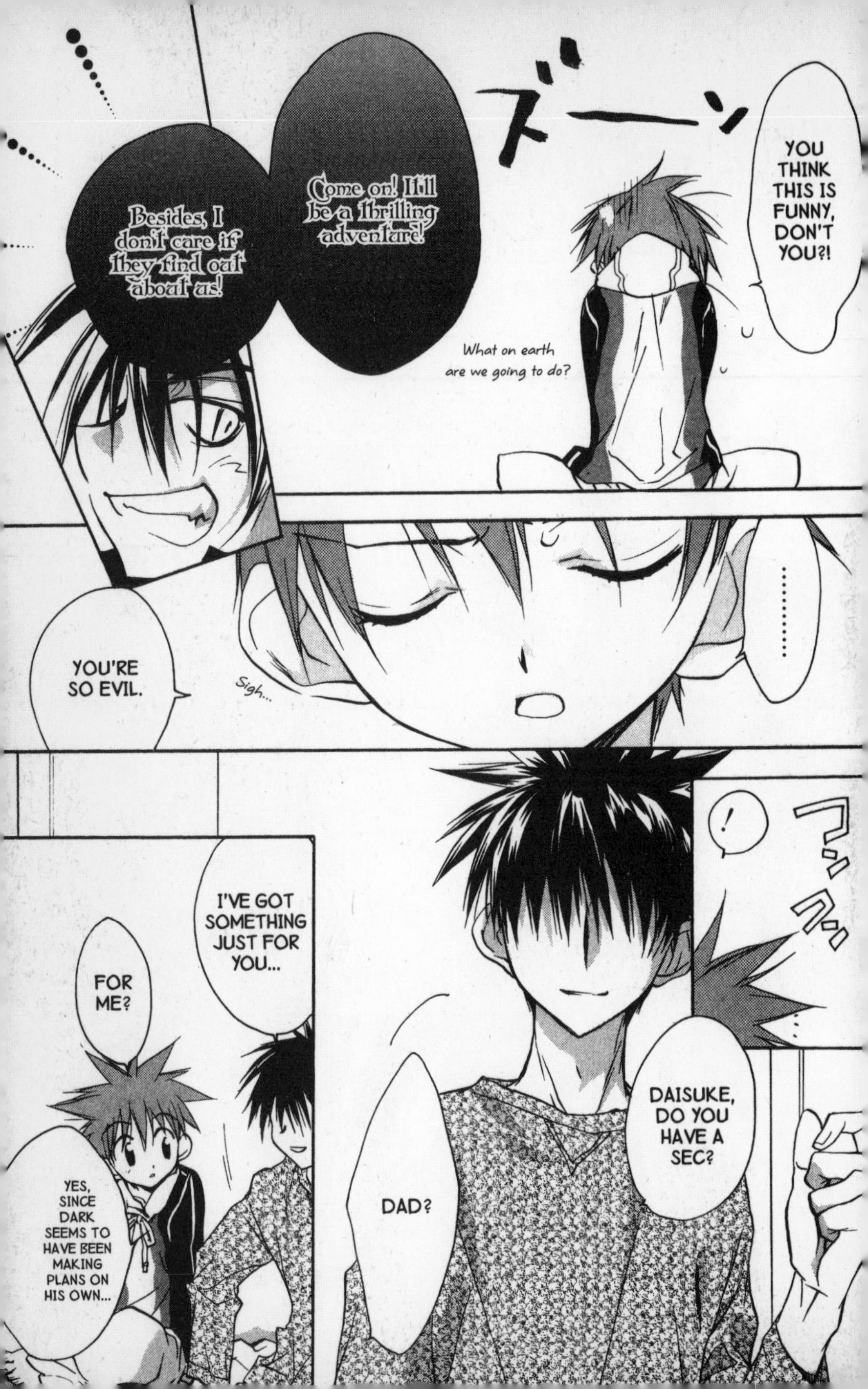
ズーン
YOU THINK THIS IS FUNNY, DON'T YOU?!
What on earth are we going to do?
Come on! It'll be a thrilling adventure!
Besides, I don't care if they find out about us!
......
Sigh...
YOU'RE SO EVIL.
!
DAISUKE, DO YOU HAVE A SEC?
DAD?
I'VE GOT SOMETHING JUST FOR YOU...
FOR ME?
YES, SINCE DARK SEEMS TO HAVE BEEN MAKING PLANS ON HIS OWN...

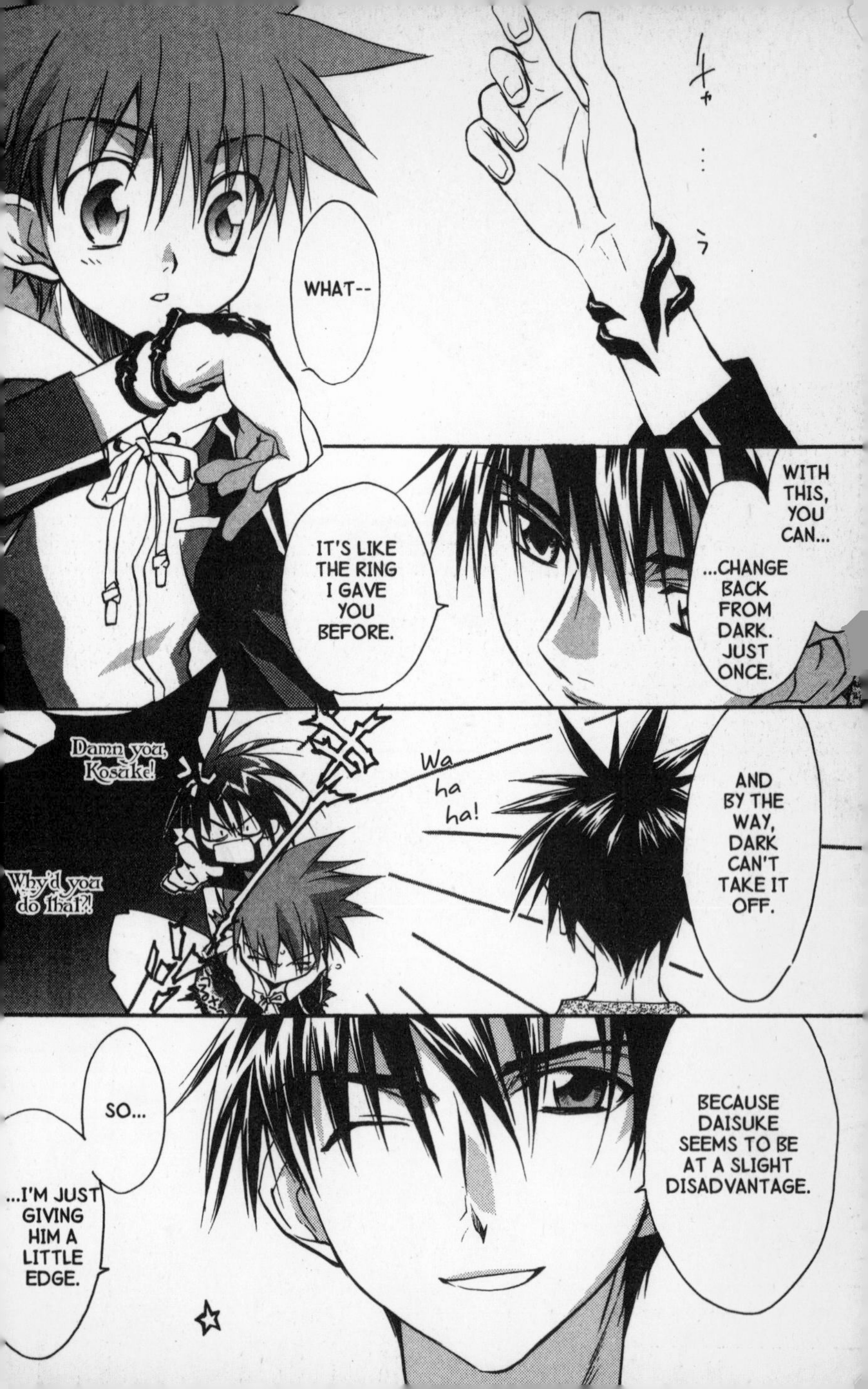
WHAT--
WITH THIS, YOU CAN...
...CHANGE BACK FROM DARK. JUST ONCE.
IT'S LIKE THE RING I GAVE YOU BEFORE.
AND BY THE WAY, DARK CAN'T TAKE IT OFF.
Wa ha ha!
Damn you, Kosuke!
Why'd you do that?!
BECAUSE DAISUKE SEEMS TO BE AT A SLIGHT DISADVANTAGE.
SO...
...I'M JUST GIVING HIM A LITTLE EDGE.

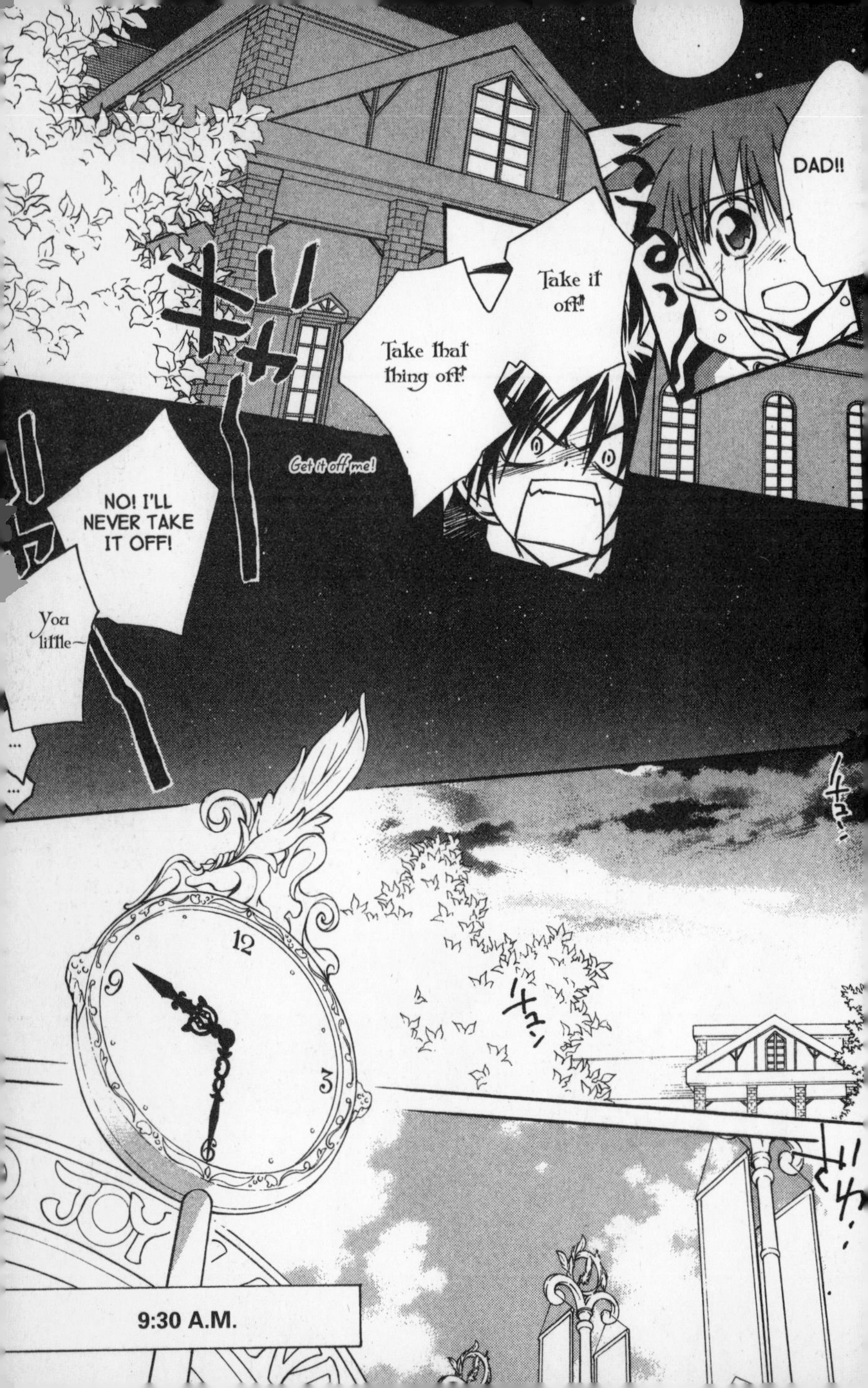
DAD!!
Take it off!!
Take that thing off!
Get it off me!
NO! I'LL NEVER TAKE IT OFF!
You little~
...
...
9:30 A.M.

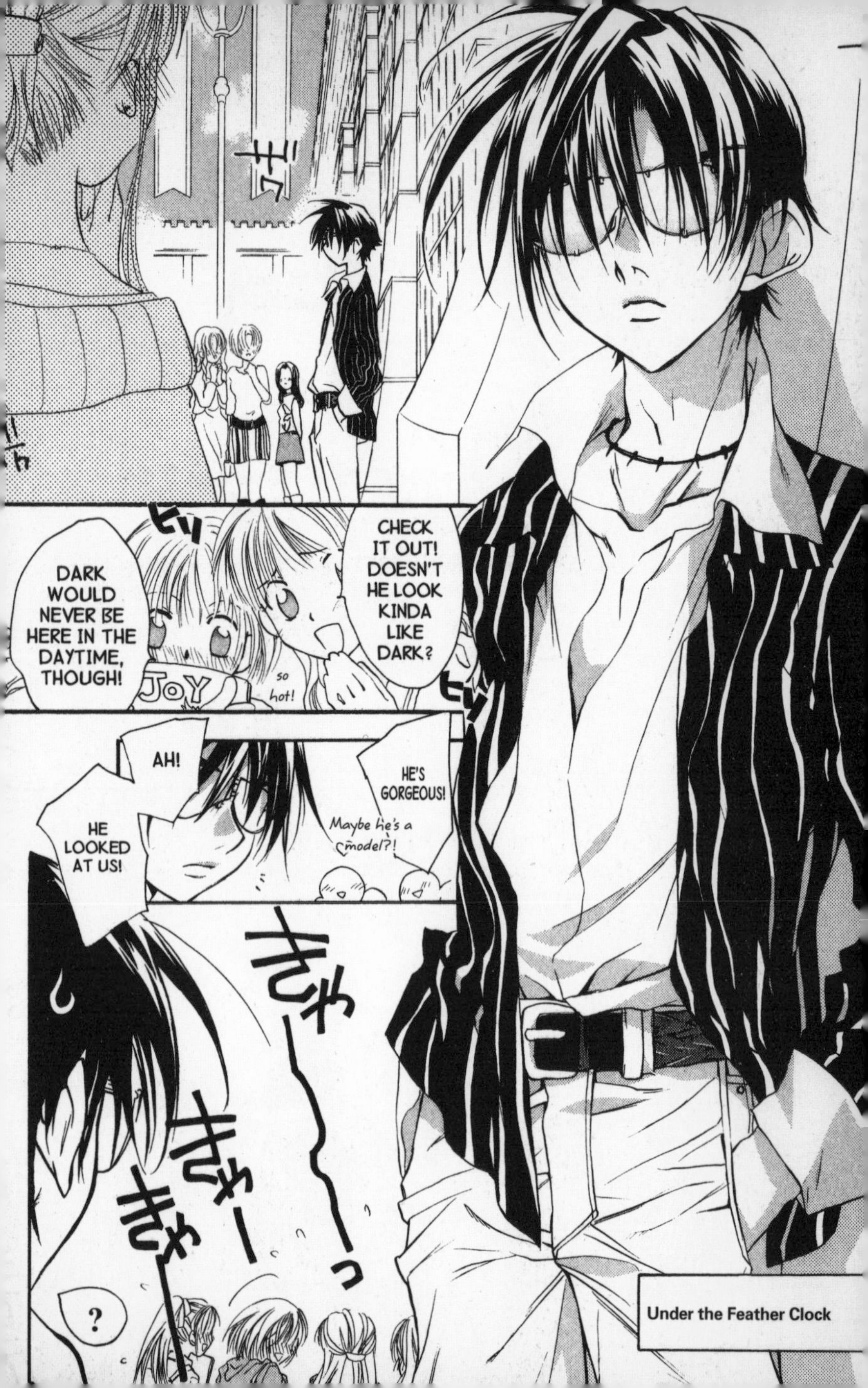
CHECK IT OUT! DOESN'T HE LOOK KINDA LIKE DARK?
so hot!
DARK WOULD NEVER BE HERE IN THE DAYTIME, THOUGH!
HE'S GORGEOUS!
Maybe he's a model?!
AH!
HE LOOKED AT US!
?
Under the Feather Clock

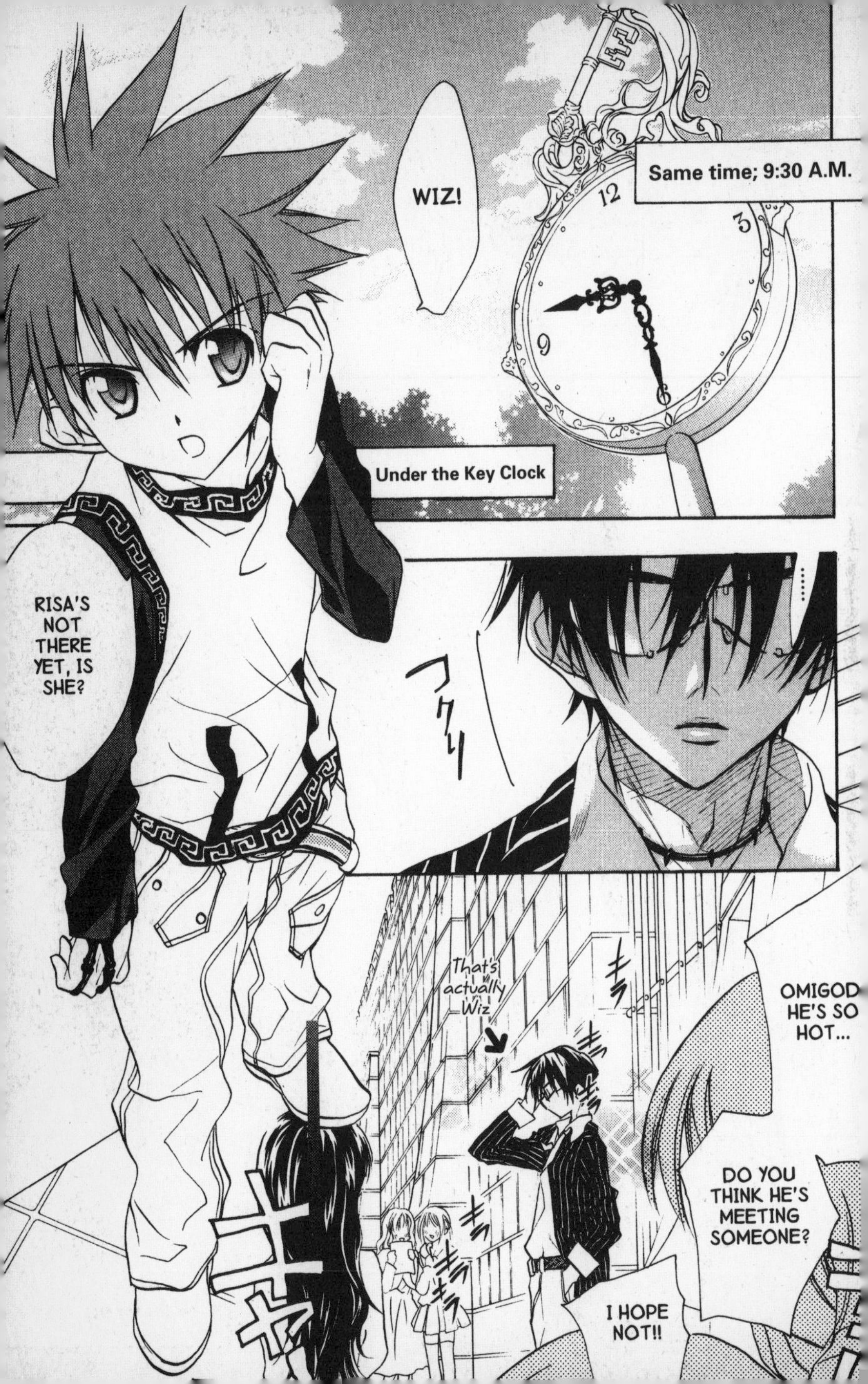
Same time; 9:30 A.M.
WIZ!
Under the Key Clock
RISA'S NOT THERE YET, IS SHE?
......
OMIGOD HE'S SO HOT...
That's actually Wiz
DO YOU THINK HE'S MEETING SOMEONE?
I HOPE NOT!!

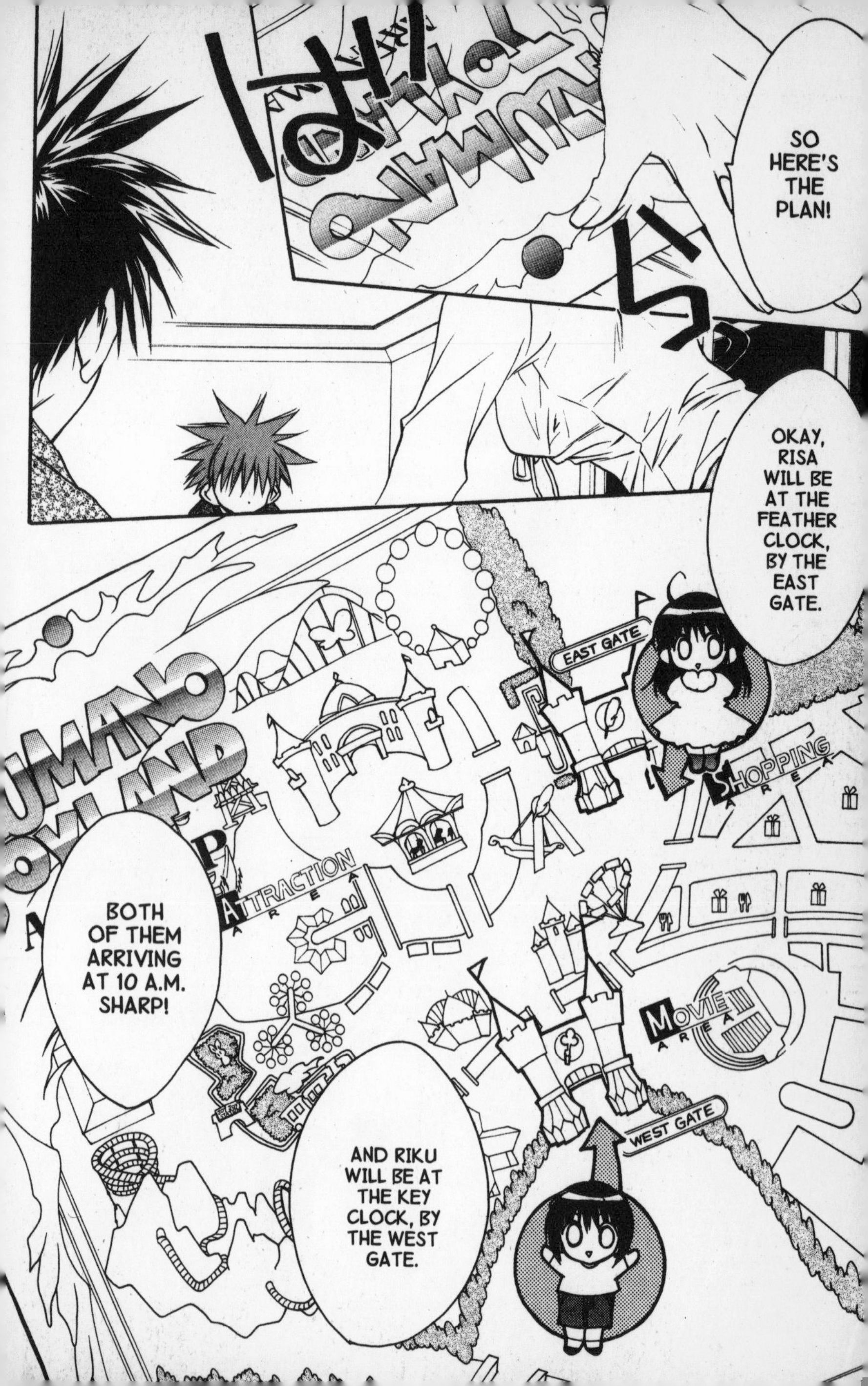
SO HERE'S THE PLAN!
OKAY, RISA WILL BE AT THE FEATHER CLOCK, BY THE EAST GATE.
AND RIKU WILL BE AT THE KEY CLOCK, BY THE WEST GATE.
BOTH OF THEM ARRIVING AT 10 A.M. SHARP!
EAST GATE
SHOPPING AREA
ATTRACTION AREA
MOVIE AREA
WEST GATE

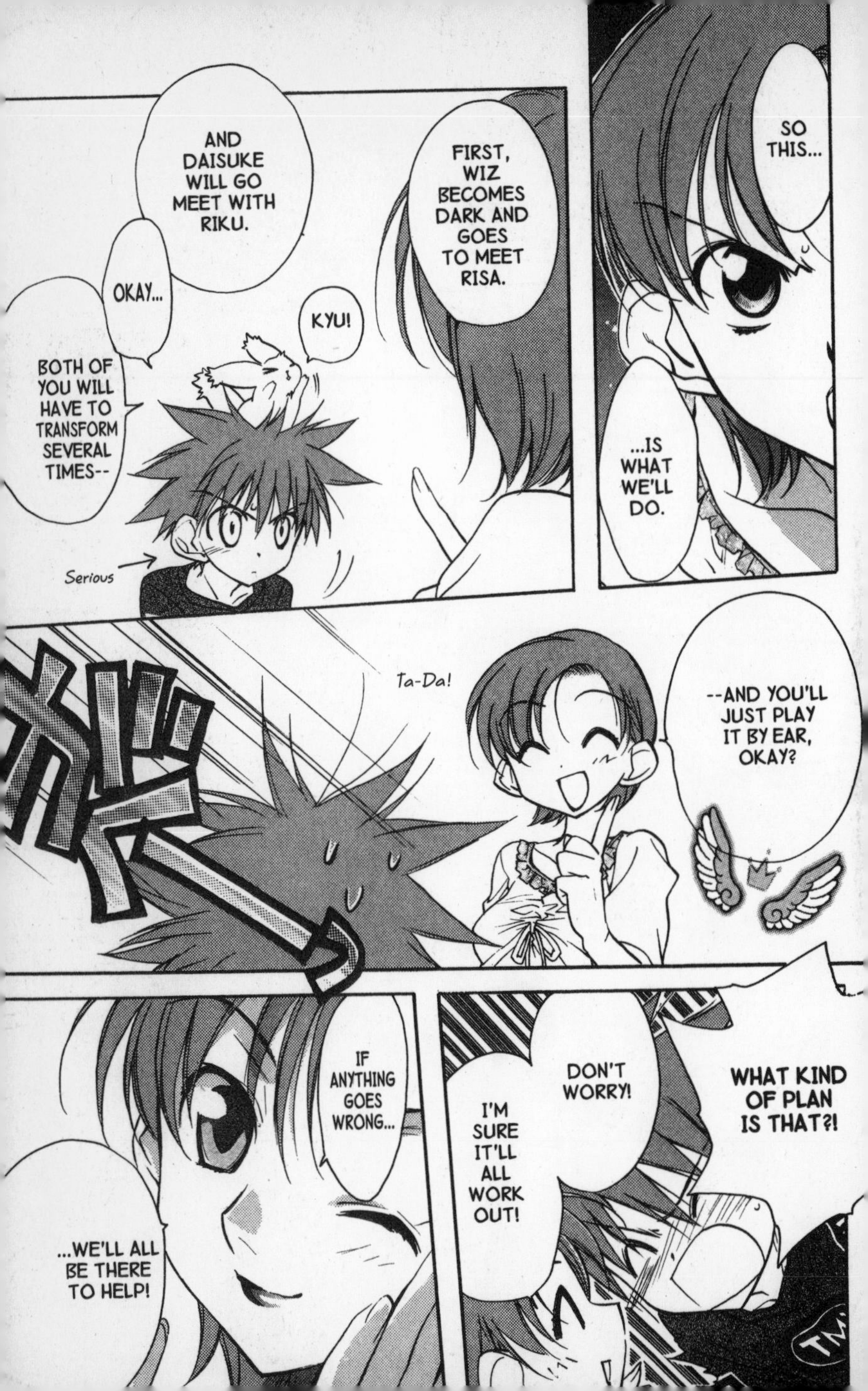
SO THIS...
...IS WHAT WE'LL DO.
FIRST, WIZ BECOMES DARK AND GOES TO MEET RISA.
KYU!
AND DAISUKE WILL GO MEET WITH RIKU.
OKAY...
BOTH OF YOU WILL HAVE TO TRANSFORM SEVERAL TIMES--
Serious
--AND YOU'LL JUST PLAY IT BY EAR, OKAY?
Ta-Da!
WHAT KIND OF PLAN IS THAT?!
DON'T WORRY!
I'M SURE IT'LL ALL WORK OUT!
IF ANYTHING GOES WRONG...
...WE'LL ALL BE THERE TO HELP!

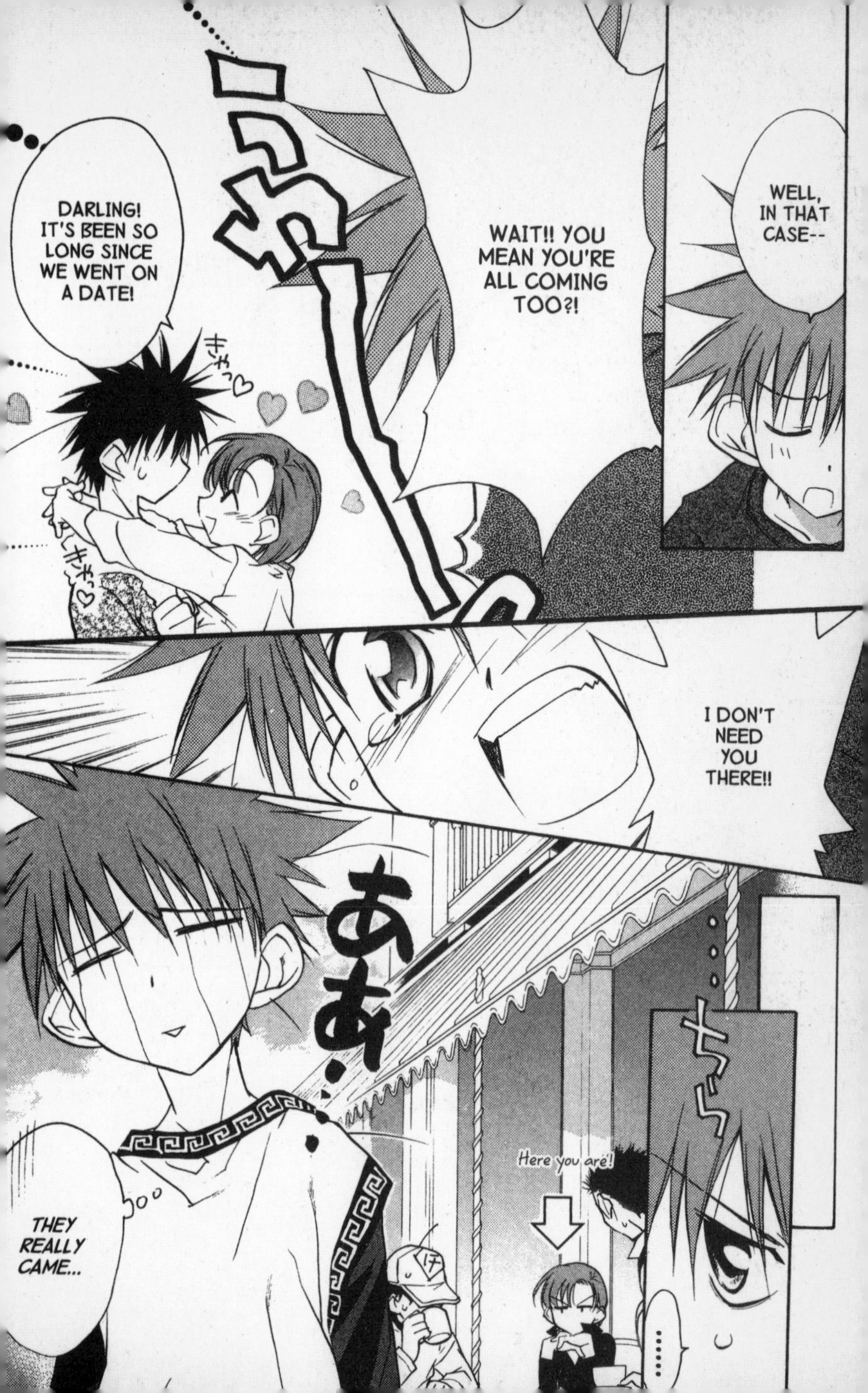
WELL, IN THAT CASE--
WAIT!! YOU MEAN YOU'RE ALL COMING TOO?!
DARLING! IT'S BEEN SO LONG SINCE WE WENT ON A DATE!
きゃっ♡
I DON'T NEED YOU THERE!!
ああ…
ちら
Here you are!
...
THEY REALLY CAME...

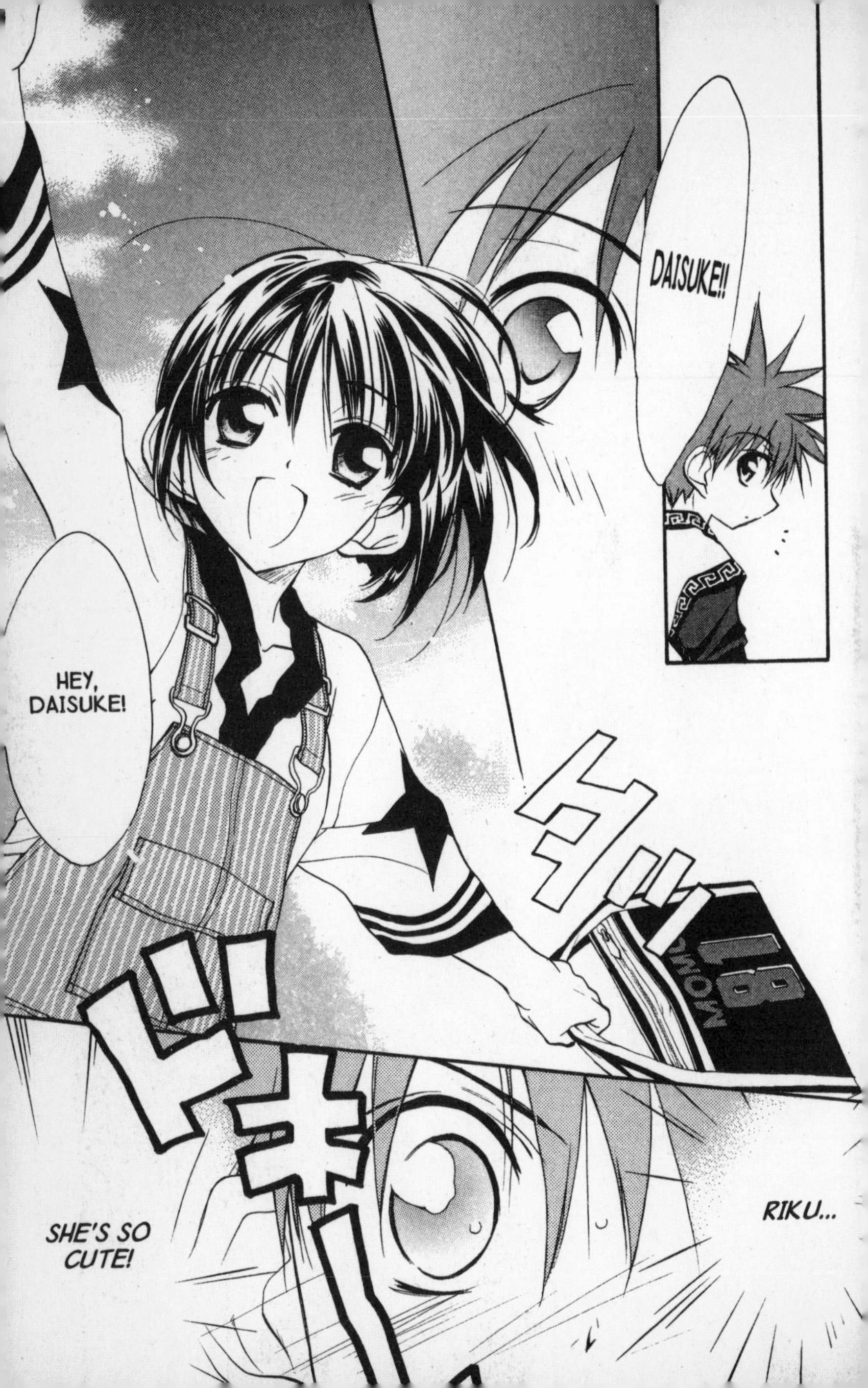
DAISUKE!!
HEY, DAISUKE!
RIKU...
SHE'S SO CUTE!

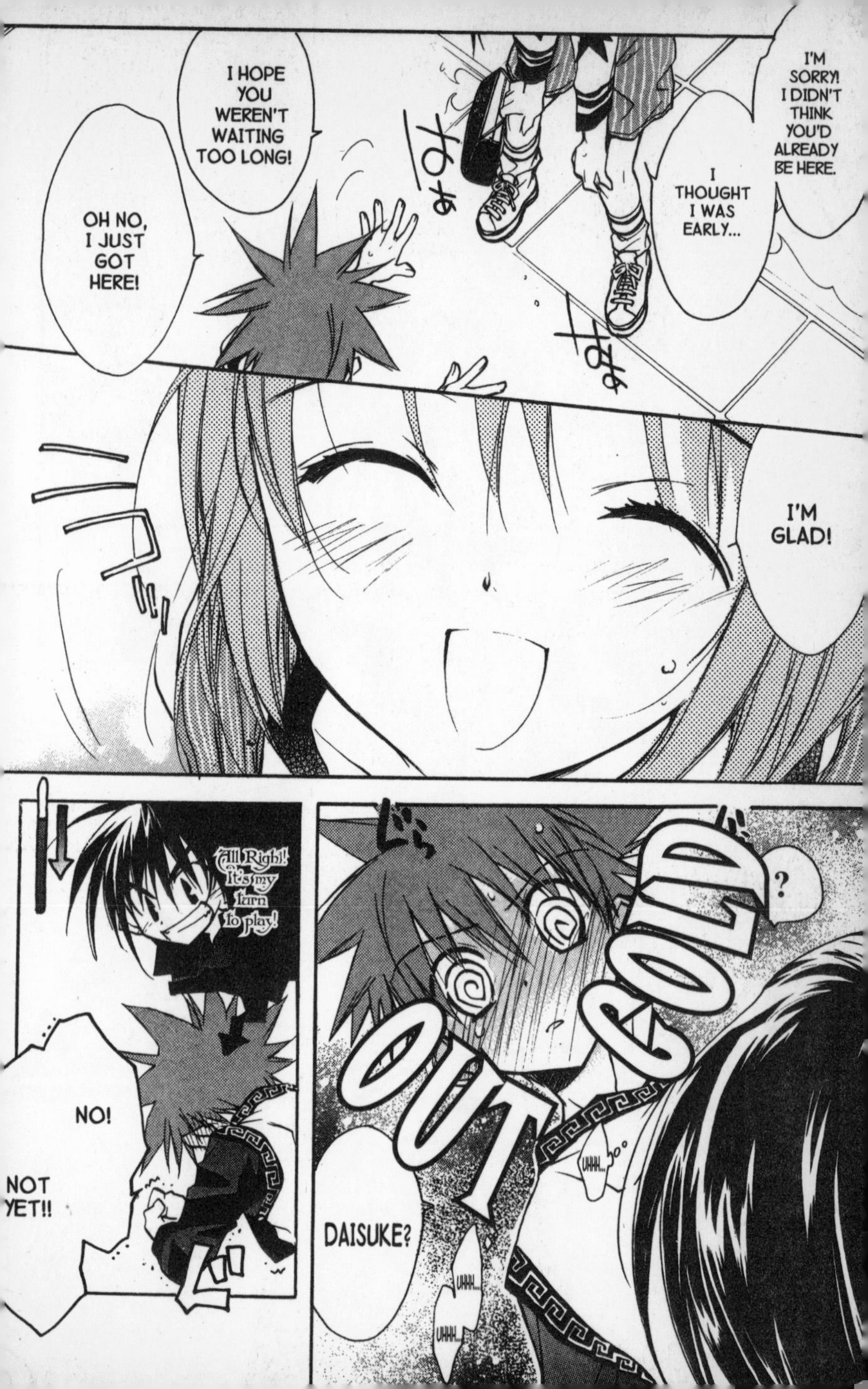
I'M SORRY! I DIDN'T THINK YOU'D ALREADY BE HERE.
I THOUGHT I WAS EARLY...
I HOPE YOU WEREN'T WAITING TOO LONG!
OH NO, I JUST GOT HERE!
I'M GLAD!
?
GOLD OUT
UHHH...
DAISUKE?
UHHH...
UHHH...
All Right! It's my turn to play!
NO!
NOT YET!!

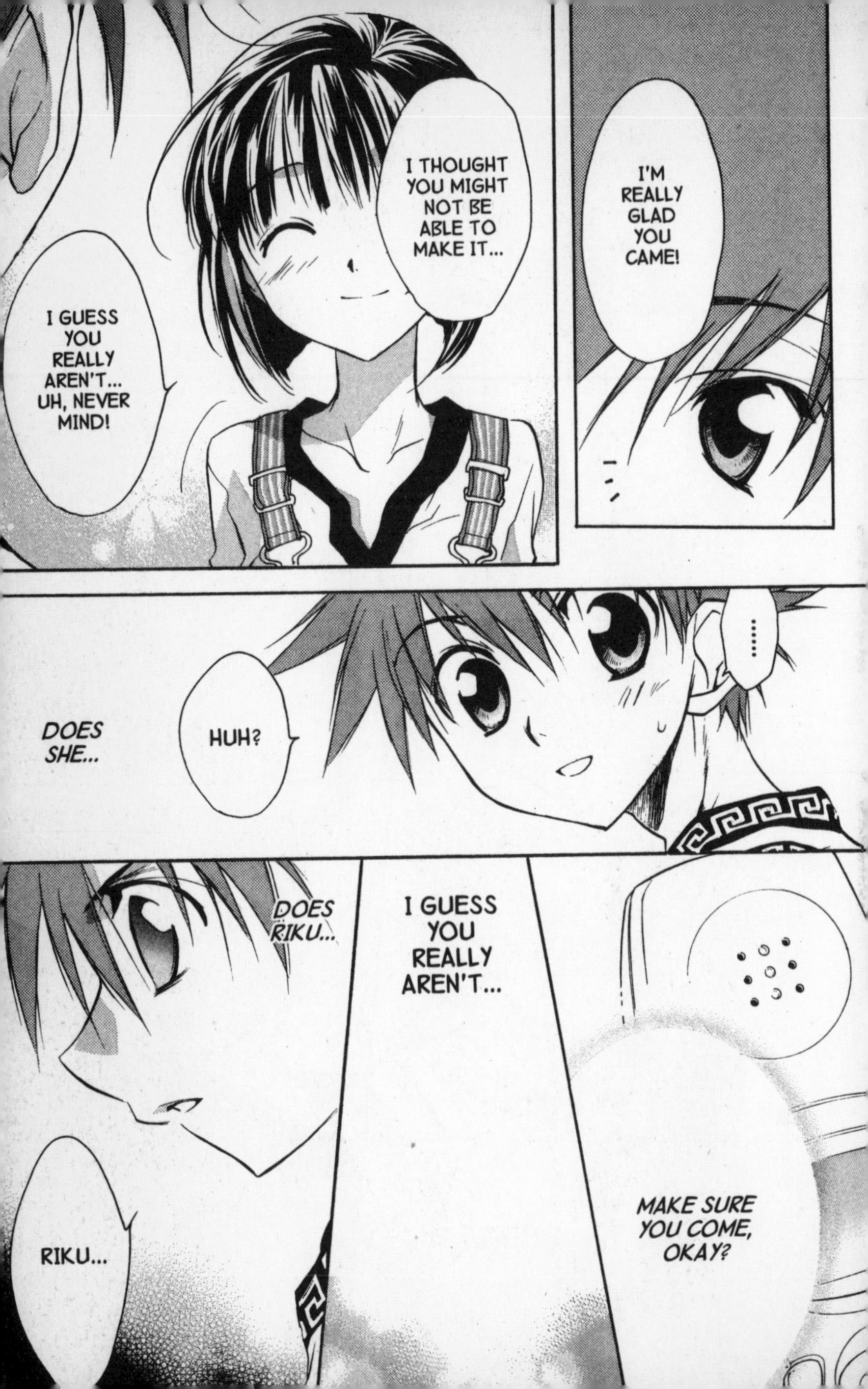
I'M REALLY GLAD YOU CAME!
I THOUGHT YOU MIGHT NOT BE ABLE TO MAKE IT...
I GUESS YOU REALLY AREN'T... UH, NEVER MIND!
......
HUH?
DOES SHE...
MAKE SURE YOU COME, OKAY?
I GUESS YOU REALLY AREN'T...
DOES RIKU...
RIKU...

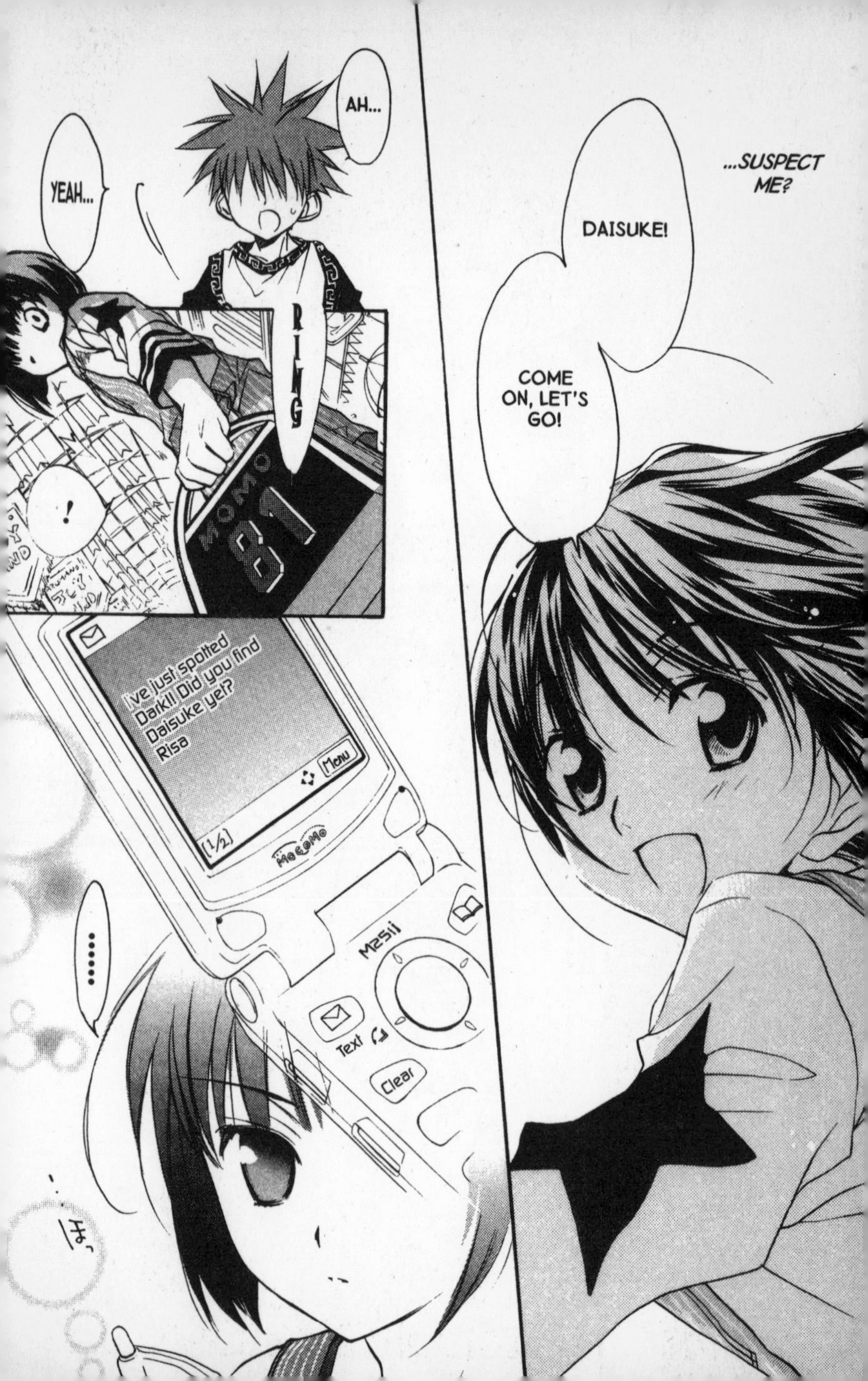
...SUSPECT ME?
DAISUKE!
COME ON, LET'S GO!
AH...
YEAH...
RING
!
I've just spoted Dark!! Did you find Daisuke yet? Risa
Menu
Text
Clear
......

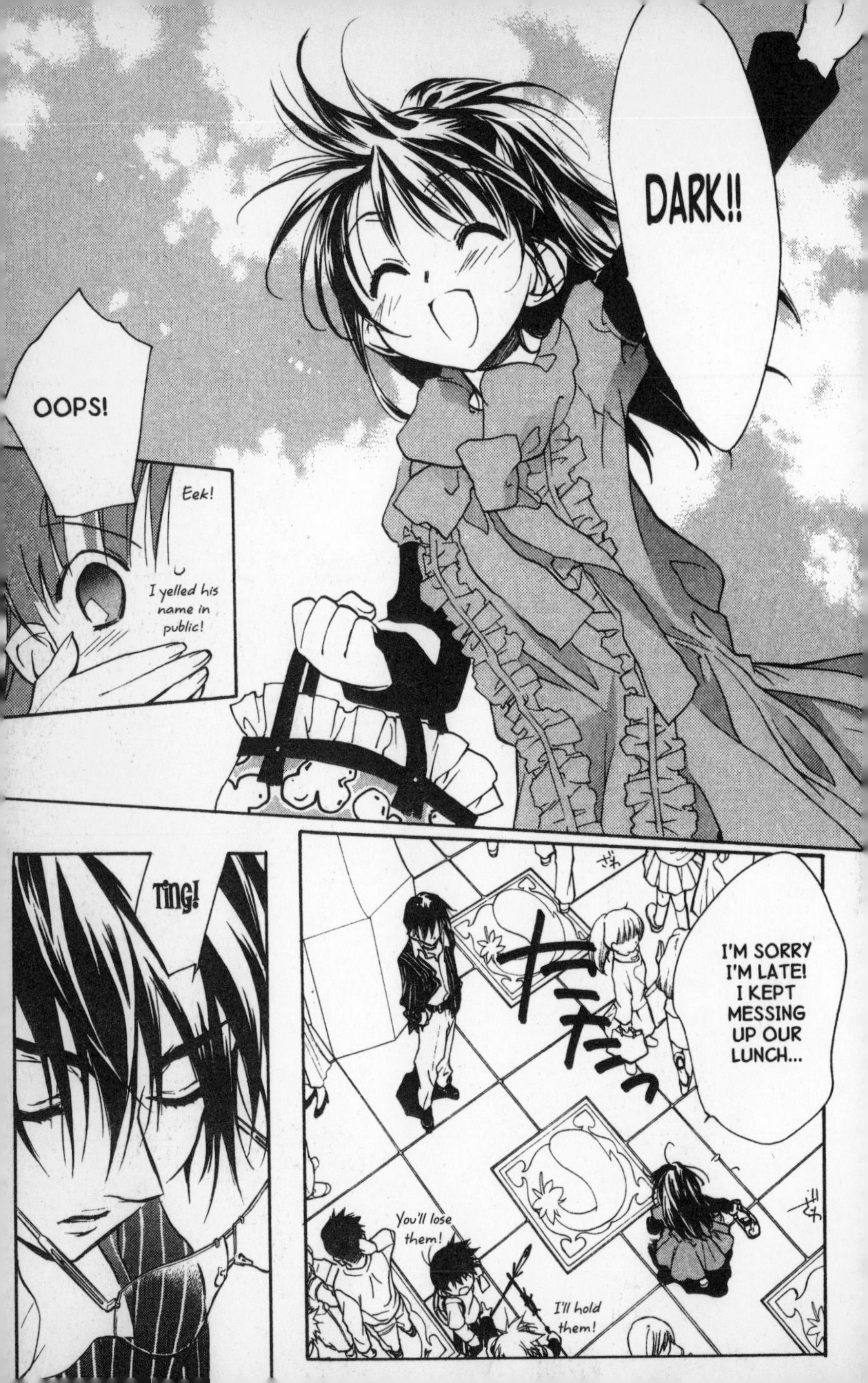
DARK!!
OOPS!
Eek!
I yelled his name in public!
I'M SORRY I'M LATE! I KEPT MESSING UP OUR LUNCH...
You'll lose them!
I'll hold them!
TING!

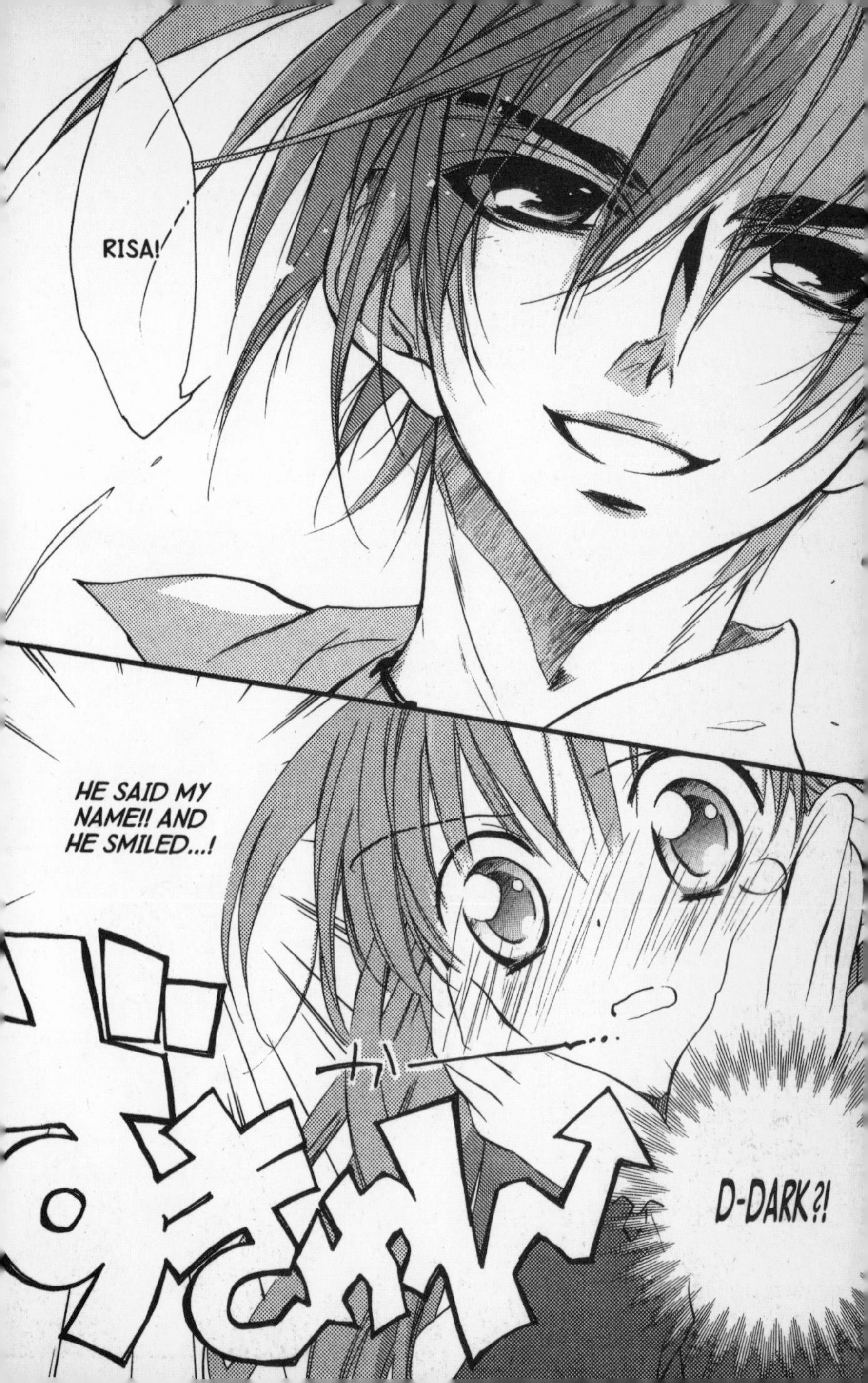
RISA!
HE SAID MY NAME!! AND HE SMILED...!
D-DARK?!

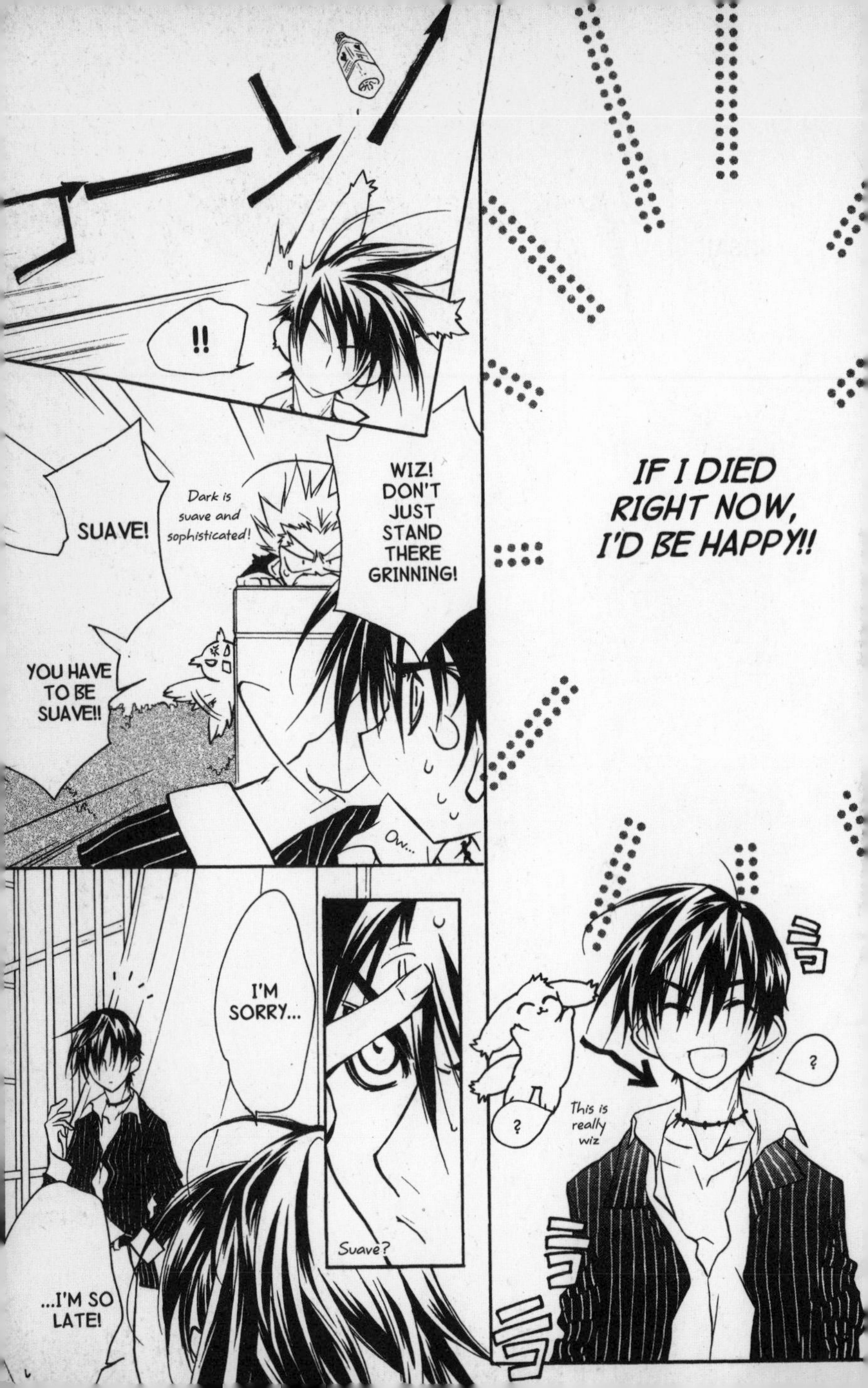
IF I DIED RIGHT NOW, I'D BE HAPPY!!
!!
WIZ! DON'T JUST STAND THERE GRINNING!
Dark is suave and sophisticated!
SUAVE!
YOU HAVE TO BE SUAVE!!
Ow...
?
?
This is really wiz
I'M SORRY...
Suave?
...I'M SO LATE!

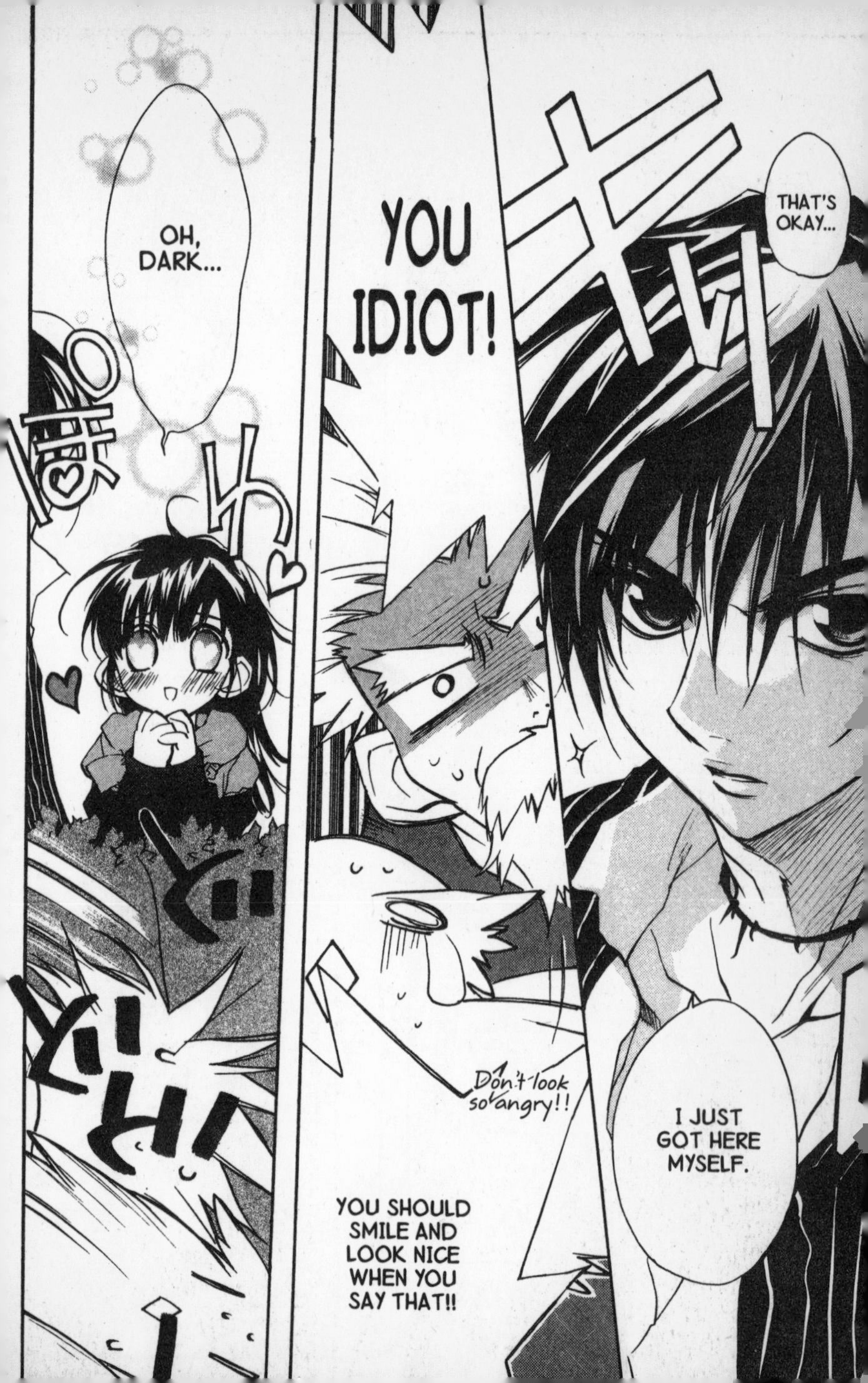
THAT'S OKAY...
I JUST GOT HERE MYSELF.
YOU IDIOT!
Don't look so angry!!
YOU SHOULD SMILE AND LOOK NICE WHEN YOU SAY THAT!!
OH, DARK...

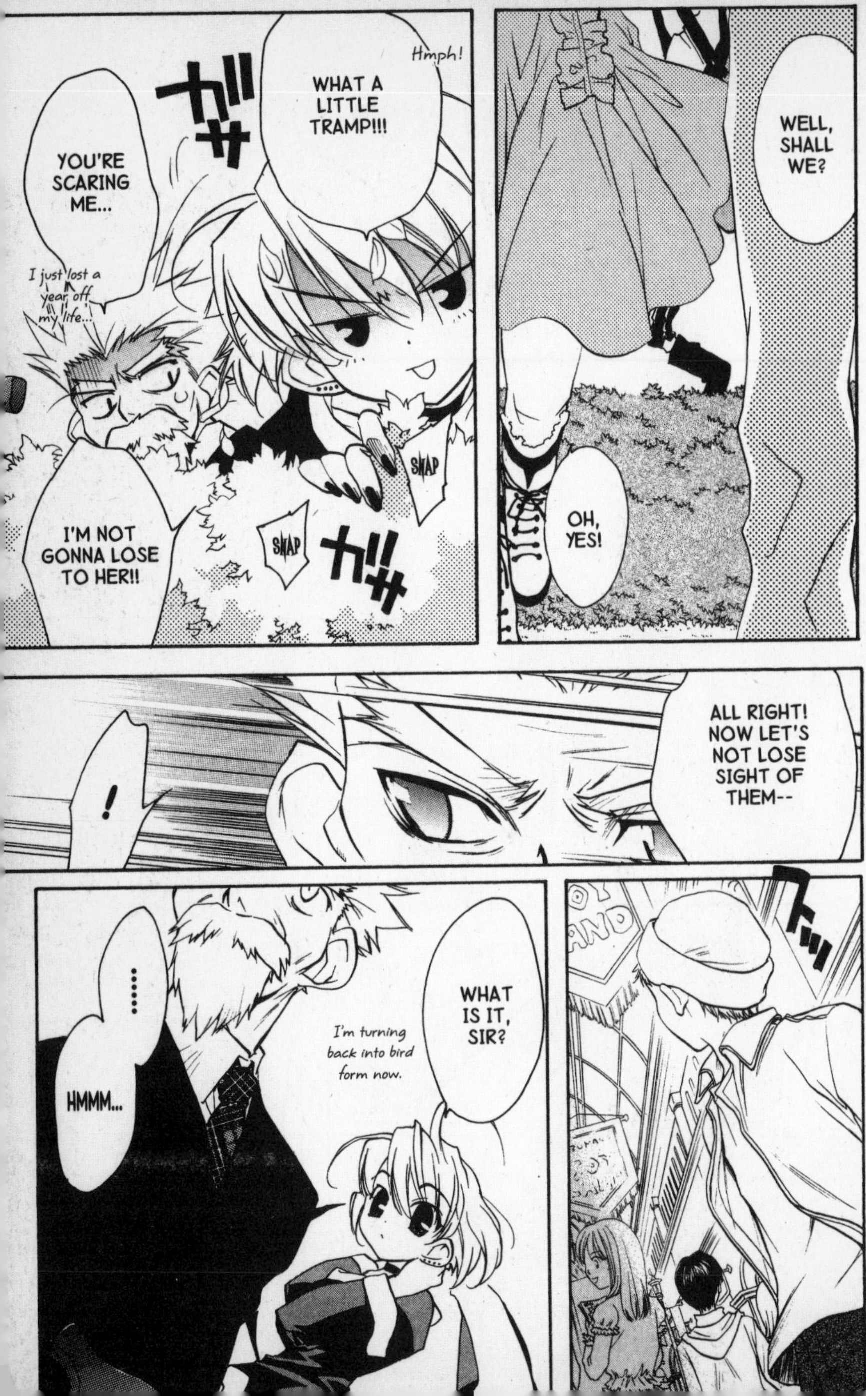
WELL, SHALL WE?
OH, YES!
Hmph!
WHAT A LITTLE TRAMP!!!
YOU'RE SCARING ME...
I just lost a year off my life...
SNAP
SNAP
I'M NOT GONNA LOSE TO HER!!
ALL RIGHT! NOW LET'S NOT LOSE SIGHT OF THEM--
!
WHAT IS IT, SIR?
I'm turning back into bird form now.
......
HMMM...

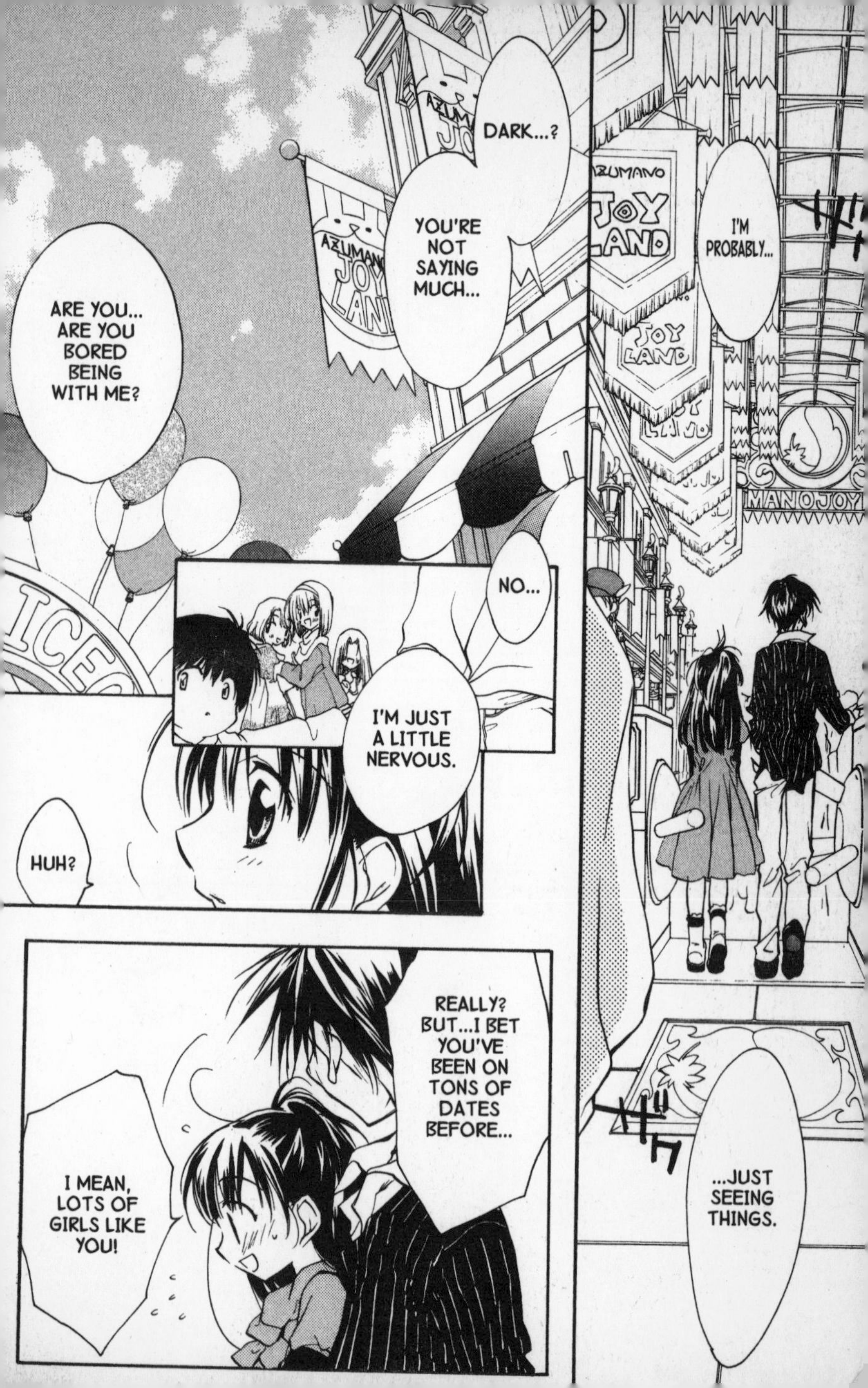
AZUMANO JOY LAND
I'M PROBABLY...
...JUST SEEING THINGS.
DARK...?
YOU'RE NOT SAYING MUCH...
ARE YOU... ARE YOU BORED BEING WITH ME?
NO...
I'M JUST A LITTLE NERVOUS.
HUH?
REALLY? BUT...I BET YOU'VE BEEN ON TONS OF DATES BEFORE...
I MEAN, LOTS OF GIRLS LIKE YOU!

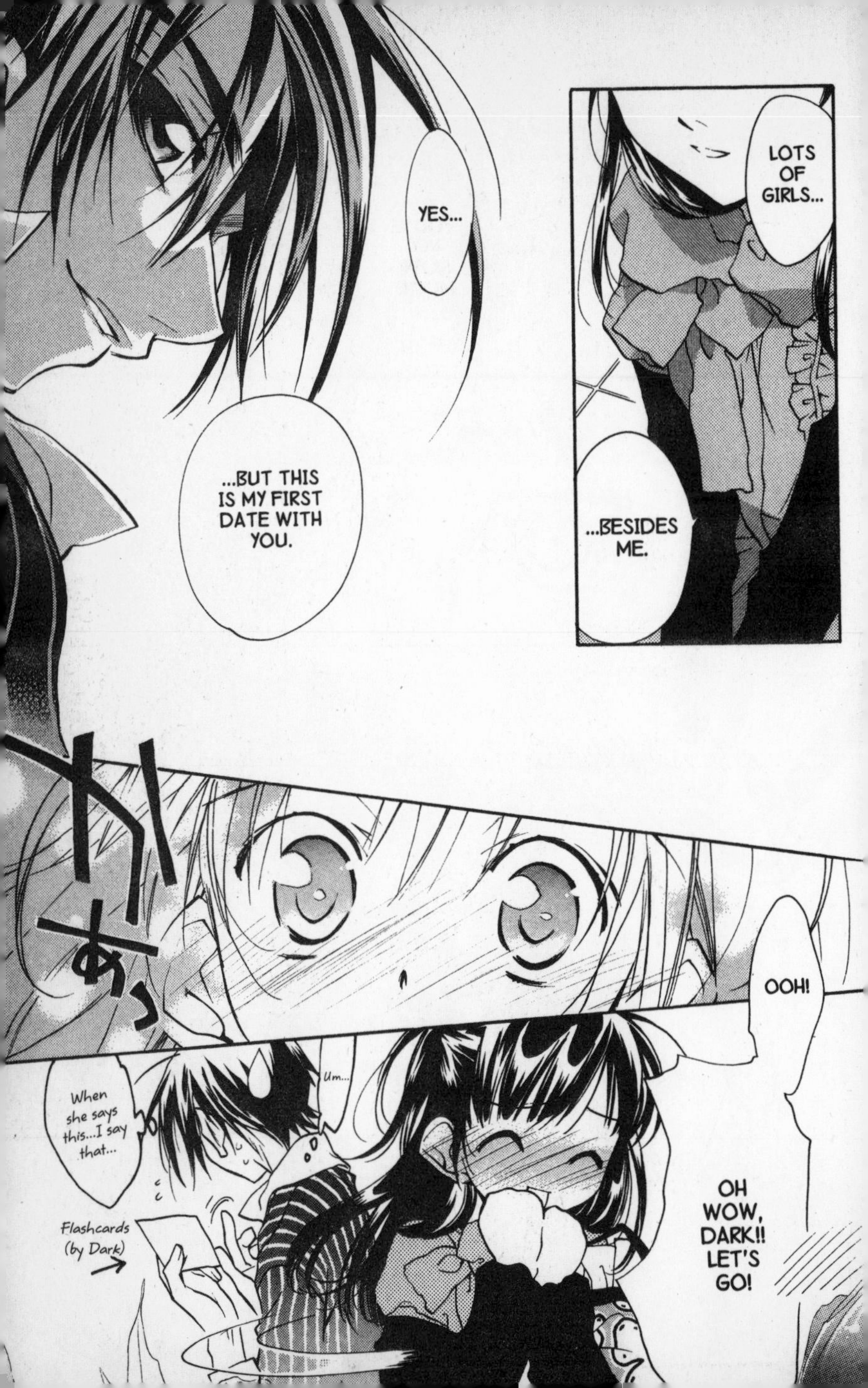
LOTS OF GIRLS...
...BESIDES ME.
YES...
...BUT THIS IS MY FIRST DATE WITH YOU.
OOH!
あっ
OH WOW, DARK!! LET'S GO!
Um...
When she says this...I say that...
Flashcards (by Dark)

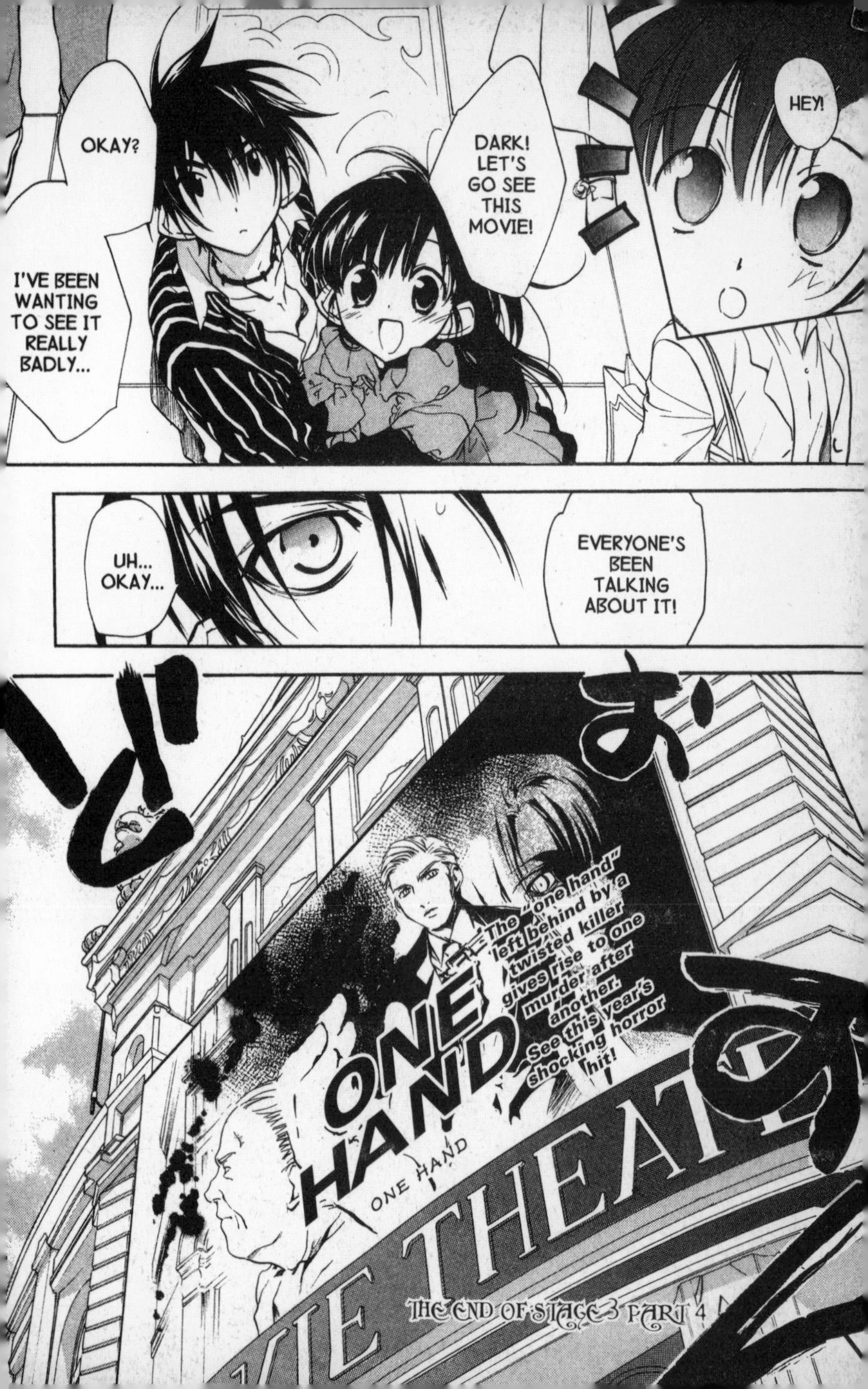
HEY!
DARK! LET'S GO SEE THIS MOVIE!
OKAY?
I'VE BEEN WANTING TO SEE IT REALLY BADLY...
EVERYONE'S BEEN TALKING ABOUT IT!
UH... OKAY...
The "one hand" left behind by a twisted killer gives rise to one murder after another. See this year's shocking horror hit!
ONE HAND
ONE HAND
THE END OF STAGE 3 PART 4

D•N•ANGEL
THINGS TO COME...

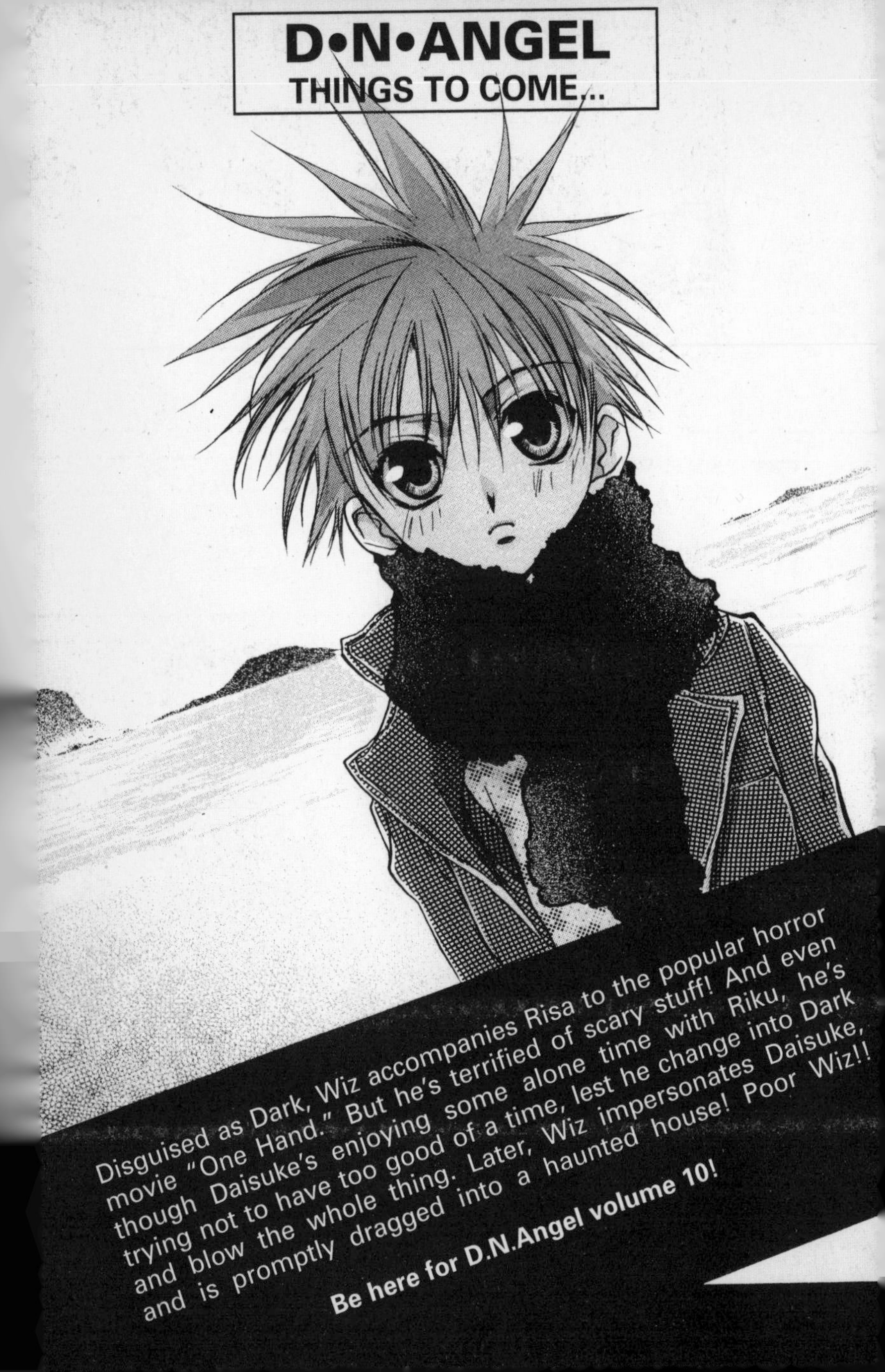

Disguised as Dark, Wiz accompanies Risa to the popular horror movie "One Hand." But he's terrified of scary stuff! And even though Daisuke's enjoying some alone time with Riku, he's trying not to have too good of a time, lest he change into Dark and blow the whole thing. Later, Wiz impersonates Daisuke, and is promptly dragged into a haunted house! Poor Wiz!!

Be here for D.N.Angel volume 10!

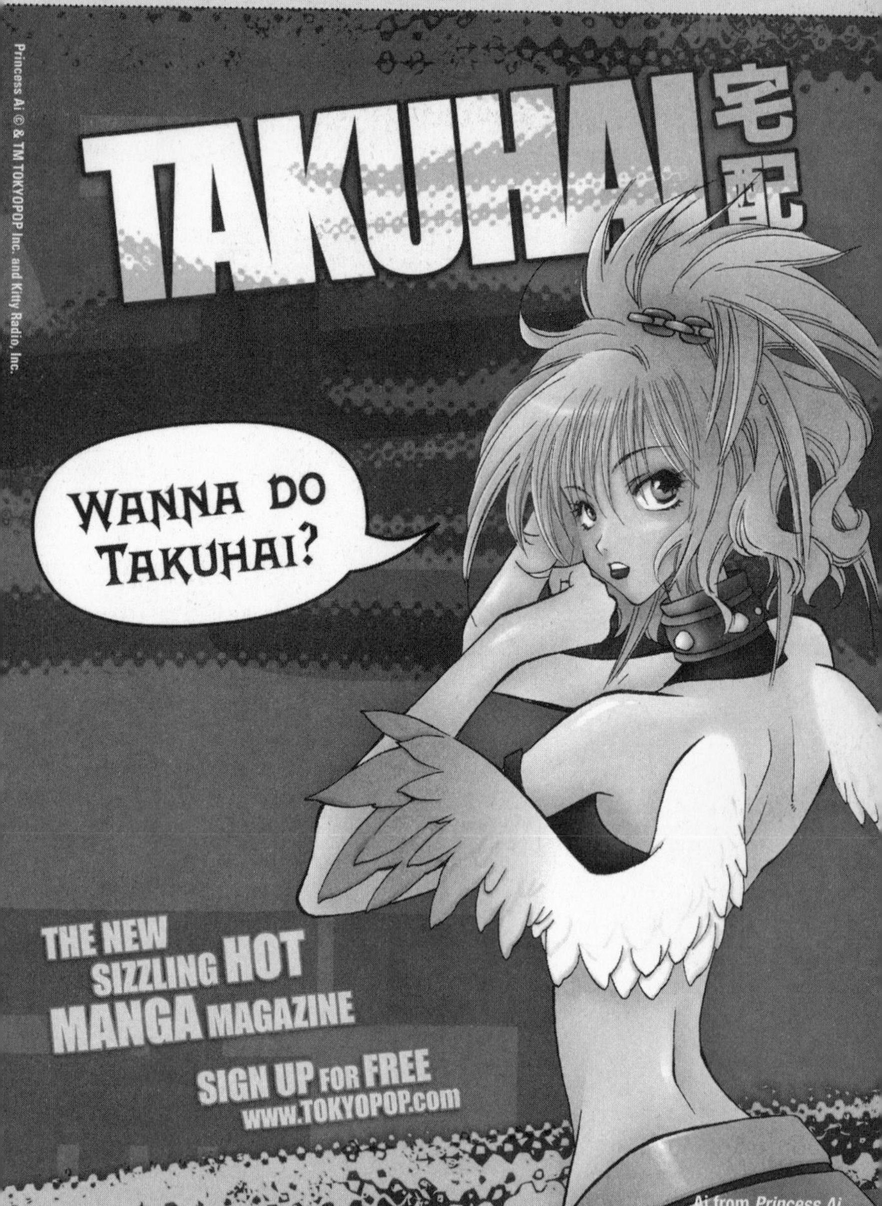
TAKUHAI 宅配
WANNA DO TAKUHAI?
THE NEW SIZZLING HOT MANGA MAGAZINE
SIGN UP FOR FREE
WWW.TOKYOPOP.com
Princess Ai © & TM TOKYOPOP Inc. and Kitty Radio, Inc.

Ai from *Princess Ai*

SIGN UP NOW FOR **FREE** AT: WWW.TOKYOPOP.COM

TOKYOPOP SHOP

WWW.TOKYOPOP.COM/SHOP

HOT NEWS!
Check out the
TOKYOPOP SHOP!
The world's best
collection of manga in
English is now available
online in one place!

GIRLS BRAVO

RIZELMINE

WAR ON FLESH

*War on Flesh
and other hot
titles are
available at
the store that
never closes!*

- **LOOK FOR SPECIAL OFFERS**
- **PRE-ORDER UPCOMING RELEASES**
- **COMPLETE YOUR COLLECTIONS**

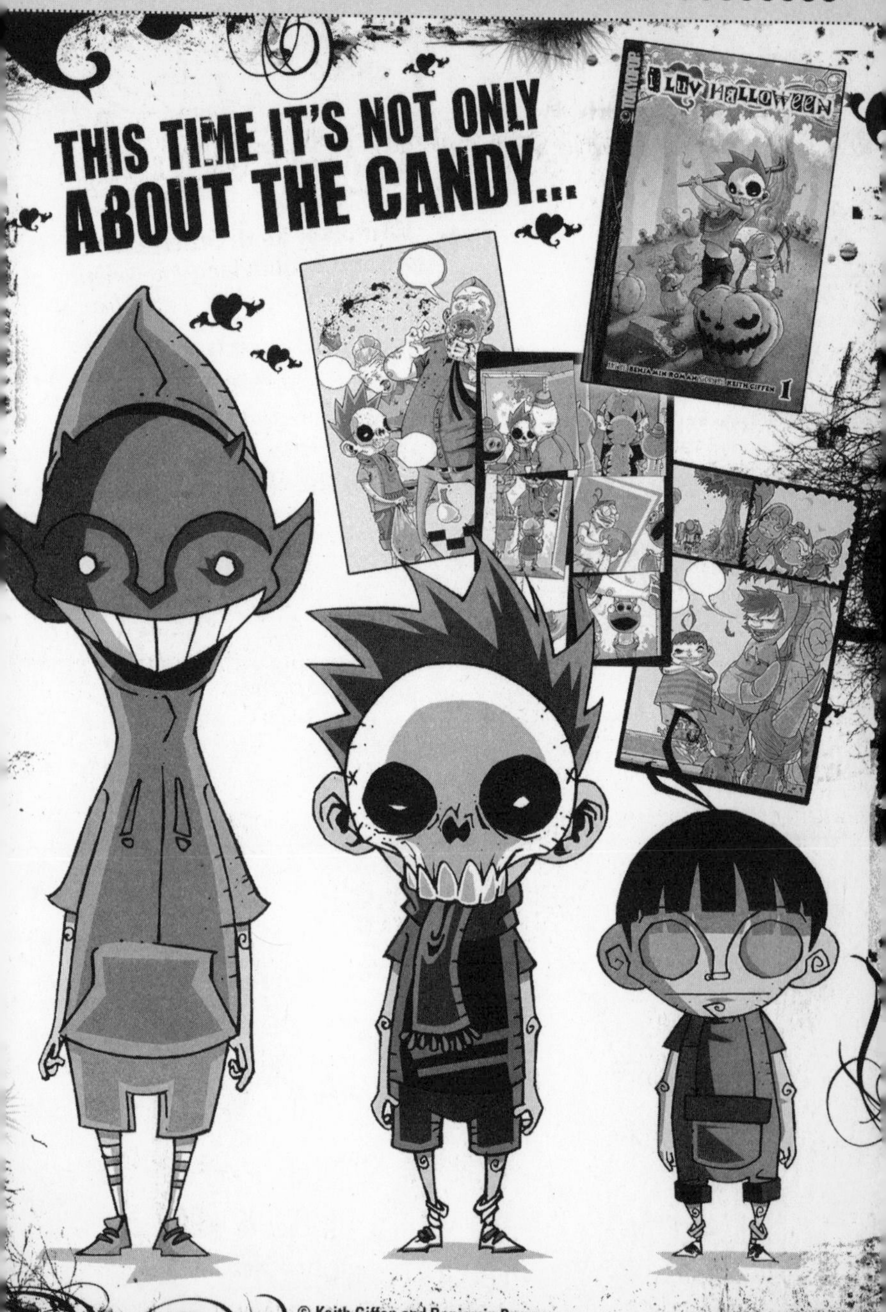
THIS TIME IT'S NOT ONLY ABOUT THE CANDY...
I LUV HALLOWEEN
BENJAMIN ROMAN
KEITH GIFFEN
1

I LUV HALLOWEEN

I LUV HALLOWEEN™

Written by Keith Giffen, comic book pro and English language adapter of *Battle Royale* and *Battle Vixens*.

Join the misadventures of a group of particularly disturbing trick-or-treaters as they go about their macabre business on Halloween night. Blaming the apples they got from the first house of the evening for the bad candy they've been receiving all night, the kids plot revenge on the old bag who handed out the funky fruit. Riotously funny and always wickedly shocking—who doesn't *love* Halloween?

OT
OLDER TEEN
AGE 16+

Preview the manga at:
www.TOKYOPOP.com/iluvhalloween

SCRAPPED PRINCESS

BY GO YABUKI, ICHIRO SAKAKI, AND YUKINOBU AZUMI

HER BIRTH FORETOLD THE DESTRUCTION OF THE WORLD!

Fifteen years ago, a set of twins—a girl and a boy—was born to the king of Linevan. Shortly after their birth, a prophecy foretold that when the girl turned 16, she would bring about the end of humanity. To avoid this terrible fate, the king ordered the girl disposed of—scrapped! She miraculously survived and was raised away from the kingdom that would kill her. But now she has turned 15, the king's guards have caught wind that she's still alive...and they set out to finish the job!

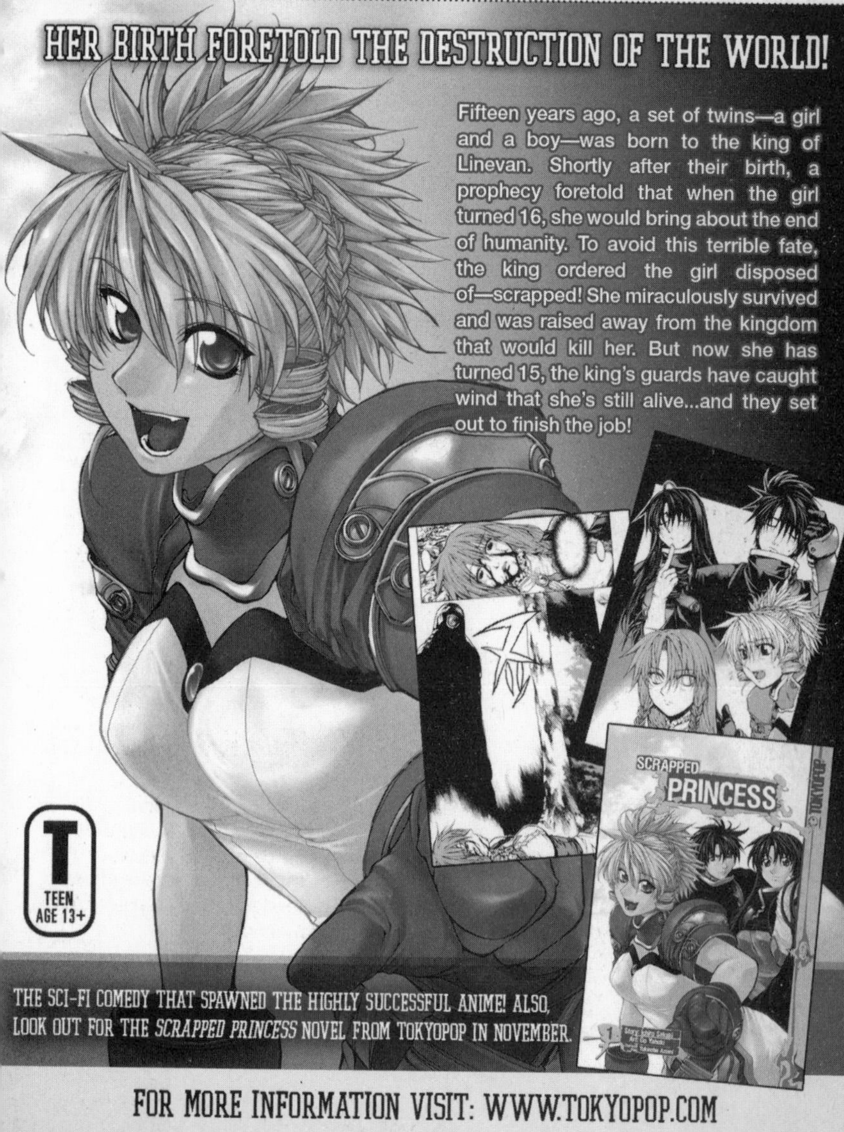
SCRAPPED
PRINCESS
TOKYOPOP

T
TEEN
AGE 13+

THE SCI-FI COMEDY THAT SPAWNED THE HIGHLY SUCCESSFUL ANIME! ALSO, LOOK OUT FOR THE *SCRAPPED PRINCESS* NOVEL FROM TOKYOPOP IN NOVEMBER.

FOR MORE INFORMATION VISIT: WWW.TOKYOPOP.COM

KAMICHAMA KARIN
BY KOGE-DONBO

Karin is an average girl...at best. She's not good at sports and gets terrible grades. On top of all that, her parents are dead and her beloved cat Shi-chan just died, too. She is miserable. But everything is about to change—little does Karin know that her mother's ring has the power to make her a goddess!

From the creator of *Pita-Ten* and *Digi-Charat!*

Y YOUTH AGE 10+

© Koge-Donbo.

KANPAI!
BY MAKI MURAKAMI

Yamada Shintaro is a monster guardian in training—his job is to protect the monsters from harm. But when he meets Nao, a girl from his middle school, he suddenly falls in love...with her neckline! Shintaro will go to any lengths to prevent disruption to her peaceful life—and preserve his choice view of her neck!

A wild and wonderful adventure from the creator of *Gravitation!*

T TEEN AGE 13+

© MAKI MURAKAMI.

MOBILE SUIT GUNDAM ÉCOLE DU CIEL
BY HARUHIKO MIKIMOTO

École du Ciel—where aspiring pilots train to become Top Gundam! Asuna, daughter of a brilliant professor, is a below-average student at École du Ciel. But the world is spiraling toward war, and Asuna is headed for a crash course in danger, battle, and most of all, love.

From the artist of the phenomenally successful *Macross* and *Baby Birth!*

T TEEN AGE 13+

© Haruhiko Mikimoto and Sostu Agency · Sunrise.

STOP!

9/06

You w... ng!

This book is ... o-left
format. Sinc... rs
get to experi...
asking for it,
and far more

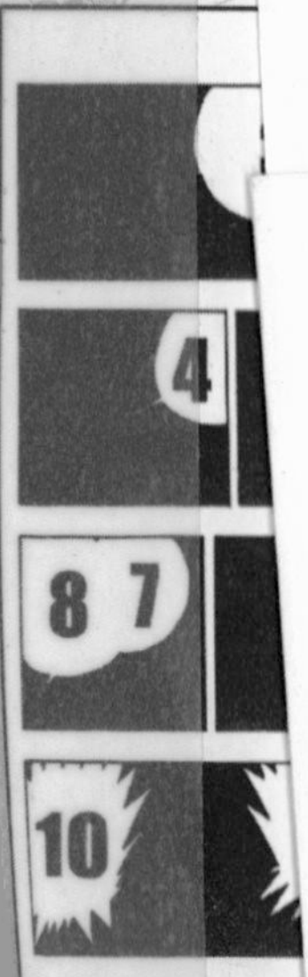
4
8 7
10